Cyberlaw

Law for
Digital Spaces
and
Information Systems

John T. Bandler

Bandler Group LLC
New York, New York

First edition published 2025 by Bandler Group LLC, 48 Wall Street, 11th Floor, New York, New York 10005

Library of Congress Cataloging-in-Publication Data

Names: Bandler, John T., author
Title: Cyberlaw: Law for Digital Spaces and Information Systems
Description: First edition. | New York, New York: Bandler Group LLC, 2025.
Includes appendix, references, index, glossary, and diagrams.
Summary: "Cyberlaw is everywhere: the intersection of law and technology. Law in the United States has evolved over hundreds of years and is now intertwined with technology, computers, the internet, and information systems. Cyberlaw affects everything we do, within traditional and digital spaces. Cybercrime is rampant and allows theft from far away, privacy is a critical concern as personal data is collected, sold, and hacked. Cyberconflict occurs between nation states, and now cyberspace provides a global method for speech, persuasion, and even manipulation. This book is for anyone desiring to learn about cyberlaw. Read it cover-to-cover or jump to the chapters relevant to your research. It breaks complexities into their simplest parts, then adds explanation and detail, then provides extensive additional references. The part and chapter titles show the book's comprehensive journey. We start by building a cyberlaw learning mindset, then introduce law in the U.S. Next, we walk through technology, cybercrime, traditional civil laws applied to cyber, data laws, cyber conflict, cyber speech, and finally apply it to organization management. Cyberlaw issues penetrate every aspect of our lives, society, and system of government and democracy. This book explores them from a comprehensive perspective." — Provided by publisher.
Identifiers:
LCCN 2024927347
ISBN 978-1-963435-03-0 (paperback)
ISBN 978-1-963435-04-7 (hardback)
ISBN 978-1-963435-05-4 (eBook)

Don't have the book yet
and want to learn more?
See the **main book page**:
johnbandler.com/cyberlawbook
Scan the QR code to go there

Already have the book?
See the **resources page**:
johnbandler.com/cyberlawbook-resources
Scan the QR code to go there

Visit John Bandler's website at JohnBandler.com

Dedication

To my parents, wife, son, and daughter.
You make it possible and worthwhile.

Contents

About the Author

John Bandler led one of the earliest cybercrime and virtual currency money laundering criminal prosecutions as an assistant district attorney under the late and great Robert M. Morgenthau.

John then entered private practice and started helping organizations and individuals navigate today's risks and issues regarding cybersecurity, cybercrime prevention, information governance, privacy, law, and more.

He began teaching a cyberlaw course for undergraduate students, built a law school course on cybercrime and cybersecurity, and taught a graduate level course on law for information systems. All of that meant creating materials relating to cyberlaw.

He now brings you this book to help you learn.

John previously served as a prosecutor for thirteen years and before that as a New York State Trooper. He also served in the U.S. Army Reserve.

He earned his law degree from Pace University's Law School and his undergraduate degree from Hamilton College, majoring in physics with a computer science minor. Since graduating law school, he continues learning through self-study and every time he writes and teaches.

Some of his other works include:

- *Policies and Procedures for Your Organization* (2024 book)
- *Cybercrime Investigations* (2020 book)
- *Cybersecurity for the Home and Office* (2017 book)
- Online courses on law, cyberlaw, privacy, cybersecurity, policies and more
- His website at JohnBandler.com

John can be reached at:

John Bandler
Bandler Law Firm PLLC
Bandler Group LLC
48 Wall Street, 11th Floor
New York, NY 10005
JohnBandler.com
JohnBandler@JohnBandler.com

More about John at johnbandler.com/about

Acknowledgments

This book would not be possible without the help of many people over the course of my life and the writing of this book.

I start with my wife, children, and parents, to whom I dedicate the book. My wife provided valuable guidance throughout the book on appearance, style, and substance.

I also would like to acknowledge all the experts, mentors, supervisors, students, and clients who gave me knowledge, feedback, and experience throughout my life.

A thanks to those who helped on my first three books and many articles, whose editing suggestions now influence my writing. Readers, editors, co-authors, and publishers. And those who gave me the means to build courses in a variety of platforms, where I further developed my thinking and content.

And a special thanks to the readers who read this book prior to publication, who made it so much better, starting with my cousin, Rob Bandler, former Deputy Director of IT Security at Cornell University, who read this book from cover-to-cover prepublication and provided valuable feedback (as he has done with each of my books), John G. Bates, Cam DiGiovanni, Janay Russo, Samantha Mathews, Maxim Kovalsky, Robert Barnsby, Scott Giordano, Mitchell Fink, Richard E. Parke, Peter Richards, Joshua Larocca, David Patariu, and others, some of whom prefer not to be named.

The usual disclaimers apply for all who helped—they get credit for the good and they made the book better than it would have been. They don't necessarily agree with everything in the book, and they get no blame for anything that is wrong. This was their personal help with no connection to their employer.

I acknowledge my website JohnBandler.com, where I built many of these thoughts and words, where I can continually tweak my writings, diagrams, and thought process. I used my prior works to help write this book and I refer the reader back there for more. The diagrams in this book are my creations and many early versions probably first appeared on my website.

I acknowledge my book, *Policies and Procedures for Your Organization* where I further evolved my thoughts, content, terminology, glossary, diagrams, and more. I always try to refine and improve, but don't rewrite just for rewriting's sake. I also acknowledge my first book, *Cybersecurity for the Home and Office*, and second book *Cybercrime Investigations* (and the co-author).

Mostly, thank you, the reader. I never know who will read what I write and what their background or interests will be. I try my best to organize the books well and write clearly. If you have constructive feedback to share, please reach out.

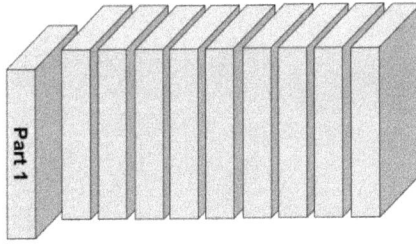

Part 1

Introducing the book and a mindset for learning cyberlaw

In this part

- Why this book
- Who it is for
- How to use it
- "Cyberlaw" vs. "traditional law"
- Learning and improving how we research, read and write

In other words:

- Let's get our journey started
- Don't skip this part or you will miss out

John T. Bandler

1

Why Cyberlaw and How to Use This Book
(Introduction)

In this chapter:

- Why read
- Who should read
- How to read
- Some good principles
- Warnings and disclaimers
- Where you can find more (resources)

1.1 Why read this book?

The areas of law that involve computers and the internet are relatively new, evolving, interesting, and important for our country.

Let's call it "cyberlaw." We will analyze this term throughout and will stop putting it in quotes.

We examine what "cyber" means. How new tools of technology change our world, how existing laws might be applied, and the new laws being put in place. It starts with learning (or refreshing our knowledge) on legal fundamentals. These basics are important on their own, and we need to see how they are applied to technology and the issues technology creates.

We examine what "law" is, an important area for every resident and citizen of our country.

Taking some time to learn about all of this will serve us well.

Some readers are motivated by more than just learning–they have an obligation.[1] Regardless, learning remains the underlying goal.

---

[1] Maybe this is assigned reading for a course you are taking.

1.2 Who this book is for

This book is for anyone wanting to learn more about cyberlaw and how law is applied to digital spaces and information systems.

We cannot avoid cyberspace and its many implications for us, nor can we avoid law, so we should learn about it.

This book is for students learning cyberlaw and is especially suited as a course book because of its modular and organized structure. Chapters can be covered either in depth or skimmed, according to the needs of the course, instructor, and students.[2]

This book is for anyone with any level of understanding—or confusion—about law, cyberlaw, and technology. It provides a foundation so any reader can understand the basics, then covers the details, then provides resources for additional learning.

Every reader is different and opens this book with a different set of knowledge about law and technology. Wherever you are, this book is for you and does not presume experience with law or technical subjects.

1.3 How to use this book

This book can be read straight through, from start to finish. In doing so an adequate foundation is laid for each important area.

Some readers will go slower on some chapters or sections but faster on others depending on their knowledge and their wishes.[3]

---

[2] Each course and each student are different.

Courses have a different focus, level of learning, prerequisites, and instructors. That is one reason I did not try to organize chapters according to a rigid semester week schedule. Instead, the chapters are their own topic, and instructors can choose to cover multiple topics during a week or focus as they see fit. It all depends upon what is most relevant for that course and expected knowledge for students.

Further, every student in each course is different, starting from a different spot, bringing different strengths and with different areas that need improvement. Some may be strong on legal knowledge, others strong on technology knowledge. It is impossible for an instructor to predict each student's starting point, so this book is understandable for all by creating foundational baselines.

[3] Even those knowledgeable in a topic area can benefit from giving it a careful read, including with an "editor's eye." They may see something from a different perspective which may reinforce or provide new insights on concepts or details.

Since this book is modular and carefully organized a reader or researcher can go right to a particular topic. Some courses may focus on certain areas and skim or skip others. The table of contents, index, chapter preambles and section headers help locate the desired material.

I drop footnotes periodically because they can provide additional information, a vignette, or citation, and they help keep the main text streamlined.[4]

Some sections, marked as "preview" provide a quick summary on a topic at hand, to be covered in more detail later. Similarly, sections marked as "recap" will refresh your memory of material in a prior chapter.

Infographics or shaded paragraphs marked "recap" will help emphasize important takeaways.

1.4 Perspective and law: The United States and New York State

This book is written from a United States (U.S.) perspective and thus concerns laws within the U.S. Where we dive into details on state law, it will focus on New York. This state is not necessarily better than anywhere else, but it provides excellent examples and I know it well from having enforced the laws, studied them, and taught them.

Trying to address the laws of all fifty states in this book would be unwieldy, to say the least. Law within New York is complex enough, so there is little benefit in trying to do a tour of every state's law and how they may differ.

Similarly, law within the U.S. can get complicated (including how it intersects with international laws), so I did not attempt to analyze this

---

Constructive feedback from experts and beginners is always welcomed, which helps ensure I have considered all perspectives and can improve future editions or build additional resources.

[4] Footnotes may provide a citation or reference when needed right then. The end of each chapter may include some more general chapter references and additional reading. Footnotes also include asides, vignettes, minutiae, and statute quotations when I feel it is too much for the main text. Skip the footnotes if you don't have the time, or read if they are of interest.

The citations are designed for convenience and are streamlined, neither official "Bluebook" (as lawyers often use) nor other official styles. I provide a webpage URL when possible. When I cite to my own work and my website, I omit certain information to keep it simpler and reduce the word count. All webpages were accessed shortly before publication in January 2025.

from the legal perspective of any other countries. That too would have been unworkable.

Through our U.S. and New York perspective, readers will obtain a solid basis in law, including how to learn more about other laws, including those of your own state.

1.5 Layered concepts

Concepts are layered throughout this book, often with a simple outer layer up front, and then we delve deeper into more complexity. Or to use another metaphor, we will climb up one level at a time (scaffolding).[5]

Readers need to understand some basics of "regular" law and technology before grasping concepts of cyberlaw. This book provides that.

All courses are built differently and may cover material with a unique focus. Instructors cannot control what a student learned prior to joining the class, and every student starts from a different place, just like every reader of this book starts from a different place.

If you find certain concepts difficult or confusing, try reading it twice, (reading aloud can help too), see the additional resources I suggest, and return to it later. If you find certain areas oversimplified, you can gallop through them at a faster pace, and then dive into additional resources.

1.6 My journey to write this book (preview)

My entry to law started as a New York state trooper, and my beginning in cyberlaw were as a prosecutor investigating cybercrime; a global world of theft that included identity theft, virtual currency payments and money laundering.

I moved into private practice in the areas of cybersecurity, cybercrime prevention, investigation, and privacy.

I began teaching and writing on these topics. Each semester, each course, each client, and each article was an opportunity to expand my knowledge and thinking, and to see what can help students better understand our legal system, government, and cyberlaw.

---

[5] This concept of "scaffolding" or "laddering" allows us to methodically climb to higher levels of understanding. We return to this in Chapter 3.

I've written three books, and each had some cyberlaw content within it. Now it was time to write this book on cyberlaw.[6]

1.7 Warnings and disclaimers

We all need to make decisions and manage our own risks, including me as a writer and publisher, and you as a reader.

This book is not legal advice nor consulting advice, just a book to share knowledge.[7] This book is not specifically tailored to your individual circumstances. You assume all risks from using this book. I disclaim all liability regarding your use of this book.

Cyberlaw—like all other areas of law—has legal consequences when things don't go right. Legal disputes can occur even when things are done properly and in good faith. There is even greater risk when laws are misunderstood or ignored.

I want to help you build good knowledge, so I give quality information to the best of my ability in a reasonably priced book. As above, I have no liability for anything resulting from the use of this book.

References in this book may become outdated. Links may cease to function. Laws may change. Even when laws seem to be static, lawyers and judges may disagree about what the law is.

When in doubt, seek legal counsel or other professional assistance.

I use utmost care, but I might make a mistake.[8] Please let me know if you find any so that I can correct it in the next version (and thank you for reading and letting me know).

My website may go down and disappear, or content could go behind a subscription wall.

I discuss actual events and legal cases to illustrate the law and factual issues. Parties to those legal disputes (and their lawyers) might disagree with how I summarize them. I create my summary based on my research and what I read, then I form an opinion about it and how best to

---

[6] If you are interested in learning more about this journey, see Part 10.

[7] If you need legal advice consult a competent, reliable attorney. You will probably need to pay money and there may be an engagement letter also. Unless that is done, you probably won't have an attorney-client relationship.

[8] Or maybe it is an Easter Egg.

condense it simply. You should read this book as you would read anything, with a critical eye and brain. You can evaluate the following:

- What is Bandler trying to say? Is it reliable and credible? Which parts are factual or law based, which parts are more opinion?
- How can I research more about this case (or law)?
- How could I research more about what Party A says about this case, including (i) about what the facts are (e.g., what happened) and (ii) what the law is? How reliable and credible are they?
- How could I research more about what Party B says about this case (the facts and law)? How reliable and credible are they?
- What did the judge and jury decide in this case? (An issue decided in court, such as with a conviction, guilty plea, or jury verdict, has significant weight, though you may still want to consider reliability and credibility.)
- Are there other reliable sources to help me determine what actually happened in this case?

1.8 Reading for a school course?

If this is required reading for a course, remember to follow all course instructions, including within the syllabus, learning management system (LMS), and from your instructor.

1.9 References, resources, and JohnBandler.com

My website has been a way to publish and evolve my thinking, writing, and diagrams over the years. I can write an article and publish it immediately so it can be accessed by students and clients. Then I can update and refine it over the years. Now this book evolves that further.

I polled my students; some prefer to read on a website, and some prefer a single book they can hold.[9] For those that wanted a reliable book with everything put together with a comprehensive and cohesive organization and terminology, this is it.

---

[9] Some admitted they would rather not do the reading at all. I appreciated that they were honest and willing to share that! But reading needs to be assigned and most student learning occurs outside of the classroom through reading and self-study. Students who read can participate and learn more in class and also aid their instructor and classmates.

My intention is that the website will have updates, additional reading, and references.[10]

Each chapter list some references, resources, and additional reading at the end. Footnotes will point to them as well. There is also a references page for each chapter on my website.

With any article or book, one challenge is including the right amount of detail and arriving at the right length. Not too long, not too short.

For each topic, this book points you to some next steps for research and investigation. Often that will start with my website, which has a page that corresponds to the chapter.

Again, I cannot guarantee the website will stay working or freely available forever. Neither this book nor my website is the sole resource—just a start. Look for reliable sources and consider their weight, authority, and reliability.

I will include a webpage address (universal resource locator, URL) and a QR code also to help you get to the main page relevant for the chapter.

QR codes found in this book will point to a webpage within my website at JohnBandler.com.

Now, I point you to my general resources page for the book (consider bookmarking it):

- https://johnbandler.com/cyberlawbook-resources

Next, here is the resources page for *this* chapter:

- https://johnbandler.com/cyberlawbook-resources-ch01

As you use the QR codes throughout the book, consider that things may not work perfectly in the future, depending on my website, future book editions, and potential realignment of chapters. The book itself is what you paid for, with an enormous amount of information and references within it. The website is a free convenience I offer.

---

[10] That's my hope, but I can't promise it or guarantee it.

1.10 QR codes

QR codes present some risk (as does everything in life) because they take you somewhere on the internet.

I believe the QR codes in this book present no risks for privacy because they are static and go only to my website.

Near the QR codes in this book, you will see which page at JohnBandler.com the code will take you to. If multiple webpages are listed, then the QR code goes to the top page in the list. When you scan the QR code, your device should indicate that it is going to my website, Johnbandler.com.

There may be some privacy implications with other QR codes (from other places) due to the data they obtain. However, the QR codes in this book do not provide me with any analytics and are "static."

Regarding other QR codes you see in other places:

- A malicious QR code could point you to a malicious website, and malicious websites can damage your computer, security, and privacy.
- If you scan other people's QR codes (unlike the codes in this book) there is a chance they are "dynamic." They might first direct you to the QR code provider company, and they can collect some information about you including date, time, location of the scan and operating system used.

To read more about QR codes, see my article at https://johnbandler.com/qrcodes.

1.11 Chapter questions

Some chapters will have questions at the end. To reduce the page count some questions will be on my website. Whether you review these questions or not is up to you or your instructor.

Some questions may be simple to ensure you have retained certain details, a first step towards more complex areas of knowledge. Some questions may call for more thought, or your opinion.

Here are some questions for this chapter:

- Why are you reading this book on cyberlaw?
- What do you hope to learn from it?

2

Cyberlaw Introduced

In this chapter:

- Cyberlaw sits on a foundation of traditional law
- We can apply traditional laws to digital circumstances

2.1 What is cyberlaw anyway?

That is a complex question with a complex answer—one could write a book about it!

Let's start simple, as indicated in the glossary:

Cyberlaw: Cyber + law. The areas of law relating to computers and the internet, including areas of criminal law, cybersecurity, privacy, nation-state conflict, and more.

This is not a legal definition, just my way of explaining it and a start.

2.2 Cyberlaw sits on a foundation of traditional law

Let's introduce this next concept:

Cyberlaw sits on a foundation of traditional law.

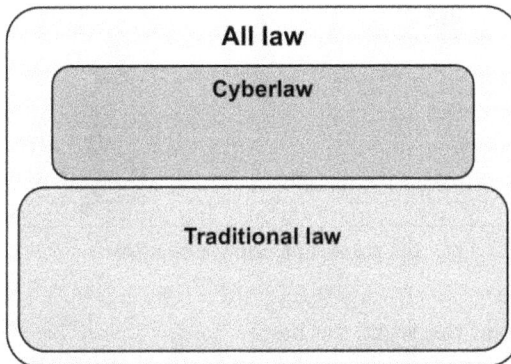

Cyberlaw sits on a foundation of traditional law

It is helpful to imagine cyberlaw as sitting on top of traditional law because we realize that "traditional law" came first, then the cyber age arrived, and law evolved in several ways. This shows we need to understand traditional law before we can understand cyber law.

We cover the basics of our legal system in Part 2, including the way humans have evolved their rules for society, our modern system of law, the way we resolve disputes, and the basics of criminal law and civil law. Later in the book we cover the traditional bodies of law (e.g., criminal, negligence, contract) and assess how they are applied to cyberspace. Then we will explore "data laws."

The main takeaway is that cyberlaw includes traditional law and requires a solid understanding of traditional law.

2.3 Cyberlaw is a subset of traditional law

The above analogy is good for some purposes but is not perfect (no analogy is).

Cyberlaw is now an integral part of our existing laws, and sometimes it doesn't matter which was built first because they are all here now. We can depict cyberlaw as a subset of all laws like this.

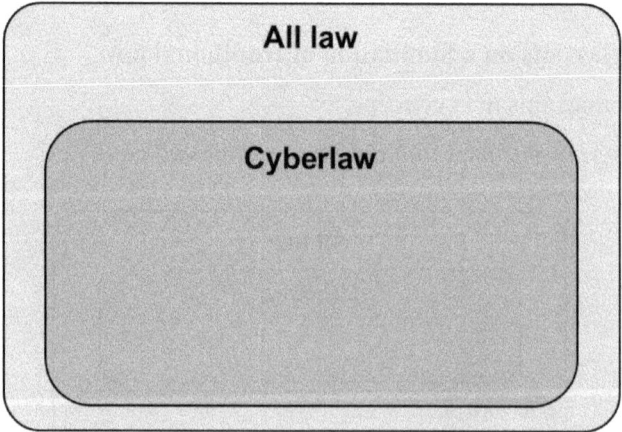

All law

Cyberlaw

Cyberlaw is a subset of all law

2.4 A word about the word "cyber"

The word cyber is used everywhere. Perhaps it is an unwarranted cliche, added in front of way too many words, and should never be used alone.

It is part of our language now. Let us lay out what it means, at least for me, and for this book.

"Cyber" basically means relating to computers, networks, and the internet, which includes all things digital.[11]

2.5 What are the "information systems" mentioned in the book title?

Information systems are systems used to manage information. A system is a group of parts, and may include software, hardware, and people. Managing information includes collecting information, processing it, storing it, and distributing it. These systems today will involve computers and networks.

Practically speaking these information systems relate to information technology (IT) and focus on various components working together in groups (systems). There is considerable overlap between the fields of information systems, information technology, computer science, data science, cybersecurity, and related fields.[12]

2.6 More on cyberlaw

We have three foundational principles to work with so far:

Cyberlaw: Cyber + law

Cyberlaw sits on a foundation of traditional law

Cyberlaw is a subset of all law.

---

[11] People may have differing opinions on what "cyber" means to them or in what context. As an initial matter, most computers are connected to networks and the internet, computers need data, all of that is digital.

Then we can have excellent discussions about what "cyber" means to us, how the word came about, and for contexts. Consider the term "cybernetics" and the relationship between humans and technology, and the exchange of information and feedback that occurs to regulate a system.

Remember that "cyber" and many other terms in this book are in the glossary. Some glossary items are borrowed and then updated from my prior book, *Policies and Procedures for Your Organization.*

[12] For example, you can check the various courses of study at Pace University's Seidenberg School of Computer Science and Information Systems (CSIS), where I teach a course on information systems and law. Study areas include information technology, information systems, computer science, and more. *See* https://www.pace.edu/seidenberg/find-your-program/undergraduate; https://www.pace.edu/seidenberg/find-your-program/graduate.

This is a way to start thinking about cyberlaw in three short sentences.[13]

Then the entire book explores what "cyberlaw" means, covering areas of law relevant to computers, information systems, and the internet.

Even though "cyberlaw" might seem like a buzzword to some, the term is now part of our language.[14] We are stuck with it, especially because I put it in the title of the book.

Let's recognize that some people can have mental blocks when it comes to technology, law, or both. We can break through those blocks by realizing it is all understandable if we start simple and break it down into individual, consumable components.

As we think about all laws and "traditional laws," we should think about those traditional legal areas that have existed long before the internet, including:

- Criminal law
- Negligence law
- Contract law.

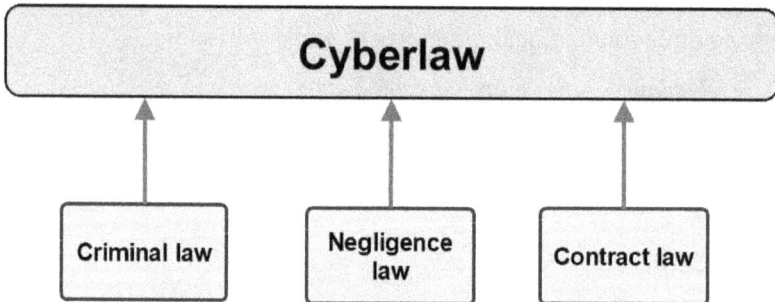

Some traditional laws in cyberlaw

---

[13] It is a challenge to summarize a complex area so briefly. This may seem too simple for some, and some may disagree, especially and including lawyers. That's what keeps things interesting. If you ask ten lawyers what "cyberlaw" means, you might get eleven different answers! Including the lawyer's famous: "it depends."

[14] "Cyberlaw" is in the name of one course I have taught for many years. Another course I have taught for years regarding law for information systems initially used a coursebook with "cyberlaw" in the title.

All these areas apply in the digital realm. Cybercrime is a part of criminal law, negligence concepts apply to cyberspace, and contract principles do too.

Then we can think about newer laws that are specific to "cyber," sometimes called "data laws" such as:

- Data disposal
- Data breach notification
- Cybersecurity
- Privacy.

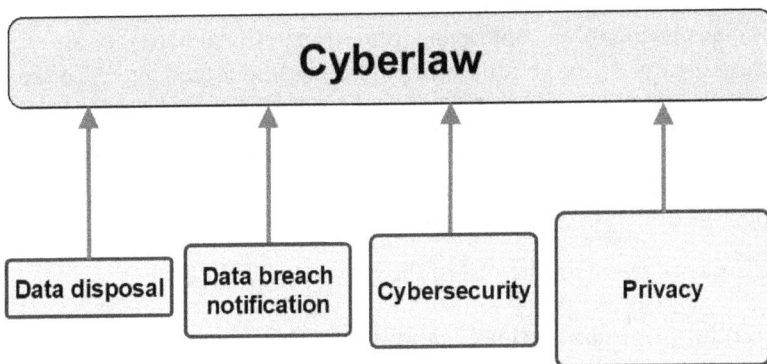

Cyberlaw

| Data disposal | Data breach notification | Cybersecurity | Privacy |

Some data laws in cyberlaw

These laws may come from either the federal government or from states. They may apply to a specific sector (such as healthcare or finance) or have more general application.

Cybercrime is an established threat that can damage organizations, the economy, critical infrastructure, and result in criminal theft and misuse of consumer data.

Cybersecurity and privacy are growing areas of compliance that are also important for every organization.

Governments have created laws and regulations that organizations need to understand and comply with. These laws relate to protecting certain sectors, protecting consumer data, notifying government and affected consumers of a data breach, and now a growing array of privacy laws.

We can apply traditional laws to digital circumstances

We can apply traditional laws to cyberspace, though there are layers of nuance. We do not rigidly apply them, but rather try to analyze what is similar to what we have seen before, and what is different. We realize that statutes have their own specific definitions which might not be applicable in cyberspace.

When lawyers and judges encounter a set of facts and a sequence of events or circumstances, they seek to analogize and distinguish. Put differently they:

- See what is the *same* as what we have encountered before, and
- See what is *different* from before.

In this book we do this from a rational, objective perspective. That is because we are not lawyers trying to win a case or represent a client; politicians trying to win approval, votes, or a political battle; or an interested party trying to influence politicians about the law.[15] We are not advocates, we are simply learners thinking about law and discussing it.

We have now explained cyberlaw very simply in three short sentences, and then with a little more nuance in this section, and this chapter as a whole.

You are now ready for the rest of the book, to dive in further.

2.6 Sayings (misconceptions?) about cyberlaw

As we explore cyberlaw we hear some sayings and we should consider whether these are accurate, misconceptions, myths, or clichés. We look past the surface to the nuances of law in cyberspace.

2.6.1 "Law is behind"

Some may say:

 ✗ *The law is too slow and needs to catch up.*

Assuming developments in law are needed, we want to avoid falling into a trap of assuming a solution is easy—that it is just a matter of snapping one's fingers to get everything aligned and "caught up." We also want to consider that if everything moved rapidly, we probably would not see great laws that please everyone.

---

[15] None of this is to downplay or belittle the important roles that lawyers, politicians, and interested parties play in society and for the development of law. The point is merely that we can be objective learners instead of partisans trying to win an argument or battle. More on this in Chapter 18.

We need to consider realities and the foundations and complexities of law and people.

History shows us that whether law moves slowly or quickly, some will be happy, some will not. There is no magic solution to achieve the "right" result.

Even when law moves slowly and deliberately, there is plenty of room for disagreement. Because of our system of government and law, there is no single authority that could magically put new laws in place. It takes a process, sometimes a messy and prolonged process.

Before we utter the phrase "the law needs to catch up," let's first research what the actual laws are now, and how they might be applied to the new circumstance, what gap needs to be filled, and how it should be filled.

A product, service or technology might seem totally new (electric cars, virtual currency, cryptocurrency, artificial intelligence) but there may be "traditional" laws that apply to it.[16]

Only after investigating the current law can we put forth a reasoned opinion about what the law should be, and how fast it should move to get there.

Consider how new laws come about in the first place in a process with many players and tensions. It is messy and far from instant.[17]

As new laws are debated and developed, we should assess pros, cons, risks, and various stakeholders. We need to assess credibility, reliability and interests of individuals and entities who support certain legal positions or proposed laws. Some groups spend a lot of money to influence the debate and the law-making process, their money does not make them "right."

2.6.2 "Cyberspace jurisdiction"

Sometimes, we hear these phrases:

- ✗ *We need a new legal jurisdiction for cyberspace.*

- ✗ *We need a global jurisdiction for cyberspace.*

---

[16] During the early days of virtual currency and then cryptocurrency, there were many who claimed that existing laws did not apply to these "new" activities. Maybe this was from wishful thinking or just lack of knowledge. More on this in Chapters 19 and 22.

[17] More in Chapter 6.

As we assess challenges in cyberspace, including for cybercrime investigation and prosecution, we should avoid thinking that there is a magic wand that can be waved or that a single person or entity can make this happen.

Before proposing global jurisdiction, we want to properly understand the existing laws and principles of jurisdiction[18] and consider the legal concept and rule of nation-state sovereignty.[19]

Then we want to consider whether it would even be a good thing if there was a global organization with authority over the entire Earth.

In sum, global jurisdiction may sound good at first, but deeper inspection reveals problems. There would not be a single government to oversee it, nor would other governments agree with it. There are a lot of countries in this world, many are adversaries and commit or allow cybercrimes to be committed against other countries. They engage in cyber operations and even war or other illegal actions. No single global entity would ever act in a way that all other countries would be happy with. The United Nations is an important and essential international body, but we can see that international relations are complex. Messy. There is no "easy" button to push.

2.7 Additional reading and references

This is our introduction to cyberlaw. The rest of the book covers it all in more detail.

- *Chapter 2 resources*, https://johnbandler.com/cyberlawbook-resources-ch02
- *Cyberlaw*, https://johnbandler.com/cyberlaw

2.8 Chapter questions

- How does the book characterize the word "cyber," and what is your opinion on that word and why?
- How does the book define "cyberlaw," and then share your opinion on that definition and why you think that.
- More questions on the Chapter resources webpage.

---

[18] In Chapter 8 and Chapter 9 we introduce jurisdiction, then cover it in depth in Chapter 12.
[19] *See* Chapter 35.

3

Reading, Learning, Researching, Writing, and Artificial Intelligence Tools

A bonus chapter to further your learning on cyberlaw
(and any other topic).

- Learning (which requires effort)
- Do not use AI tools to do your learning for you
- Scaffolding and layering
- Research (investigation)
- Writing and citing

3.1 Learning introduced

Learning is a way to improve ourselves, to build our knowledge, build our brains, our skills, and our ability to make good decisions.

You are learning about cyberlaw and maybe this is assigned reading in a course. Perhaps that course will also require additional research and some writing; maybe even a final paper.

For all these circumstances, this chapter can help you, starting now. That's why it is here, early in the book, rather than in an appendix.

I learned a lot in my life so far, studied a lot, and taken a lot of tests. I have also taught a lot, to many students with many different backgrounds and levels of knowledge and skills for research and writing. With my two children I realize much of parenting is teaching.

Teaching is not just about presenting information and knowledge. Students need motivation, they need to put in their own effort, and they need certain skills for learning and for later in life. They need to understand that their education and learning is in their own hands.

Parts of my courses involve writing, including weekly assignments and a final paper. I read those submissions and I think about whether students are learning and what is needed to improve. I created and refined some processes and resources over the years and decided to put some of that into this book.

3.2 This book is meant to be read

This book is written in plain language. Simple and clear. No lawyerly legalese. Reading is a skill that needs to be practiced, and requires thinking and brain engagement.

I understand why some students might not want to do the assigned reading. Some have trouble reading or just do not like to read. Some may be tired or bored (see tips for that coming up).

Failing to do the reading is ultimately a loss for the learner.

Practice reading to learn the material and get better at reading and thinking.

There are no true shortcuts here, the material needs to be read.

3.3 Do not use AI tools to "learn" cyberlaw or do your work

Some might think:

> ✘ *Reading about law is hard, can't I have artificial intelligence (AI) read it for me?*

Or perhaps:

> ✘ *Writing is hard, and writing about law is harder. Can't I have artificial intelligence (AI) write it for me?*

Please do not use AI tools to "read" it for you or summarize it for you. It won't help you understand the material any better than just reading it. You will cheat yourself of an opportunity to learn and internalize concepts we cover and build skills you need and confidence in yourself.

Getting a quick and easy answer does not substitute for putting in time and effort. Avoid those "shortcuts" because they do not get you to the right destination. They take you to a place where you missed the chance to improve yourself.

Learning is both a process and a destination. It is not about submitting an assignment with minimal work but a process of thinking, evaluating and choosing. We should exercise and build our skills to write, think, decide, and choose words and meaning.

With effort you will build yourself, your confidence, and your skills. You will eventually thank yourself for having done so.

John T. Bandler

3.4 Your learning comes with your effort

You learn only by putting in time and effort.

That is the truth. There are no magic ways to learn.

It is hard yet possible to learn when tired, bored, confused, or lost. Some techniques that can help you include:

- Stand up
- Read aloud
- Reread
- Take notes, underline, mark
- Read like an editor [20]
- Scaffold (more next).

Learning does not come automatically with academic credits or a degree. Learning comes with your genuine effort.

3.5 Scaffolding and layering

Scaffolding and layering are similar concepts to help us learn and is how the book is organized. Simple concepts up front, more complexity later.

With scaffolding, the idea is that learners can start at the ground level and build a scaffold to climb up level by level and build knowledge. Sometimes this is called "laddering," as in climbing a ladder, one rung at a time.

Some complex concepts may be initially beyond our reach, but we can start with basic concepts and fundamental details. Learn the categories, then what they mean, then try further complexity. With repetition and thought and effort, we can clear the confusion. Basic concepts are in your easy grasp and complexities become reachable.

We build this scaffold little by little. We practice climbing up it each day, we add to it every day and week. Then by the end of our semester, we have built a scaffold forty stories tall, and we can quickly climb from bottom to top with ease.

---

[20] Reading like an editor means you read it as if you are correcting it; as if you are editing your own writing, editing it for a friend or as part of your duties as a book editor or article editor. You think and make notes to question, correct punctuation, sentence structure, or other issues.

3.6 Your research on cyberlaw starts here

Your research on cyberlaw starts right here, in this book.

If you are researching a particular topic, start with the relevant chapters and sections, and use the glossary and index.

If this book is required reading in your course, read it and use it for your research, don't overlook what is here, right in front of you. This is your solid start for learning and research. It is not the end, so eventually read the relevant additional references and laws that the book points to.

Identify the laws and legal authorities—important yet frequently overlooked. Identify their names, and where to find them, cite them and provide the link to them.

Then expand even further. There is a lot of good information out there, from many reliable sources. This book is your starting point but is not the end of your research.

3.7 Research, legal research, investigation, and analysis

We all need to research and investigate—it is part of life. We make decisions, and these decisions need facts. To get facts, we need to conduct research and due diligence, assess information and sources, and consider what is accurate, reliable, and important. We assess what to make of all this information, apply logic and reason, and arrive at conclusions. opinions, and decisions.

Many things in life require research and investigation; writing a paper, choosing a school, looking for a job, and voting for a candidate in an election.

We can follow a process. It starts by seeking and obtaining evidence and facts from multiple sources. For each source, we need to assess their reliability, credibility, motive, and authority.

Our preference is *reliable* sources. We remember that even a very reliable source could be wrong, and even a source that lies frequently could be telling the truth.

We assess facts, evidence, statements, information and whether they are accurate. Do they make sense? Are they corroborated?

We analyze facts and evidence, apply logic and reason, and arrive at inferences, conclusions, opinions, and options to decide from.

Let's dive in a little deeper.

3.7.1 Research

Research is the process of finding and analyzing information. Research is simply a type of investigation.

We research many things throughout our life, so why not work to improve and practice these skills now? Whether you are buying a product online, buying a car or home, looking for a job or looking to hire someone, it all requires research. Good research can lead to better decisions and outcomes.

As you research, your notes should include your sources. This is because not all information you come across is equal in reliability and weight, and you may need to cite it later. If you copy something from a source to your notes, be sure to include quotation marks and indicate the source so you don't forget this was copied.

3.7.2 Legal research

Legal research is simply research about what the laws are.

It means finding and analyzing information that applies to law, including analyzing "what the law is."[21]

Some government rules have higher authority than others. Some conflict with each other, and many are open to interpretation, especially with new circumstances or facts. Much has been written about laws, which evolve, and not every person writing about these laws and rules is correct or stays correct forever.

As you conduct legal research, include the sources in your notes, and evaluate what the source is and how much weight it carries, its legal "authority."

The highest authority is the U.S. Constitution, so start there and see if it applies.[22] Also consider state constitutions. While the constitutions are the ultimate legal authority, they are subject to considerable interpretation by courts, meaning human judges.

---

[21] Lawyers spend a lot of time (and client money) arguing and disagreeing on what the law is. Even neutral judges disagree about what the law is. Sometimes there is no simple magic answer about what the law is since it is not an exact science.

[22] For example, if your cyberlaw issue relates to speech and expression, you start with the First Amendment. If your cyberlaw issue relates to a government intrusion, search, or seizure, start with the Fourth Amendment.

Consider statutes, those duly enacted laws passed by the legislature and signed by the executive. They are another important place to start.

Then consider U.S. Supreme Court (USSC)[23] decisions, which interpret the U.S. Constitution and federal statutes as well as state actions. The USSC decides what the law is and is the ultimate legal authority in the country.[24]

Even though the USSC is the ultimate authority, they do not rule on every legal issue or fact pattern,[25] so your research should consider case decisions from other courts. As judges review facts and laws, they lay out what the law is and how it should apply to the facts of that case. Consider what court issues that opinion, because the decisions of some courts carry more weight than others.[26] Case decisions may have precedence (*stare decisis*) that create law to decide future cases.

Consider regulations, passed through the regulatory process by a regulator. These regulations (rules) are usually more detailed than a law, and the regulator was empowered by a law to issue (promulgate) them.

---

[23] Sometimes this is referred to as the Supreme Court of the United States (SCOTUS) though within this book we use USSC.

[24] That said, the judges on the USSC are still human beings and are not infallible. Their legal decisions and legal reasoning can be influenced by personal viewpoint and politics. Even well-established legal precedents about what the "law is" can be reversed from time to time.

[25] A "fact pattern" is a set of facts outlining a circumstance and might also be called a "hypothetical situation" or simply a "hypothetical." It allows lawyers to imagine a sequence of events and then discuss how the law might be applied to it. In science, this might be called a "thought experiment" or "*gedankenexperiment*." Albert Einstein wrote *gedankenexperiments* that helped illustrate and prove his important scientific discoveries.

[26] For example, a decision from the U.S. Court of Appeals for the Second Circuit is binding within the Second Circuit federal district courts (trial courts), but merely persuasive in other circuits. While this case is binding law within the second circuit, lawyers may still argue that the case does not apply (they will "distinguish" the case and say why it is different).

A decision from the New York State's First Department Appellate Division is binding on state courts within the First Department, but merely persuasive elsewhere.

Consider guidance put out by the regulators and enforcers, which interpret and state what the law is.[27] See what enforcement actions they have brought regarding the law.[28]

Look at news articles and legal scholarship and articles about laws and cases. These articles do not have legal authority, but they might summarize the laws or facts of a case well and they might influence a judge or lawmaker in the future. Remember that "legal experts" are not infallible, and even excellent legal scholars disagree with each other. It is your job as an investigator and researcher to assess what they say and work towards authoritative legal sources.

3.7.3 Briefing a case[29]

"Briefing a case" means reading and analyzing a legal case, a court decision written by a judge (or by several judges).

When reading a case decision, which is a court's opinion written by one or more judges, identify or consider these things about the decision.

- Caption/title of case (names of the parties)
- Citation of case (how to cite it, find it)
- The court issuing the opinion (trial court, appellate court, state or federal, location, etc.)
- The date of the decision
- What type of case is it? (civil, criminal, regulatory)
- Further identification of the parties? (Plaintiff, defendant, appellant, appellee, etc.)
- What are the facts of the case? (e.g., what happened before the case got to court)
- What facts are agreed upon. What facts are in dispute?

---

[27] For example, the New York State Attorney General enforces violations of New York's cybersecurity and data breach reporting statutes. See what they say about these laws and how to comply with them at https://ag.ny.gov.

The New York State Department of Financial Services put forth a cybersecurity rule for financial services companies which they enforce. See what they say about how to comply at https://www.dfs.ny.gov.

[28] Each of these regulators (or regulatory type agencies) publicize certain enforcement actions to improve public awareness and for deterrence. See their press releases and the underlying documents for the cases they bring.

NYAG *Press Releases*, https://ag.ny.gov/press-releases.

NYS DFS *Newsroom* (press releases), https://www.dfs.ny.gov/Newsroom.

[29] *Briefing a case (summarizing a case)*, https://johnbandler.com/briefing-a-case.

- What is the prior procedure of the legal case? (How did the case start in the legal system, and where has it been to get to here)
- Who wrote the main opinion? Are there concurrences or dissents?
- What issues and laws are being interpreted and decided? How are they decided?
- What level of authority/precedent does this ruling carry? (Binding upon the U.S.? Upon a state? Highly or mildly persuasive? etc.)
- Summarize the court's holding (ruling on law) in one or two sentences.

3.7.4 Investigation and Analysis: Assess the source

Investigation is a type of research, and vice versa.

We look for avenues of investigation, a path to take, things to focus on. We lift up stones to see what is underneath—sometimes nothing, sometimes a gold nugget or clue.

We obtain information from various sources. Knowing the source is an important part of research, investigation, and analysis. It helps us pinpoint where the information is really coming from and assess how reliable it is.

Consider these statements, from extremely vague to more concrete:

"I heard that X did Y"

"A told me they heard that X did Y"

"A told me that B told A that B saw X do Y"

"B told me that they saw X do Y"

"I saw X do Y"

Citing sources is an important part of writing. Assessing the source is important for research and investigation. We look for sources with greater credibility and weigh. We also evaluate hearsay considerations.[30]

---

[30] The legal rule on hearsay indicates that the law prefers testimony about firsthand observations, not testimony about what someone else said.

To avoid a hearsay objection in the above example, the lawyer would want to call a witness to the stand to testify about what they themselves saw. Then that witness can be cross examined by the opposing lawyer, and the factfinder (e.g.,

Citing ensures that the source is properly attributed.[31]

As we research, we look to see if we can move towards sources of greater authoritativeness and corroborate existing sources.

3.8 Writing starts in your brain

Your writing should start in your brain.

It then goes from the thoughts in your head, to your fingers, to the keyboard.[32]

Don't use AI to write for you, since that would cheat yourself of the practice you need to grow and improve. It might also violate school rules and course rules.

Put in effort, read the material, form your own thoughts, write your own words. Then …

3.9 Edit your words

Few people write their first draft perfectly. Most of us need a second draft. A third. Probably many more.

Whatever draft number we are on, we can probably improve upon it in some way. This means we read what we wrote and edit it to make it better. You can make yourself a better writer.

Read it aloud to better understand how it sounds. This will also force you to slow down and pay attention to each word and every punctuation mark.

Editing tools are available, including those with AI capabilities. Use the tools wisely and you must remain the decider about what edits to make.

---

jury) can decide whether the witness is credible and should be believed as to whether X did Y.

    Of course, there are many exceptions to the hearsay rule as well.

[31] When writing academic or legal papers, citing also ensures proper credit is given where due. Where things are not cited or quoted, the writer is presenting the words as their own. More on this shortly.

[32] Some prefer to put pen to paper. Whatever works for you.

3.10 Citation

Citation is essential, especially for papers and research.

Here are four important principles:

- Follow the spirit of the rules, write with academic integrity, do your own work, and never plagiarize.
- Always cite where appropriate (any borrowed thoughts).
- Always quote and cite where appropriate (any copied text).
- Cite so that the reader can find the material you cited.

Now let's focus on citing and quoting:

- *Citing* is for ideas, thoughts, or facts you are borrowing or using from another. You are crediting the original author, but you have not directly copied them.
- *Quoting and citing* is for when you have copied someone else's writing. You are giving proper credit to the original author, and letting everyone know it is their writing, not yours.

Remember these basic rules, then you can get into the details of citing, which can be complex. I have guides for that[33] and see the rules of your school, course, or chosen citation format.

Remember that AI may be new, but that does not mean the rules for citation and academic integrity do not apply to this technology. You still need to cite your sources and cite what you quote, whether it is a human or an AI tool.[34]

Finally, if you do your own work, put in honest effort, and properly read and cite your sources, then you will never need a plagiarism checker to check your work before you submit it.[35]

---

[33] *See A guide to citations and references*, https://johnbandler.com/guide-citations-references.

[34] Remember that AI tools may not cite their sources, neither may papers written by someone else. There are so many reasons to do your own writing.

[35] Some students ask about using these checkers and seem to worry about false positives from these checkers. If you are doing things properly and honestly there is nothing to worry about. Good instructors know that plagiarism checkers are just a tool.

If someone never intends to rob a bank, they don't need to worry that they might have a *doppelganger* (look alike) who is robbing banks, and that there

3.11 Additional references and resources

- *Chapter 3 resources*, https://johnbandler.com/cyberlawbook-resources-ch03
- *Writing*, https://johnbandler.com/writing
- *How to Write a Paper*, https://johnbandler.com/how-to-write-paper
- *A guide to citations and references*, https://johnbandler.com/guide-citations-references
- *Artificial Intelligence and Human Writing and Thinking*, https://johnbandler.com/artificial-intelligence-writing-thinking
- *AI's promise and problem for law and learning*, https://johnbandler.com/ai-promise-and-problem
- *How to Take an Exam*, https://johnbandler.com/how-to-take-an-exam
- *How to Learn and Study*, https://johnbandler.com/how-to-learn-and-study/
- *Briefing a case (summarizing a case)*, https://johnbandler.com/briefing-a-case
- My Udemy course on *How to learn, study, take an exam, write, and research*, https://johnbandler.com/udemy-courses

3.12 Chapter questions?

- As you read this book, are there concepts from this chapter that you can apply for yourself that can help you better learn cyberlaw?
- As a student taking formal courses (whether you are a current, past, or future student), what concepts from this chapter could help you to better learn in your studies?
- Is it helpful or beneficial to consider being a life-long learner, rather than just a temporary student?
- How are researching and investigating similar?
- When in your daily life do you need to research and investigate?

---

might be a mistaken identification as the robber. There is no need to drastically change one's appearance to avoid this error.

If you are doing your own research and writing, you don't need to worry that someone else wrote the exact same words as you. It's not going to happen.

John T. Bandler

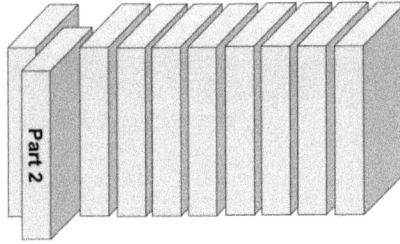

Part 2

Introducing Law and Our Legal System

In this part:

- Rules humans create
- Foundations of law
- The U.S. legal system
- Our U.S. Constitution and Amendments
- Criminal law
- Civil law
- The First Amendment
- The Fourth Amendment

In other words:

- We know that cyberlaw rests on a foundation of traditional law.
- Let's understand those foundations of law and our system.
- Build our own foundation of knowledge.

John T. Bandler

4

Rules Humans Create, Live By, and Break

In this chapter:

- Rules are a simple way to think about law
- What should the rules be?
- How should the rules be enforced?
- What process to enforce rules and resolve disputes?

4.1 Rules in perspective

Rules are everywhere, law is just a type of rule, and cyberlaw is an area of law.

Law does not have to be a confusing concept. We realize that laws are simply rules that come from the government. Our entire lives are surrounded by rules of many types, so this rule-based understanding makes law accessible and understandable.

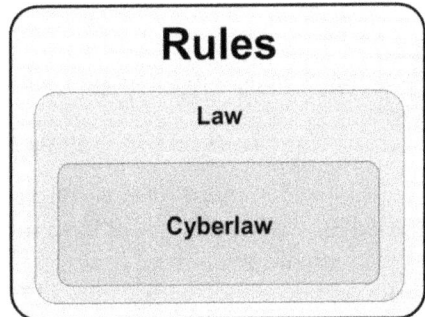

"Rule" is a broad term that generates varying responses. Some people have a negative view of rules because they want to do things without being constrained by someone else's rule. Others are more rule oriented, abiding by them and annoyed when others do not.

Most agree that some degree of rulemaking and enforcement is needed in many places, even when we disagree on what those rules should be or how they should be enforced.

Here are five main places that rules come from:

- Parents and family
- Ourselves

- Society
- Organizations
- Government.

We can depict these categories like this.

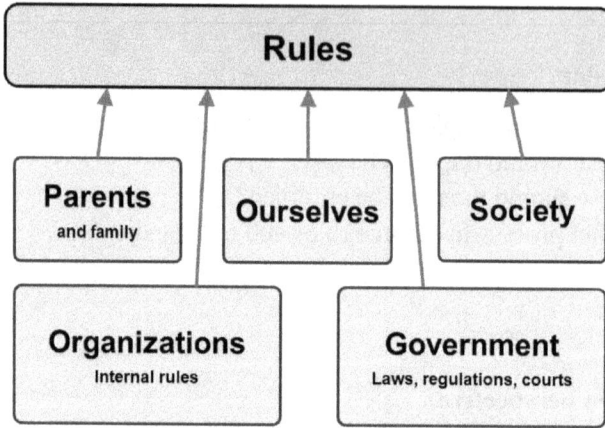

Rules come from many places

Now let's spend a moment on each of the five categories.

4.2 Our first rules as individuals come from our parents

We first experienced rules as children from our parents and those who raised us. Early rules might have included not eating dessert until we are done with our main meal or when to go to bed. Hundreds of parental rules and teachings were imposed upon us, many become part of our own personal rules. Parents and family continue to provide rules and guidance throughout our life, which influences what we do, our decisions, and who we are.

As we get older, we become subject to more rules from other places.

4.3 Societal rules

Ever since humans began living together in communities, they created and enforced rules. These rules were helpful for safety and to obtain and distribute food and shelter. People needed order and a division of labor regarding who might hunt, gather, farm, cook, build, clean, or fight.

These rules were generally for the greater good, with punishment (a deterrent) for those who broke the rules.

John T. Bandler

"Society" has a vague meaning and overlaps with other areas, but we can think of cultural or neighborhood rules and customs, including many that people perceive differently or disagree on.

Societal rules are influenced heavily by government, religion, organizations, family, and individuals. They existed long before formal laws and included mechanisms to deter violations.

4.4 Our personal rules (from ourselves)

We develop personal rules that guide our conduct based on our upbringing, experiences, and all the other influences in our life. Sometimes this is known as one's conscience, ethics, integrity, moral compass, values, or personal honor. For example, some may follow the "Golden Rule" which is to do unto others only as you would wish done to you.

Different people faced with the same circumstances may make different choices. Often, there is a personal code of conduct, even if instinctual or inarticulable, that influences that decision.

Personal rules are heavily influenced by external forces and are not fixed in stone nor always consistent. Nor is human decision making always according to rules and logic.

4.5 Organizational rules

People are part of organizations, and those organizations have rules. Organizations include:

- Work (the organizations that employ us)
- School
- Religious groups
- Others.

Organizations create rules to properly manage themselves and their people and sometimes those rules are written down, perhaps called policies, procedures, handbooks, or something else.[36]

These organizational rules can be called "internal rules" because they are internal to the organization (compared to "external rules" which come

---

[36] If you are a student, your school has many rules; if you are an employee, your employer does too.

from outside the organization). Organization management requires rules, including regarding cyber related matters, as we discuss in Part 9.

4.6 Government rules ("laws")

The rules that come from the government are "laws."

This concept helps demystify law, by thinking of it simply as a rule from government. Government has created laws for conduct (what to do and not to do) and laws for the process of resolving disputes, including when someone is suspected or accused of breaking a rule.

4.7 Principles for rules and their enforcement

Rules should be created and enforced with:

- Reasonableness
- Fairness in the written (or spoken) rule
- Fairness in enforcement of the rule, often with a process
- Sufficient room for common sense and human decision making.

Rules should leave sufficient room for common sense and decision making. Then a process is needed when enforcing the rule to ensure fairness, such as:

- Some fact finding
- Allow the alleged rulebreaker to provide their version of events and anything that explains or mitigates their conduct
- Decide if a rule violation occurred
- If a rule violation occurred, decide on a fair consequence.

The concepts of "fairness" and "reasonableness" are a good starting place.

4.8 Who interprets the rule?

Rules are interpreted by humans, and humans are not perfect. They make mistakes and reasonable humans may disagree. Some of our species are plain unreasonable. All of this means the interpretation of a rule can change based on the human.

We hope for a process to ensure that rules and their creation, modification, interpretation, and enforcement proceeds reasonably and deliberately.

4.9 Debating a rule and the process

When analyzing and debating a rule, it is helpful to separate two important issues:

- Is the rule itself fair?
- Is enforcement of the rule fair?

Rules can be fair, unfair, somewhere in between, or unclear. The same can be said for enforcement of rules, and there is often room for agreement and debate.

This type of analysis can be applied to any type of rule, whether it comes from parents, school, employer, or government.

4.10 Ethical, criminal, and civil rules in context

Ethics (*e.g.*, "morals" and "character") is an important trait and could be part of a personal set of rules.

Ethical rules are usually a higher standard of conduct than criminal or civil laws. Criminal laws prohibit the most extreme types of bad conduct. Civil law may prohibit many actions already disallowed by criminal law plus more. Ethics is an even higher standard of conduct encompassing all the above plus more, including a duty to act or speak.

This diagram shows how criminal law prohibits a relatively small area of conduct, civil law a larger area, and ethics an even larger area.

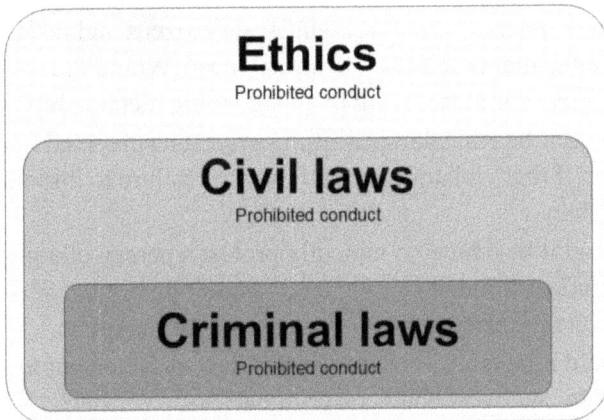

Ethics
Prohibited conduct

Civil laws
Prohibited conduct

Criminal laws
Prohibited conduct

**Conduct prohibited by ethics,
civil laws and criminal laws**

Ethics is an important trait to build in oneself and to seek out in candidates for a job (any job including a government job or political office). Like most traits, it can be learned and practiced and improved—if the person truly desires to. It can be hard to identify because deceptive or unethical people will make attempts to appear trustworthy and honest.

Ethics is about the process as much as the result. Doing the right thing, for the right reason, and looking out for the people that may be owed a duty. For example, a government official elected to office has a duty to use that office to serve the government and citizens (not to enrich themselves, family, friends, or bribe givers).

4.11 Additional reading and references

- *Chapter 4 resources*, https://johnbandler.com/cyberlawbook-resources-ch04
- *Rules*, https://johnbandler.com/rules
- *Ethics*, https://johnbandler.com/ethics

4.12 Questions

- List the five main places rules come from.
- Consider the five main places rules come from, as laid out in the chapter. What do you think of them? Are some more important than others, and why? Are there categories you think should be added or removed and why?
- In what ways are laws just like rules, in what ways are they not?
- In a democracy and free country, do citizens and residents have an ethical duty to follow criminal laws? Would the result be different for those living in an autocratic dictatorship?
- Could it be ethical to peacefully protest a perceived injustice, even if that violates a minor law (e.g., failure to disperse, etc.)? Explain.
- Could it be ethical to violently protest a perceived injustice, including through spitting on or assaulting police, or damaging private property or government property? Explain.
- Could it be ethical for someone in law enforcement to violate a law to catch and convict a criminal?
- Could it be ethical for a private organization to break criminal laws to try to catch a cybercriminal?

5

Laws Introduced: Rules from Government

In this chapter:

- Laws in context
- Sources of law
- Areas of law
- Laws for conduct
- Laws for process

5.1 Laws are just rules from government (recap)[37]

Laws are essentially rules that are made by the government, including constitutions, statutes, regulations, and court decisions. Those are essentially our "laws."

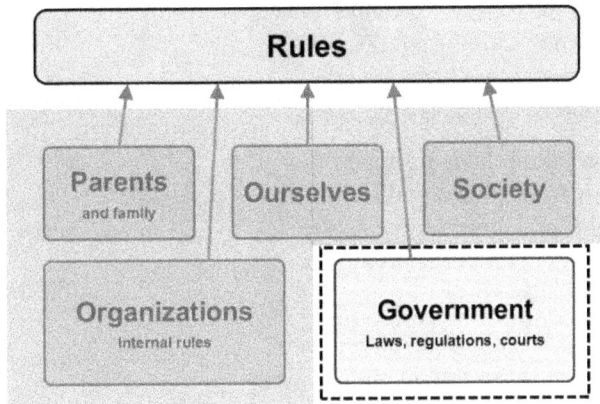

Rules

Parents and family

Ourselves

Society

Organizations Internal rules

Government Laws, regulations, courts

Rules from government are laws

---

[37] The prior chapter discussed "rules" more generally. Much of that discussion is applicable here to laws.

By viewing laws as a type of rule from government, some of the mystery is removed.

Still, laws are created and enforced with a complex process and have a significant effect upon society.

Most people agree that governments need to impose some degree of rulemaking and rule enforcement—even if we disagree on what those rules should be and how they should be enforced.[38]

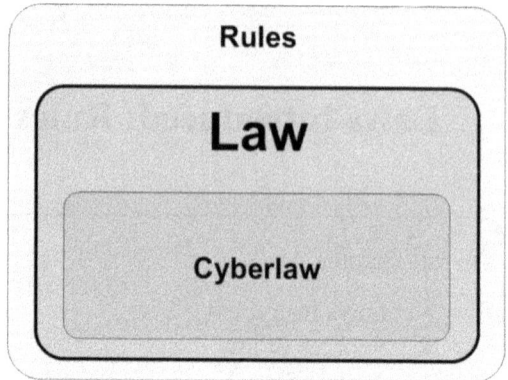

5.2 Laws include rules for conduct and rules to resolve conflict

Here are two important categories of laws to consider:

- Substantive laws (about conduct: what to do and what not to do)
- Procedural laws (a process for resolving disputes).

Substantive laws provide rules on what to do or not do. Areas of substantive laws include criminal laws and civil laws.

Procedural laws provide rules on how to resolve a conflict. This conflict is going to be about whether someone violated a substantive rule.

For example, if the government alleges that a defendant violated a criminal law, there is a process and system for resolving that allegation. If one party alleges a civil wrong was committed by another, there is a civil process and system to allege and resolve that dispute. These are areas of procedural law.

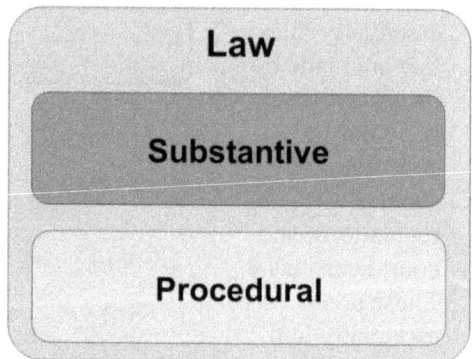

---

[38] Occasionally there are groups of anarchists that proclaim they hate government and all its oppressive rules and laws, and they decide they will create their own free society where people can do whatever they want. Even these types of organizations inevitably begin creating their own rules and processes.

5.3 Sources of laws

Law needs to come from somewhere, and different countries look to different places for their systems of government and law.

In a dictatorship or autocracy, the system of law comes from a single person.

In a theocracy, leaders rule in the name of God (or a god), which is subjective and open to varying interpretation about God's wishes.

Other countries begin with a governmental founding document such as a "constitution," and a process for enacting laws, reviewing laws, reviewing disputes, and governing the day-to-day activities of a country. Many countries at founding were wary of becoming a dictatorship and wanted to protect rights. They may have branches of government such as:

- Executive
- Law making (legislative)
- Courts and judges (judicial).

Most countries have different government units, such as:

- Country
- Smaller units (state, county, province)
- Even smaller units (city, town, village).

5.4 Judges interpret the law

Legally speaking, law is interpreted and decided by judges, and this occurs as they decide individual cases which are litigation between two or more parties. These decisions have legal effect beyond that particular case and become judge-made law. That is the concept of precedence (*stare decisis*).

Judges are humans, almost always an attorney, hopefully experienced, wise, and impartial. Humans are not perfect; attorneys and judges are not either. Reasonable people will often disagree, and not every person is reasonable.

Most people have opinions on legal issues, and opinions on political or social issues where they may not fully appreciate the legal tie-ins.

Our job in this book is to explore cyberlaw so that you can form a reasonable understanding and develop your own thoughts and opinions.

Judges and lawyers should not be the only people who have opinions that matter regarding law and cyberlaw.[39]

5.5 Principles of law

The principles and theories of law are wonderful.

In a country *with* the rule of law, truth and justice and fairness are paramount. We strive for a fair system with rules of conduct and a fair process for consequences when people do not abide by these rules.

In a country *without* the rule of law, those principles do not matter. Whoever has the most power, the most strength, and the greatest ability to force, coerce, or manipulate will get their way.

Even in a nation with the rule of law, the realities are messier, as we will explore in the next chapter.

5.6 Fairness of the law and fairness of enforcement

We can assess laws just as we assessed rules, and it helps to separate two issues:

1. What is the law, and
2. How should the law be enforced.

After that, we can dive into greater detail to fully analyze the situation:

- What is the law
- What should the law be
- How is the law enforced now
- How should the law be enforced
- What process to determine what happened (the facts)
- How to protect people's rights from the government's power
- What consequences if a law is broken.

A law, as written, could be fair, unfair, or somewhere in between. There will always be room for reasonable people to debate those issues (remembering that not every person is reasonable).

The next issue is enforcement of laws, and whether that is fair or not. Laws can be interpreted and enforced fairly, with consequences tailored

---

[39] We want to give due respect to a legal education and legal experience, while realizing that does not give a person the right to an unchallengeable opinion.

Lawyers often disagree, and for any lawyer that has one opinion, you can find another lawyer who has the opposite opinion. We see this in any litigation, cable news show, and even with a panel of appellate judges hearing the same case.

to the circumstances. Or they can be enforced unfairly, arbitrarily, or capriciously, including against political enemies. As always, reasonable people will debate whether enforcement is fair or not.[40]

5.7 Areas of law (preview)

There are dozens of areas of law, and layers to each of them, with entire books devoted to them. Some lawyers might specialize in one area but know little about others. Books are written on each area of law, and even on micro-components in a legal area.

An interesting part of cyberlaw is that it spans so many of these other areas of law.

5.8 Additional reading and references

For more on the concepts discussed above, you can visit:

- *Chapter 5 resources*, https://johnbandler.com/cyberlawbook-resources-ch05
- *Law*, https://johnbandler.com/law

5.9 Chapter questions

- Laws are just a type of R_____ that come from the G_____
- Laws are essentially a type of rule that come from _____
- List two main types of law, S_____ and P_____
- List two main areas of law, Cr_____ law and Ci_____ law
- Law includes rules for conduct (known as _____ law) and rules for process (known as _____ law)
- What group of people in the legal system are the official interpreters of what the law is?

---

[40] As an example, most people would agree that there should be speed limits on most roads, meaning a prohibition on speeding above that limit. Some might disagree on what the speed limit should be on a particular road, and some might disagree on what level of enforcement is appropriate. Most would agree it would be unfair if police stopped and wrote tickets to only certain motorists for going a single mile per hour over that speed limit (*e.g.* 31 in a 30 zone).

- As we assess or debate a law, it is helpful to separate two components, (1) the law as it is _____ and (2) how the law is _____

6

Introducing the U.S. Legal System:
Substantive Laws and Procedural Laws
(Laws for Conduct, and a Process to
Investigate and Resolve)

In this chapter:

- Our U.S. legal system
- A democracy with many freedoms
- Sources of our laws
- Substantive laws (laws for conduct)
- Procedural laws (laws for process)
- Practice and theory are beautiful, but reality is messier
- New York's system

6.1 Sources of law in the U.S.

U.S. law is a system of rules from our government that establish standards of conduct and a process for resolving conflicts peacefully. These legal conflicts usually occur when someone alleges someone else broke those rules.

Laws come from different places. First, we can look at the government authority issuing the rule, such as:

- Federal government (U.S. government)
- A state government (New York, Connecticut, California, etc.)[41]

---

[41] The term "state" in this book refers to one of our fifty states, such as New York. When I use that term, consider if you should also be thinking about the District of Columbia and territories such as Puerto Rico which may also have their own laws. I might say "check your state laws" but you might want to read

- A "state type" level government, including District of Columbia, territories like Puerto Rico
- A smaller governmental unit: county, city, town, village, etc.

Then we can look at the type of rule that is issued on behalf of that governmental unit. These rules include:

- Constitution (founding documents establishing the government and certain duties and rights)
- Statutes (laws duly passed by a legislature, signed by executive)
- Regulations (rules put forth, or "promulgated," by a regulatory body)
- Court decisions (decisions by a judge or judges that affects the parties of that case and may create legal authority over other cases).

For example, our federal (US) government and laws include:

- U.S. Constitution (with amendments)
- U.S. statutes
- U.S. regulations
- U.S. court decisions.

The U.S. Constitution is the foundation for our system of government and a framework for all laws. State constitutions serve a similar purpose for each state.

The U.S. Constitution establishes our three branches of government (executive, legislative, judicial) and their powers, and has twenty-seven amendments. The first Ten Amendments are the Bill of Rights.[42]

Statutes are enacted into law by the legislature with the signature of the executive (President or Governor).

Regulations are more detailed legal requirements that are put forth by a regulator (such as a financial or health regulator). That regulator will have their legal authority pursuant to a statute.

---

that as "check the laws of your state, district, or territory." Also consider tribal governmental units.

In a Chapter 35 we will use the term "nation-state" to refer to countries. Within international law the term "state" could mean a country, but not in this book.

[42] More on the U.S. Constitution in the next chapter.

Courts resolve legal disputes. Court decisions set forth how a particular case is decided, affecting the litigants (parties). These decisions also have broader legal weight that can apply to future cases. This principle of broader legal weight is known as "precedent," "*stare decisis,*" "judge made law" and "common law." As an example, court decisions have crafted the areas of negligence law and contract law.[43] Court decisions have continually evolved the law as first put forth in places such as the First Amendment and Fourth Amendment.

As we look to state law, we should consider that each state may have a legal framework that parallels the federal framework, including:

- State constitutions
- State statutes
- State regulations
- State court decisions.

Remember there are fifty states, plus the District of Columbia and territories like Puerto Rico and Guam. Each of those may have a constitution, statutes, regulations, and court decisions.

We can't become experts on the laws of every state, but we can start with our home state (mine is New York).

This diagram shows these sources of law in a simple fashion.

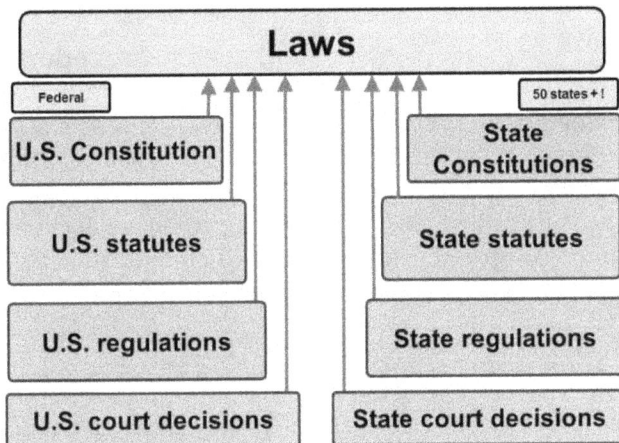

Laws

Federal   50 states + !

U.S. Constitution	State Constitutions
U.S. statutes	State statutes
U.S. regulations	State regulations
U.S. court decisions	State court decisions

Laws in the U.S. come from many sources

---

[43] Occasionally legal scholars summarize a body of case law in Restatements of the Law, such as for contracts, torts (civil wrongs) and product liability, and more.

6.2 Federal laws and state laws

An important category to identify is whether a law is federal (from the U.S. Government) or from a state. A federal law has force throughout the country, a state law has force within that state.[44]

This distinction can make law confusing but also makes it interesting. There are a lot of laws from many places!

> **Recap**: As you come across a law, regulation, or court decision, figure out where it is from. Either:
>
> - Federal (U.S.), or
> - State (and identify which state).

6.3 Substantive law and procedural law

Consider laws within the U.S. as being either substantive or procedural.

It helps to envision whether it is a rule of conduct (what to do, or what not to do), or a rule to resolve a conflict or investigate something (process and procedure oriented).

Law

Substantive

Procedural

Substantive laws relate to conduct. Criminal substantive laws prohibit certain conduct, someone could be arrested and prosecuted for violating those laws, and jail could even be a penalty. Civil substantive laws also prohibit certain conduct or require certain actions. Someone could be sued civilly for violating those rules and be required to pay money to compensate the plaintiff.

Procedural laws relate to process. They try to ensure the process for resolving a legal dispute is orderly and fair to both sides.

If the police and prosecutor allege a defendant violated a criminal law, the criminal procedure laws set forth how the government can go about investigating this supposed crime, and then proving it in court, from

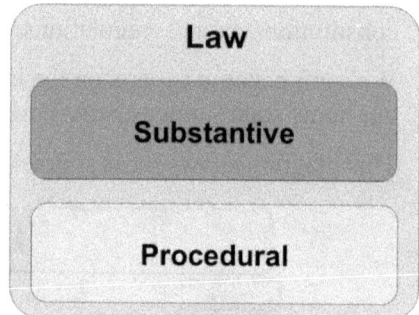

---

[44] We will see that many cyberlaws have effect and force beyond that state's geographic borders.

arrest through trial and appeal, ensuring the defendant receives due process.

If a civil plaintiff alleges the defendant wronged them (e.g., through negligent driving or by defaming them) then the civil procedure laws set forth the process for filing that lawsuit and litigating it.

***

Recap: As you come across a law, figure out whether it is:

- Substantive law (a law about what not to do), or
- Procedural law (a law of process, how to resolve a dispute).

***

6.4 Criminal law and civil law

Another category to focus on is criminal law versus civil law. They have many important differences.

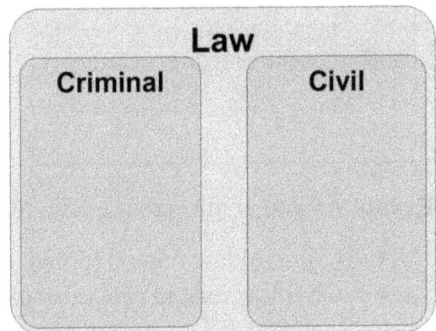

Criminal law concerns government bringing criminal cases against individuals and sometimes against organizations. The government participants include police, special agents, prosecutors, and all the other people who work with them.

The government acts on behalf of society, and the law seeks to recognize the immense power of government in this area and level the playing field. The government has the power to take away an individual's freedom and has created constitutional and statutory protections for defendants.

Civil law is about more individualized and mostly monetary harms. Anyone can bring a civil case, including individuals, companies, and the government. Consequences of a civil case almost never involve jail (except in extreme cases where a party is flagrantly and repeatedly contemptuous of the court). There are fewer protections for civil defendants compared to criminal defendants.

This diagram summarizes some of the differences between criminal and civil law.

Criminal Law vs. Civil Law

Criminal law
- Government brings the case on behalf of society
- **Goals**: Protect society, deter, punish, rehabilitate
- Defendant can be held in custody
  - Arrested
  - Jail pending trial possible
  - Jail a possible sentence
- **Beyond a reasonable doubt** (BRD) is the burden of proof
  - Highest burden of proof in legal system
- Protections of U.S. Constitution

Civil law
- Anyone can bring a civil case
- **Goals**: Typically to recover money (monetary damages)
- Defendant gets a summons to appear in court
- **Preponderance of the evidence** is the typical burden of proof
  - More likely than not

Recap: As you come across a law, identify whether it is:

- Criminal law related (police could arrest someone for it), or
- Civil law related (police could *not* arrest someone for it).

As we assess these important categories:

- Civil law or criminal law
- Substantive law or procedural law.

We can see four important categories that come from these:

- Criminal substantive law
- Criminal procedural law
- Civil substantive law
- Civil procedural law.

We can evolve the diagram to show the four areas like this:

John T. Bandler

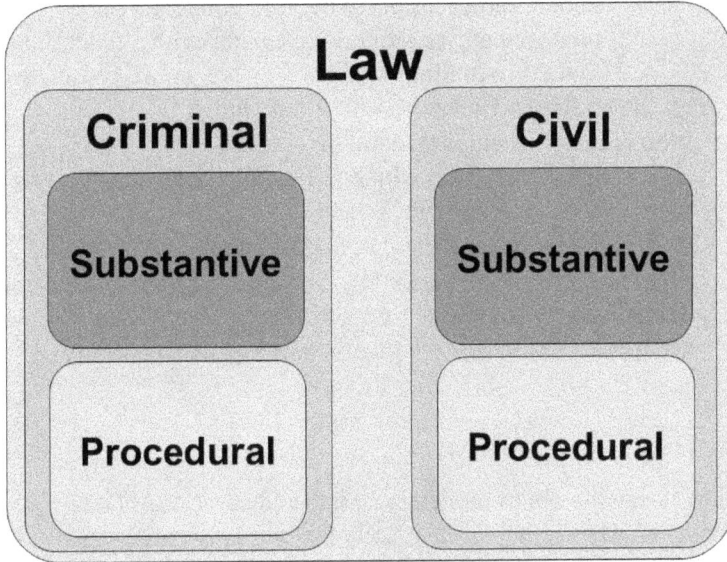

6.5 Criminal law basics (preview)[45]

Criminal law is significant, and the criminal justice system is vast and sprawling. It is of great interest to the public through news and entertainment with television shows and movies based upon police, prosecutors, criminals, and crime.[46]

We can group criminal law first according to whether it is:

- Federal criminal law, or
- State criminal law of any of the various states.

Then we can group criminal law according to:

- Substantive laws (the criminal statutes that offenders are charged with breaking) and
- Procedural laws (the process of investigating and prosecuting).

When assessing a criminal case, students should consider:

- What criminal court is it in?
- Is it in federal court or a state (or local) court, and which court?

---

[45] We dive into criminal law in Chapter 8, and cyber-criminal law in Part 4.
[46] For all its importance and interest, relatively few lawyers practice in criminal law.

- o Federal prosecutions will be in a federal court, prosecuted by a federal prosecutor with a federal judge.[47]
- o State prosecutions will be in a state court, prosecuted by a state prosecutor, with a state judge.[48]
- Who is the prosecutor (federal or state)?
  - o If federal, from which federal district?
  - o If state, from which state?
- Who is the judge, and in what court do they sit?
- What are the criminal laws alleged to have been violated (federal or state, identify section, title, etc.)?
- What law enforcement is involved in the investigation and arrest?

6.6 Civil law basics (preview)

Civil law is usually about monetary harms and suing to obtain compensation (damages). Occasionally the court will order a party to do something or *not* do something.

Civil law has two components:

- Substantive civil law (the rules of conduct), and
- Procedural civil law (how civil litigation conflicts are resolved).

In a civil case, we also want to assess what court it is in. We want to identify first whether it is a federal or state court, then learn more details (the venue, which state, etc.).

Then we want to ask what laws are being applied. This is known as "choice of law," and in civil cases the court in one location occasionally applies the law of another location.

There are fewer protections for defendants in civil court compared to criminal court. The burden of proof on civil plaintiffs is lower; the parties are deemed to be on a more equal level.

---

[47] Federal prosecutors are typically called Assistant U.S. Attorneys, and the federal judge is typically a District Court Judge or U.S. Magistrate Judge.

[48] Each state is different. Even within New York it can get complicated, our state prosecutors are usually Assistant District Attorneys but could be an Assistant New York State Attorney General or appointed by a city, town, or village. Judges could be from the New York Supreme Court (our highest-level trial court), a district court, county court, or from a city, town, or village court.

A person wishing to bring a civil case usually needs to pay their attorney, or have the attorney agree to take the case on a contingency, meaning the attorney receives a percentage of any recovery.

A person defending in a civil case usually needs to pay their attorney as well. (In a criminal case, defendants who cannot afford an attorney are usually appointed one at no charge).

Because of this heavy financial component to civil cases, money and cost are a significant factor. Parties must evaluate costs to litigate and potential outcomes.[49]

There are many areas of civil law, which we will cover more in Chapter 9, and then Part 5.

6.7 Litigation and procedural law (preview)

When one side to a dispute alleges the other side violated a rule of conduct, they may bring a legal case. Then comes the process to resolve that case.

We call each side to a dispute a "party." That party could be an individual or entity, such as a business, governmental unit, or nonprofit.

The party bringing the case is the plaintiff.

In criminal cases, the government brings the case so they may be called the "Government," "United States," "People of the State of New York," or "New York." They are usually not referred to as a "plaintiff."

The party defending the claim is the "defendant" (no surprise).

Litigation is a legal dispute brought before a court, and it has these basic steps:

- The complaining party (plaintiff) files the legal complaint with the court to commence the legal action
    - Criminal case: filed by prosecutor or police
    - Civil case: filed by plaintiff
- Legally require the defendant to come to court to answer the charges
    - Criminal case: arrest, criminal summons, etc.

---

[49] For example, a rational plaintiff would not spend $100,000 in legal fees to recover $10,000 in damages, nor would an attorney agree to take a case on contingency (paid a percentage of any recovery) unless it seemed likely the recovery of significant compensation would offset their time spent.

- o Civil case: civil summons
- Motion practice by both sides to address legal issues and resolve certain claims
- Discovery (disclosure) – the sharing of information between sides
- Hearings for the court to hear pretrial information and facts
- Court decisions
- Trial to adjudicate the claims
- Verdict
- Post-trial motions
- Judgement
- Appeal.

More details in each of the chapters on criminal and civil law.

6.8 Theory and principles of law in the U.S.

The principles of law in our country are beautiful.

In our representative democracy, citizens elect the government that creates and then enforces and administers the law. Citizens also serve as jurors.

Here are some important points:

- Our country is a nation of laws.
- No person should be above the law.
- Our highest law is the U.S. Constitution.
- We have a process for creating laws.
- We have a process to enforce the law fairly and impartially (hence the blindfold on lady justice).
- Juries decide the facts in many legal disputes.
- We have a process for electing government officials.
- The officials we elect create laws and enforce laws.
- Citizens play an essential role in our legal system and government by:
  - o Serving as jurors
  - o Voting.
- Citizens have both a right and responsibility to fulfill these duties by:
  - o Serving as fair and diligent jurors, following judicial instructions
  - o Casting informed votes after doing diligence.
- Law affects every one of us.

- We should all know something about law.[50]

6.9 The theory is wonderful, reality is messier

Theory is important, but even within a perfect theoretical world, reasonable people will disagree, and some people will be unhappy with the result. It will be messy. There will be dissent whether it is picking a candidate, passing a law, a judicial decision, an individual criminal prosecution and trial, or an opinion about how the criminal justice or civil justice legal systems work. Even our theory—beautiful as it is— realizes that nothing will be perfect from everyone's perspective.

Our reality is even messier.

First, citizens are people, and they can be influenced and even manipulated. Their thoughts and actions, including their votes, can be influenced. The digital realm makes this influence and manipulation a reality for foreign powers, candidates, businesses, and more.[51]

Second, other factors indicate that not every law is fair, and not everyone gets equal justice. For example, a billionaire and wealthy corporations or groups can influence the law and regulation by hiring lawyers, lobbyists, public relations firms, and former government officials to influence the legislation and regulation, including public perception of it.

Third, parties to a legal dispute can purchase legal representation or other access that may grant them a different result. They can fund litigation that might push smaller adversaries into defeat. Some litigation can simply be a war of attrition, costing each side in lawyer's fees until one or both decide it is time to cut losses and settle. Lawyers try to get a win for their side—litigation is a battle even when done legally and ethically. Not every lawyer is ethical and does their job within the bounds of the law and attorney ethics. If juries ultimately decide the facts in a trial, the

---

[50] Our system of law, like our democracy, is fragile. If our citizenry do not properly understand and appreciate it, and if bad actors are allowed to manipulate or cause damage, it can be undermined.

[51] In Part 8 we assess speech and thought and how it can be influenced online. Even the foundation of our democracy, one person one vote, can be affected if (for example) a foreign government, domestic organization or social media platform could improperly influence sufficient citizens to affect the outcome of an election.

highly funded legal team has a number of advantages towards convincing that jury.[52]

Litigation involves lawyers as advocates, advocating for their own client. Each lawyer will express the facts and laws in a way to benefit their own client. Some lawyers go further than others in how far they will spin, stretch, or even distort the facts and law.[53]

Finally, our system presumes certain norms will be followed, and that important government positions will be staffed by competent people of good character, serving the good of the country. This is not always the case.

We want to be realistic and practical, not overly optimistic, nor pessimistic and cynical. Here's one way to think about it:

> *The U.S. legal system is the worst, except for everyone else's system.*

And here's another:

> *The U.S. legal system is not perfect, but it is one of the best systems around.*

Other countries recognize our rule of law, and that is why they trust it to store their assets, investments and to do business.

We are a nation of laws, and we all play a role in our country and legal system and should not take it for granted, nor assume it is immune from improper influence.

We can appreciate the beauty of law and learn to think like a lawyer who is objective, reasonable, without a client to serve, and without a stake in the outcome. With that perspective we can assess facts and law.

We realize that not all lawyers in all situations are equal nor objective and impartial. We can see the beauty of law and our system of

---

[52] Consider the advantages if one side can spend millions of dollars on expert jury consultants and other resources designed to pick the most favorable jurors and then to present a case designed to persuade them.

[53] Attorneys have a duty to zealously represent their clients within the bounds of law and attorney ethics. Even ethical attorneys will view facts and law in the light most favorable to their own client. Some attorneys may stretch the bounds of ethics and law.

Most government attorneys are a little different because they have a unique duty to justice, not just to "win." That is because their "client" is both the government and the people the government represents.

government while realizing how messy and imperfect it can be. Even subject to grave error or corruption.

We also need to realize it is a system made up of people, requiring constant vigilance to maintain its integrity and not become subject to partisanship, corruption, or service to a single individual.

6.10 A New York frame of mind[54]

Law in the U.S. means federal law (from the U.S. Government) plus the law of our fifty states.

We cannot cover the law of *every* state in this book, so we use New York as an example.[55]

First, let's put New York in the context of all the other states.[56] It is just one of fifty states, but it has a strong influence on law and the country. Some call it the financial capital of the country—even the world.

The New York State Court System is large, and some parts are named differently compared to other states.[57] It is divided into four Departments, then into Judicial Districts. Consider these courts:

- New York Court of Appeals (highest appellate court, located in Albany)
- Appellate Division and Appellate Term courts (an intermediate level appellate court, for appeals right after a trial)

---

[54] This section title is a nod to the song by Billy Joel, *New York State of Mind.* New York state stretches from the beaches of Montauk to the Niagara Falls, including rural farms and the mega metropolis of New York City.

[55] Become familiar with your state's laws and relevant websites. Each state will have official websites where they make their laws available to the public including about state enforcement actions. There will be reputable private sites that do this too, and reputable law firms that provide excellent summaries.

Consider the National Conference of State Legislatures (NCSL) which has many helpful compilations of states laws across a particular area. *See* https://www.ncsl.org. Then consider sites like Cornell Law School's Legal Information Institute (LII) which has a wealth of legal resources, including on state law. *See* https://www.law.cornell.edu.

[56] International students and readers from other countries may be unfamiliar with our system of a federal government and state governments.

[57] For more about the New York State Court System, *see* https://www.nycourts.gov.

- State Supreme Court, a trial level court that can hear the most serious types of civil and criminal disputes[58]
- County Courts (can hear serious criminal disputes and civil matters under a certain amount)
- District Courts (sort of like County Courts but in Long Island)
- City courts
- Town and village justice courts (misdemeanors and traffic infractions and certain civil matters).[59]

6.11 Additional reading and references

- *Chapter 6 resources,* https://johnbandler.com/cyberlawbook-resources-ch06
- *Law in the United States Introduced,* https://johnbandler.com/law-in-united-states-introduced

6.12 Chapter questions

- List three important ways we can categorize laws to help identify them
- Categorize laws based on whether they are Federal or _____
- Categorize laws based on whether they are substantive or _____
- Categorize laws based on whether they are criminal or _____
- Four types of laws are (i) constitutions, (ii)_____, (iii) _____, and (iv) _____

---

[58] In New York it is called a "Supreme Court" because it is the most powerful trial level court. Other states call their highest-level appellate court the "Supreme Court."

[59] Fun fact: At the time I was a state trooper, when I issued a traffic ticket it would be returnable in either a town, village, or city court. If the motorist pleaded not guilty, I would appear in court on the designated date and act as both prosecutor and primary witness.

7

U.S. Constitution and Amendments:
The Foundation for Law and Government

In this chapter:

- The highest, foundational law in our country, the U.S. Constitution

7.1. The U.S. Constitution

The U.S. Constitution is the highest law in the United States. It establishes our system of government with three branches and a system of checks and balances. It gives power to the government, limits the power of government and guarantees certain rights to the people.

The U.S. Constitution became effective in 1789, and has been amended many times, starting with the Bill of Rights. As our highest law, other laws and actions by the government must comply with it.

If a judge finds that a law violates the U.S. Constitution, the judge could declare the law unconstitutional and render the law void. If a judge finds a government action unconstitutional, the judge could order the government to stop doing it.

Every state in our country also has their own constitution. Thus, it can be helpful to specify "U.S. Constitution" instead of merely "Constitution" to be clear which constitution you are referring to.[60]

---

[60] Since "U.S. Constitution" and "First Amendment" and other amendments are proper nouns, they get capitalized.

7.2 We the People

Our Constitution starts with "We the People." The first paragraph reads:

> *We the People of the United States, in Order to form a more perfect Union, establish Justice, insure domestic Tranquility, provide for the common defence, promote the general Welfare, and secure the Blessings of Liberty to ourselves and our Posterity, do ordain and establish this Constitution for the United States of America.*
>
> *— U.S Constitution, preamble*

This basically means our government is formed by the people, for the people, and with a process in place for elections and governance.[61] We are not a monarchy, not a dictatorship, not a theocracy (religion-based government), nor subject to mob rule or riot. We are a government of the people with processes in place to resolve our differences peacefully and lawfully.

7.3. Articles within the Constitution

There are seven Articles within the Constitution.

- Article I establishes the legislative branch. It provides for a bicameral Congress, with the U.S. House of Representatives and U.S. Senate, and lays out the powers of Congress. (Bicameral means "two chambers").
- Article II establishes the executive branch. E.g., the President, powers of the president, etc.
- Article III establishes the judicial branch. This includes the U.S. Supreme Court and other federal courts.
- See the text for other Articles.[62]

---

[61] Of course, every phrase or term can be misused and misunderstood, and "We the People" is no exception. Rest assured the Constitution does not grant individuals the right to violate criminal laws nor overthrow the government with force just because they disagree with it. Instead, the Constitution provides for elections, a process, and peaceful resolutions of disputes and transitions of power.

[62] The U.S. Constitution can be found online many places, including: National Archives, https://www.archives.gov/founding-docs/constitution-transcript; Cornell LII, https://www.law.cornell.edu/constitution.

No matter where you find it, you would cite to the U.S. Constitution.

These three branches are co-equal and provide for checks and balances. We did not want our executive branch becoming all powerful (like a monarchy), so each branch can temper ("check") the others.

The U.S. Constitution grants the federal government only certain powers, so it is in theory a "limited" government.

7.4 A limited U.S. government?

The U.S. Constitution (in theory) provides for a "limited" federal government, and specifically provides ("enumerates") certain powers to the federal government. If powers are not specifically given to the federal government, it cannot assert those powers, and they are reserved for the states, or for individuals.[63] This means the federal government does not have a general "police power" (general blanket authority) whereas states do.

Where you hear the term "state's rights," that refers to the right of the state to set certain rules and make certain decisions, independently from the federal government.[64]

In practice, the federal government has enormous powers. It can tax and spend, regulate interstate commerce (an expansive power), provide for national defense, and more. This gives it the power to impose all sorts of rules upon the states and individuals.

7.5 Interpreting the U.S. Constitution: fixed or evolving?

Legal scholars and regular folks debate which of these statements should be followed:

- The Constitution is a living, evolving body of law, that judges can interpret in accordance with the times.
- The Constitution is fixed words with a fixed meaning, we need to see what the exact text says to interpret it.

---

[63] The Tenth Amendment reads:
> *The powers not delegated to the United States by the Constitution, nor prohibited by it to the States, are reserved to the States respectively, or to the people.*
> *— U.S. Constitution, Tenth Amendment.*

[64] As with all things in life and law, people can be selective in whether or how they support states' rights or the right of the federal government. That may depend upon which side they agree with in each situation.

- We need to interpret the text of the Constitution and to do so we must consider the founding fathers' "original intent" when they drafted the document.
- The Constitution can live and evolve only through the process of amendment—not through judicial interpretation.
- Laws should be changed through the legislative process—not through judicial interpretation.

Some of the terms relating to various legal theories of constitutional interpretation include:

- "Originalism"
- "Textualism"
- "Founders' intent."

The reality is that the law evolves, even when the fixed words of the Constitution remain unchanged and without amendment. Interpretation of the Constitution evolves. This evolution cannot be without bounds, it needs to be tempered, and judges should not stretch nor shrink the Constitution to arrive at their desired outcome. Neither can we pretend it is still 1789.

Clearly, interpretation of the U.S. Constitution has progressed over the years, even as certain text remains unchanged. Fourth Amendment case law is proof of this evolution.

As we debate whether and how law should evolve, including interpretation of fixed words of the Constitution, we should consider a few principles.

One is the principle of precedence, also known as *stare decisis*. Once a court of high authority rules on what the Constitution says, that has legal weight. A general rule is that subsequent decisions should be bound by that.

Another is that law should evolve with the times. The Fourth Amendment was written long before the cyber age, and courts have evolved it to address today's issues.

Another is that many people (including lawyers and even some judges) are advocates for a cause. This means that textualism, originalism, and precedence can sometimes be fickle concepts, which are embraced when convenient but discarded when suitable to arrive at the desired result.

7.6. Who gets to say what the U.S. Constitution means?

The U.S. Supreme Court has the ultimate legal authority to decide what the U.S. Constitution (with amendments) means. Let's examine that.

People (and lawyers especially) debate about what written laws really mean, and how laws should be applied. Ultimately, it is judges who decide what the law is. We have a system of appeals, and the highest court in the country is the United States Supreme Court (USSC or U.S. Supreme Court).

We would like our legal system to be free of political influence regarding individual cases, and we would like every judge to be fair and impartial, judging the case and the law based on the facts and the law—not personal beliefs or opinions. The legal doctrine of precedence provides some stability, indicating that prior decisions on law have great weight for pending and future decisions, but that is not always the case.[65]

We also need to be realistic. Judges are humans, and humans are imperfect. Further, politics works to influence the legal system and the U.S. Supreme Court. While the USSC decides the supreme law of the land, there is room to question whether their decisions are purely about law, or whether and how they might include political or personal judgments. Indeed, Presidents might nominate Supreme Court Justices based upon how they might rule in the future on certain issues.

7.7 The U.S. Constitution: a legal foundation for peaceful decisions about our country

> *"A republic, if you can keep it."*
>
> — *Benjamin Franklin*

Our Constitution is the oldest written national constitution still used. Our system of government has lasted over 225 years, with [mostly] peaceful transfer of powers between administrations. Cyberspace is a powerful influencer about what people think, their view of the facts, their view of

---

[65] A prominent recent example concerns abortion, the "right to choose," the "right to life" and related issues. Consider the U.S. Supreme Court (USSC) cases of *Roe v. Wade* in 1973 which granted certain Constitutional rights to pregnant women and then *Dobbs v. Jackson* Women's Health Organization in 2022 which reversed that decision. We will return to this in Chapter 32 on privacy, and then perhaps in a future book.

Whether you support the *Dobbs* decision or abhor it, it serves as a reminder that the U.S. Constitution, and law itself, is not absolute but subject to interpretation by humans.

the law, and government. We should not take our system of government for granted, nor assume that democracy and the rule of law is destined or predetermined to continue forever in this country.[66]

7.8 The oath to the Constitution

Our country is a nation of laws and process, not of individuals. Officials take oaths to the Constitution, sometimes to an office, but never to an individual.[67]

Here is the federal oath:

> *I _____, do solemnly swear (or affirm) that I will support and defend the Constitution of the United States against all enemies, foreign and domestic; that I will bear true faith and allegiance to the same; that I take this obligation freely, without any mental reservation or purpose of evasion; and that I will well and faithfully discharge the duties of the office on which I am about to enter. So help me God.*

In contrast, dictators, authoritarian governments, monarchies, and cults require loyalty and devotion to an individual. Allegiance is sworn to the person although that is contrary to the best interests of the people.

All our elected officials have sworn oaths to support and defend the Constitution of the United States, to look out for the good of country and constituents.[68]

---

[66] Consider the disruption following the 2020 election, and how some people may have been influenced to believe things that may not have been true, or angered to do things that they might not otherwise have done. On January 6, 2021, many individuals swarmed the U.S. Capitol (the home of our legislative branch) while Presidential election electoral votes were being counted. Some viewed this as an attempt to stop the vote count and stop the peaceful transfer of power from occurring. It is worth considering what influenced them and what has occurred since. That brings us back to cyberlaw, speech online and thoughts in our brains, which we cover more in Part 8, and then maybe in a future book.

[67] I was an Army officer, police officer, and assistant district attorney. Each time I started, I swore oaths to uphold the U.S. Constitution and the New York State Constitution.

[68] Not every elected official lives up to that oath. Some look out for personal gain or profit, to retain power improperly, or prioritize serving their party or party leader at the expense of the country.

7.9 The Amendments

The Constitution can be amended, though that is a long and difficult process. There are now twenty-seven amendments, and the first ten are the Bill of Rights. The First Amendment (speech) and Fourth Amendment (search and seizure) are the most important for cyberlaw.

Here's a quick and partial list of some of them with a quick summary:

- Bill of Rights – Amendments 1-10
  - 1st Amendment: Freedom of speech, religion, assembly, press
  - 4th Amendment: Freedom from unreasonable search and seizure
  - 5th Amendment: Grand jury, double jeopardy, due process, right to remain silent
  - 6th Amendment: Fair speedy public trial by impartial jury, right to attorney
  - 10th Amendment: Reservation of rights to states and people
- 13th Amendment: Abolish slavery
- 14th Amendment: U.S. citizenship for former slaves. States cannot violate citizen rights, must provide due process and equal protection.
- 15th Amendment: To ensure voting rights for formerly enslaved people.
- 19th Amendment: To ensure voting rights for women.

I have skipped many amendments for brevity. To see all the amendments, visit the National Archives or Cornell law site.[69]

7.10 The First Amendment (preview)

The First Amendment protects us from government restrictions on speech, religion and more.

Notice that the First Amendment *protects against government interference* with speech. This has implications for both criminal and

---

[69] Find the Bill of Rights and subsequent amendments at the National Archives, https://www.archives.gov/founding-docs/bill-of-rights-transcript, https://www.archives.gov/founding-docs/amendments-11-27.
Also find it at Cornell LII at https://www.law.cornell.edu/constitution.

civil law. Certain speech or expression cannot be criminally prosecuted or be the basis of a successful civil lawsuit.

The First Amendment does not protect against private interference with speech (though other laws might).

There is an enormous body of case law (legal precedent) that interprets what the First Amendment means.[70]

7.11 The Fourth Amendment (preview)

The Fourth Amendment protects us from unreasonable search and seizure by the government.

It does not protect against private searches, seizures, or takings (though other laws may).

From the Fourth Amendment an enormous body of case law has developed and evolved.[71]

7.12 Reviewing government laws and actions

When a party in a legal action challenges the constitutionality of a law or government action, courts will apply different levels of scrutiny to the legal issue, depending on the type of question.

Simply put, there are three levels of scrutiny:

- Rational basis review (a low level of scrutiny)
- Intermediate scrutiny (a medium level)
- Strict scrutiny (a high level of scrutiny).

Rational basis review is a low hurdle for the government to meet, they merely need to show the law is "rationally related" to a "legitimate" government interest.[72]

Intermediate scrutiny is a medium level of review, the government needs to show that the law is "substantially related" to an "important"

---

[70] More on the First Amendment in Chapter 10. We discuss it further in our discussion of civil and criminal cyberlaw and again in Chapter 36 where we examine speech in cyberspace.

[71] We dive into the Fourth Amendment in Chapter 11, and then in Part 4.

[72] Cornell LII, *Rational basis test*, https://www.law.cornell.edu/wex/rational_basis_test.

government interest.[73] Intermediate scrutiny would be applied to content-neutral restrictions on speech (restrictions on time, place, or manner).

Strict scrutiny is the most detailed review of government laws or actions, and the government must show the law is "narrowly tailored" to achieve a "compelling governmental interest."[74] Strict scrutiny is applied to content specific restrictions on speech.

7.13 Conclusion

The U.S. Constitution and Amendments are the country's highest law. The Constitution establishes our government and how it operates, with three branches and a system of checks and balances. As we assess rules for government conduct and laws, our first thought and our research starting point should be the U.S. Constitution.

7.14 References and additional reading

- *Chapter 7 resources*, https://johnbandler.com/cyberlawbook-resources-ch07
- *Law in the United States Introduced*, https://johnbandler.com/law-in-united-states-introduced
- *U.S. Constitution and Amendments*, https://johnbandler.com/us-constitution
- *U.S. Constitution* at Cornell LII, https://www.law.cornell.edu/constitution
- *U.S. Constitution* (full text via National Archives), https://www.archives.gov/founding-docs/constitution-transcript
- Chapter 10, First Amendment
- Chapter 11, Fourth Amendment

7.15 Chapter questions

- Name the highest law in the U.S.
- Who has the final say in interpreting what the U.S. Constitution means?
- What does the First Amendment protect against?

---

[73] Cornell LII, *Intermediate scrutiny*, https://www.law.cornell.edu/wex/intermediate_scrutiny.
[74] Cornell LII, *Strict scrutiny*, https://www.law.cornell.edu/wex/strict_scrutiny.

- What does the Fourth Amendment protect against?
- What year did the U.S. Constitution become effective?
- What document establishes our system of government and is the highest law in the country?
- List the three branches of U.S. government
- Briefly summarize what Articles I, II, and III of the U.S. Constitution establish
- Since many states have their own constitutions, the best way to be clear that you are writing about the U.S. Constitution is to call it _____ and not just the "Constitution."

8

Crime, Criminal Law, and Criminal Justice Introduced

In this chapter:

- Crime
- Criminal law
- Criminal justice
- Our criminal justice system
- Jurisdiction introduced

8.1 A unique body of law

Criminal law involves the government and its process of investigating, arresting, prosecuting, and punishing.

Criminal law is enforced by the government on behalf of society, one of the several important distinctions from civil law.[75]

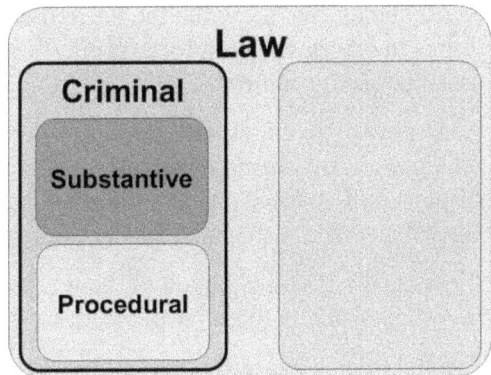

Consider how the three branches of government are involved in criminal law:

- Legislative branch enacts the criminal laws
- Executive branch (police and prosecutors) investigates and enforces the laws
- Judicial branch hears the cases and tries to ensure a fair process.

---

[75] Civil law involves more individualized harms and typically private parties. Consequences in a civil law case usually include monetary damages.

Consequences in a criminal case can include punishments such as fines and jail. Criminal cases have a higher burden of proof than other areas of law (beyond a reasonable doubt).

One arm of government brings the cases (executive branch with police and prosecutors) while another arm of government (judiciary) seeks to ensure a fair process and protect individual and societal rights.

Criminal law is a unique area where relatively few lawyers practice. It plays prominently in television, film, and news, and in the personal lives of individuals (and their families) if they are unfortunate enough to fall victim to crime, or if they are arrested for alleged commission of a crime. It is where the most serious harms that people do are addressed. The government protects residents and can exercise its most powerful domestic powers, including arrest and incarceration.

I have spent over twenty years in criminal law, both as a police officer and prosecutor.

8.2 Crime and our criminal justice system introduced

Since humans have walked the Earth there have been some who do bad things to others. Stealing food, property or land, or attacking others with assault, rape, or murder.

As society evolved, private actions of deterrence, retribution, and retaliation were deemed inadequate. A lack of formality and responsibility caused chaos. Individual action or mob action lacked consistency and justice and was not desirable for stable society.

It eventually became the job of the government to protect, deter, investigate, and enforce laws to address certain ill conduct.

Eventually this evolved into our current criminal justice system.

To call it a "system" is an oversimplification because it implies a single, overarching management and structure. In practice it is a sprawling network of interconnected parts. Sometimes the connections are smooth, sometimes the connections are disjointed or dysfunctional.

There are police and other sworn law enforcement at the federal, state, county, city, town, and village levels, with agencies ranging from a few people to thousands.[76] There are prosecutors in hundreds of different offices at the federal, state and county level who represent their respective government to pursue criminal investigations and prosecute cases.[77]

There is a court system to resolve these disputes. The court requires the prosecutor to do certain things throughout a litigation, and ultimately to prove their case beyond a reasonable doubt at trial if needed. The court can also accept guilty pleas.

If the litigation results in a guilty plea or conviction after trial, the court will sentence the defendant to what it feels is fair, within the bounds of the law, with considerations of deterrence, rehabilitation, punishment, and restoration. The sentence could be treatment, community service, probation, a fine, or jail.

There are jails and prisons to hold prisoners.[78] This is often called the "corrections" system under the concept it is correcting their behavior for eventual release and so they will make better decisions. Corrections is a significant part of the criminal justice system because of the number of people who are incarcerated. There are other employees of this system to supervise defendants living in regular society but who are on parole, supervised release, or pre-trial release.

---

[76] For example, when I was a state trooper in the New York State Police (NYSP), I was one of about four thousand sworn police officers in the agency at the time, one of the ten largest police agencies in the country. My station had a relatively small patrol unit, with about thirty troopers assigned, big for NYSP and the region, but small compared to city police departments. Within in our patrol area were dozens of other police agencies at the county, city, town, and village level. Since I left, NYSP absorbed some other state agencies and is even larger, at about 5,000 sworn members.

Read more about the NYSP at https://troopers.ny.gov.

[77] I was an assistant district attorney (prosecutor) at the New York County District Attorney's Office (Manhattan DA) along with about 500 other assistant district attorneys. It is a very large prosecutor's office with unusual national and international reach and depth of some of its cases.

Read more about the Manhattan DA's office at https://manhattanda.org.

[78] Some believe the term "prisoner" or "inmate" is a stigmatizing term so a better term might be "incarcerated individual." Others go further such as with "person or individual with justice system involvement." *See e.g.*, The Fortune Society, *Words Matter: Using Humanizing Language*, https://fortunesociety.org/wordsmatter.

Criminal laws were established and formalized to define what conduct was prohibited such that it could result in arrest and prosecution. Defendants, cops, prosecutors, judges, juries, and the public needed it put into writing. These criminal codes (sometimes called penal codes and in New York called the "Penal Law," abbreviated "PL") are *substantive* criminal law. They specify what cannot be done, under penalty of criminal action. Theft, burglary, assault, rape, murder, money laundering, and hundreds of other crimes are spelled out, with plenty of definitions too.

Some criminal laws also specify what law enforcement can do to investigate criminal activity, the process of arrest, and how the litigation will proceed after arrest through motion practice, plea, or trial, sentencing, appeal, and so forth. This is the area of criminal *procedure* law.[79] In New York this is aptly named the Criminal Procedure Law (C.P.L.).

This procedural law is the process of how the criminal justice system works and how cases are brought and resolved. It describes when an arrest can be made, when a search warrant can be issued, what happens at an arraignment, and the entire process up through trial, during trial, and after.

8.3 Federal vs. state vs. city and other localities

Since our criminal justice "system" is really a network of governmental entities that sometimes work together and sometimes operate separately, let's think of how to categorize the players.

Our first category is to assess whether we are dealing with a federal or state criminal justice system or prosecution. While there is sometimes overlap or interaction, they are mostly separate, operating under separate bodies of law.

If there is an active prosecution, you want to consider what court it is in, what laws are charged, and who is the prosecutor and judge. Specifically, is it:

- A federal prosecution, charging a violation of federal law.

---

[79] If "criminal procedure" sounds stuffy or complex, just think of it as the *process* used to resolve a criminal case.

- o This will be in a federal court, with a federal judge, and a federal prosecutor (Assistant U.S. Attorney).[80]
- A state prosecution, charging a violation of state law.[81]
  - o Identify which state and which state law. This will be in a state court, with a state-empowered prosecutor and judge.
    - That prosecutor might be a county level prosecutor, acting on behalf of the state.
    - On rarer occasions, that prosecutor could be a state level prosecutor, or at the level of a city, town, or village locality.

As recap: The first things to consider from our legal perspective are:

- Which laws are involved (federal or state),
- Which court is presiding, and
- Which prosecutor is bringing the case.

8.4 Police, agents, and other sworn law enforcement

Police ("cops") and agents do the "action-y" things more suitable for Hollywood, so they are the focus of television and movies. A prosecutor typing at a keyboard is less dramatic.[82]

Federal law enforcement (special agents, agents, postal inspectors) investigate to build and support cases brought by federal prosecutors.

---

[80] The federal government's criminal justice apparatus is massive but relatively well organized.

There is a single U.S. court system (*e.g.*, federal judicial branch). You can read more at https://www.uscourts.gov.

There is an enormous U.S. Department of Justice, led by the federal Attorney General. One component of this are federal prosecutors (U.S. Attorneys), and other components include the FBI, DEA, U.S. Marshal's Service, and federal prisons. Read more about the DOJ: Department of Justice, *About DOJ*, https://www.justice.gov/about; *Agencies* (U.S. DOJ organization chart), https://www.justice.gov/agencies/chart/map.

Then there are other federal law enforcement agencies outside of DOJ, including from within the Department of Homeland Security (DHS), which includes the United States Secret Service (USSS, formerly within the Department of Treasury) and more.

[81] Each state has their own system, with their own names and titles. There will be a lot of similarities but also many differences.

[82] Rest assured that most law-enforcement work is not action or glamor.

State and local law enforcement (police officers, state troopers, deputy sheriffs) make arrests and investigate to bring cases to state and local prosecutors.

That is how things typically work but there are also instances where state and federal entities interact. State and local law enforcement can work on federal investigations and cases, and federal law enforcement can work on state investigations and cases. There may be task forces established, and individual cases sometimes benefit from the cooperation.[83]

These "sworn" law enforcement personnel are sworn to act as law enforcement and carry a sidearm (gun) and are empowered to make arrests and perform other law enforcement duties. Their primary authority may come from either federal law or state law (and sometimes both).

New York state law enforcement has powers from New York law. The Criminal Procedure Law (C.P.L.) defines the term "police officer," and this includes sworn individuals, carrying a sidearm and with arrest powers, from all sorts of agencies and with all sorts of titles, including:

- Police officer
- State trooper[84]
- Deputy sheriff.

New York state also has "peace officers" which have slightly less powers compared to police officers.[85]

---

[83] In the Western Express case, federal special agents from the U.S. Secret Service worked closely with us, as we investigated and prosecuted violations of New York State law. Many other sworn law enforcement personnel from a variety of state, local, and federal agencies also assisted, especially on those days where we executed multiple search warrants simultaneously. Many support personnel (such as analysts who are not sworn and do not carry a sidearm or have enforcement powers) assisted as well, their help equally valuable to build the case.

[84] For eight years, my title was "state trooper" and I also had the powers of a "police officer" as defined in the New York Criminal Procedure Law (C.P.L.).

[85] Corrections officers are "peace officers" as may be many other titles, such as park rangers. Federal Special Agents may have "peace officer" status under New York law, in addition to their powers under federal law.

8.5 Substantive criminal law

Substantive criminal laws are the rules that define what the crimes and offenses are.

Put differently, they are the laws about what individuals and entities cannot do. If they break these rules they face potential investigation, arrest, prosecution, and punishment.

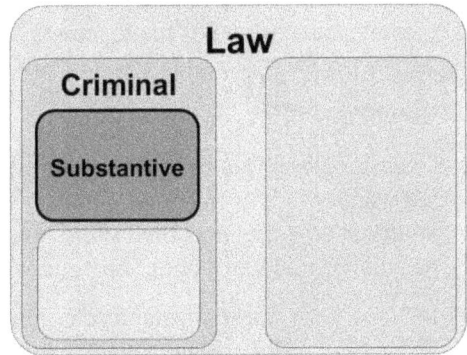

For a person to be arrested and prosecuted, there needs to be a specific statute prohibiting that conduct—that is the substantive criminal law we are talking about.

These offenses are of different degrees, with different ranges of punishment. In New York, they are classified as traffic infractions, violations, misdemeanors, and felonies, and there are different degrees of misdemeanors and felonies, each with different maximum punishments.

Most offenses have at least two elements:

- *Mens rea* (guilty mind, or a culpable mental state)
- *Actus reus* (guilty act, the action).

There are occasionally a few offenses that do not require a *mens rea* (guilty mind), and this includes traffic infractions and a few other typically minor offenses.[86]

These culpable mental states (*mens rea*, guilty mind) may include:

- Intentionally
- Knowingly
- Recklessly
- With criminal negligence.

---

[86] Speeding is an offense without a *mens rea*. It doesn't matter if the motorist *knew* they were speeding, or if they *intended* to speed, or if their speedometer was broken. All that needs to be proven is that they were speeding. Cases of "statutory rape" based on an underage victim also do not have an intent or knowledge element as to the age of the victim. The prosecutor does not have to prove the defendant knew (or should have known) how old the victim was, they just must prove that the act occurred and what the actual age of the victim was.

This means that a criminal substantive statute will specify one of these mental states as one of the elements of that crime.

The *actus reus* (guilty act) typically is an affirmative act such as stealing, punching, killing, or possessing.

Occasionally a failure to act (an omission of action) can be criminalized, but usually only if the person had a duty to act. For example, a parent or guardian who neglects their child through omission (failure to feed or provide proper care) could be penalized for this omission.

In New York, most substantive criminal law is found in the Penal Law (P.L., or N.Y.P.L.). The New York Penal Law defines terms and specifies a wide range of criminal offenses, and the wide ranges of sentences for each.

For example, P.L. Article 155 contains many sections relating to larceny (theft). They define it and specify the offenses of Petit Larceny (any theft) and four degrees of Grand Larceny, defined based on the amount stolen and what is stolen. For example, Grand Larceny in the Fourth Degree P.L. § 155.30 prohibits stealing anything valued at over $1,000, and Grand Larceny in the First Degree P.L. § 155.42 prohibits stealing anything valued at over a million dollars. Other sections and subsections penalize various methods of theft depending on the object stolen (*e.g.*, credit card, automobile, firearm, secret scientific material) and the manner of theft (*e.g.*, by extortion, by instilling fear, etc.).

New York has other bodies of law that prohibit certain conduct, and which can be enforced criminally by police and prosecutors.

The Vehicle and Traffic Law (V.T.L.) prohibits a range of traffic offenses, most of which are classified as minor offenses ("traffic infractions") but some of which can be punished as misdemeanors or even felonies. Examples of offenses in the New York V.T.L. include:

- V.T.L. § 1180 Speeding
- V.T.L. § 1192 Driving While Intoxicated
- V.T.L. § 511 Driving with a Suspended License.

There are also other state laws which have substantive criminal provisions which can be enforced in criminal courts, including:

- Environmental Conservation Law

- Banking Law[87]
- Alcoholic Beverage Control Law
- Education Law
- Executive Law
- General Business Law
- Judiciary Law
- And more.[88]

Every state has their own bodies of substantive criminal law, and of course the federal government does too.

The bulk of federal substantive criminal law is in Part 1 of Title 18 of the United States Code (U.S.C.). That covers a range of sections which we can cite as 18 U.S.C. §§ 1–2725.[89]

For example, 18 U.S.C. § 1030 defines Fraud and related activity in connection with computers.[90]

8.6 Procedural criminal law

Procedural criminal law is the process of how criminal law is administered. It is the procedures that are used by law enforcement officers and agents, prosecutors, judges, and defense attorneys.

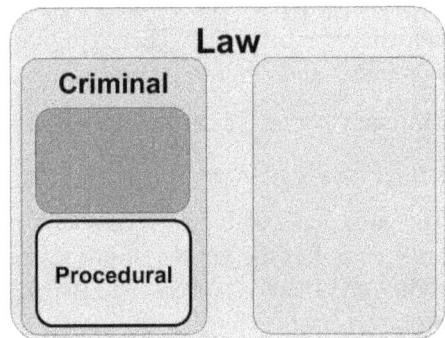

---

[87] Western Express International, Inc., the virtual currency money launderer organization, was charged with violations of the Banking Law for operating a check cashing and money transmitting business without the appropriate license. More on this case in Chapter 19.

[88] All of New York's laws are available online, including at https://www.nysenate.gov/legislation/laws/CONSOLIDATED. Only a small portion of all these laws can be considered substantive criminal law. The most important substantive criminal laws in New York are the P.L. and V.T.L.

[89] The symbol "§" means "section," and when we put two together, "§§" that means "sections" – a range of them.

[90] Also known as the Computer Fraud and Abuse Act. More on this in Part 4. You can view this statute at https://www.law.cornell.edu/uscode/text/18/1030.

This is typically referred to as criminal procedure law and is an important law school course and part of law.[91]

Criminal procedure law deals with two important areas:

- Before arrest: The investigation, collecting evidence, seizing people, things, and data.
- The arrest and litigation: The process of arresting a defendant and then litigating the matter through trial and beyond.

Let's introduce each briefly.

8.6.1 Investigation, evidence collection, seizing people and things

This area of investigation, arrest, and finding and seizing evidence derives directly from the Fourth Amendment. When the government seizes a person or evidence it needs to comply with the Fourth Amendment's requirements, including related statutes and case law.

There are procedural laws that describe when a police officer can make an arrest, when a search warrant may be issued by a judge, and when evidence can be seized. There are other provisions including for subpoenas and other legal processes.

More in Chapter 11 on the Fourth Amendment, and then in Part 4.

8.6.2 Process of litigation

This area deals with the process of litigating a criminal case. The prosecutor has the burden of proof, the defendant has many procedural rights, and there is a process to [try to] ensure rights are protected and the process is fair.[92]

The criminal law process to resolve the case (litigation) may include:

- Pre-arrest investigation
- Arrest
- Arraignment in court (formal notice of charges)
- Ensuring defendant has defense counsel
- Plea negotiations or pleas (at any time)
- Bail, bond issues

---

[91] Don't let words like "procedure" and "procedural law" make you think this is painful. It is simply "process" and is an important part of law, especially for defense attorneys alleging their client's procedural rights were violated.
[92] Some of these procedural rights are based upon the Bill of Rights, perhaps enacted into statute, and there are plenty of other statutes and case law.

- Discovery (exchange of information, almost all from the government to the defendant)
- Motion practice to decide issues (motions to dismiss the case, to suppress evidence, etc.)
- Pretrial hearings to flesh out issues
- Judicial decisions to decide issues
- Trial and verdict (more next section)
- Sentencing (if convicted)
- Appeal (if convicted).

At any point there can be plea negotiations and a guilty plea, and the decision on whether to plead guilty or go to trial is solely for the defendant. Very few criminal cases go to trial, but it is the defendant's absolute right to proceed to trial if they want.

8.6.3 New York criminal procedure

New York's Criminal Procedure Law (C.P.L.) lays out all the criminal process basics for New York.[93] It defines police officer, peace officer, the criminal court system, jurisdiction, statute of limitations, speedy trial requirements, rules of evidence, standards of proof, proceedings from arrest to sentence and beyond.

8.6.4 Federal criminal procedure

18 U.S. Code Part II (18 U.S.C. §§ 3001 - 3772) lays out federal criminal procedure, and The Federal Rules of Criminal Procedure (F.R.C.P.) have more detailed rules.[94] Rules for evidence in a federal criminal trial are laid out in the Federal Rules of Evidence.[95]

8.7 Criminal jurisdiction introduced

Jurisdiction is a special part of criminal procedure law, highly relevant for cyberlaw and cybercrime, and often misunderstood.[96]

---

[93] N.Y. C.P.L., https://www.nysenate.gov/legislation/laws/CPL.

[94] There are rules about every part of the federal criminal process—similar to New York's rules but perhaps clearer—and it is worth a few moments just to browse the categories and section headers. *See* 18 U.S. Code Part II, https://www.law.cornell.edu/uscode/text/18/part-II; Federal Rules of Criminal Procedure (F.R.C.P.), https://www.law.cornell.edu/rules/frcrmp.

[95] Federal Rules of Evidence (F.R.E.), https://www.law.cornell.edu/rules/fre.

[96] In Chapter 2 we introduced that jurisdiction is not the main issue with cybercrime, and that establishing a "global jurisdiction" would not be a magic cure. We cover jurisdiction more in Chapter 12, then in Part 4.

Jurisdiction in a criminal case basically means the authority of the court to preside over the offense. By extension, this also affects the authority of prosecutors and law enforcement over the offense.

Jurisdiction as a comprehensive concept (for both criminal and civil cases) can be divided into two main categories:

- Personal jurisdiction (*in personam* jurisdiction, over the person)
- Subject matter jurisdiction (over the subject matter, or topic, of the legal dispute).

A court needs both types of jurisdiction to hear a case.

Personal jurisdiction is usually not an issue in criminal cases.[97] Criminal litigations essentially start with an arrest of the defendant and bringing that person in front of the court which establishes this type of jurisdiction.

In criminal law we focus on subject matter jurisdiction—jurisdiction over the events that allegedly occurred.

Jurisdiction has a very different analysis for state and federal prosecutions.

States have a general authority over everything that happens within the state which means it is generally simpler to establish a state court's criminal jurisdiction.

The Federal government (including its court system and prosecutors) has "limited" jurisdiction, meaning it only has that power and authority granted to it by the U.S. Constitution.

This means the federal government (which includes federal prosecutors and the courts they use) needs to establish their authority (jurisdiction) over certain acts. It's not enough to say it happened within the U.S., or that it victimized a person in the U.S. There also must be a specific

---

[97] To be more precise, often the criminal action begins when the accusatory instrument (indictment or complaint) is filed with the court. But the litigation is essentially paused until the defendant finally appears in court, whether voluntarily or after arrest.

Once the defendant has been brought before the court personally, personal jurisdiction is established.

I never thought much about "personal jurisdiction" during my twenty-one years of law enforcement, but did think about how to find and arrest the defendant, and occasionally perform an extradition from another state to New York, and on a few exciting occasions, extraditing from another country to ours.

reason why the U.S. has power to prosecute it. Sometimes this is called a "jurisdictional hook."

We will talk more about jurisdiction in Chapter 12 and then in Part 4.

8.8 Venue introduced

Venue is a different concept from jurisdiction and is a significant issue for the federal criminal justice system because our country is so big.

Venue is about whether the case is being heard in the proper courthouse. Put differently, assuming that jurisdiction is established, there may be multiple courthouses within that jurisdiction to hear the case, and some may be proper, others may not be. More in Chapter 12.

8.9 Preview to a criminal trial

If plea negotiations do not result in an agreement, or if the defendant for any reason decides not to plead guilty and to exercise their right to a trial, the case proceeds to trial.

The burden is on the prosecutor to prove every element of every crime beyond a reasonable doubt. Typically, the defendant has a constitutional right to a jury trial, and that means the prosecutor must prove it to every single juror's unanimous satisfaction.[98]

If the defendant does not have a right to a jury trial, or if the defendant chooses to waive their right to a jury trial, they could have a "bench trial" where the judge decides the facts, including whether the prosecution proved their case to the legal standard – beyond a reasonable doubt (BRD).

Before the criminal trial starts, many issues need to be addressed and resolved by the judge, including what evidence should be excluded from the trial if it was collected in violation of the Fourth Amendment.[99]

Then the criminal trial process generally includes:

- Final pretrial issues
- Jury selection (if a jury trial)
- Trial officially starts

---

[98] For traffic infractions, violations, and minor misdemeanors, there may not be a right to a jury trial, meaning a judge would decide the facts.
[99] During the trial itself the judge will continue to make many evidentiary rulings.

- Prosecution opens and says what the evidence will prove (opening statement)
- Defense may open to present their view to the jury
- Prosecution presents its case (witness testimony, exhibits, etc.)
- Prosecution rests
- Defense may present a case
- Prosecution may rebut the defendant's case
- Defense may make closing arguments
- Prosecution makes closing arguments
- Judge instructs the jury on the law
- Jury deliberates (to decide the facts, and whether the prosecution proved the defendant's guilt beyond a reasonable doubt for each element of each crime charged)
- Verdict (guilty or not guilty as to each count).

8.10 New York, and my time as a state trooper and prosecutor

I spent over twenty years in the criminal justice system, starting as a police officer (state trooper) for eight years in the New York State Police,[100] in one of their busiest stations in the state at the time.

It was a challenge knowing all the various substantive laws, and what charges were appropriate in each circumstance. The size of our patrol area was enormous, my station covered over a dozen different towns and villages, and encircled a few cities. Each held court on a different day.[101]

When I made an arrest it was my job to write out the criminal complaint (charging document), and then the defendant needed to be arraigned before a judge or issued a ticket to appear in court.

Next came my experience as a prosecutor, an Assistant District Attorney for thirteen years at the Manhattan (New York County) District

---

[100] The New York State Police (NYSP) is one of the country's finest, largest, and oldest police agencies. They provide full police services to many communities, and support services to other communities including homicide investigation, crime scene, canine, helicopter, emergency services, and more. They also conduct highway patrol throughout the state. Sworn members of the NYSP are "police officers" as defined in the New York Criminal Procedure Law. For more about the NYSP, see https://troopers.ny.gov.

[101] With some skills typing and with computers and organizing, it eventually became my job in the station to update the document summarizing all these courts, their addresses, what day and time they held court, the names of all the various judges, and so forth.

Attorney's Office.[102] In New York City the prosecutors drew up the criminal complaints, so I was still writing these, but now doing them with much better precision. Soon enough I was handling an enormous caseload of over 200 misdemeanors, preparing for trials every week and conducting many trials.

Many cases proceeded right up until the trial, requiring an exhaustive preparation for that trial. A year or more might have elapsed after the arrest and a defendant's case would be in court scheduled for trial, and I would appear personally to answer, "ready for trial." That sequence might go something like this:

> *Judge: This case is on for trial today, are the People ready?*
>
> *Prosecutor: Yes, Your Honor, The People are ready for trial.*
>
> *Judge: Defense counsel, are you ready?*
>
> *Defense attorney: Judge, I am not ready, I need an adjournment to prepare more.*
>
> *Judge: This is the third time this has been on for trial; it is going to trial today. Let's find a trial part.*

At which point there might be more attempts to adjourn the case, discussions and perhaps a plea, or the trial might actually proceed.[103]

---

[102] The District Attorney of New York County (DANY) serves one of New York City's five counties (also called boroughs) representing the People of the State of New York. New York County's borough name is Manhattan. Because of two long serving visionary heads of the office (District Attorneys Frank Hogan and then Robert Morgenthau) and the office's location in a financial center, the office has brought cases typically reserved for federal (U.S.) prosecutors. For more about DANY, *see* https://manhattanda.org.

[103] Ironically, a "speedy trial" procedural law often means that cases can take much longer to get to trial. Any delays attributable to the prosecutor were added up and if they eventually reached a certain number of days the case would be dismissed forever. This law is important for defendants but also creates a strong incentive for them to delay the case, because each adjournment that took place was an opportunity for more time to be charged to the People, with the possibility of a future dismissal.

Every time I prepared for trial (hundreds of cases) I learned more about the facts of that case, the process of preparing and conducting a trial, and more about legal issues relating to each case.[104]

Soon enough I moved on to felonies, and eventually an identity theft case came to me which would lead to an enormous global cybercrime investigation. That is the Western Express cybercrime case, which would last eight years, culminating in a trial that lasted almost four months. That's how I came to learn about cybercrime and what eventually led me to cyberlaw. More in Chapter 19.

8.11 The value of thinking like a [good] prosecutor

Learners and practitioners of the criminal justice system should "think like a prosecutor," even if they never want to be one.

This means to think like a *good* prosecutor, who tries to do the right thing, for the right reason, properly assessing criminal laws and our criminal justice system.[105]

That requires important knowledge and skills and thinking about:

- Facts
- Law
  - o Substantive laws (the crimes that could be charged)
  - o Procedural laws to investigate (to gather evidence)
  - o Procedural laws to prosecute (to litigate and prove guilt)
- The interests of justice (what is fair)
- How others will think about it (more next).

As the prosecutor thinks, they also think like a defense attorney (who will attack the case—that's their job), as a judge (who will make many

---

[104] It might seem like a waste of time to prepare a case for trial only to get a guilty plea, but that was a fact of life in prosecution practice. Many defendants (presumably on the advice of their defense counsel) would not plead guilty until the People answered "ready" for trial, and sometimes not until the People answered ready on multiple occasions and it was clear the case was going to trial imminently.

[105] By thinking think like a "good" prosecutor we consider all proper factors, including the facts, law, interests of justice, and perspectives of others who will view and judge the case. Reasonable people will disagree about the actions of an ethical, competent, and well-intentioned prosecutor. We also acknowledge that prosecutors and prosecutor's offices are rarely perfect, made up of humans, and mistakes happen, sometimes outrageous conduct, and on rare occasions even criminal conduct.

legal rulings on the case), as a juror (who will make the ultimate decisions on the facts of a case, if it gets there), and as the public.[106]

The most important thing, once the prosecutor properly understands the facts of the case and the law, is justice, which allows the prosecutor a unique ability to do what is right and fair.[107]

The prosecutor's function will include making important decisions and taking actions relating to:

- The process of investigating
- Deciding what charges to bring against a defendant
- The process of litigating a case (from arrest through plea or trial and appeal)

Thinking like a prosecutor is a helpful way to accurately learn the issues and consider the complex decisions involved. The prosecutor will always be second-guessed, and for good reason (that is the way our system is designed). To properly understand our criminal justice system, it is not enough to blindly criticize with a knee-jerk reaction, we need to better appreciate how and why those decisions are made.

8.12 Criminal issues in cyberlaw (preview)

Many cyberlaw issues start with crime.

Cybercrime is simply the merging of "cyber" and "crime." The investigation and prosecution of cybercrime takes place within our existing system of criminal law and justice. Cyberspace presents new opportunities for criminals and thieves all around the world to steal from us, and challenges investigating, identifying, and apprehending those responsible.

---

[106] The prosecutor's focus must remain on justice. They should never follow the incorrect views of others but should merely consider their perspective. They should not take actions that are politically expedient, nor should they simply blow with the winds of politics or public opinion. Their duty is justice.
[107] While the prosecutor is an advocate and attorney who represents the government, they also have a unique duty to justice, rather than to win. This is different from the duties of most attorneys who represent a client and have a duty to try get the best possible outcome for the client, even when the client is wrong.

8.13 References and additional reading

- *Chapter 8 resources*, https://johnbandler.com/cyberlawbook-resources-ch08
- *Criminal law*, https://johnbandler.com/criminal-law
- Chapter 12, Jurisdiction
- Part 4, Criminal Cyberlaw
- NY Penal Law, https://www.nysenate.gov/legislation/laws/PEN
- NY Criminal Procedure Law, https://www.nysenate.gov/legislation/laws/CPL/-CH11-A
- Title 18 U.S. Code, https://www.law.cornell.edu/uscode/text/18
- My forthcoming online course on criminal law, crime, and our criminal justice system, at Udemy (coming someday), https://johnbandler.com/udemy-courses

8.14 Chapter questions

- What is the most important law that governs government search and seizure?
- How is the federal government's criminal jurisdiction "limited"?
- States have a general "police power" which the federal government does not. What does that really mean? And how does it affect policing and prosecutions?
- Who brings more cases each year, state and local prosecutors or federal prosecutors? Why do you think that is? What reliable statistics can you find and cite to?
- What is the difference between jurisdiction and venue?
- What is the difference between substantive criminal law and procedural criminal law?
- What is the difference between criminal law and civil law?
- What is the difference between federal criminal law and state criminal law?
- How can you tell if a particular criminal case is federal or state/local?
- List the two elements present in almost every criminal offense.
- *Mens rea* is Latin for _____
- *Actus reus* is Latin for _____

9

Civil Law Introduced

In this chapter:

- Civil law
- Substantive and procedural civil law
- Civil jurisdiction

9.1 Civil law is substance plus procedure

Civil law is designed for individuals and entities to bring claims to recover monetary damages. It is all the areas of law within the U.S. that are not criminal law.[108]

Civil law has rules for conduct that could result in civil consequences, such as the paying of monetary damages to compensate someone who was wronged. These areas of civil substantive law are varied, and lawyers may specialize in just one of them. Far more lawyers practice in civil law compared to criminal law.

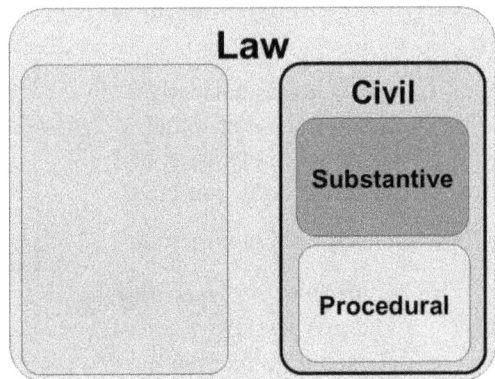

---

[108] Criminal cases involve the government as a party; prosecutors and police bringing cases on behalf of society. Defendants can be held in custody and because of the power of the government, criminal law gives many protections to criminal defendants.

Civil law is for more individualized harms, and anyone can bring a claim against anyone else, usually for monetary damages.

Civil procedure is simply the process of navigating civil cases. It includes the process of bringing a civil claim to the court, and then litigating it.[109]

Civil law exists to address individualized disputes among organizations and individuals (parties). While the government can be a party to a civil case (as plaintiff or defendant) most civil cases do not involve the government as a party.

The judicial branch of government runs the court system which hears these civil cases (as it does for criminal cases), with less focus on the rights of a civil defendant.

While consequences in a civil case typically include monetary damages, occasionally there might be an order from the court that a party do something or not do something. Only in the rarest and most extreme of occasions would jail be involved, and that would only occur if the court needed to compel or punish certain egregious conduct.

9.2 Civil substantive law – areas (bodies) of civil law

We start with a general principle that U.S. civil law is basically everything that is not criminal law.[110] There are many areas of civil law, also called "bodies of law."

Some areas of civil law include:

- Cyberlaw, cybersecurity and privacy law[111]
- Personal injury (negligence torts, intentional torts, etc.)
- Defamation
- Invasion of privacy
- Fraud
- Product liability

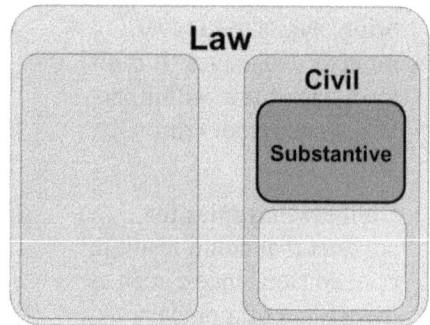

---

[109] Civil procedure can seem intimidating and was a dreaded law school course for some. Think of it simply as the rules and process for resolving civil cases.

[110] Note that some areas of law and society straddle both civil and criminal law, and some areas might be neither. Part 7 and 8 address those areas.

[111] I put cyberlaw first since that's what this book is about, though many other lawyers may think of it as a niche and newer area of law. As we explore, we will see how many other areas of law it touches.

- Employment law
- Transactional law (contracts)
- Construction law
- Real estate law
- Intellectual property law
- Immigration law
- Family law
- Financial sector laws
- Health sector laws
- Education sector laws
- Election law
- Tax law
- Any area of life where there might be a dispute between two or more individuals or entities, whether over money, property, or any right or slight, real or imagined.

And more.

9.3 Civil procedure law

Civil procedure law addresses the process of bringing and resolving a civil claim. At each stage of a civil litigation, there are rules about the process.

Even though rules are written down, there is always plenty of room for lawyers to fight about what the process should be, and why the other side is in violation.

At the start of a civil litigation, the plaintiff's attorney drafts a civil complaint, alleging how the defendant has wronged the plaintiff. This complaint needs to be properly served upon the defendant, with a summons to appear in court.[112]

Properly serving the defendant (*e.g.*, a process server hands a copy of the summons and complaint while in a proper location) will give the court

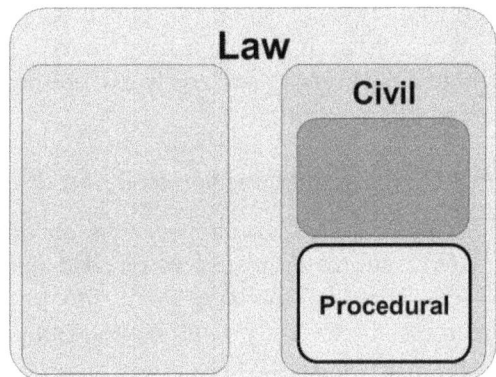

---

[112] The summons could be served first, without a complaint, but many litigators choose to file and serve both together.

personal jurisdiction over the defendant. There are also other ways to achieve proper service of process.

The defendant needs to appear in court and will usually hire an attorney. Through defense counsel the defendant might challenge service of process, jurisdiction, adequacy of the complaint and more. The civil litigation process continues through settlement or trial.

In all, the civil litigation phases can include:

- Civil complaint and summons
- Motion to dismiss
- Decision
- Discovery (exchange of information, by both sides)
- Motions
- Hearings
- Trial
- Verdict
- Appeal (by either or both sides).

At any point there can be settlement negotiations and a settlement. Since litigation is costly and the dispute is usually about money in the first place, most civil cases settle before trial. Much of civil litigation revolves around the bruising and costly disputes resulting from discovery and other pretrial motions.[113]

9.4 Civil jurisdiction: personal and subject matter

Civil jurisdiction is an important issue, often highly contested. If the defense attorney can succeed on challenging it, they could win the case—or at least force the plaintiff to start all over. As a matter of fairness, the law only wants courts with proper jurisdiction exercising authority over cases. It would be unfair to require a defendant to travel to a distant location with little connection to their actions to defend a suit.[114]

---

[113] Practical advice: avoid getting yourself into a civil litigation if you can. Make your litigation decisions based on facts and reason, and usually money too, never emotion.

[114] In civil cases (unlike criminal cases) a plaintiff can obtain a default judgement against a defendant if they were properly served but fail to answer the complaint or fail to respond during important phases of the litigation.

Remember to think of jurisdiction in two parts:

- Personal jurisdiction
- Subject matter jurisdiction.

The principle of personal jurisdiction seeks to protect individuals from being hauled into far away courts or be subjected to judgements of these distant courts. It is often obtained by personally serving the defendant with the summons while the defendant is within the jurisdiction. There are other ways to establish it, and they usually involve showing an adequate connection of the person (or organization) to the jurisdiction.

Subject matter jurisdiction and venue may be at issue too. Subject matter jurisdiction is whether the court has the legal power to hear the case and what it is about. If events happened within the jurisdiction, or a party resides in the jurisdiction, that might be sufficient for state cases.

Since federal courts have "limited" jurisdiction, federal subject matter jurisdiction needs to be established to bring a case in federal court. There are two ways to establish federal jurisdiction if the dispute:

1. Involves a federal issue or statute ("federal question jurisdiction"), or
2. Involves parties from different states. Here, federal jurisdiction is appropriate to avoid giving one of the parties a home field advantage in a state court and to properly address interstate issues ("diversity jurisdiction" based on diversity of state citizenship).

Venue is different from jurisdiction, and concerns whether the case is within the proper location (courthouse), of all the courthouses within that same jurisdiction.[115]

9.5 The civil trial

Civil trials are even less common than criminal trials. A civil case is usually about money, civil trials are expensive for both sides, which means they have strong incentives to settle before the trial.[116]

---

[115] As in criminal law, venue is important for federal civil cases, because it can mean the difference between going to court in California or New York (for example).

[116] Imagine you are pursuing a civil claim, and your lawyer tells you a trial will cost $10,000, $100,000, or even $1,000,000. Your lawyer then informs you of

In civil cases and trials, there is less emphasis on protecting the rights of defendants, and each side is on a more equal plain. Since most discovery (exchange of information) has occurred before trial, many of the issues are streamlined and many facts are known. Not every case is entitled to a jury trial, in which case the judge would decide the facts after hearing the evidence. If it is a jury trial, a unanimous verdict might not be required (some states might allow a verdict with five-sixths of the jury in agreement).

Whatever the verdict, either side can appeal.

9.6 Civil issues in cyberlaw (preview)

As you can imagine, civil issues in cyberlaw are everywhere.

The digital world is essential to life and business. Things go wrong in the digital world (or in a manner related to it) and when they do individuals and organizations will sue each other.

Imagine if a cybercriminal breached an email system, learns about a pending transfer of $400,000, and then impersonates various individuals to misdirect that transfer and steal the money. With so much money stolen, it is reported to law enforcement who begin an investigation but are unlikely to solve the case. The parties disagree on whose fault the theft was, and who should bear the loss, so threats of litigation start, and perhaps a lawsuit is filed.[117]

9.7 References and additional reading

- *Chapter 9 resources*, https://johnbandler.com/cyberlawbook-resources-ch09
- *Civil Law*, https://johnbandler.com/civil-law
- Cornell LII, Civil Law, https://www.law.cornell.edu/wex/civil_law
- Part 5, Civil Cyber Law I
- Part 6, Civil Cyber Law II - Data Law

---

the approximate chances of winning at trial, and that even if you win, the other party will appeal, and you will have to pay for that process too. A settlement starts to seem like a good idea, a certain amount of money to resolve the case forever.

[117] This is a prevalent crime. *See* Chapter 13 and *Email Based Funds Transfer Frauds*, https://johnbandler.com/email-based-funds-transfer-frauds.

9.8 Chapter questions

- What is the difference between civil law and criminal law?
- What are two important areas of civil law?
- Why do people generally bring a civil case, and what do they usually hope to gain from it?
- Why might civil trials be a relatively rare thing?
- What are two important ways to categorize civil law? (Hint, S_____ law and P_____ law)
- A civil case could be brought in either a F_____ court or a S_____ court
- What action commences a civil lawsuit?

John T. Bandler

10

The First Amendment
and Protections for Speech
from Government Interference

In this chapter:

- What the First Amendment protects
- What it does not
- We value freedoms for speech and expression in this country
- These freedoms are not absolute
- PS: Just because you *can* say something doesn't mean you *should*

10.1 The First Amendment

The First Amendment protects us from government restrictions on speech, religion and more.

It reads:

> *Congress shall make no law respecting an establishment of religion, or prohibiting the free exercise thereof; or abridging the freedom of speech, or of the press; or the right of the people peaceably to assemble, and to petition the Government for a redress of grievances.*
>
> —First Amendment, U.S. Constitution

Any time we assess the laws surrounding speech and expression, the first legal authority to consider is the First Amendment. It is the foundational law on this subject, and other laws flow from it and must comply with it.

It is only 45 words, so it cannot provide much detail. Hundreds of millions of words have been written about what it means, and now I add to that word count.[118]

This amendment is important for cyberspace and cyberlaw, straddling criminal law, civil law, and broader issues of expression, thought, communication, propaganda, disinformation, and conspiracy theories.[119]

10.2 The law on speech starts with the First Amendment

The law on speech and expression in the United States starts with the First Amendment. That is the most important takeaway of this chapter.

The First Amendment is a restriction upon what the government can do about the speech and expression of individuals and organizations (including the press).

The First Amendment restricts:

- When the government can bring a *criminal* case based upon someone's speech or expression.
- When government civil courts can be used to hold someone *civilly* liable based upon their speech and expression.

As we assess relevant laws and what to apply to a fact pattern,[120] we consider when the First Amendment applies and when it does not. It applies when the government is involved, it does *not* apply when we are addressing entirely private actions, not conducted by the government.[121]

---

[118] This word count estimate is back of the envelope and rudimentary based on court decisions, books, articles, and more. If anyone has a math + law inclination and wants to work up a more precise figure, I would be happy to see it.

[119] Organizing this book was a process, especially with issues surrounding speech because it straddles so many different areas of law and life, and because the law is often misunderstood. We cover it a little in each relevant area and by Chapter 36 the reader has a solid understanding of it.

[120] Fact pattern meaning a set of facts, whether real or imagined (hypothetical).

[121] Government action is also known as state action. The First Amendment applies directly to the federal government, and then to the states (and local governments) through the process of incorporation (as with many other parts of the Bill of Rights). Therefore, New York state, New York city, and all other states and localities need to abide by the First Amendment.

10.3 Speech and expression considerations through time

Considerations about speech and expression have long existed, especially at the founding of our country and for religious freedom. Our new country wanted to avoid having a government with excessive power to tell individuals what they could say (or not) and how they could worship.[122]

Previously, those wishing to speak and be heard faced many gatekeepers in their way. It was harder to create and distribute speech and writing. Stand on a soapbox in a park and only a few would hear you. Write a letter to an editor and only a few would publish it, and once published only a few would read it.

Today, people can express themselves in many different forums, to be heard around the world, thanks to technology. There is more speech than ever. It is easy to communicate, write and distribute. We can even use AI tools to create content, meaning it can be created without much thought or effort.

A main purpose of writing is to communicate and influence. Now businesses, politicians, billionaires, and nations can expand their influence, including throughout the world.

The laws surrounding speech and expression existed long before this era of internet speech, and they are even more relevant today.

10.4 "Free speech" vs. "protected speech"

As we learn about laws for speech (and other laws too) work for precision and clarity.[123]

Try to avoid using this term:

> ✘ *Free speech*

---

[122] From our founding, we did not like the idea of the government telling us which religion was proper or not. Other countries throughout history—and in existence today—have close ties between government and religion, even rules for citizens concerning religion and worship and what women can wear. Those governments might be called theocracies.

[123] First, don't be afraid to express yourself and your opinions and thoughts about the law, and don't be overly anxious about making a mistake or using the wrong word. Imperfections and mistakes are OK and part of learning. Try to push yourself for increasing clarity and precision with the words and terms you use, finding the right balance as you discuss and write.

"Free speech" is a vague term, meaning different things to different people, and does not address the protections of the First Amendment.

A better phrase to use is:

> *Speech protected by the First Amendment.*

We could increase the precision by framing it this way:

> *Speech that cannot be <u>criminally</u> punished because it is protected by the First Amendment.*

> *Speech that cannot be <u>civilly</u> actionable because it is protected by the First Amendment.*

There are many other issues in society about speech that fall outside of First Amendment analysis, including what is acceptable in society, what should be acceptable, and so forth.

Our first focus should be on the facts and the law, assessing the legal issues. Then we can address separate issues, including what is acceptable, ethical, decent, or desirable.

10.5 The First Amendment applies only to government actions

The First Amendment applies only to government actions. In legal terms, this might be referred to as "state action," meaning an action of a government entity, whether it is the federal government or a state or local government.

Therefore, when assessing what laws apply or not, we must review whether the person or entity restricting speech is:

- From the government ("state actor" or taking a "state action") or
- Not related to the government (private).

Since the First Amendment only applies to state action (not private action), this is a critical distinction.

If a private actor—whether a business, school or individual—restricts speech, it does not implicate nor violate the First Amendment. The speech restriction might be unwise or reprehensible, it might violate other laws or considerations of decency, but it does not violate the First Amendment.[124]

---

[124] Obviously, there are nuances to this, and lawyers and politicians are crafty.

10.6 Introducing the first categories of speech: Whether you can bring it to court

We can identify a few different categories of speech that will help us analyze a particular speech or expression.

We start this journey by asking some threshold questions about speech in the context of the First Amendment, to focus on the protections of the First Amendment and the distinctions of criminal and civil law.

These questions ask whether a claim based on speech can be brought in criminal court or civil court. By asking these questions, we assess whether and how the First Amendment applies.

> *Question 1:*
>
> *Is the speech protected from criminal prosecution or is it prosecutable?*

This requires us to analyze whether the First Amendment protects that speech from criminal prosecution or not. Could the police make a valid arrest, which prosecutors could successfully prosecute?

More precisely, is the speech itself illegal and criminal?[125]

Then we ask our next question:

> *Question 2:*
>
> *Is the speech protected from civil action, or is it the proper subject of a civil claim?*

This requires us to analyze whether the First Amendment protects that speech from civil lawsuit or not. Could a plaintiff bring a lawsuit successfully to recover damages because of that speech?

When we ask these two questions for any example of speech, there are two possible answers, with three main possible outcomes.[126]

---

[125] A separate question is unrelated to this analysis—whether the speech itself is legal and proper but creates liability for the speaker. For example, a confession would incriminate a defendant for a separate crime, but the speech itself is legal.

[126] Technically, there are four possible outcomes, but we can merge two of them for simplicity's sake and arrive at three.

- **Protected speech** (speech that is protected by the First Amendment)
- **Civilly actionable speech** (speech that someone could sue for and make the person pay money in damages)
- **Criminally actionable speech** (speech that could get someone arrested and prosecuted).

These three categories are the most important to start with.

10.7 All of our categories of speech

We need more categories to address the realities of life. How speech affects us and fits into our legal analysis and the First Amendment.

Let's first introduce a new category of all speech, *everything* that could be said or expressed.

- **All speech** is the category that includes any speech or expression.

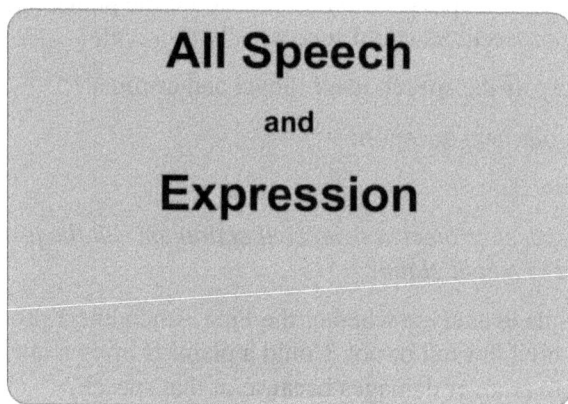

All Speech

and

Expression

Speech categories

"All speech" is an infinite category, including anything you could say or write, any hand gesture or facial expression, any music and art.

Next, we know that a lot of speech is going to annoy someone. Out of all that speech out there, most of it annoys someone, somehow. We can name it and define it like this:

- **Annoying speech** is speech that annoys at least one person. This is highly subjective and a fact of life among humans and the discomfort or conflict our speech can cause.

And depict it like this.

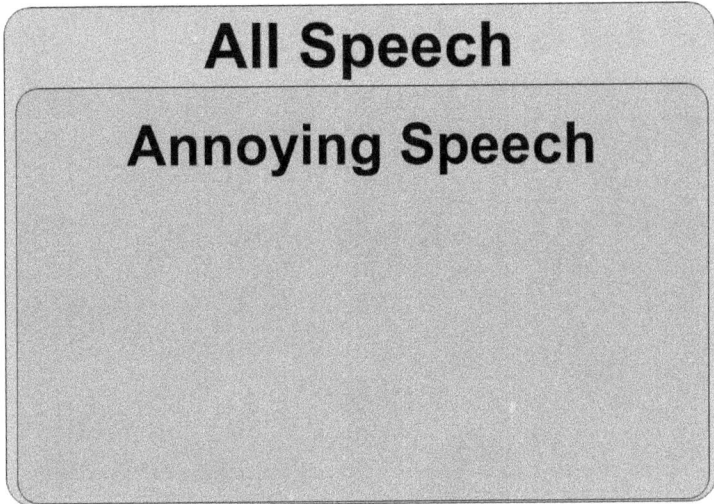

All Speech

Annoying Speech

Speech categories

Many people get annoyed but do not do or say anything about it. Their annoyance rests with themselves, and they do not take any action based on their displeasure.

Examples of annoying speech that is also protected by the First Amendment might include:

- Read chapter 10 for next week.
- Pushup position, now!
- You're fired (or more nicely; We're going to have to let you go).
- I support position A, and position B is wrong.
- I like candidate X, and candidate Y is an idiot.
- Anyone who votes for candidate Y is an idiot.
- I don't like your pizza.
- Your appearance is [insert insult].
- Other insults (use your imagination).

Another category of speech is the portion of annoying speech that is sufficiently irritating that a person decides to do something about it. They might "unfriend someone" online or in person, reply with their own speech, or take another action. Let's define that like this:

- **Unfriending speech** is speech that annoys a person enough that they take some type of action. That action might be their own speech, unfriending, boycotting, and more.

We can add "unfriending speech" to the diagram like this:

Speech categories

The responses in reaction to unfriending speech might be appropriate, inappropriate, or even criminal. The annoyed person might make a report to the police, claiming the speech was criminal, such as in the case of threats to cause physical harm. The annoyed person might hire an attorney to evaluate a civil claim against the speaker. Still, most unfriending speech is neither criminally nor civilly actionable.

The annoyed person might take an action that does not involve the legal system, including:

- Clicking the button to unfriend, dislike, unfollow
- Speaking back
- Protests
- Boycotts
- Punching, assaulting, and even murder.[127]

Now let us examine how some "unfriending speech" can find its way as the proper subject of a court proceeding, starting with what might be "civilly actionable."

---

[127] These last actions would not be justified, but many crimes of assault and even murder are preceded by a verbal dispute.

Speech categories

A civil action might occur if the person consults an attorney who agrees to represent them and bring a civil case against the speaker, such as for defamation, harassment, or invasion of privacy.[128]

If it is a meritorious lawsuit, then it is within the category of "civilly actionable" and a court might make that person pay money for the civil wrong they committed with their speech.

Now let us examine what might be "criminal speech" and how we might get there. Suppose someone makes a direct threat of harm to another person which gets reported to law enforcement who might make an arrest.

Alternatively, law enforcement may be doing their investigation and come across statements made by suspects, including statements that are part of a criminal conspiracy.

Assuming that speech can be properly criminalized, we can add that criminal speech to our diagram like this:

---

[128] We discuss these intentional torts in Chapter 24.

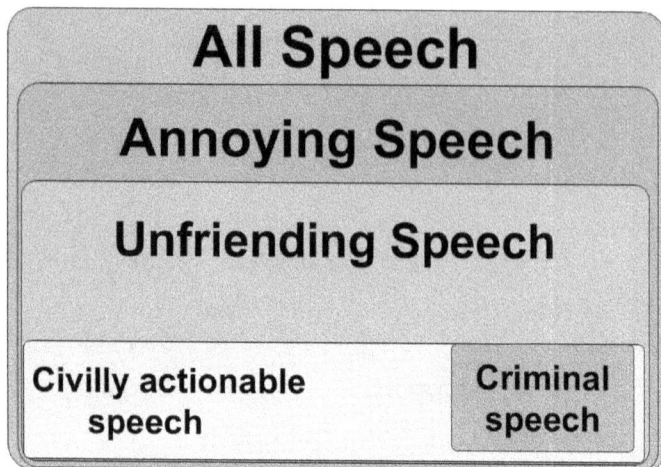

Speech categories

When any of these speech related cases are litigated in court there will be arguments from both sides. One party will allege the statements are not protected by the First Amendment, and the other party will argue the opposite. It is the judge that initially decides that issue, and thus would essentially be deciding where in the diagram the conduct lands.

If speech is the proper subject of a meritorious criminal or civil action, it is not "protected speech." Conversely, if speech cannot be the proper subject of criminal prosecution or civil lawsuit, then it is "protected speech."[129] We can depict this with the following diagram:

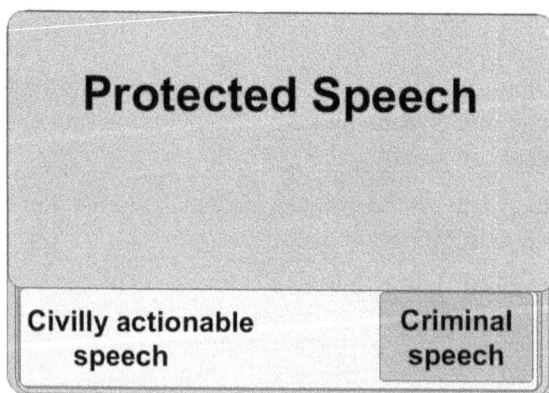

Speech categories

---

[129] Note that there are areas of speech that are protected from criminal prosecution but not protected from civil action, such as defamation.

John T. Bandler

A vast majority of speech is protected by the First Amendment, so the diagrams have not been to scale so far. Of all the speech and expression that has been made, or could be made, only a small portion of that could possibly be civilly actionable, and then only the tiniest fraction of all speech could be criminally actionable.

We can show that like this:

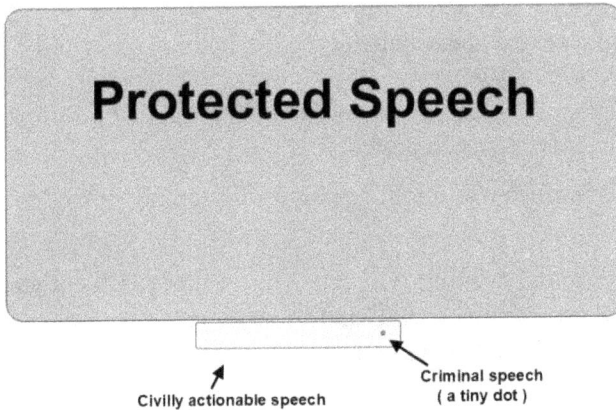

Protected Speech

Civilly actionable speech

Criminal speech
(a tiny dot)

Speech categories (a better scale)

Whatever the law is, two things are true:

Just because you can say it, doesn't mean you should.

Just because you can sue about it, doesn't mean you should.

Recap: There are three areas of government consequences (or not) regarding speech (according to the chapter):

- Protected speech
- Civilly actionable speech
- Criminally actionable speech.

Recap: There are six categories of speech, according to the chapter:

- All speech
- Annoying speech
- Unfriending speech
- Protected speech
- Civilly actionable speech
- Criminally actionable speech.

10.8 Speech: Protected from criminal prosecution or prosecutable?

Let's explore further whether speech is protected from criminal prosecution by the First Amendment, or if it is properly prosecutable.[130]

Speech and expression that could be properly prosecuted includes:

- Direct imminent threats of violence.
- Speech that is part of the commission of a crime.
- Child sexual abuse content (formerly known as child pornography).
- Deliberately leaking or mishandling classified information when you have a duty to protect it.

Examples of speech that might be part of the commission of a crime include:

- Menacingly stating "Give me your wallet or I'll cut you."
- Pay me money or I will do this unlawful act.
- Other words that are part of a criminal act.
- Falsely shouting "Fire!" or "Bomb!" in a crowded theatre causing panic and injury.
- Direct threats to harm someone.
- Saying words that incite violence or a riot.
- Creating or distributing or possessing child sexual abuse content (sometimes referred to as child pornography).

Our assessment is *whether the speech and expression itself is a crime,* not whether it relates to other criminal activity, or is evidence of a crime.[131]

---

[130] As mentioned, only a tiny portion of speech is prosecutable, the rest is protected. Also, some speech is "protected" by the First Amendment from criminal prosecution but can still be used as evidence in a criminal prosecution to prove another crime. A confession such as "I killed X" is evidence that the defendant killed X, but this statement itself does not violate any laws.

Compare that to the situation where a crime boss tells their subordinate "Go kill X;" that statement is part of the crime and is prosecutable.

[131] Again, if a defendant makes a confession to a crime, such as by stating "I killed X" or "I hid the weapon in location A," their speech does not constitute a crime. It is merely evidence of the commission of another crime.

I gave this a double mention because student answers and AI chat bots frequently provide incorrect examples.

10.9 Speech: Protected from civil action or proper subject of civil action?

Now let's explore whether speech might be protected from civil action by the First Amendment.

Generally, we are free to say a whole range of things without fear of a meritorious lawsuit. We can express our opinions on almost anything.

Speech that can be the subject of a civil suit include speech that:

- Is defamatory (asserts falsities that cause monetary damage)
- Threatens
- Invades privacy or causes emotional distress
- Violates a contractual obligation (non-disclosure, non-disparagement).

Examples of speech that might be civilly actionable include:

- Many of the criminal speech examples provided previously which cause civil harm to an individual.
- "There are pedophiles in the basement of the pizza restaurant" (when that statement is false).
- "The relatives of murder victims are faking it and are merely crisis actors" (when that statement is false).
- "I found an X object in my food." (when that statement is false).
- "The voting systems tampered with the votes and changed the votes" (when that statement is false).
- "Those voting workers tampered with the vote ballots" (when that statement is false).

10.10 Standards of review (recap)[132]

Government laws relating to speech will be reviewed by courts according to one of the three tests for constitutional questions.

Remember the three levels of scrutiny:

- Rational basis review (a low level of scrutiny)[133]
- Intermediate scrutiny (a medium level)[134]

---

[132] *See* Chapter 7 where we introduced this concept.
[133] Whether the law is rationally related to a legitimate government interest.
[134] Whether the law is "substantially related" to an "important" government interest.

- Strict scrutiny (a high level of scrutiny).[135]

When there is a government restriction on speech, these rules apply:

- If the restriction is "content neutral" (the restriction does not relate to what the content of the speech is) then it gets intermediate scrutiny.
- If the restriction is "content based" (restriction does relate to the content of the speech) then it gets strict scrutiny.

A general prohibition on yard signs (regardless of what they say) is "content neutral." Similarly, reasonable restrictions on the time, place, and manner of public assembly or protest (regardless of the reason for the assembly) is also content neutral.

Strict scrutiny is applied to content specific restrictions on speech. The government is very limited on how it can restrict speech based upon content.

For example, if the government passed a law that restricted criticism against the government, that law would get strict scrutiny and surely not survive.

Government can restrict or punish speech that presents a "clear and present danger" or "imminent" danger.[136]

The government can also prosecute people who improperly disseminate classified information. The restriction is content based, but narrowly tailored and necessary to protect our nation's secrets.

10.11 Speech and expression in cyberspace (preview)

There is more speech and expression than ever before, growing exponentially. Most humans have a computer attached to their fingers ninety percent of the time, and AI tools make it all too easy to generate words and images.

---

[135] Whether the law is "narrowly tailored" to achieve a "compelling governmental interest."

[136] In *Brandenburg v. Ohio*, 395 U.S. 444 (1969) the USSC held that the government cannot punish inflammatory speech unless it was "directed to inciting or producing imminent lawless action..." In *Chaplinsky v. New Hampshire*, 315 U.S. 568 (1942) the USSC put forth the "fighting words" doctrine and that they can be punished, though today the definition of those fighting words is reserved for very extreme statements.

This means the laws surrounding speech are more relevant than ever.

Forty years ago, there were fewer ways for people to threaten, defame, influence, or manipulate, but today the opportunity to do that is even greater.

Our analysis for this chapter was based upon protections of the First Amendment and the legal standpoint, so we focused on perceived negative effects (annoyance, unfriending) that might lead to a legal dispute.

Another issue arises when the listener *likes* the message and is influenced and persuaded by it. They will not complain, there will be no legal dispute, but it is an important issue to consider, as we do in Part 8.

10.12 References and additional reading

- *Chapter 10 resources*, https://johnbandler.com/cyberlawbook-resources-ch10
- Part 8, Chapter 36 on cyber speech
- *First Amendment things to know*, https://johnbandler.com/things-to-know-first-amendment
- *First Amendment, speech, social media*, https://johnbandler.com/free-speech-first-amendment-social-media-2
- First Amendment via Cornell LII, https://www.law.cornell.edu/constitution/first_amendment

See Chapter 10 resources webpage for review study points

10.13 Chapter questions

- Summarize what the First Amendment protects against?
- List three areas of government consequence (or not) regarding speech
- List all six categories of speech, according to the chapter
- If the speech is protected by the First Amendment, can someone be arrested for saying it? Why or why not?
- If the speech is protected by the First Amendment, can someone be sued civilly for saying it? Why or why not?
- Give an example of speech that is protected by the First Amendment (keep the example appropriate for school)

- Read the 45 words of the First Amendment. What do you think of when you read them? Is this your first time?
    - Here's the text of it:
      "Congress shall make no law respecting an establishment of religion, or prohibiting the free exercise thereof; or abridging the freedom of speech, or of the press; or the right of the people peaceably to assemble, and to petition the government for a redress of grievances."
- When we are assessing laws around speech and expression, what is the first and most important law we should consider?

11

The Fourth Amendment
and Government Search and Seizure

In this chapter:

- Fourth Amendment
- Rules for government search and seizure
- A protection against unreasonable government intrusions

11.1 The Fourth Amendment

The Fourth Amendment protects us from unlawful and improper searches and seizures by the government.

It reads:

> *The right of the people to be secure in their persons, houses, papers, and effects, against unreasonable searches and seizures, shall not be violated, and no warrants shall issue, but upon probable cause, supported by oath or affirmation, and particularly describing the place to be searched, and the persons or things to be seized.*

> —*Fourth Amendment, U.S. Constitution*

As with the First Amendment, it is a protection from *government* action.

11.2 The law on government searches and seizures starts with the Fourth Amendment

Any time we assess what the government is allowed to do with respect to a search or seizure, we start with the Fourth Amendment.

Conversely, any time we are assessing whether the Fourth Amendment applies or not, we need to assess whether the government was involved in the search or seizure.

11.3 The Fourth Amendment applies only to government actions

To analyze whether the Fourth Amendment applies, we look to see whether there was government action, also known as "state action."[137]

If a police officer, investigator, or agent (whether state, local, or federal) stops and detains a car or person, or recovers evidence (drugs, guns, electronics), then there is clearly "state action" and we need to assess whether their actions complied with the Fourth Amendment.

If a private security guard, doing screening for a concert identifies and seizes evidence (drugs, guns, knives) and then calls police and gives this evidence to police, then—at first glance—it seems like there was no state action for this seizure, and thus the Fourth Amendment might not apply.

If a loss prevention agent in a store observes a suspect shoplifting, makes an arrest and recovers the stolen merchandise and other contraband (drugs, etc.), and then gives all this evidence to police for arrest and prosecution, it seems like we reach the same result—no state action. If there was no state action for the seizure, then the Fourth Amendment does not seem to apply.

Still, defense attorneys are creative, and judges interpret facts and law to arrive at their vision of justice. Additional inquiry might be required to properly determine if there was state action or not,[138] and judges might look to other facts and law to ensure evidence is properly admissible.

11.4 A search warrant requirement, then exceptions to that requirement

The Fourth Amendment imposes a search warrant requirement on law enforcement. That's the first general rule and it means that law enforcement generally needs to obtain a search warrant from a judge before searching something or someone.

---

[137] Remember that "state action" in this context just means "government action." We look to see whether the government did the act, including individuals acting on behalf of any level of government whether federal, state, or local. We assess state action for both First and Fourth Amendment analysis.

[138] For example, suppose in our concert example, there was a meeting between police and security screeners before the concert, and a police supervisor instructed the security screeners to conduct searches a certain way for certain purposes. A judge could find that this relationship and instruction meant there was indeed "state action."

Then there are exceptions to this rule because it is time consuming and cumbersome to obtain a search warrant, and it would be unreasonable for law enforcement to obtain a warrant every single time they need to do a reasonable search or seizure.

The law has developed several exceptions to the search warrant requirement, including for:

- Consent (if consent is truly voluntary and knowing)
- Plain view (contraband is plainly viewable from a lawful vantage point of the officer)
- Search incident to lawful arrest
- Pat down frisks upon reasonable suspicion
- Automobile searches upon probable cause (the "automobile exception")
- Emergencies and hot pursuit (exigent circumstances)
- Automobile inventory.

Let's cover each of those briefly.

11.4.1 Search incident to lawful arrest

When a police officer makes a valid arrest, they can search the arrestee, including the area within arm's reach ("grabbable area"). Any contraband or evidence recovered is fair game and lawfully seized.

Of course, most defense attorneys will challenge the lawfulness of the arrest and search, so that will be an area of litigation and ultimately for the judge to decide.

11.4.2 Pat down frisks upon reasonable suspicion

When police are investigating crime, if they have reasonable suspicion (knowledge that is less than probable cause) that a person is involved in criminal activity, they can temporarily detain them. If they also have reasonable suspicion the person might be armed, they can do a "pat down" frisk to check for weapons. If weapons are found, they can be properly seized, and an arrest made.

11.4.3 Automobile searches (the "automobile exception")

If police have probable cause that evidence of a crime is within a car, they can search the car, and do not have to obtain a search warrant. This is the automobile exception to the search warrant requirement. It is based upon vehicles being movable and it being difficult or unreasonable to require police to obtain the warrant, by which time the car and evidence will be long gone.[139]

11.4.4 Hot pursuit

When police are in hot pursuit of a suspect, the law has decided that they should be able to continue their pursuit, even if the suspect flees into buildings or residences.

As a slightly separate but related doctrine, most states allow hot pursuit into adjoining states.[140]

11.4.5 Exigent circumstances

Exigent (emergency) situations mean police have greater latitude.

Imagine some of the circumstances depicted in movies and television, where the criminal or terrorist is about to do something bad within hours, minutes, or seconds.

There is no time to get a warrant. Should the police do nothing? Or should they break down the door, open the package, etc.?

The law recognizes that these actions might be needed and might be lawful, even in the absence of a warrant.

11.4.6 Automobile inventory

The automobile inventory might not technically be a "search," though that might be a matter of articulation and who is speaking.[141] Police should have an established procedure to inventory property they recover to ensure there is nothing dangerous within it, and to reduce false claims of theft or loss of valuables. If police inventory a vehicle according to this process, evidence recovered should be admissible and in accord with the Fourth Amendment.

---

[139] As a state trooper, there were occasions when I pulled over a car and could smell the strong odor of burning marijuana because the occupants had been enjoying a smoke just before I pulled them over. At the time, this provided probable cause that contraband (marijuana) was in the car, thus I had legal authority to search it, with a search warrant not required.

[140] This legal authority to pursue does not mean they will pursue. On one occasion I was instructed to terminate the pursuit at the state line.

[141] Some might call this "semantics," but words matter, especially in law.

11.5 The exclusionary rule

The exclusionary rule holds that when law enforcement violates the Fourth Amendment, any evidence they seized improperly will be excluded from the trial ("suppressed" or "excluded"). The jury will never see or hear about it.

It is an important part of Fourth Amendment law because it is the penalty law enforcement must face, and their incentive to do things properly.

The exclusionary rule was not always in place. For a long time, the Fourth Amendment was toothless because there was no penalty if law enforcement violated it.

Illegal stop and search? Without a penalty or remedy, law enforcement had no incentive to do things the right way.

In 1914 the case of *Weeks v United States* was decided by the U.S. Supreme Court, and that is where the exclusionary rule was born. The Court decided to impose this penalty on government. Eventually (in the 1961 case of *Mapp v. Ohio*) this rule was expanded to all law enforcement, including state and local.

The exclusionary rule also applies to other areas of criminal law, including almost every area where law enforcement takes an action that obtains evidence. This includes:

- Stops, searches, and seizures
- Confessions and statements by defendants
- Witness identification of a defendant.

The exclusionary rule has been used to help enforce rights beyond the Fourth Amendment, including rights against self-incrimination, to confront witnesses, and for due process.

11.6 An evolution of Fourth Amendment law on government searches and seizures

Here is a summary of some important Fourth Amendment chronology and case progression. This evolution helps us see that Fourth Amendment law has evolved, including with changes in technology.

Consider that initially there were no consequences for violations of the Fourth Amendment, then consequences applied only to the federal government, later becoming applicable to state and local governments.

- Fourth Amendment ratified in 1791. A protection against unreasonable searches and seizures, and a search warrant requirement. Yet toothless and without enforcement for over a hundred years.
- *Weeks v. United States*, 232 U.S. 383 (1914).[142] Warrantless seizure by federal law enforcement from a private residence violates the Fourth Amendment. Illegally seized evidence must be excluded (suppressed).
- *Burdeau v. McDowell*, 256 U.S. 465 (1921). Searches by private parties, even illegal searches, do not implicate the Fourth Amendment, and suppression is not a remedy.
- *Gambino v. United States*, 275 U.S. 310 (1927). Searches by local or state law enforcement (in 1927) do not implicate the Fourth Amendment unless it is on behalf of the federal government ("silver platter" doctrine). This case is no longer good law because today the Fourth Amendment clearly applies to all government actors, whether federal, state or local, based upon the 1961 case *Mapp v. Ohio* (next).
- *Mapp v. Ohio*, 367 U.S. 643 (1961). The Fourth Amendment applies to states (not just the federal government) via the Due Process clause of the Fourteenth Amendment. Illegal searches by local law enforcement do implicate the Fourth Amendment, and suppression (exclusion) is a remedy.
- *Katz v. United States*, 389 U.S. 347 (1967). The USSC addressed the wired telephone and law enforcement's ability to listen in—a wiretap. Though telephones and payphones had been around for

---

[142] That citation, "*Weeks v. United States*, 232 U.S. 383 (1914)" is the full and correct citation for the U.S. Supreme Court (USSC) case. It includes the party names (*Weeks v. United States*), the location in the book of decisions (232 U.S. 383) and the year of the decision (1914). For courts other than the USSC, a case citation will also indicate what court it is, and occasionally which judge.

Today most major cases are publicly available, including through Google Scholar and other resources. For example, *Weeks* can be found:
> https://scholar.google.com/scholar_case?case=8676110639881267815
> https://www.law.cornell.edu/supremecourt/text/232/383
> https://www.oyez.org/cases/1900-1940/232us383
> https://supreme.justia.com/cases/federal/us/232/383/
> https://caselaw.findlaw.com/court/us-supreme-court/232/383.html

Weeks is one of those famous cases that is available everywhere and other cases may not be as widely available. But consider those resources when doing your legal research and finding the text of an actual case. Wherever you find the case, your citation is to the case itself first, not to the place hosting the decision.

a while, this was the first time the Supreme Court assessed law enforcement's listening in on conversations. They decided that the Fourth Amendment applies to conversations and this newish technology too.[143] They put forth the concept of a "reasonable expectation of privacy" (REP) from the government. This is one of the first technology related evolutions for Fourth Amendment law.

- *Terry v. Ohio*, 392 U.S. 1 (1968). Police may temporarily detain (stop) and possibly pat down frisk a suspect based upon reasonable suspicion (which is less than probable cause). This allows police to act and investigate even if they do not yet have probable cause. The detention needs to be based upon reasonable suspicion the person is involved in criminal activity. The pat down frisk needs to be based upon reasonable suspicion the person might be armed. In sum, "stop and frisk" is Constitutionally permissible based on this case.[144]

11.7 Searches and seizures in cyberspace (preview)[145]

Does the Fourth Amendment apply to our "new" digital world?

The answer is "of course."

Legal interpretation of the 54 words of the Fourth Amendment has evolved over the years so that it does address technology and cyberspace.[146]

Judges, including those on the U.S. Supreme Court—the ultimate authority on the Fourth Amendment and what it applies to—have

---

[143] In 1967, wired telephones and payphones had been around for a while so were old in one sense, but in comparison with when the Fourth Amendment was put into force, they were relatively new.

[144] The term "stop and frisk" means different things to different people and has been the subject of public debate and considerable litigation concerning the New York City Police Department (NYPD) including in 2013 and 2014. A trial level federal judge decided that the NYPD's stop-and-frisk program and practices were improper and violated the law and Constitution. Stop and frisk remains a constitutionally permissible police activity, if done properly.

[145] We'll cover this more in Part 4 on criminal cyberlaw. Also keep in mind that the government accesses and captures data for national security reasons, which gives targets less protections as we cover in Part 7.

[146] Even judges who claim to be "textualists" or "originalists" have recognized the application of these words with the evolution of life and technology.

rendered decisions over the years that address all the complex issues that come with cyberspace and government search and seizures. This includes:

- Wiretaps on "landline" phone lines (*Katz v. U.S.*, above)
- Location data that may be available in stored data
- Obtaining live location data
- Obtaining live transactional data about calls placed or received
- Obtaining live content on what people are saying, texting, emailing, or doing on their computers
- Accessing stored data from a cloud provider (e.g., Google, Microsoft, Apple)
- Accessing stored data from an electronic device (smartphone, laptop, etc.)
- And so forth.

11.9 References and additional reading

- *Chapter 11 resources*, https://johnbandler.com/cyberlawbook-resources-ch11
  - o Includes study points
- Chapter 21 on gathering evidence in cyberspace
- *Fourth Amendment and cases things to know*, https://johnbandler.com/things-to-know-fourth-amendment-cases
- Fourth Amendment, U.S. Constitution, https://www.law.cornell.edu/constitution/fourth_amendment

11.10 Chapter questions

- What is the highest law in the U.S. regarding government searches and seizures?
- What does the Fourth Amendment protect against?
- If a judge decides police obtained evidence unlawfully, what might the judge do?
- If the Fourth Amendment imposes a search warrant requirement, list some exceptions to that requirement
- True/False: The Fourth Amendment was ratified in 1791; thus it couldn't possibly be applied to cyber and digital evidence.
- Read the 54 words of the Fourth Amendment. What do you think of when you read them? Is this your first time?

12

Jurisdiction

In this chapter:

- Jurisdiction for criminal and civil cases
- Mostly criminal jurisdiction so we are ready for Part 4

12.1 Jurisdiction basics (recap)[147]

Jurisdiction is essentially the authority of the court to hear a case.

There are two types of jurisdiction:

- Jurisdiction over the **person** (defendant), known as *in personam* jurisdiction or personal jurisdiction.
- Jurisdiction over the **subject** of the dispute, known as subject matter jurisdiction.

In civil cases, both are required and highly litigated. They are an opportunity for the defense to get a case thrown out for good, or make the plaintiff start over.

In criminal cases and investigations, subject matter jurisdiction is the main jurisdictional issue which influences which prosecutors and law enforcement can investigate and prosecute a crime. Personal jurisdiction is not as important of a legal issue, because it is satisfied if a defendant is arrested and brought before the court.

---

[147] We introduced jurisdictional concepts in Chapter 8 on criminal law and Chapter 9 on civil law.

12.2 Civil jurisdiction basics (recap)[148]

Civil jurisdiction requires both:

- Personal jurisdiction (*in personam* jurisdiction, over the person), and
- Subject matter jurisdiction.

The plaintiff obtains personal jurisdiction over the defendant usually by personally serving a copy of the summons and complaint on the defendant. A process server is usually hired to do this, and we've seen it on television enough. Since this personal service is sometimes hard to do, there are other ways to achieve service, such as through mailing and leaving at a residence or place of business.[149]

Statutes require a defendant to have a sufficient personal connection to a jurisdiction to be sued in that jurisdiction.

Subject matter jurisdiction is usually a simple matter in a state court, because states have a general authority over what happens within the state (the so called "police power").

In a federal court, subject matter jurisdiction can be harder to show, because our federal government is of "limited" jurisdiction. Federal courts have:

- Federal question jurisdiction (subject matter involves a federal issue)
- Federal diversity jurisdiction (there is diversity of state residences among the plaintiffs and defendants).

12.3 Criminal jurisdiction basics (recap)[150]

Jurisdiction is a special part of criminal procedure law and is rarely an issue in routine traditional criminal cases.

Jurisdiction in a criminal case simply means the authority of the court to preside over the offense. By extension, this also affects the authority of prosecutors and law enforcement over the offense.

---

[148] We introduced this in Chapter 9 on civil law.

[149] "Nail and mail" service refers to taping a copy on the defendant's door and also mailing a copy. The invention of sticky tape means process servers don't have to actually nail the documents to the door, which would cause damage.

[150] We introduced this in Chapter 8 on criminal law.

Since criminal litigation effectively starts with an arrest of the defendant and bringing that person in front of the court, this means that once a criminal litigation is in process, the defendant has been physically arrested and brought to the court. Personal jurisdiction is not really an issue in criminal cases.

In criminal law we focus on subject matter jurisdiction. When we say "jurisdiction" in a criminal case, we are usually talking about jurisdiction over the "subject matter," meaning the crime that [allegedly] occurred.

Jurisdiction has different analysis, depending on whether we are dealing with a state prosecution or a federal prosecution.

12.4 State and federal jurisdiction compared (recap)

States have general "police powers" over everything that happens within their state. "Police power" is a legal term and means more than just law enforcement and policing—it means that states have general authority over mostly everything happening in their state.

In contrast, the federal government has "limited" power because of the U.S. Constitution.[151] This means the federal government needs to establish their authority (jurisdiction) over certain acts.[152] One common way to do this is if the crime affects interstate commerce, an area the federal government is specifically authorized to exert power over.

Imagine a suspect shoplifted a candy bar from a grocery store in Manhattan. That is an offense the Manhattan DA clearly has jurisdiction to prosecute because the offense occurred within the borders of New York County and within New York State. In contrast, the federal government cannot prosecute this case (even if they wanted to) because they would not be able to establish federal jurisdiction.[153]

---

[151] Remember that the Tenth Amendment says that powers not specifically given to the federal government are reserved for the states or for individuals.
  We put "limited" in quotes because while the federal government has limited powers (in theory), when it does have the ability to act, its powers are immense.
[152] As we mentioned in Chapter 8, it is not enough to say it happened within the U.S., or victimized a U.S., person, there needs to be a specific reason why the U.S. has power to prosecute it.
[153] Suppose that theft was from a small store or kiosk within a federal building. In that case the federal authorities might be able to assert U.S. jurisdiction because it was on federal property. Still, they would probably use their discretion and decline the case and be happy to let local prosecutors handle it!

Similarly, for any criminal act within New York County, the Manhattan DA's office would have clear and default authority to prosecute by mere virtue of the act occurring within the county borders. In contrast, federal prosecutors would need to establish federal jurisdiction, find that jurisdictional hook.

Sometimes both federal and state authorities have jurisdiction over the same offense. This is the case with many cybercrimes, and in TV shows and movies where city cops and FBI agents argue about "jurisdiction" after a bank robbery. No surprise, but Hollywood often frames these arguments improperly.

The true jurisdictional question is not about what law enforcement individuals can or cannot do, but which court can hear the case.

Often, *both* state and federal courts have jurisdiction. Meaning either—or both—law enforcement could investigate to gather facts and evidence. Separately, either or both state and federal prosecutors could bring charges, using any combination of local, state, and federal personnel.

In practice, there may be good reasons why one or the other should take charge, and individual and organizational dynamics means friction occurs.

Keep your focus on the legal question as to which courts have legal jurisdiction (subject matter jurisdiction) to hear the case.

12.5 State criminal jurisdiction

Typically, state jurisdiction is established by the prosecutor showing that the conduct occurred within that geographic area. This is a simple issue for crimes like traditional theft, burglary, assault, or murder.

The prosecutor typically needs to show the required state and county jurisdiction. It is possible that multiple states might have jurisdiction, but the relevant question is only whether *this* county and state has the power to proceed.

The prosecutor asks the witness:

Where was this?

What county and state is that in?

Because it is such an obvious factual issue, the Judge at trial might even allow a leading question, and combining two questions into one:

Is that in the County and State of New York?

Based upon that, the county and state where those acts took place is established and so is jurisdiction.[154]

This can get complicated. Consider these hypothetical situations (fact patterns).

- Theft or assault happens on a train or plane going between counties or states.
- Threatening phone call is made from one state to another.
- Defendants are involved in a complex conspiracy committing crimes all over the country, including some acts in a particular county?
- Defendant shoots a rifle from State A killing victim in State B.
- Defendant kills Victim in an unknown location, and dumps the body in State A.
- Defendant (identity thief) assumes the identity of Victim in State A, but Victim resides in State B.

Chances are state laws on jurisdiction address these issues. New York's C.P.L. certainly does.[155]

We can already see some issues with cybercrime and jurisdiction, but also consider that the law may have applicable provisions. Consider these scenarios:

- A victim within the state.
- Theft from a victim within the state.
- An electronic communication into the state.
- A data breach into the state.

Traditional provisions can apply, and we will dive in further in Part 4.

---

[154] As a prosecutor, proving jurisdiction was a basic, foundational requirement for every Grand Jury presentation and trial evidence. In street crime type cases, where a harm was inflicted at a physical location somewhere in Manhattan, we would elicit that jurisdictional component by asking about the address, and then by asking:

"Is that in the County of New York?"

And then the witness would reply,

"Yes."

In more complex cases, including cybercrime, establishing jurisdiction requires more attention to detail.

[155] *See* NY C.P.L. Article 20, *Geographical Jurisdiction of Offenses*, https://www.nysenate.gov/legislation/laws/CPL/A20.

12.6 Federal criminal jurisdiction

We see that the federal government, and thus the federal criminal courts, are of "limited" jurisdiction, only with authority over areas specifically listed in the U.S. Constitution.

That's the rule. But let's look at the practicalities.

First, when we say "limited," we mean it is not over everything that happens within the country. But in those cases where the federal government does have jurisdiction over something, their power is enormous. You've heard the saying:

"Don't make a federal case out of it."

That saying reflects the significance and power of their cases. The federal government does not bring a lot of prosecutions each year (compared to state and local prosecutors), but when they do, the cases reflect a large investment of resources.[156]

Second, they can obtain jurisdiction over so many things, simply by showing the offence affects "interstate commerce" – which is often a minimal hurdle. Similarly, if the offense happens on federal land, property, or victimizes a federal entity or individual, that could be sufficient to establish jurisdiction.[157]

Third, the feds often decline to pursue a matter even when they have jurisdiction because it does not meet their monetary threshold. They know they can only bring a small number of cases each year, so are very selective about the cases they work on.

12.7 Jurisdiction over cyber conduct

Remember the thoughts (misconceptions?) we discussed in Chapter 2?

✘ *We need a new legal jurisdiction for cyberspace.*

✘ *We need a global jurisdiction for cyberspace.*

---

[156] For example, of all the cases brought in the U.S. each year, both criminal and civil, 98.5% are brought in state courts, and 1.5% in federal courts. *See* Court Statistics Project, *Federal and State Caseload Trends, 2012-2022*, https://www.courtstatistics.org/court-statistics/state-versus-federal-caseloads.
[157] As we will cover in Chapter 20 internet connected computers are deemed "protected" computers under the main cybercrime federal statute and thus properly subject to federal jurisdiction (in theory).

It is true that actions "happen in cyberspace," and data gets transmitted through it, and it can be hard to know the path it took or where it was in that nebulous area.

But cyber conduct is committed by a person, who is in a physical location, even if that location is usually hard to identify and unknown at the start of the investigation. And cybercrime has an effect and causes harm, and usually that is where the victim is, a physical location.

By understanding the existing laws for criminal jurisdiction over the crime itself, we see that they can be applied for most cybercrime.

We will talk more about cybercrime jurisdiction in Part 4.

12.8 Venue compared

Venue is a different concept from jurisdiction and is a significant issue for the federal criminal justice system, less so in the state systems.

Venue relates to whether the case is being heard in the proper courthouse. Put differently, assuming jurisdiction is established, there may be multiple courthouses within that jurisdiction, and some may be the proper venue, others may not be.

The U.S. as a country may have jurisdiction to prosecute a defendant for allegedly committing an offense, but there are federal courthouses all around the country in 94 different federal districts. Which district should it be in, and in which courthouse?

A defendant deserves to have their case in the proper venue. A defendant who allegedly committed a crime in California should not have to travel to New York to answer the charges, if nothing happened in New York.

If the main events of a crime occurred in California, and that is where the victims and witnesses are located, then it seems the charges should be brought there. If the main events of a crime occurred in New York, that seems like a proper venue. The jurisdiction of the U.S. remains constant, but the federal venue is different.[158]

---

[158] Consider the case of Michael Avenatti, formerly a California attorney who rose to prominence representing Stormy Daniels and appearing on cable news. Ultimately, he was charged with extortion by New York based federal prosecutors, theft by New York based federal prosecutors, stealing from clients (including Stormy Daniels) and tax evasion by California based federal prosecutors. Each charged him in the federal district (venue) which had the most logical connection to the crimes. All established federal jurisdiction.

While the U.S. Department of Justice has oversight over every federal district prosecutor's office, each is led by a United States Attorney who is appointed by the President and confirmed by the Senate. There can sometimes be rivalries and disputes among the various districts.

Venue in the state system also relates to whether one is in the right courthouse. New York has a very complicated system with many different types of trial courts (where litigation is brought) and those types vary depending on whether one is in New York City, Long Island, or upstate.

12.9 References and additional reading

- *Chapter 12 resources*, https://johnbandler.com/cyberlawbook-resources-ch12
- NY C.P.L. Article 20, Geographical Jurisdiction of Offenses, https://www.nysenate.gov/legislation/laws/CPL/A20
- 28 U.S. Code Part IV - Jurisdiction and Venue, https://www.law.cornell.edu/uscode/text/28/part-IV
- Federal Rules of Criminal Procedure (FRCP) Title V, Venue, https://www.law.cornell.edu/rules/frcrmp/title_V

12.10 Chapter questions

- List the two types of jurisdiction.
- Summarize the two types of jurisdiction.
- If a court does not have jurisdiction over a case, can it do anything about that case? Why?
- What is the difference between jurisdiction and venue?
- In criminal cases, which type of jurisdiction would be at issue and why?

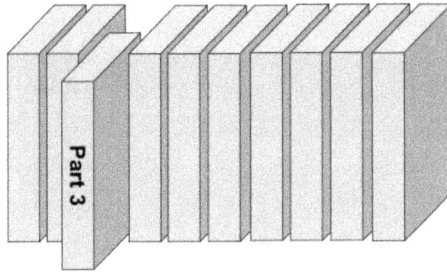

Part 3

Entering the Digital Domain of "Cyberspace" Introducing Technology, Cybersecurity, Cybercrime, and Data Privacy Issues

In this part:

- Some cyber basics, such as:
  - o Today vs. yesterday
  - o Cybercrime
  - o Markets for data about you
  - o Introduction to technology
  - o Introduction to cybersecurity

In other words:

- A foundation in cyber, so we can apply traditional law to cyberspace
- This helps us better understand cybercrime laws, data laws, and how traditional laws are applied to cyber issues

John T. Bandler

13

How We Got to Cyberlaw:
Today's World Compared to 30 Years Ago

In this chapter:
- The advance of technology
- Its impact on five main areas
- The intersection of cyber and law

13.1 The advance of technology

Society and technology have evolved. Changes may be small and large. We should think about:

- What is new?
- What is the same?[159]

Throughout human history some things remain true:

- Some people steal from others and victimize them
- People create and use new tools
- People innovate
- People need to send and receive payments to transfer value
- Criminals need to send and receive payments, and hide their improper activity
- Tools can be misused by accident
- Tools can be used deliberately for bad.

As we think about cyberlaw and society, we can think about five main areas:

- Law
- Technology
- Crime

---

[159] This is a method of legal thinking: to analogize and distinguish.

- Privacy
- Business and commerce.

These five areas have been around for hundreds (even thousands) of years but have evolved and expanded over time.

Consider life in the early 1990s, with a desktop computer, a dial-up internet connection, and no cell phones.[160] We can think of our five areas overlapping and with relative sizes like this.

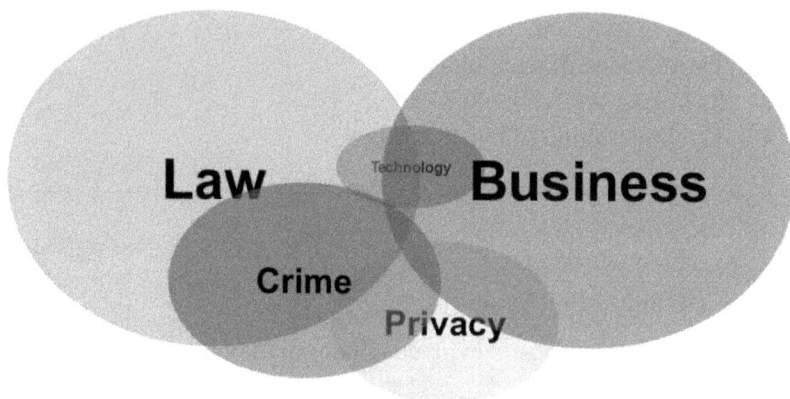

Law   Technology   Business

Crime

Privacy

30 or so years ago (1990s)

The intersection of law and technology ("cyberlaw") was a very small area then and many were unaware of it, especially regarding crime and privacy.

Today, technology advancements mean we have:

- An ever-present internet and constant connectivity
- Computers everywhere, in our pocket, on our wrist
- Enormous amounts of data and constant data flow
- Global communication
- New ways to steal

---

[160] That was me at twenty-something, and I was working as a young trooper. Initially, no cell phone, no pager, no personal computer. When working, we had the radio, but for details I needed to call the station which required stopping somewhere and asking to use their phone. Eventually I got a pager, which let people contact me, but required me to find a phone to make a call. Eventually, cell phones arrived. At home, I eventually had a personal computer with dial-up internet. NYSP resisted computers for a longer time.

- New ways to send value to another person (payments)
- New ways to launder money
- Anonymity for criminals.[161]

With the explosion of technology its intersection with law is now very large–that is essentially the area of "cyberlaw," and affects both criminal law and civil law. It looks something like this:

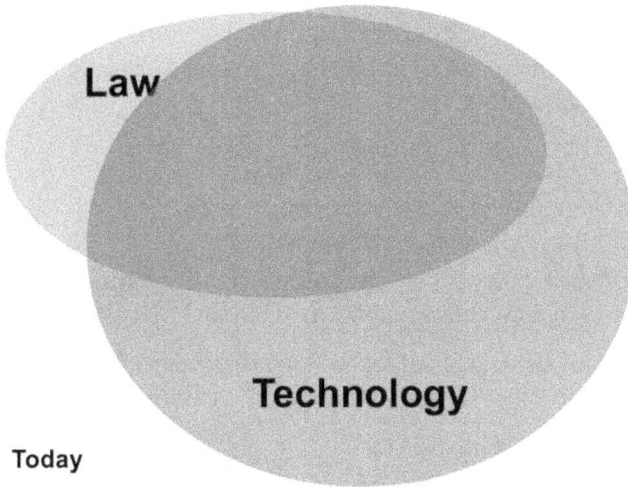

Law

Technology

Today

When we layer in all the other bubbles of business, crime, and privacy, we see technology permeates everything like this:

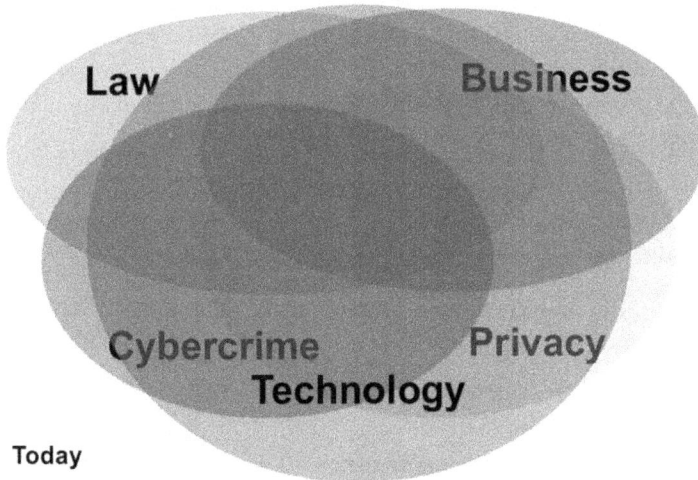

Law   **Business**

Cybercrime   **Privacy**

Technology

Today

---

[161] Or consider it "attempted anonymity" or "pseudonymity."

Think of the tools and advances over the course of human history. We started with basic tools and things have evolved, with this approximate sequence:

- Brains
- Abacus (a human operated mechanical computer)
- Accounting machines (cash registers, desktop calculators, etc.)
- First digital computers
- Enormous, expensive main frame computers
- Era of ubiquitous computers in the home (personal computers, or desktop computers)
- Creation of internet
- Smartphones and mobile devices
- Ubiquitous, constant internet connections
- Cloud storage and cloud computing
- Constant connectivity and computing with a multitude of devices, applications, and networks.

Along the way, some areas of technology receive excitement, hype, and marketing buzz. Whether warranted or not, we have seen:

- Internet of Things (IoT)
- Blockchain
- Cryptocurrency (a type of virtual currency)
- Machine learning
- Artificial intelligence
- Quantum computing
- Metaverse
- Quantum Artificial Intelligence Algorithmic Blockchain Warp Speed Computer Next Generation Cryptoverse.

I made up the last one. People can debate the importance or significance of some of these inventions as well as future inventions. Those who stand to profit from them will market them and hype them.

With learning, thinking, and communicating among humans, consider these advances:

- Non-verbal communication
- Verbal communication
- Cave writings and stone writings
- Writing on papyrus and paper
- Hand copying to reproduce written work
- The printing press

- Newspapers
- Typewriters
- Early computers and early word processing
- The internet and search engines ("Google")
- Internet instant communication (news, X/Twitter, YouTube, etc.)
- Today's word processing tools (Word, Google Docs)
- Chat-GPT, Artificial Intelligence (AI), and "Generative AI."

Each advancement might allow future generations to have a jump start on information and education, allowing them to learn and explore even faster and further. Perhaps not every invention does this.[162]

With value and payments, consider these evolutions:

- Valuable items and services (food, labor)
- Barter
- Currency substitutes (gold, salt)
- Currency of a government
- Other currency substitutes
- Technology based currency substitutes (virtual currency, cryptocurrency, virtual assets).[163]

New products, services, inventions, and practices are always being created. Even with real change comes marketing and hype for sales and investment, and sometimes hype comes without underlying substance.

13.2 Changes in law with tech

Technology is now everywhere and that means "cyber" is everywhere, including with law, and all the areas that intersect with law.[164]

Think how the law has evolved over hundreds (and even thousands) of years along with the evolution of society, and how that continues with technology. Technology has created many changes over the last thirty years.

---

[162] Ironically, it is possible that AI could have an opposite effect for some people. If students and learners use AI to substitute for their efforts to read, think, and write, then those important skills might not be developed properly when compared to students who expended the effort and thought. *See* Chapter 3.
[163] More on this in Chapter 22 on virtual currency.
[164] Hence this entire book on cyberlaw which became bigger and bigger as I dug into the topic.

Some of that evolution is case-by-case. A judge hears a case involving an existing legal concept (*e.g.*, the crime of theft, a contract dispute, a claim of negligence) but the facts involve something new: the use of a computer, providing computer services, or something that involves computers. That judge issues a decision applying the existing law to some of these new circumstances.

Some of that evolution is based upon new laws and regulations. The government decides there needs to be new written legal requirements to address the issues of the day. Perhaps this includes secure disposal of consumer data, cybersecurity, data breach reporting, privacy, artificial intelligence, or some other new issue.

The evolution of law in a constitutional democracy is complex and without a single central authority to impose it.

13.3 Crime to cybercrime

Crime has been occurring since the first humans. One individual or group tried to steal from another, to take property or land. Rules have evolved and today we have a complex structure of criminal law to define crimes and adjudicate allegations of crime.

Theft has been around since the beginning of human interaction, where one individual or group steals from another.

As criminal groups became more organized, as the government realized that a lot of crime is profit oriented, the government looked to identify illegal criminal profits, enforce tax laws, and create rules to identify the flow of illicit funds. Money laundering and anti-money laundering was born.

As tools and platforms relating to computers and the internet were developed, it is no surprise that thieves began to use them. As new methods for payments and value transfer were developed, criminals began to use them for money laundering too.

Cybercrime can steal funds directly, and cybercrime can steal data (or take it hostage) to make money.

With technology, the era of cybercrime was born. With the high profitability of cybercrime, the era of cybercrime money laundering was also born.

Cybercrime is "new" in the sense that it uses new technology and can be done from anywhere. Theft used to be a local crime and now can be committed from anywhere in the world. While a pickpocket or burglar needed to touch a wallet or enter a house physically, a cybercriminal can steal data and funds from anywhere in the world.

Cybercrime is "old" in the sense that it is mostly just theft, similar to what selfish humans have been doing for thousands of years.

13.4 Privacy

Privacy is an old concept, including the privacy of our person and our home.[165] Debates have continued regarding the right of the individual to be left alone versus the rights or demands of other individuals, society, and government.

Information about people has long had value for marketing, including print advertising and then radio and television advertising.

Today in our constantly connected society, consumer data is even more valuable. This data is collected, stored, shared, sold, and stolen.

Privacy is a bigger issue than ever. Never have so many details of an individual's life been stored in a single device—our smartphones. Never have people's movements and interactions been captured and stored by so many different private companies. It is a worthy area for law and discussion.

13.5 The explosion of speech

There is more speech and expression today than ever before in human history.

More speech online means more discussion about speech issues like what should be criminalized or have civil consequences, and issues beyond the law.

With technology today, almost every person in the world has the potential to create or post words or videos to a platform where anyone else in the world could read it or see it.

That's why we laid a foundation for law and speech by discussing the First Amendment, and we will return to it later.

Thirty years ago, far fewer written communications existed between individuals and for public consumption. It was laborious. A letter needed

---

[165] We can imagine cave dwellers being protective of their abodes, and the 1300s England had laws against peeping toms. Chapter 32 covers privacy and privacy laws.

to be written and mailed. A note needed to be delivered. Now we communicate constantly. All this data is shared and often stored.

Thirty years ago, we took relatively few photos. Cameras were expensive, not everyone had one, and they were carried mostly just by photographers and tourists. Purchasing and developing film was also expensive. Now people take thousands of photos a year, many are stored by tech behemoth companies and are shared with the world.

13.6 Government investigation and surveillance in cyberspace

There are unprecedented pools of data which the government may try to access and use for law enforcement or national security purposes. There is so much communication and data in our new world; individuals carrying smart phones with a host of tracking abilities, and online platforms that collect and store massive troves.

Government searches and seizures implicate the Fourth Amendment, including in digital spaces. Various individuals within government sometimes complain about some new challenges of investigating in the cyberage, an issue we will also address later.[166]

13.7 Business, commerce and marketing

Business and commerce expand with technology. With every new tool is a business opportunity for many. The tool may be touted as the savior for society, but there is also an individual or organization trying to make money from it.

Technology related services are ubiquitous and include IT, managed IT, cloud services, email, websites, tools to do new things, to do old things faster, for ecommerce, customer relationship management, sales, and more.

Businesses choose to offer "free" technology services and products to the world. But the well-worn saying is:

If the service is free, you are the product.

Put differently, if Facebook (Meta), X (formerly Twitter), Google, or Microsoft offer a free service to the world, they are probably not doing it as a public service or charity. They are offering the "free" service to cultivate users, to learn about them, and be able to monetize that or sell something. A large platform learns a lot about their users and can sell

---

[166] We will discuss the encryption debate in Chapter 23.

advertising or data to others. Big business with massive privacy implications.

Digital advertising is an enormous industry. Organizations pay billions of dollars a year to influence consumers to purchase their goods or services.

These payments might be to obtain views (a user view of the advertisement or message), clicks (that take the user to a particular webpage or app), and purchases.

All these systems and techniques that are used to influence the purchasing decisions of consumers can also be used to influence people in other ways. To inspire outrage, donate, support or vote for a particular candidate or issue, to protest, and more.

13.8 References and resources

*   *Chapter 13 resources*, https://johnbandler.com/cyberlawbook-resources-ch13

13.9 Chapter questions

*   What technology did you grow up with, and how is it different from what you have today?
*   Does technology make our lives easier? How so?
*   What are the five areas that have evolved, as outlined in the chapter?
*   Would you add any other areas to these five areas, or remove or consolidate any?

John T. Bandler

14

Cybercrime and Identity Theft: Stealing from Others Using Digital Spaces and Creating a Black Market for Data

In this chapter:

- Cybercrime
- Cybercrime is mostly theft
- Identity theft
- Stealing through cyberspace
- Geography is no longer a hindrance to crime

14.1 Cybercrime defined

Here's my working definition of cybercrime:[167]

> **Cybercrime**: Cyber + crime. When someone violates a criminal statute using computers and the internet.
> (Most cybercrime is ultimately about theft but there are many typologies and other motives.)

You may hear the other terms as well, or see that some subdivide cybercrime into categories, so those terms might include:

- Computer crime
- Digital crime
- Internet crime
- Data crime
- Cyber-enabled crime
- Cyber-native crime
- Cyber-dependent crime.

---

[167] Many of these definitions within the book are also in the glossary. Remember that different people have different understandings of what terms mean, few definitions are universally agreed upon, and people may disagree.

If "cyber" encompasses the digital realms, then it includes computers, data, and the internet. It is hard to have an event that involves one of these areas but not the others. "Cyber" seems to be essentially synonymous with "computer," "internet" and "data."

For this book, let us work with a basic definition and meaning of cybercrime. (cyber + crime).[168]

Cybercrime cases will need lots of digital evidence, but also some traditional evidence and investigative techniques. The converse is also true—traditional crimes will require digital evidence as well as traditional evidence.

14.2 Identity theft defined

Identity theft is essentially when the defendant assumes the identity of the victim to obtain goods or services, steal, or commit additional crime.

Identity theft is stealing, but with a twist. It might not steal directly from the person impersonated, but from a company. With a single act, there may be multiple victims, and perhaps cascading entities who bear the ultimate financial cost. There may be multiple jurisdictions involved, with the victim in Place A, the defendant in Place B, and other companies involved in Places C and D. Identity theft relies on the use of the victim's personal information, creating another market for this data.

Personal information has long been valuable for the legitimate credit industry, which obtains, buys, and sells it for legally permitted purposes. Credit is based on one's identity.

That brought the criminal market for this personal information to commit identity theft. Computers and networks meant people were applying for credit and using credit cards, and stores were making instant decisions to allow purchases or not.

In the 1990s our government[169] realized that criminal substantive laws needed the addition of identity theft statutes. They recognized a need to

---

[168] We will address the "enabled" vs. "native" vs. "dependent" terminology in Chapter 23.
[169] "Government" meaning our federal government and the many state governments.

protect personal information and criminalize the illegal use of it for crime.[170]

Simple theft statutes apply simply to traditional theft. Consider this typical fact pattern:

- Defendant (thief) steals from Victim
- Both were in proximity in the same jurisdiction, both are available to law enforcement
- Victim can state and testify that Defendant lacked permission and authority to take whatever was stolen.

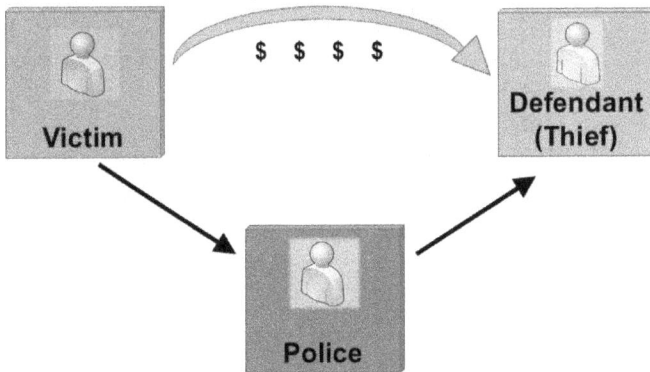

Theft before cyber

Now consider a simple fact pattern of identity theft and how a simple occurrence might be more difficult to prove and investigate:

- Victim A has a credit card from Bank B.
- Store C sells expensive electronics.
- Defendant D obtains Victim A's credit card information and creates a forged credit card and goes to Store C to purchase merchandise.
- Victim A later sees this fraudulent transaction on the Bank statement, reports it to the bank and to Police E in their state.

---

[170] In statutes, this type of personal data might be called "personal information," "personal identifying information" (PII), "personal health information" (PHI), and more. It may have extensive definitions of what that term includes, to include name, address, birthdate, social security number, credit card or financial account numbers, biometric information, usernames, passwords, and more.

- Police E might tell Victim they need to report it in the state where the crime happened (Police F).
- Police F might even tell Victim they cannot help, or that a personal visit is needed to file a report.
- Bank B might reverse the charge for Victim A, meaning Victim A does not bear the theft loss.
- Bank B might refuse to bear the cost of the fraud, and do a "chargeback" to Store C, making the store bear the theft loss.
- Police and prosecutors seeking to investigate, solve, and prove the case would need to:
  - Interview victim and get them to appear for grand jury or trial.
  - Obtain records and video and statements from the store and its employees.
  - Obtain records from the bank.
  - Try to identify, find, and apprehend the defendant.
  - Ensure they can prove their case in grand jury or court with appropriate witness testimony and records.

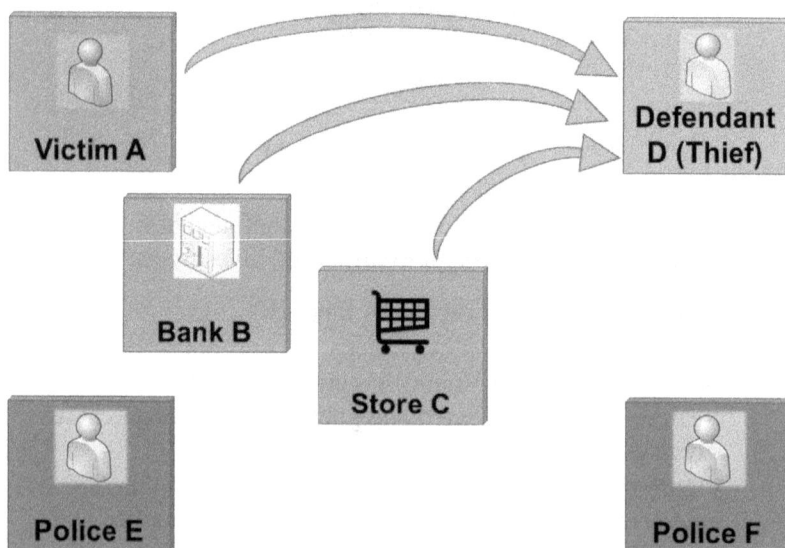

Identity theft has many victims

Defense attorneys would seek to weaken or dismiss charges on jurisdictional grounds and based upon uncertainty about who the victim is, and sow confusion about what the records and video show.

John T. Bandler

Identity theft statutes (including from New York) address this crime and provide clear jurisdiction for the state if the theft occurs in the state (such as in-store shopping) or if the victim resides in the state.

Cybercrime often involves identity theft and is required for identity theft. The identity thief may have obtained stolen personal information online from cybercriminals who committed data breaches. Cybercrime often involves victims being impersonated online, including through fraudulent account logins (and attempts) and impersonating emails.

14.3 The cybercrime and identity theft economy

The rise of identity theft and cybercrime came jointly, and they remain intertwined. Victim "personal information" is valuable to identity thieves so they can commit identity theft; it provides access to credit to obtain goods or services.

Stores and banks request this information and then make determinations about whether to extend credit, approve a transaction, and more. They should verify the applicant's identity and consider whether they are a good credit "risk."

Since personal information is valuable to commit identity theft, identity thieves will pay for it. Since identity thieves will pay for it, someone else (cybercriminals) can make money by stealing it and selling it.

There are many ways to obtain and steal this valuable information. Huge troves of data are available in online repositories, so a data breach can yield millions of consumer records, which can be resold and used for identity theft.

Some cybercriminals have significant technical skills, and some may specialize in committing data breaches and obtaining this data. Others may specialize in reselling this data to make money.

Other methods of obtaining this information include dumpster diving, pickpocketing, and using corrupt employees in a retail establishment.

Identity theft occurs any time a victim's information is used to impersonate them or assume their identity. This identity theft is used to commit many types of crimes to steal and earn an illicit profit.

Cybercriminals are never going to use their real name or identity to commit a crime, so they will either make up information or impersonate a real person when needed.

In sum, there is an enormous black-market economy of criminals who steal via cybercrime and identity theft. They need to steal, gain profits, pay each other and remain anonymous and undetected by law enforcement.

14.4 Theft is no longer local (thanks to cyber)

Once upon a time, to steal, a thief needed to get close to your wallet, purse, or home. Now, that thief can steal from anywhere in the world.

Thieves in any country can now steal from victims in the United States. Hundreds of billions of dollars are stolen through cybercrime every year, and much of this ultimately leaves the country.

It is fascinating to think about. A mind-bending concept that I came to know intimately in the Western Express case. Money is stolen from inside this country, somehow leaves this country and gets to the criminal in another country. We can try to trace those funds individually and, in the aggregate, (overall trends).

Sometimes this movement of funds can be complex. Since the goal of almost all cybercrime is greed, profit, and theft, this means they want money; and the illegal profits need to reach the cybercriminal.

14.5 Payment methods and virtual currency (preview)[171]

Most cybercrime is about stealing and making money because cybercriminals want to get paid. Cybercrime is a large economy with many participants, and each contributes goods or services to further a scheme and to get paid for their illegal efforts.

The payment method needs to be reliable and hard to detect by law enforcement (anonymous or pseudonymous). Criminals need to be able to pay each other anonymously and with confidence that the payment is irreversible, anonymous, and reliable. They do not want to be ripped off or reported to or detected by law enforcement.

The solution for this is virtual currency which was pioneered in the 1990s. An informal value transfer method that does not directly involve any government currency.

Virtual currency's main start was in 1996 with Egold, and 1998 with WebMoney. By 2005 I was a prosecutor starting to investigate these transactions and compiling records and evidence regarding cybercrime

---

[171] We will talk more about all of this in Chapter 22 on virtual currency.

activity that went back to 2001. Cryptocurrency arrived around 2008 with Bitcoin.

14.6 Western Express (preview)[172]

My introduction to cybercrime was the Western Express case which started in 2005.

Western Express International, Inc. was a virtual currency exchanger located in Manhattan (New York County), the same county where I happened to be a relatively junior prosecutor. The case started with a routine identity theft case, and we followed payments and learned about the use of Egold virtual currency that went through this exchanger.

Review of the exchanger's activities and connections made clear that they trafficked in virtual currencies for customers who were identity thieves and cybercriminals. In this early world of virtual currency and cybercrime, it was fascinating to see the financial interaction between Western Express, U.S. based identity thieves, foreign cybercriminals, and legitimate financial institutions.

While working on this case for eight years I learned about cybercrime, money laundering, current and evolving investigative techniques, and did some exciting things including obtaining evidence and prosecuting defendants from other countries. This was by far the biggest investigation and trial of my career.

14.7 Three priority cybercrime threats

There are three main categories of cybercrime which are important to know:

- Email based funds transfer frauds
- Data breach
- Ransomware.

Understanding these three types is important to understand both cybercrime and how to protect against them (with cybersecurity).[173]

---

[172] Chapter 19 discusses this case.
[173] There are a lot of other cybercrime typologies out there, and others may lay out differently. I find these three categories are helpful for informing students and clients.

14.7.1 Email based funds transfer frauds

Cybercriminals steal funds large and small through their clever abuse of email communication. They impersonate people via email to divert funds and steal them. This fraud is mostly trickery and con artistry ("social engineering"), though it often involves a data breach first.

The funds may never be recovered, are not insured, and litigation and other disruption ensue.

This fraud is sometimes called CEO or CxO fraud (when executives are impersonated to engineer a funds transfer) or business email compromise (BEC) when individuals in a business are impersonated to engineer a fraudulent transfer.

Criminals use many techniques to attempt and succeed with these frauds.[174] Organizations need to evaluate if email systems were accessed, and if a data breach occurred.

14.7.2 Data breach

A data breach is the unauthorized access to confidential data. This occurs when a cybercriminal breaks into an email account, network, or stored data. The cybercriminal can use this breach to steal data from the victim for resale in a criminal marketplace, such as when payment card information is breached, or credit information. The criminal might try to commit a follow-on crime against the victim, such as a theft by email-based funds transfer fraud, or by inserting ransomware into the victim's system (see next).

This breach can have many negative consequences, require notification to government and affected parties, damage reputation, and more. There are many ways a cybercriminal can breach an information system to access and steal data.[175]

14.7.3 Ransomware

Ransomware locks the data within computer systems making it unusable. The cybercriminal uses malware and encryption to encode data and then extorts the victim to pay a significant ransom to obtain the code to regain access to systems and data. Business disruption can be immense,

---

[174] For more details, *see Email Based Funds Transfer Frauds*, https://johnbandler.com/email-based-funds-transfer-frauds; *Email Based Funds Transfer Fraud - The Details*, https://johnbandler.com/email-based-funds-transfer-fraud-details.

[175] *Data breach*, https://johnbandler.com/data-breach.

reputational harm follows, and organizations need to evaluate if a data breach occurred.[176]

14.8 The impact of cybercrime on law

Cybercrime came with technology and with enormous consequences. It is a critical area of criminal law, and a serious threat to all of us.

It is an important component for cyberlaw in general.

First, law enforcement cybercrime investigations and prosecutions are an integral part of cyberlaw. We can call this "criminal cyberlaw."

Second, cybersecurity civil laws have been created to require organizations to better protect themselves against cybercrime. It is a recognition of a criminal threat, and implementation of civil rules and standards of conduct to protect against that crime and its consequences.

Law aside, the discipline of cybersecurity exists because of cybercrime.

14.9 References and resources

- *Chapter 14 resources*, https://johnbandler.com/cyberlawbook-resources-ch14
- *Cybercrime*, https://johnbandler.com/cybercrime
- *Identity Theft*, https://johnbandler.com/identity-theft
- *The Three Priority Cybercrime Threats*, https://johnbandler.com/priority-cybercrime-threats
  - *Data breach*, https://johnbandler.com/data-breach
  - *Ransomware*, https://johnbandler.com/ransomware
  - *Email based funds transfer frauds*, https://johnbandler.com/email-based-funds-transfer-frauds
- Part 4 Criminal Cyberlaw, especially:
  - Chapter 19, Western Express
  - Chapter 22, Virtual Currency
- Prior books:
  - *Cybersecurity for the Home and Office* (2017), Chapter 2, The Black Market for Your Data: The Cybercrime Economy

---

[176] *Ransomware*, https://johnbandler.com/ransomware.

- *Cybercrime Investigations* (2020), Chapter 2, What is Cybercrime and Why is it Committed

14.10 Chapter questions

- List the three priority cybercrime threats.
- How is cybercrime similar to "traditional" crime, and how is it different?
- What is most cybercrime really for? Why do they do it?
- How is identity theft harder to investigate compared to traditional theft?
- Why do identity theft and cybercrime go together?
- What was the first main virtual currency and what year?
- What came first, Egold or Bitcoin, and in what years?

15

The Other Markets for Your Data Which Create the Need for Data Privacy

In this chapter we introduce:

- Personal privacy
- Data privacy
- Digital advertising and marketing
- Cyber influence
- The battle for your data
  - For your views and dollars
  - And your brain

We saw in the prior chapter that criminals want to steal our data and use it to commit crimes, including identity theft. While that is a critical black-market for information about us, here we explore other markets for our data.

15.1 Yep, we are a product

As stated previously:

If the service is free, you are the product.

We obtain free use of social media, email accounts, and search engines. There is a reason tech companies provide this to us for free. It is not charity, but because there is value for them when people use it.

If Google (and others) provide excellent free services for indexing and searching the internet, watching videos, using email, document storage, and more; it is because it provides them with a business advantage. They learn about what their users are doing and who they are, so they can sell advertisements that the users will view.

Paid services have privacy implications as well, and you should not assume that just because you are paying for something that your privacy is protected adequately. The business model probably includes gaining value from learning about you.

Many companies learn a lot about their customers, and then obtain value from that information. They may sell or share that data, or work with "partners" and other companies to target you for services or ads.

Cell phone service providers know everywhere you go, who you speak with, and get a good look at many of your habits and data surfing characteristics. Some have received government rebukes and fines for failing to properly notify consumers about the extent of this data collection and use. Some now offer rewards programs in exchange for this data. Your cell phone terms of use and privacy policy are extensive documents that may specify this, assuming you can understand them.

Providers of eBooks, audiobooks, and video streaming services get to know what you read and watch. Gathering this detailed information about our interests would have been impossible in years past.

Websites and advertising networks track our online activities in detail. Behemoth tech companies like Google, Apple, Microsoft, Amazon, and Meta get to know much about our lives. These enormous companies are certainly not perfect, but usually have teams of lawyers and other professionals working to analyze and comply with legal requirements.

There is an enormous industry devoted to advertising, marketing, and targeting consumers like you and me. Some of these companies work hard to understand and comply with the law, others may flagrantly violate the law, others fall somewhere in between.

15.2 Digital advertising

Digital advertising is an enormous industry. Companies pay to try to get people to see a digital ad, see an email, click on an ad or link, or make a purchase.

If you see an ad on a website, in a video, or anywhere on the internet, someone paid for you to see it. Within that process are many entities that probably were paid for some part of that process. This is a highly complex area, far from transparent, and there is quite a bit of shady behavior involved.

When companies pay money to advertise, they want to target their advertisement, so the more they know about who might see the ad, the better.

We have all experienced eerie feelings as we are served with ads that seem to read our minds. If you recently searched about researching or purchasing a laptop computer, that might be the perfect time to serve you with an ad for such a product.

Every time you searched for a product in one place, and then got served with a related ad in a different place, that is advertising technology tracking you. Someone paid money to target you as a type of consumer.

Companies may try to target certain demographics, grouped by age, gender, location, and other characteristics. The more they know, the better for them.

A great deal of money is spent on these pursuits, and then trying to identify if their ads were effective in securing a purchase.

15.3 Monetizing the internet

Imagine a company with an advertising budget, whether a few hundred dollars, thousands of dollars, even millions of dollars. They will spend that money to get the right consumer to see their product or service, for a chance to get them to make a purchase.

There are thousands of these companies, collectively spending billions of dollars each year.

To capture these advertising dollars, an enormous industry of digital advertising companies sells products and services to help others spend their advertising budget. They promise the ability to reach the "right" consumers.

Advertising dollars are best spent if they reach the right person, already inclined to make a purchase, or easily influenced to do so.

The advertiser might pay by view, click, or conversion (sale). Think of these terms:

- *View*: The advertiser pays a certain amount for every user who theoretically "viewed" the ad, such as by scrolling past it in their social media feed, or seeing it displayed on a website.
- *Click*: The advertiser pays a certain amount for every user that clicked on a link (or a graphic or ad that is clickable) and that took them to the advertiser's website.
- *Conversion*: The advertiser pays a certain amount for every user that took the desired action (filled out a form, signed up for an email list, making a purchase).

- *Commission*: A payment (fixed fee or percentage) for driving traffic to the advertiser where a sale is completed.

15.4 The battle for your brain (preview)

Digital advertising is a battle for your brain and your attention, to influence you to purchase a product or service. They are investing a lot of money, time, and research on that, knowing they will see a return on their investment.

There are several layers to this. The final layer is making a purchase or sale, but many things happen before that, including the click, view, or simply time spent on the site or platform.

This can be capitalistic, businesslike, professional, or shady. Some companies have good products and advertise accurately. Other companies have inferior products and advertise deceptively. Each consumer is susceptible to different types of advertising. Fear, anger, or urgency often work well.

The more the platforms and advertisers know about us, the better they can keep us attached to their platform, and the more precisely they can target us with advertising.

The business of advertising technology is in tension with our privacy, but that is not the only issue this technology poses. There are many other people who want to influence us, not just to buy a product or service, but for a variety of other reasons.[177]

15.5 Facebook and Cambridge Analytica (preview)

The Facebook-Cambridge Analytica scandal highlights important points about privacy, digital advertising, and the targeting of individuals to influence them about important national and global issues.

Facebook (and its parent company Meta) makes a lot of money from selling information about its users. This information is valuable and can be used to influence those users and others too.

Every one of those users gets a "free service" they can use, a social media platform they can use to interact with others, and every user is also a "product" that Meta can sell to others for a profit.

---

[177] More in Chapter 36.

Meta made promises to its users about how information would be collected and shared. These promises were conveyed through their terms of use and privacy policy, which become similar to a contract.

As borne out in government press releases and regulatory action, Meta broke their privacy promises, and improperly shared data with Cambridge Analytica.

To settle the privacy claims, Meta paid a $5 billion dollar penalty.[178]

We will return to this case later as we discuss privacy (Part 6) and speech and thought (Part 8).

15.6 References and resources

- *Chapter 15 resources*, https://johnbandler.com/cyberlawbook-resources-ch15
- Chapter 32, Privacy and privacy laws
- Chapter 36, Cyber speech and the battle for our minds
- *Privacy*, https://johnbandler.com/privacy
- *Facebook - Cambridge Analytica case*, https://johnbandler.com/facebook-cambridge-analytica-case
- *Cybersecurity for the Home and Office* (2017), Chapter 3, Advertising: Another Market for Your Data.

15.7 Chapter questions

- If the service is free, you are the _____
- Explain what is meant by the phrase, "If the service is free, you are the product."
- Review a privacy policy for a free service you use (social media, etc.) Does it seem like they use your information to make a profit?

---

[178] That's "billion" with a "B." If the penalty seems large, imagine the profits Facebook obtains through its use of information about platform users.

See FTC *Press Release, FTC Imposes $5 Billion Penalty and Sweeping New Privacy Restrictions on Facebook* (July 24, 2019), https://www.ftc.gov/news-events/news/press-releases/2019/07/ftc-imposes-5-billion-penalty-sweeping-new-privacy-restrictions-facebook.

See Facebook - Cambridge Analytica case, https://johnbandler.com/facebook-cambridge-analytica-case.

- If a social media platform does not charge most of its users, and provides an enormous platform with many resources, how do they make money?
- Do social media platforms have an influence on what content we see? How so?
- How should social media platforms moderate the content on their platforms, and how should they decide what content a particular user should see in their feed?
- What are some ways that digital advertisers monetize user behavior?

16

Introduction to Technology, Computers, and Networks

In this chapter:

- Technology in four parts:
  - You the human
  - Computers
  - Data
  - Networks

16.1 Why a technology chapter?

Why do we need a chapter on technology to learn about cyber law?

- Imagine taking a class on traffic law or automobile accident liability and you did not understand the basics of a car, what the steering wheel does, what the pedals do, what a crash entails, etc.
- Imagine being a hotel owner and taking a class on premises liability law, and you do not know how to close a door, or lock it, and you have never heard of video surveillance.
- Imagine speaking to your doctor about a health issue, and you don't have a basic understanding of human biology, your organs, common medical conditions, or science.

Similarly, to understand cyberlaw we need to know some basics about technology. We don't have to be tech experts, we just have to get a little more comfortable with it and informed about it, so relax and learn one step at a time.

16.2 Technology has four components

Think about your technology as having four components:[179]

- The human that configures and uses technology (you)
- Computer devices
- Data and online accounts
- Networks and the internet (how computers talk to each other).

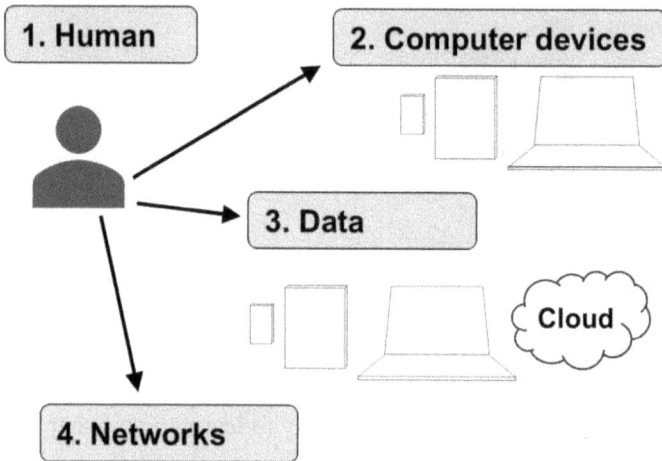

Four technology components

Technology may be confusing at first glance, and we may never understand all the intricacies of it, but we can understand the basics. And we can work to unravel one technological mystery at a time.[180]

---

[179] Breaking a complex topic into four understandable parts helps, and these parts also align with my Four Pillars of Cybersecurity.

[180] In my journey with technology, I find that things can seem overwhelming at first, whether it is analyzing huge troves of data via Excel, using digital forensics tools, website administration, or writing and formatting a book for publication. This feeling of general confusion can be put aside if you simply try to learn one technological task at a time. Five or fifteen minutes is sometimes all you need to research how to get over that one hurdle. Then the next hurdle can be tackled another day.

By technology, I really mean "information technology" (IT) and "information systems" (IS).[181] As we discuss IT, we should also think about "information assets," which generally means things like computer devices, data, online accounts, networks, internet and phone access, and all the related things, including people.

16.3 People as drivers of their technology

As individuals, we operate our technology just like we drive our car or live in our home. We make decisions about how to configure it and how to use it.

If we are administering an organization's information systems, we make decisions to manage and configure it as well.[182]

People are the decision makers (even when they decide to let technology decide for them). They make many decisions from routine to critical, and they are the ones who configure and use technology. People are also assets of an organization. While they are not "property" they are the most important part of an organization and store and communicate an incredible amount of knowledge and information.

16.4 Using technology efficiently and securely

Let us address the physical and virtual technology itself, including computers, data, and networks.

One important question is how to use technology efficiently and to the proper degree of security.

There are many technology providers who compete, and lots of technology to be integrated so that they hopefully work smoothly together.

An important first step is to identify what technology you are using. Technology can be complicated even for a single individual and gets much more complicated for organizations. If we do not know what we have, we will not know how to secure it or improve how we use it.

---

[181] IS can be used to abbreviate "information security" and not just "information systems." Check for context. You see it does depend on what the definition of "IS" is.

[182] Some organizations could be more diligent on how they make these decisions.

We will review the next three categories of:

- Devices (computers)
- Data
- Networks.

16.5 Computers introduced

Computers are simply tools for calculating and storing. They include

- Smart watch
- Smart phone
- Tablet
- Laptop computer
- Desktop computer
- Servers (powerful computers) that serve other computers, including on the cloud.

At their most basic level, computers simply store and process binary bits of information. A binary bit is a single value that can only have one of two values. It is either "0" or "1" (put differently "on" or "off," "yes" or "no").

A single bit of data is not much data, so we look to larger chunks of data, like bytes, kilobytes, megabytes, terabytes and so forth. Their various approximate[183] size is:

- 1 bit contains either a "yes" or a "no" value
- 8 bits is a byte
  - A single byte could describe a character, such as a, b, c
- 10^3, or 1,000 bytes is a kilobyte (KB)
- 10^6, or 1,000,000 (one million) bytes is a megabyte (MB)
- 10^9, or 1,000,000,000 (one billion) bytes is a gigabyte (GB)
- 10^{12}, or 1,000,000,000,000 (one trillion) bytes is a terabyte (TB).

---

[183] These figures are in Base 10, meaning the counting system we are all used to, where numbers are expressed as powers of 10, *e.g.,* 10^3, 10^6, and so forth. Computers use binary, which is Base 2, so actual storage will be based on powers of 2, such as 2^{30}. There has been litigation over this discrepancy, and you may be able to see the fine print when you go shopping for hard drives or storage. Engineers have created alternate terms for greater precision by modifying the words with "bi" (for binary). Gigabyte (GB) means 10^9 bytes, or 1,000,000,000 bytes, whereas actual storage is probably moving to Gibibyte (GiB) which means 2^{30} bytes, or 1,073,741,824 bytes.

With enough bits, computers can store data, emails, documents, photos, videos, and entire hard drives with all our life's documents and data.

Our computers need memory to "think" while processing and calculating. Memory is often expressed in megabytes (MB) and gigabytes (GB). Memory is also known as random access memory (RAM) and needs to be very fast.

Our computers need storage to hold data so it can be available later and that stays even when the computer is turned off.[184] This storage is often expressed in gigabytes (GB) and terabytes (TB). The physical storage for this used to be hard disk drives (HDD) which were rotating platters that can store magnetic charges. Now solid-state drives (SSD) offer faster operation and no moving parts.

Computers store data, process data, and communicate with other computers. The communication between two or more computers is what networking is about.

Computers are made up of many parts. Modern computers are sleek and self-contained, so most users never see their inside and it is tempting to think of them as a single undividable organism. But they are still made up of parts, just like they were thirty years ago.

Important hardware parts include:

- Case
- Power source or converter (battery, power conditioner, etc.)
- Processors to think (central processing unit, CPU)
- Memory to store data temporarily while thinking (RAM)
- Internal storage (persistent storage that stays when the computer is turned off) (HDD/SSD)
- Interfaces for input and output with the human user (screen, keyboard, mouse)
- Physical ports (to connect data cables, electricity, thumb drives, audio)
- Network interface controller (NIC) to communicate with other computers.[185]

---

[184] Stored data is referred to as "data at rest" (compared to "data in transit").
[185] The NIC will have its own unique MAC address. MAC stands for media access control.

Then important software components include

- BIOS (Basic Input/Output System) or UEFI (Unified Extensible Firmware Interface) as the first thing a computer loads when it wakes up before it can even ask "Where am I?")
- Operating system (the main software application that manages the computer and applications, such as Windows, MacOS, Chrome, iOS, Android)
- File system (a method of storing files and folders that comes with the operating system)
- Applications (Apps) or software (Microsoft Office, Google Docs, etc.)
- Virtual ports, a software representation of ports used for communicating and networking.

16.6 Data introduced

Data is stored on computers, transmitted by computers, and often stored in the cloud—meaning the computers you cannot see and are in a data center somewhere.

The amount of data we create, store, and transmit is staggering.

From an individual perspective, we want to consider:

- What data is on our devices (smartphone, tablet, laptop, desktop)
- What data is stored in the "cloud" (Google, Apple, Microsoft, our email accounts)
- What data is on other cloud-based applications (social media such as Instagram, Facebook, LinkedIn, and other applications too).

Online accounts are used to access software services and more of our data is stored there. People and organizations maintain dozens or hundreds of online accounts.

16.7 Encryption at rest

Encryption at rest is an important way to secure sensitive data that is stored on a device, whether a smartphone, tablet, laptop, or on the cloud.

When data is stored somewhere it is "at rest." If it is not encrypted, then anyone who is able to access that data can see what the data is.

If the data is encrypted, then it is encoded, and a person who accesses it would need the secret key code to unlock (decode) that data.

16.8 Networks introduced

Networks are simply a mechanism for one computer to communicate with another. Most networks have multiple computers on it, and even a home network may have dozens of computers on it today, including laptops, tablets, smartphones, smart TVs and other streaming services, security devices and "smart home" devices.

Computers and networks have a "protocol" for communicating, which is basically the language they use. Some protocols to be aware of include:

- "Internet protocol suite," to communicate on the internet, made up of TCP and IP.
- TCP: Transmission control protocol (joined with IP for internet communication), has error checking to ensure the entire message was received.
- IP: Internet protocol for communicating on the internet (and local networks). Associated with "IP Address" for addressing.
- UDP: User Datagram Protocol. A way to send a lot of data without checking to ensure all data was received (good for streaming services).

Networks require some hardware and functions including:

- Network interface controller (NIC)[186] (a part of each computer for interacting with the network)
- Cables
- Wireless signals
- Network switches
- Modem
- Router.

For consumer convenience, often the cable internet company supplies a combined modem-router unit, and the router portion of it establishes the wireless network. The router connects computer devices within the network and is the gateway (middleperson) to locations on the internet, such as cloud data (perhaps stored with Google or Microsoft), websites visited, streaming services, and so forth. We can envision all the wireless connections of various devices in the home to this router with this diagram.

---

[186] The "C" used to stand for card, but now this hardware part is smaller and does not need to be its own card.

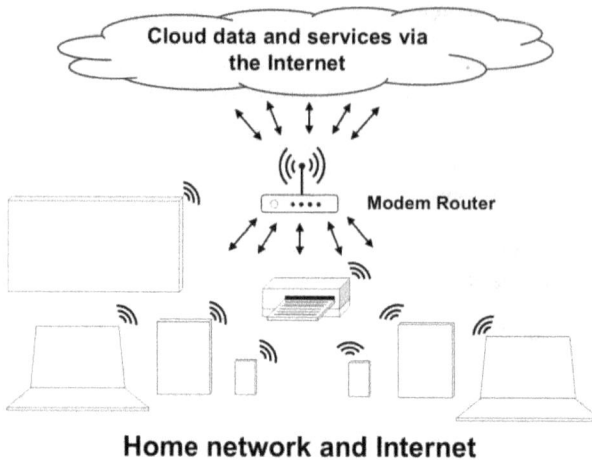

Home network and Internet

16.9 MAC addresses and IP addresses

For computers to communicate with each other using TCP/IP they need IP Addresses.[187]

Computers have NICs (network interface controllers) which have a unique MAC (media access control) address. Each method of networking in a computer may have its own MAC address; ethernet port for wired communications, Wi-Fi adapter, Bluetooth, etc.

On a local home network, a local IP Address is assigned by the router. The router is like a traffic cop and mailroom for the network. It collects the MAC address of each computer on the network and assigns it a local IP address (a private IP address). It routes traffic and information to and from the outside world (the internet) and within the home.

We obtain internet service from an internet service provider (ISP) such as Spectrum or Verizon or our university. They assign us a public IP address through which we can access the internet. When we visit a website (such as JohnBandler.com), the website sees our IP address, and we see its IP address. Knowledge of those IP addresses allows exchange of information between the two computers as we navigate the site.[188]

---

[187] My education on IP addresses started when trying to find the people who used them to commit various crimes. I learned how people can hide their true IP address.

[188] To keep things simple for us humans, the domain name system (DNS) translates "JohnBandler.com" to the IP address where the website is hosted.

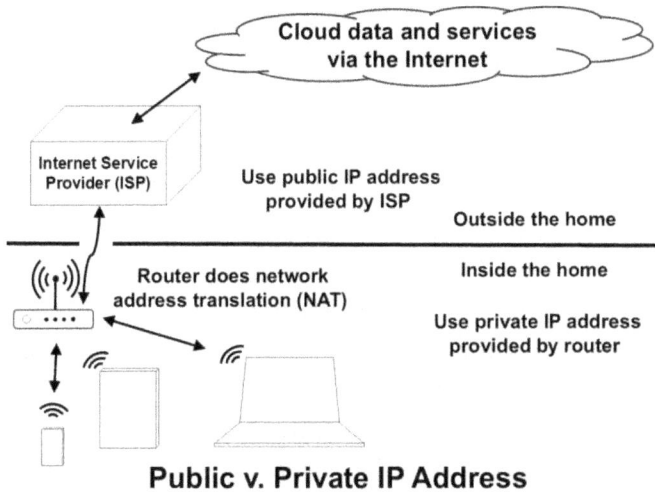

Cloud data and services via the Internet

Internet Service Provider (ISP)

Use public IP address provided by ISP

Outside the home

Router does network address translation (NAT)

Inside the home

Use private IP address provided by router

Public v. Private IP Address

Our home router does the routing of this data from the internet source to get it to the correct device in our home network. Through network address translation (NAT) it translates from public IP addresses (to access the world) to the private IP address of the device on that local network.

One part of the protocol to communicate is computers need to identify each other using an IP address. Think of it like a phone number to call someone. Or, like an address and return address on a letter or email as messages are transmitted back-and-forth.

IPv4 is version four of the IP addressing protocol and worked great until there became too many devices on the internet. Under IPv4, you see IP addresses with a range from:

0.0.0.0

to

255.255.255.255

There are four numbers, each separated by decimal points, and they can be anywhere from 0 to 255.[189] You can check your own public IP address, and if it is IPv4, maybe it looks something like this:

66.63.182.121

---

[189] 0 to 255 allows for a total of 256 possibilities, that's 2^8 possibilities, exactly one byte of information is needed to store this value.

You can also check your own private IP address, and if it is IPv4, maybe it is formatted something like this:

192.168.0.84

IPv6 is the new addressing protocol that things are switching to, little by little. It may look scary, but that's because it is using hexadecimal base (rather than our typical base-10).[190] To count in hexadecimal, we start at 0 and count to F (which really represents 15), like this:

0, 1, 2, 3, 4, 5, 6, 7, 8, 9, A, B, C, D, E, F

Now that you know something about hexadecimal counting, you will recognize it when you see an IPv6 address, which might look like these:

0000:0000:0000:0000:0000:ffff:423f:b679
2001:4860:0007:070e:0000:0000:0000:0000

And there are ways to shorten each of them, such as:

::ffff:423f:b679	or	0:0:0:0:0:ffff:423f:b679
2001:4860:7:70e::	or	2001:4860:0007:070e:0:0:0:0

16.10 The internet

The internet is simply a giant network, used for websites, email communication, and everything else. Some of us grew up without it and life seemed fine but now it seems that no individual or organization could exist without it. If our internet goes down for a few minutes, it is a problem.

As above, internet addressing is now a combination of IPv4 and IPv6.

The domain name system (DNS) servers help translate between words (helpful for humans) to numbers (the language of computers), for visiting websites. When you type "johnbandler.com" into your web browser address line, your browser consults the DNS server system, which responds with the IP address of where my website is hosted, and it takes you there.

The internet also allows for email and all the cloud, social media, and other tech products and services. In the simplest form, it is one computer communicating with another to obtain that service, and each computer knows the public IP address of the other.

---

[190] Hexadecimal can store 16 values, from 0 to 15, which can be represented with four bits of data, which is half a byte, also known as a "nibble."

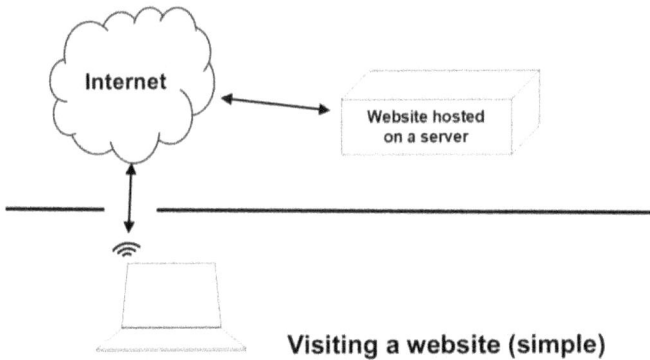

Visiting a website (simple)

A little more detail needs to be layered in to show that the laptop gets to the internet via the router, modem, and then the ISP (e.g., Verizon or Charter or Comcast), then to the ISP of the website, and to the website itself.[191] With that added information, the diagram looks like this:

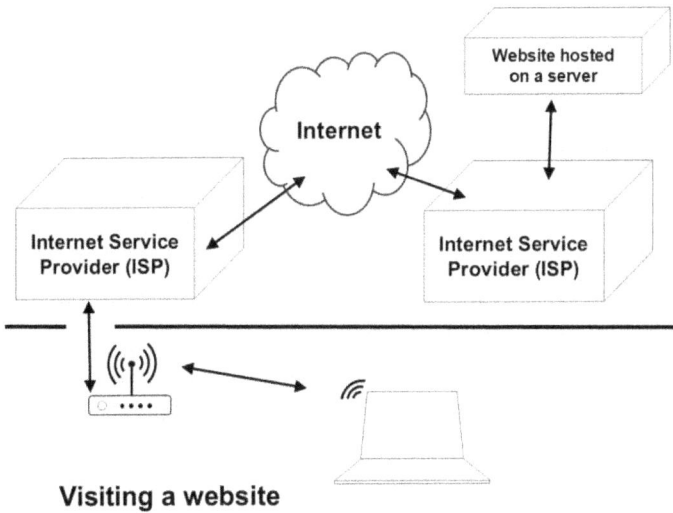

Visiting a website

---

[191] We are using the term internet service provider (ISP) broadly. A consumer may use an ISP such as Comcast, Spectrum, or Verizon, and the public IP address resolves to that company. A webhosting or proxy or large internet company will lease their internet service directly, so doing a public lookup of their IP address may show it resolving directly to that company, e.g., GoDaddy, Amazon, Microsoft, Google, etc.

16.11 Proxies, VPNs and Tor

Proxies, VPNs, and Tor can be used to protect user's privacy and for criminals to conceal themselves. They add a step in the internet communication process, which can also slow things down.

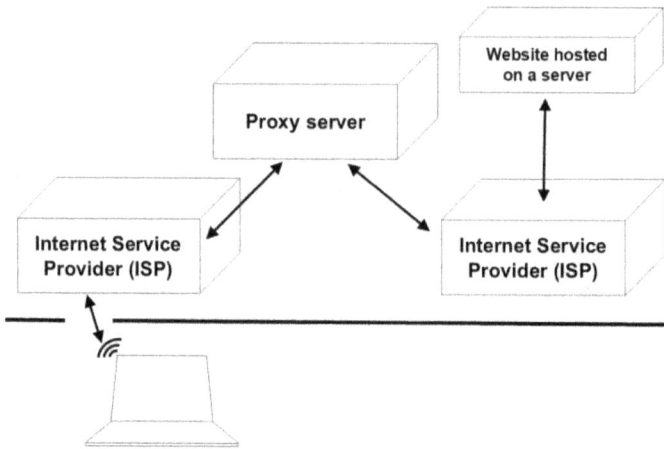

Using a proxy

Sometimes a computer user does not want to interact directly with another computer, but wants to add a middle stop, that's a proxy. A proxy can be used to protect privacy and to conceal one's true origin on the internet. A virtual private network (VPN) is a proxy that also provides encryption abilities for the data while in transit.

In this diagram, we see the proxy is in between the user and the website they are visiting. The website cannot see the user's true originating IP address and only sees the IP address of the proxy. Not depicted in the diagram is the proxy's own ISP, they need a way to access the internet too.

Tor, sometimes referred to as The Onion Router, is essentially a door to the "dark web."[192] It is like a super proxy, providing many proxy steps to conceal a user's origin. Tor can be used to visit a website on the regular

---

[192] The "dark web" requires special software (like the Tor browser) to access and is not searchable through our regular search engines. Read more about Tor and its history at https://www.torproject.org and https://www.torproject.org/about/history.

Then consider the "deep web" which is on our "regular" internet but is not searchable because it requires a login password to access.

internet, in which case the visitor is essentially disguised by many layers of proxies, as depicted here.

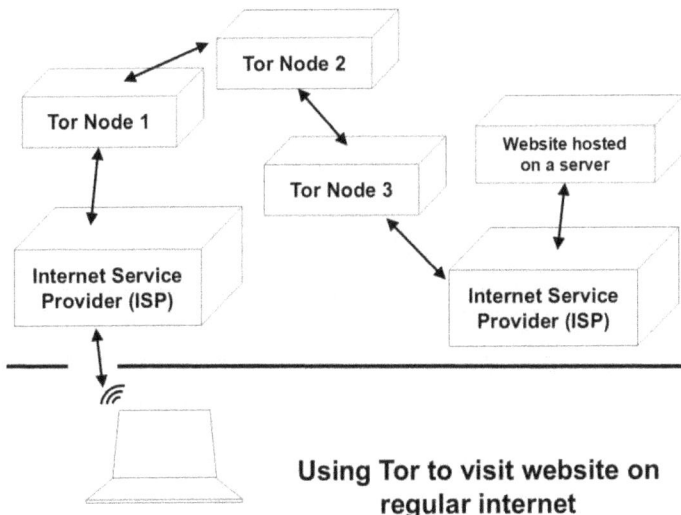

Using Tor to visit website on regular internet

Tor can also host websites, meaning the website's true location can also be disguised. This means computers can interact without knowing each other's true IP address.

16.12 Encryption in transit

Encryption is the encoding and decoding of data. Unencrypted information transmitted via networks and the internet can be readily inspected by anyone along the path of that communication, so encryption is the technique to keep that data secure and private.

Encrypting data that is transmitted is called encryption in transit.

One way to think about the need for encryption in transit is to imagine that every network or internet communication is like sending the message on a postcard, which anyone could read. Only by writing in code can the confidentiality of the message be protected.

16.13 References and resources

- *Chapter 16 resources*, https://johnbandler.com/cyberlawbook-resources-ch16
- *Technology Basics*, https://johnbandler.com/technology-basics/

- *Cybersecurity for the Home and Office* (2017)
  - o Chapter 5, Basic Computer Principles
  - o Chapter 6, Basic Networking and the Internet
- *Cybercrime Investigations* (2020), Chapter 3, Introduction to Computers, Networks, and Forensics
- To improve your knowledge of technology, explore what is already at your fingertips, including:
  - o Your devices, settings, applications

16.12 Chapter questions

- Review the section headers of this chapter and provide a summary of each term, as if you were explaining it to a senior parent or grandparent
- Name the main computer parts
- Identify your local (private) IP address on your local network
- Find your public IP address
- Find the public IP address for a website you trust and use a lot and see if using that IP address in the address line will take you there.
- Identify your computer's make, model, operating system, hard drive type, storage space on the hard drive, RAM space

17

Introduction to Cybersecurity and Cybercrime Prevention

In this chapter:

- Four Pillars introduced
- Decision making and risk
- Cybersecurity and information security basics

17.1 Start with the Four Pillars of Cybersecurity (preview)[193]

Cybersecurity starts with people, their knowledge and the decisions they make. Then it proceeds towards securing computer devices, data, and networks.

These four pillars of cybersecurity are:

- Knowledge and awareness
- Secure computer devices
- Secure data
- Secure networks and internet usage.

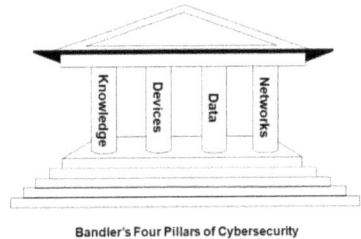

Bandler's Four Pillars of Cybersecurity

I developed this concept because it focuses upon simple, practical, and effective areas to understand and implement cybersecurity. We need to understand cybersecurity to understand all the areas of cyberlaw, especially cybersecurity laws.

This means we need a simple way to think about and implement cybersecurity, even for people who are not technology or security experts.

---

[193] After years of working with individuals and organizations on cybersecurity, it becomes clear that this process needs to start with the human. That's why I lead the chapter with this main point and introduce my Four Pillars of Cybersecurity which emphasizes people and their knowledge as the first pillar.

There are many other ways to think about and organize cybersecurity and cybercrime prevention, with many different philosophies, this is just a starting point for you.

17.2 Cybersecurity and information security defined

Here is a rough definition of cybersecurity to get us started.

> *Cybersecurity is cyber +security. Cybersecurity means securing things in cyberspace and protecting against cybercrime.*

Cybersecurity is a subset of information security, which is an area that has been around for thousands of years, long before the internet and computers. Information security is the process of protecting information, whatever form that information takes. Cybersecurity is a newer and essential subset of information security, focused on protecting information assets in digital form, and protecting from cybercrime. We can see their relationship in the below diagram.

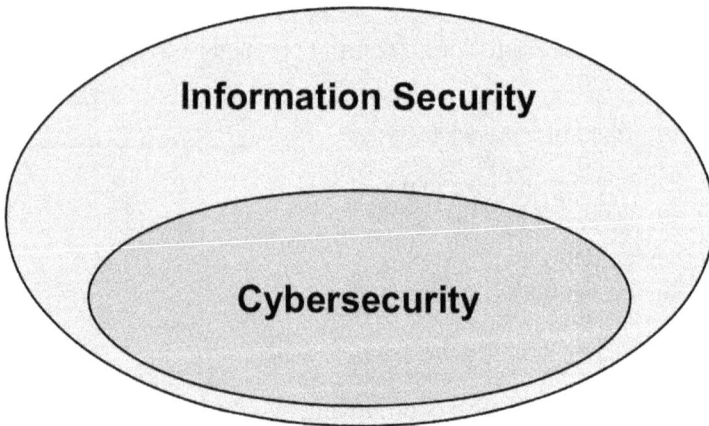

Information Security vs. Cybersecurity

Think about "cybersecurity and information security" together because they are interrelated and our work on one can be done comprehensively with the other.

17.3 Manage information assets well and apply good decision making

Cybersecurity starts with people and the decisions they make to manage their information systems and risks.

These decisions need to assess organization mission, legal requirements, cybercrime threats,[194] accidents and natural disasters.

Information systems are a group of information assets working together.

Information assets can be grouped in alignment with the Four Pillars of Cybersecurity, and include:

- People
- Computer devices
- Data and online accounts and applications
- Networks and the internet.

Decisions need to be made (by employees, managers, and the organization itself) about how to protect and manage the information assets and systems, including what products and services to buy.

17.4 Risk management and decision making (preview)[195]

Decisions need to be made about risk, and this requires assessing what those risks are and considering options to reduce (or "mitigate") risks.

At its heart, risk management is about planning, evaluating options, and trying to make good, reasonable decisions.

We evaluate risks every day in our regular lives, we make decisions all the time. Hopefully we do so by obtaining the facts, reviewing options, and making a reasonable decision.

The same principles of decision making can be applied for cybersecurity risk and decision making.

Here are some simple considerations:

- Try to predict the future (not easy)
- Consider what might happen (good or bad)
- What decisions do we need to make?
  - What options for each decision?
  - Weigh pros (benefits) and cons (negatives).

---

[194] As laid out in an earlier chapter, the three main cybercrimes to know about and protect against are (i) data breach, (ii) ransomware, and (iii) email-based funds transfer frauds (business email compromise, CEO fraud).
[195] We cover risk and decision making from an organization management perspective in Part 9.

Books have been written about risk.[196] They may include highly technical terms and many ways to quantify potential harms and evaluate risk. We start with the simple basics outlined here and in Part 9.

17.5 Objectives of cybersecurity

There are three main objectives of cybersecurity, remember them with "CIA," [197] and they are:

- *Confidentiality* means keeping unauthorized users from accessing the systems or data.
- *Integrity* means that only authorized users can make changes.
- *Availability* means that authorized users can access their systems and data when needed.

Recap: The three objectives (goals) of cybersecurity are:

- Confidentiality
- Integrity
- Availability.

17.6. Controls (safeguards) to achieve cybersecurity

To achieve the three objectives, organizations (and individuals) should apply appropriate controls, also known as safeguards. You can remember these with the initialism of "PAT."

---

[196] Start with the free and reliable information from NIST (the U.S. National Institute of Standards and Technology). They have a manual on IT risk (itself 183 pages) with considerable supplemental materials, including some quick start guides.
- NIST *Risk Management Framework* (main landing page), https://csrc.nist.gov/projects/risk-management.
- NIST Special Publication 800-37, Revision 2 (Dec 2018), *Risk Management Framework for Information Systems and Organizations: A System Life Cycle Approach for Security and Privacy*, https://nvlpubs.nist.gov/nistpubs/ SpecialPublications/NIST.SP.800-37r2.pdf.
- NIST *Risk Management Framework (RMF) Small Enterprise Quick Start Guide*, NIST SP 1314 (July 2024), https://nvlpubs.nist.gov/nistpubs/ SpecialPublications/NIST.SP.1314.pdf.
[197] This is referred to this as the "CIA Triad."

These three control types are:

- *Physical* controls restrict physical access in one way or another.
- *Administrative* controls include rules, policies, and training.
- *Technical* controls are electronic protections, such as a firewall, antivirus, or monitoring software.

There are other ways to categorize safeguards, but the PAT method is your simple and practical start.[198]

Recap: The three types of cybersecurity controls (safeguards) are:

- Physical
- Administrative
- Technical.

17.7. Authentication

Authentication is the process through which an information system identifies the user and determines they are the actual ("authentic") person they claim to be.

There are three factors that can be used to make this identification ("factors of authentication").

- Something you *know* (like a password)
- Something you *have* (like a smartphone), and
- Something you *are* (like your fingerprint or facial features).

Many data breaches occur because the user relied upon a password alone, a single factor of authentication, to secure their online account. Using a second factor of authentication (2FA, MFA) such as by proving you have your smartphone, can greatly increase security.

Recap: The three factors of authentication are something you:

- Know
- Have
- Are.

---

[198] For example, another way to categorize them is preventative, proactive, detective, and corrective/responsive, but these categories are less intuitive and are independent of the PAT type categories.

17.8. Authorization and the principle of least privilege

Once the information system has authenticated a user, it can grant the user access to data and rights to do certain things with the system.

Authorization is configured by the system administrator and should be done according to the "principle of least privilege." This means that users should get the abilities they need to do their work, but no more than that.

By giving users what they need to do their job, but not more, the risks are reduced if the employee goes rogue or if the employee's credentials are compromised ("hacked").

The principle of least privilege can be applied to computers and applications as well. Give those things what they need, but not more.

17.9. Encryption at rest and in transit

Encryption is the process of encoding data so that is unreadable to anyone except those who are authorized and who have the proper key to decode it. Encryption is part of the area of cryptography.[199]

Encryption can be done for data at rest (stored on a laptop computer, smartphone, or in the cloud) and for data in transit (being sent on a network or through the internet).[200]

There are two primary types of encryption: symmetric encryption and asymmetric encryption. The names give clues regarding what each means.

Symmetric encryption uses the same key to lock and unlock the data, which is great in many circumstances but problematic in others. When sharing data, one needs to share that key, which needs to be done securely.

Asymmetric encryption (asymmetric cryptography) uses different paired keys to lock and unlock the data. This is sometimes called "public key encryption" or "public-private key encryption." One key can be made public, while the other is retained privately and kept secret. Asymmetric encryption is useful for both sending data confidentially, and for proving identity.

---

[199] Cryptography has been essential for governments, militaries, and spies throughout history.

[200] We introduced these concepts in Chapter 16.

17.10 Cybersecurity frameworks (preview)

Cybersecurity frameworks are best practices to help organizations manage all the areas of cybersecurity, with information and checklists so that they do not have to reinvent the wheel.

Cybersecurity is complicated, especially for organizations, and it becomes more complicated with increasing size. Frameworks help manage that complexity.

There are many cybersecurity frameworks out there, many from reputable organizations with smart people working there.

The simplest framework is the Four Pillars of Cybersecurity (introduced earlier with a chapter devoted to it in Part 9).

The most popular freely available framework is the National Institute of Standards and Technology (NIST) Cybersecurity Framework (CSF) which we will cover in Part 9.

17.11 Cybersecurity laws (preview)[201]

Laws, regulations, and legal standards may require that organizations maintain a certain level of cybersecurity.

We can summarize all those legal requirements with ultimate simplicity:

Have reasonable cybersecurity.

Of course, we will dive deeper than that in this book.

Traditional laws can be applied to cybersecurity, such as negligence and contract. Organizations that are negligent in their cybersecurity, or that violate contractual agreements relating to cybersecurity, could be liable for monetary damages.

There are also specific laws that may require cybersecurity. These laws may come from the federal government or from various states. Each law may apply generally (to any type of organization) or only to a specific sector (such as health or finance).

Typically, these rules focus on protecting consumer data. Each law is slightly different, and usually leave room for discretion, interpretation and adaptation.

---

[201] Cybersecurity laws are covered in Part 6.

17.12 References

- *Chapter 17 resources*, https://johnbandler.com/cyberlawbook-resources-ch17
- *Cybersecurity*, https://johnbandler.com/cybersecurity
- *Information security*, https://johnbandler.com/information-security
- *Introduction to cybersecurity and information security*, https://johnbandler.com/introduction-cybersecurity-information-security
- *Four Pillars of Cybersecurity*, https://johnbandler.com/bandlers-four-pillars-of-cybersecurity
- *Cybersecurity things to know*, https://johnbandler.com/things-to-know-cybersecurity
- *Risk*, https://johnbandler.com/risk
- Udemy course, *Cybersecurity for the Home and Organization*, https://johnbandler.com/udemy-courses
- *Cybersecurity for the Home and Office*, Chapter 4 and throughout (2017 book)
- *Cybercrime Investigations*, Chapter 4 (2020 book)

17.13 Chapter questions

- What is the difference between information security and cybersecurity?
- List the three information security objectives (CIA)
- Briefly summarize the three information security objectives (CIA)
- List the three types of controls (safeguards) to help achieve good cybersecurity (PAT)
- Briefly summarize the three types of controls (safeguards) to help achieve good cybersecurity (PAT)
- What is authentication (in the context of computers)?
- List the three factors of authentication (and give an example of each).
- What is two factor authentication?
- Why should we employ two-factor authentication on email and other important cloud and internet accounts?

18

Assessing and Applying Law
to the Digital Domain

In this chapter:

- Think like a lawyer and consider:
  o What is different, what is the same
  o What issues are related, what issues are separate
  o What current laws apply

18.1 We apply law to the digital realm by analogizing and distinguishing (just like we apply it to other "new" situations)

In life and law, some things are similar, some things are different. Some issues are related and connected to each other; some are separate.

Part of "thinking like a lawyer" is assessing these similarities and distinctions and separating the issues. We want to think like a rational, objective, unbiased, and good lawyer.[202]

As we encounter a circumstance in a digital space, we ask:

- What is the same?
- What is different?
- What laws apply?
- What laws don't apply?

The answers to this are rarely easy or simple so we need to be prepared to justify and explain our answer.

This is what lawyers should do when they advocate, and what judges should do when they decide. The analysis goes like this:

---

[202] As we mention throughout the book, to understand law you want to *think* like a good lawyer, even if you never want to *be* a lawyer.

- To what extent is this the same—or similar—to what we have seen before, such as in traditional law? If it is the same, we might be able to apply prior rules to reach a decision.
- To what extent is this different from what we have seen before, such as in traditional law? If it is different, perhaps the prior rules do not apply, and maybe we need a new rule.

This is the process of analogizing and distinguishing. Put simply:

- Assess what is similar (analogize)
- Assess what is different (distinguish).

First, we build a list of laws that could apply, whether the Constitution, statutes, or case law. We seek to understand those laws, and the facts of the circumstance we are assessing, and be critical thinkers and good investigators (researchers).

We realize that some of the things we hear are not the absolute truth but perhaps:

- Marketing language for a product or service
- Technologists promising perfection
- A lawyer representing one side's view of the facts or law
- Proponents or opponents of a law presenting their view
- The way one side chooses to frame an issue.[203]

We strive to be objective researchers and investigators, assessing facts and law, then use reason and logic to arrive at conclusions and opinions.

18.2 Separate issues when appropriate

We need to separate issues when appropriate, just as we do for other areas of law that we analyze. This means we assess what issues are related, which are separate, and why.

Here's an example relating to criminal law's exclusionary rule, where all too often, some people might say something like:

---

[203] For example, "network neutrality," "net neutrality," "open internet," and "restoring internet freedom" are terms that may mean different things to different people and be designed to persuade based on the term.

Similarly, "right to life," "right to choose," "abortion rights," "anti-abortion," "reproductive rights" and others are terms that may be designed to persuade.

When we encounter broad or vague terms we often need to dig for more specificity.

✗ This criminal justice system is ridiculous, the judge threw out the evidence on a technicality, and now the criminal goes free?! That is so unfair and makes no sense. The case should proceed and we've got to stop these judges from coddling these criminals.

Instead, we want to separate the issues of the Fourth Amendment from the broader issue of holding offenders accountable for what they do. We would do that this way:

The judge found that the police seized the evidence unlawfully, and as a result suppressed (excluded) that evidence from being used at trial under the Fourth Amendment and exclusionary rule. Here's what I think about how the police collected the evidence and the judge's decision and why ....

Separately, I understand that the exclusionary rule is an established part of our criminal justice system, and if the judge finds the evidence was seized unlawfully, it can't be used. But here's how the defendant could still be prosecuted...

The point is there are several issues here, some are not controversial (if one knows the law) and others are more open to reasonable debate.

18.3 We are the rational, objective, and unbiased lawyer

We want to think like a rational, objective, unbiased, and competent lawyer. We remember that many lawyers do not fit this description.

We build the helpful lawyerly skills of gathering facts, analyzing them, researching law, applying the facts and the laws together, and explain it clearly. Those are the purer aspects of law.

We set aside some of the other aspects of lawyering which are less altruistic and less savory. Lawyers engage in activities ranging from persuasion, spin, gamesmanship, to winning at all costs and self-promotion.

We are not a lawyer representing a client in a litigation or lobbying campaign, focusing on winning a case or achieving a goal. In those situations, the lawyer writes or says things that are probably not their actual opinion, but advocacy to serve the client.[204] Nor are we a company selling a product needing to present a rosy view.

In court and when a lawyer represents a client, they have a duty to zealously represent that client within the bounds of the law and ethics. That lawyer interprets the law and facts in a way that benefits their client. They are supposed to be tethered to the law and facts, but it is advocacy with a goal of winning or getting the best possible outcome.

Opposing lawyers often make opposite arguments about the law and facts. They take opposite positions about why a particular prior case should—or should not—be considered precedent in the current case.[205] Put more simply:

- Lawyer A may say this is a similar (analogous) situation as in Case 1, therefore the case *does* apply, and the judge should rule in Client A's favor.
- Lawyer B may say this is different (distinguishable) from what happened in Case 1; therefore it does *not* apply, and the Judge should rule in Client B's favor.

Each lawyer may be acting entirely appropriately and within the bounds of law and ethics despite arguing opposite points. A lawyer's statements in court and on television usually have a goal to persuade towards a goal.

With this book and your learning, we can be the lawyer giving strategic advice to an organization or individual, before a litigation has occurred, advising them on the risks and potential issues in the future. Or we can be the lawyer simply teaching or learning law.

As learners we have no stake in the outcome, no client paying us, and no products or services to sell, and we are free to have a reasonable and honest discussion. We can approach law objectively and impartially even as we bring existing opinions and experiences on life and law.

We assess reasonably:

- What the law is (and why we think that)
- What the law should be (and why)

---

[204] No lawyer speaking to the media about their client's pending case has ever said "Our case is terrible, and we are going to lose."
[205] Legal precedent ("*stare decisis*" or "it stands decided") is the principle that prior cases decided on a similar matter with similar facts and law has legal authority in the current case.

- What the facts are in a particular case, and what evidence proved it.

18.4 Do not assume that no existing laws apply

Avoid casting a superficial glance at a situation with new technology and then quickly assuming existing law cannot apply.

Try avoid thinking like this:

> ✘ *The law needs to catch up. This technology is new, there are no "new laws," so law currently applies.*

As examples, the below statements would be proven wrong:

> ✘ *Those old-time speeding laws could not possibly apply to my new electric car. I can go as fast as I want.*

> ✘ *Those old money laundering, money transmitting, and anti-money laundering laws could not possibly apply to this new virtual currency (or cryptocurrency). There are no rules here so I can do what I want.*

> ✘ *Those defamation laws are so old, they couldn't possibly apply to what I say on the internet.*

> ✘ *Blockchain, cryptocurrency, artificial intelligence and [insert other tech term] are so new the law hasn't caught up yet. No law applies to it, so it is a free-for-all and I can do whatever I want.*

> ✘ *The Fourth Amendment is so old, it couldn't apply to phone calls.*

> ✘ *The Fourth Amendment is so old, there is no way it applies to smartphones and cloud accounts.*

Imagine you are a lawyer in a case involving one of these new technologies and you are seeking to enforce a legal right. You will search for a law that might apply to support your case and argue that it should.

As we assume the role of an objective lawyer, we examine what each side might rely upon, and why.

18.5 What traditional laws might apply? The likely suspects

With a new technology, consider what laws might apply. Start with the most obvious, and work from there.

If we are assessing something related to speech and expression online, we need to start with the First Amendment.

If we are assessing something related to a governmental search, we start with the Fourth Amendment.

If we are assessing a cybercrime criminal prosecution (Part 4), we start with the Constitution, and then look at the written criminal statutes and their definitions. We take special note that a criminal defendant gets the benefit of the doubt if statutory words seem unclear.

If we are assessing a contractual dispute between two parties that involve cyberspace, a cybercrime event, or privacy, we look to the contract between them, and the body of contract law.

If we are assessing whether a party is negligent for allowing the commission of a cybercrime by an unknown actor, we look to negligence law. And we will draw analogies with previous brick-and-mortar situations.

Our foundation in traditional law will serve us well to interpret cyberlaw.

18.6 New laws that have been created to address cyberspace

Sometimes traditional laws cannot be applied adequately to situations we now face in the digital realm. In these cases, it is fair to say that the law needed to "catch up," or at least that the law makers thought so. Because of gaps, newer laws were created to address the newer issues. Rest assured, whatever the new laws are, some people will be happy with them, but many will not be.

New criminal laws were created to prohibit certain cybercrime acts such as data breaches, malware, and other malicious acts.

New civil data laws were created to impose requirements for data breach notification, cybersecurity, and privacy.

There will be gaps in the future and room for new legislation and new judicial decisions.

18.7 Virtual currency and cryptocurrency (preview)

When virtual currency arrived and continuing when cryptocurrency came, there were many people, including the owners and founders of certain platforms, who claimed that existing laws did not apply. Many claimed the "laws needed to catch up."

History shows the laws were indeed in place. Perhaps it was just the government was a little slower to enforce those laws for new circumstances, or that individual criminal and civil enforcement cases take time to mature.

Some past virtual currency platforms had claimed those existing laws did not apply, the prosecutors claimed they did, and generally the courts sided with the prosecutors. Those "old" money laundering and money transmitting laws were relevant to this newer method of transferring value. More in Part 4.

18.8 The Fourth Amendment in digital space[206]

Cyber related issues arise frequently in areas of criminal law.[207]

Before computers and the internet, judges were applying the Fourth Amendment's rules on law enforcement search and seizure to all sorts of circumstances, including:

- Searches of residences and offices
- Searching or "patting down" a suspect for weapons
- Searching a suspect after an arrest.

The Fourth Amendment did not foresee technology advancements such as the telephone and certainly not computers and the internet. Nevertheless, judges were soon enough applying the Fourth Amendment to new areas such as:

- Listening to phone calls
- Searching personal computer devices (smartphone)
- Searching computers from a residence or office
- Searching cloud accounts (Google, Microsoft, Apple)
- Obtaining other records from companies providing various internet service
- Searching cloud accounts (Microsoft, Google, etc.) where the data is in a data center in another country.

---

[206] Chapter 11 introduced the Fourth Amendment and Part 4 applies it to cybercrime in more depth.
[207] Criminal law forces many new issues to the forefront, as the stakes are high, and prosecutors seek evidence and to hold offenders accountable while defense attorneys challenge what prosecutors do in order to protect their client.

The takeaway is clear. Cybercrime investigation requires a solid understanding of "good old traditional law," including the Fourth Amendment.

18.9 References and resources

- Chapter 18 resources, https://johnbandler.com/ cyberlawbook-resources-ch18
- Read on as we cover how law is applied to cyber situations throughout this book.

18.10 Chapter questions

- True or False: We should look to see what "traditional laws" apply in cyberspace.
- True or False: Repeating "the law needs to catch up," is not a substitute for assessing the facts and what current laws might apply.
- Summarize the processes of analogizing and distinguishing.
- Assess two situations and summarize how they are "the same" and how they are "different." Then summarize which position is most accurate (should control, e.g., whether the two situations are more "the same" or more "different") and why.
- The process of analogizing and distinguishing is apparent in the sentencing of a convicted defendant. You are a judge sentencing a defendant who has been convicted of shoplifting. The law provides for a sentence anywhere between nothing (conditional discharge) and one year in jail, with everything in between (fines, probation, community service, less jail, etc.). The prosecutor is duty bound to recommend a sentence they think is fair and just. The defense attorney recommends what would be best for their client (the minimum, a conditional discharge). What facts and circumstances would be relevant to determine what sentence is appropriate? What might each side argue? How is it the same or different from other shoplifting cases and other defendants? What factors would you use to decide if you were the judge?

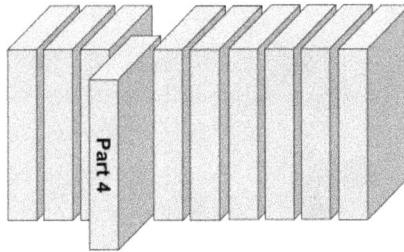

Part 4

"Criminal Cyberlaw:" Cybercrime and Cybercrime Investigations

Much of cyberlaw is related to cybercrime, so let's start there.

In this part:

- The Western Express case
- Substantive criminal laws (the laws that get charged)
- Criminal procedure (the process)
- Search and seizure
- Virtual currency
- Money laundering
- Solving cybercrime

John T. Bandler

19

The Western Express Cybercrime Case

┌───┐
In this chapter:
- A groundbreaking case
- My introduction to cybercrime and financial crime
└───┘

19.1 The case in a nutshell

Western Express International, Inc. (Western Express) was a virtual currency exchanger located in Manhattan, and one of the earliest major U.S. based exchangers.[208] They helped customers exchange funds between various government currencies and the virtual currencies of the time. In doing so, they facilitated payments between U.S. based identity thieves and cybercriminals located in former Soviet countries.

I started investigating this exchanger and their customers in 2005 while I was a relatively junior prosecutor at DANY.[209] The case continued until the trial of the last three defendants took place in 2013.

For eight years we investigated this company and its customers who were located around the country and world, learning a lot about these types of crimes and how they are committed. I also learned about the process of investigating, litigating, and conducting a trial of a complex cybercrime and money laundering case.

---

[208] Obviously, this company had no relation nor connection to other companies which may have similar words within their own names. I avoid using individual defendant names here since we can hear the story of the case without naming them, and since enough time has passed that they should be able to put these events behind them.

[209] I had just over two years of prosecutorial experience at the time. DANY stands for District Attorney of New York, also known as the Manhattan DA's Office. My formal title was Assistant District Attorney (ADA). *See* DANY's website at https://manhattanda.org.

19.2 The start of the investigation

The investigation started in 2005, when I had just joined the newly created Identity Theft Unit. This was not a plum assignment, but an added duty, on top of a grueling caseload and court assignments.

I still had so much to learn about law, investigation, and prosecution, even if I had experience from eight years as a state trooper.[210]

As a prosecutor, the power of a subpoena and search warrant to obtain records and evidence was significant. Clues and data resided in the records of various companies, and these legal tools could be used to obtain them.

The legendary District Attorney Robert Morgenthau had built DANY into a respected prosecution powerhouse. He was first elected in 1975 and would ultimately retire from the role in 2009. He realized the scourge of identity theft and the need to properly investigate and prosecute it, so he authorized the creation of a new Identity Theft Unit.

This new unit operated on a shoestring budget but had excellent leadership who mentored the junior prosecutors who made up the bulk of the unit.[211] The leaders gained the cooperation of other law enforcement and financial institutions. The unit's investigations, including Western Express and many others, were wide ranging and hard to match.

Other than the supervisors, this new unit had no full-time staff, just mostly newer ADAs with an additional duty on top of all the other assignments and cases. Eventually, the unit would hire some investigative analysts (similar to paralegals) to assist with the cases, and their help was indispensable.

These identity theft cases were laborious because they involved financial records, multiple witnesses, and often search warrants and surveillance to prove the crime and connect it to the defendants.[212]

The scale of the theft was amazing. If you detected a single offense committed by an identity thief or cybercriminal, a deeper look would

---

[210] As a trooper my investigative tools were quite basic and time was scarce because whenever the radio called, I had to answer and respond.

[211] Like me, many were essentially drafted into the unit, but it worked out great. Those early unit leaders obtained training for us in digital forensics and more, and we all built some great cases.

[212] In contrast, many street crime cases can be relatively simple with much fewer witnesses and exhibits. *See* Chapter 14.

reveal dozens, hundreds, or thousands of other criminal acts. Since this was their business, scratching the surface of one identified crime revealed an iceberg of criminal conduct just waiting to be found.

While I was in this unit, the Western Express case started with a report of a single instance of identity theft. A fraudster used a victim's credit card to make a purchase online.

A little digging and a few subpoenas made it clear that this was not an isolated fraud. The cybercriminals had committed tens of thousands of dollars of credit card fraud with dozens of victims across several ecommerce sites. Online orders were being placed with stolen credit card numbers, but the internet protocol (IP) addresses[213] were not consistent. Investigating the IP addresses was a learning experience but a wild goose chase. Still, the merchandise was shipped to a common address, and that ultimately revealed clues for the next steps.

By now this was a significant case for a junior prosecutor, even if still tiny compared to other financial cases the office handled. Soon enough, with more research and investigation, we would see a sprawling global cybercrime economy, and a new typology with virtual currency. It was in its infancy at the time but already facilitating a hidden world of international cybercrime.

Eventually we uncovered evidence spanning back to 2001, the dawn of the cybercrime economy, and up until 2017 and 2018, when the last of our targets were apprehended.

19.3 Learning about early virtual currencies

Early on, it turned out one of the participants was using Egold, the earliest viable virtual currency. I had never heard of it, so my research began.

One person paid another, they paid someone else, and I followed the Egold trail. Eventually it led to Western Express.

Virtual currencies were born in 1996 with Egold, and then WebMoney came in 1998. Cybercriminals were early adopters of this internet

---

[213] As laid out in Chapter 16, an IP address is like a return address on the internet, necessary for communicating, but also something which can be disguised. Criminals (and others legitimately concerned about their privacy) do not want their true IP address to be known or tracked.

payment mechanism and today we are all familiar with Bitcoin and hundreds of other cryptocurrencies.

In the Western Express case, cybercriminals and identity thieves paid each other with Egold and WebMoney. Following these funds and identifying the purpose of the payments became key. By gleaning voluminous records relating to Western Express International, Inc. and other sources we were able to identify, charge, and extradite some of these customers.

19.4 The first indictment

The first indictment[214] was in 2006, charging the company (Western Express International, Inc.) and their leaders (high managerial agents)[215] with illegal check cashing, illegal money transmitting, and submitting false paperwork to their banks to hide the true purpose of their bank accounts.

This was my introduction to financial regulation. I learned about the state and federal laws designed to license companies in the finance sector, protect consumers, prevent money laundering, and keep our financial system reliable and secure.

New York state laws required anyone in the business of cashing checks or transmitting funds to obtain licenses for those activities, and once a license is obtained, to engage in certain practices and record keeping. Western Express had neither a check cashing nor money transmitting license, so it was appropriate to charge them with the criminal offenses of operating this type of business without the license. They were also

---

[214] An indictment is a formal charge, issued by a Grand Jury, made up of citizens called to this type of jury duty. The Grand Jury hears evidence and if it believes there is probable cause a defendant committed a felony, they can vote to indict.

[215] New York's Penal Law (N.Y.P.L. or P.L.) has provisions to hold organizations accountable for conduct by their leaders and employees, and vice versa. N.Y.P.L. §20.20 defines "agent" and "high managerial agent" and lays out that a corporation can be guilty of an offense if the conduct is done or authorized by people in positions of high responsibility. *See* N.Y.P.L. §20.20, available at https://www.nysenate.gov/legislation/laws/PEN/20.20.

Then N.Y.P.L. §20.25 provides that an individual can be criminally liable for conduct they cause an organization to do. *See* N.Y.P.L. §20.25, available at https://www.nysenate.gov/legislation/laws/PEN/20.25.

John T. Bandler

charged with submitting false paperwork to their bank based upon their misrepresentations about the true purpose of the account.

Search warrants were obtained for Western Express offices and related residences, executed on a single day by dozens of DANY investigators and U.S. Secret Service (USSS or Secret Service) agents and other law enforcement.[216] A mountain of computers and documents were recovered.

These initial defendants eventually pleaded guilty, but our investigation continued. There were hundreds of customers sending considerable funds through Western Express, and we wanted to learn why.

19.5 The second indictment

A review of the computers and documents seized from Western Express, plus volumes of other records and evidence revealed the true purpose of the payments. Many of the exchanger's customers were cybercriminals and identity thieves using the exchanger to pay each other, launder illegal profits, and convert funds between virtual currency and traditional (fiat) currency.

Our partnership with the Secret Service helped us to learn about these offenders and the online platforms they used to communicate and do business.

With considerable work, we identified some of those cybercriminals and identity thieves, exposed their money laundering activity, and obtained enough evidence that we believed we could charge them by indictment (probable cause standard) and sufficiently prove it at trial (beyond a reasonable doubt standard).[217]

This second indictment focused upon cybercrime theft (larceny), money laundering, an organized crime charge (New York's version of the federal RICO statute) and other offenses.

---

[216] The Secret Service is well known for protecting the president and other important protection related duties, but they also have an investigative mission for financial crimes and electronic crimes. Thus, they are called a "dual mission" agency. Learn more about them at https://www.secretservice.gov.

   Other law enforcement agencies assisted on these search warrants, including the NYSP and many other law enforcement agencies.

[217] No prosecutor can predict the end of their litigation. The main point here is that a prosecutor needs to look to trial before they decide to charge someone.

19.6 The first arrests and interstate extraditions

In various stages, defendants were arrested and eventually arraigned in New York County on the indictment's charges. If they were arrested outside of New York State, they needed to be properly extradited into the state.

U.S. arrest locations included New York (Manhattan, Brooklyn, Queens), New Jersey, Louisiana, California, and Oregon.

The first arrests concerned identity thieves who operated within the U.S. Though there was publicity about that, we kept details about the international cybercriminals sealed (secret) to better our chances of catching them.

As a defendant is arraigned, they either hire defense counsel or one is appointed for them. Next, a motion schedule is set, and the defense counsel often moves to dismiss the indictment and to suppress evidence.

19.7 The organized crime count and other pre-trial litigation

There was a lot of litigation around the top count of the indictment (as charged by the Grand Jury) and this process lasted years. This count was called "Enterprise Corruption," under New York P.L. §460.20, part of the state's Organized Crime Control Act (OCCA) of 1986.

This was New York's version of the federal Racketeer Influenced and Corrupt Organizations statute (RICO). The premise of RICO and Enterprise Corruption is that organized crime leaders typically insulate themselves from the actual criminal acts, but the statute can hold everyone accountable who participates in the enterprise. It requires proof that there was a *structure* to the criminal enterprise, a *purpose*, and that certain felony crimes ("*predicate acts*") were committed to further that criminal enterprise.

The original focus of these laws was "traditional" organization crime, like the mafia (La Cosa Nostra) and how they corrupted legitimate businesses to achieve their illegal aims, and how foot soldiers committed the physical acts of the crimes, while leaders kept themselves at a distance.

The New York statute had never been updated to include newer crimes such as identity theft as predicate acts. It also prohibited joining (charging together) Enterprise Corruption and non-predicate acts. This procedural requirement meant that we could not charge identity theft as a crime along with Enterprise Corruption.

The defense moved to dismiss all the counts (including the Enterprise Corruption) count on the grounds that we did not sufficiently prove it within the Grand Jury.

We disagreed, and argued this was a longstanding cybercrime network of participants, with long running business ties working together in a corrupt criminal enterprise.

The trial court sided with the defense attorneys, and the Enterprise Corruption count was dismissed (the other counts remained).

We (the People) appealed, and the First Appellate Department reversed the dismissal of that count, reinstating it.

The defense appealed to the New York Court of Appeals (New York's highest court)[218] and they agreed with the defense. The Court of Appeals decided that the Enterprise Corruption statute could not be applied to the facts of Western Express, finding that the capitalistic organization across great distances was not the type of criminal enterprise structure that the statute envisioned.

Our Enterprise Corruption count remained dismissed, and the case had to proceed without it. This process illustrated how judges may disagree with prosecutors (and the Grand Jury) and dismiss certain counts.

It was disappointing to lose this count, especially after so much litigation. On the bright side, the rest of the case survived the other challenges, and we still had almost 300 counts, including conspiracy, grand larceny, money laundering, scheme to defraud, and more.

Defendants also moved to suppress evidence, and we replied. Because most of the evidence was seized by search warrants, which are presumptively valid, the defense had a heavy burden which they did not meet. The only pretrial hearing for an evidentiary issue concerned pedigree information provided by defendants upon their arrest, such as their name, address, phone number, and other information.[219]

---

[218] Most states call their highest appellate court their "Supreme Court," but New York does it differently. Our highest appellate court is called our "Court of Appeals," and our "Supreme Court" is the most powerful trial level court which could hear any type of case at the trial level (if it wanted to).

[219] In New York, after an arrest warrant is issued, law enforcement cannot question a defendant without their attorney present and with consent, meaning we could not question them about the crimes. But it was appropriate to ask for their basic pedigree information, which was part of the booking process and also relevant evidence to prove identity.

19.8 International extraditions and search warrants

While the litigation was proceeding, we were working to apprehend defendants who resided overseas. This was an extreme challenge, but we were eventually successful with three of the international defendants.

One was a resident of a former Soviet country who went on vacation in Greece, where we were able to have him arrested and ultimately extradited to the U.S. There was a flurry of activity when we learned he was in Greece. He was apprehended and then search warrants were executed in his home country. It would take two years to getting him to the U.S.

Two other citizens of former Soviet countries were living in the Czech Republic where they were arrested and ultimately extradited. This took about a year of planning until arrests and search warrants were executed, and then another year to get them extradited.

All of this involved paperwork, writing, time, effort, and assistance from the U.S. DOJ Office of International Affairs and their experienced federal attorneys, the U.S. Secret Service, sometimes the FBI, the U.S. Marshall's service for the final plane ride to New York, and our District Attorney's Investigators for the airport transfer and rest of the process.

19.9 A purgatory

There was a long period of uncomfortable uncertainty while the appeals were pending. We had a case with a top count that had been dismissed by the trial court, but we hoped the appeals process would reinstate it.

Some defendants were convinced they could prevail at trial, with such a complicated case, and a significant favorable decision.

This was no simple street crime case that could be prepared for trial quickly. It was massive, with computer evidence to be analyzed, dozens of boxes of documents to be reviewed, exhibits to be prepared, translations to be obtained.

I knew it would require many months, and thousands of hours of team labor. The DA's office was incredibly busy and there are limited resources available for any case, much less to devote to a case that might never get to trial. Remember that most criminal cases never go to trial, and many plead only when trial becomes certain. Every day there are other urgent issues requiring people to work on it, including for the Secret Service, whose work was needed to prepare, including with the massive amount of digital evidence that needed examination.

There had been many changes in the DA's office, with a new DA and new supervisors in the Identity Theft Unit, which by now had been renamed the Cybercrime and Identity Theft Bureau.[220]

This was a tough time, especially with all the other duties as an ADA, but fortunately there was a core crew to help. As a trial date seemed certain, the work was crushing and daunting, but it came together.

There were tasks I dreaded, hoping a more junior prosecutor would be brought on to complete them. Ultimately it was fortunate I did them myself, because I learned the case in even more detail.

19.10 The trial

Most of the defendants pleaded guilty, but three proceeded to trial.

The entire investigation was put to the test, and it was our job to prove every count beyond a reasonable doubt, and to the unanimous satisfaction of all twelve jurors.

This trial lasted about four months and included about fifty witnesses and considerable evidence of many types, from physical search warrant items, to records from dozens of places, digital evidence and more. It was so massive that we had to transport it in carts including a large "U-boat" platform cart as depicted.[221]

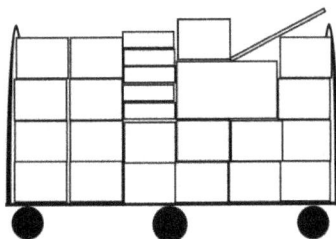

We presented our case and rested. Some of the defendants presented witnesses with outlandish tales, and I was able to cross examine them.

---

[220] In 2024 the unit was again renamed to the Cyber Crime Bureau, under a third DA. Regardless of the name, hopefully they will remember the strong connections between cybercrime and identity theft. We can debate the minutiae also: should it be "cybercrime" or "cyber crime;" one word or two?
Press releases announcing such changes often characterize it as creating a *new* unit or bureau, an innovative development. It is a matter of degree and interpretation as to how new this is or whether it is renaming or reorganizing.
[221] One of the fantastic investigative analysts would use it to transport what we needed for the day. For closing arguments, it was almost everything, requiring more carts and people. Often, he wrapped it up with plastic to transport it, so nothing fell out as he travelled from the DA's office to the courthouse across the street.

Our trial team did a fantastic job preparing and trying the case, also preserving my sanity.[222]

Closing arguments are when the attorneys summarize the evidence and explain why the jury should vote a certain way. The general rule is to be brief, but this was a complex case involving a lot of records and one hundred counts for each defendant. I needed to walk the jury through the case and evidence. If I could spend time now, it might speed their deliberation and avoid any confusion or misunderstanding. I was never one to "wing it" in court and my closing argument was typed out and exceeded a hundred pages.

During my preparation for the closing argument, I saw new clues and connections, contained within existing evidence and I was able to point these out to the jury. A criminal investigation is truly never complete until the jury receives the case.[223]

With closing arguments complete, it went to the jury for them to decide if we had proven our case.

19.11 The verdict

Waiting for the verdict is stressful. Every good prosecutor and supervisor want justice to prevail. They should not be bringing the case if they don't think it is in the interests of justice; to hold someone accountable who deserves to be held accountable.

---

[222] Protecting my peace of mind was no small feat as this was the culmination of a many years-long investigation and litigation that was highly stressful in many ways. The team took care of logistics excellently (on top of their other important work) which would have otherwise caused my brain to melt.

At trial, the courthouse where the trial took place has the worst elevator system in the developed world. There are about ten elevators each closet-sized, yet about half are out of service and the other half operate without any coordination, as if striving for the least efficient method of navigating among the floors. Every day my co-counsel and paralegal would wait for and navigate the elevators with our trial cart and witnesses. I bypassed that annoyance and took the stairs up, burning off some steam, getting my daily exercise, and then reviewing my notes until they arrived in the courtroom.

[223] Some may think the investigation is over at arrest or at some later stage. More accurately, the process of finding clues and facts and analyzing them for connections continues until the litigation is over. I discovered a new connection among various burner phone numbers already in evidence that added yet another strand of proof connecting a defendant to the cybercrimes.

Prosecutors don't always win, and the outcome was far from certain. Every member of the jury needed to be convinced beyond a reasonable doubt, based on the evidence presented. They are twelve people randomly selected from the population that you have never met. When do twelve random people ever agree on anything in regular life? Defense counsel can be skillful. Judges rule and those rulings are not always in the prosecutor's favor.[224]

I still remember those DANY career supervisors who came to visit me while the jury was deliberating, before anyone knew the outcome. They said words to the effect of:

> *"Whatever happens, you did your best, put years into this, and left it all on the playing field. Good job and be proud."*

Implicit in this is that they knew that you could do your best, be in the right, and still lose the case. And they were willing to deliver their well-wishes before the result was known—win or lose.

The verdict came.

Guilty as to every defendant, every count.

The clerk would ask:

> *"As to defendant A, Count X, how do you find, guilty or not guilty."*

And the response would be:

> *"Guilty."*

This continued for each of the three defendants, one hundred counts each, three hundred total, and each time the jury foreperson said:

> *"Guilty."*

Eight years of exhausting and stressful work had survived the final test and come to a successful end. Except for sentencing.

The judge set a sentencing date and court was adjourned.

The trial team packed up and we left the courtroom, including with the U-Boat large cart of trial evidence which needed to go out the back entrance of the courtroom and through the service elevators.

---

[224] In this case, the judge was excellent, highly respected and gave both sides a fair trial. Even if we had lost, I could not have had any complaint about him and how he oversaw the trial and litigation.

Outside the courtroom we looked at each other and reality started to set in. Justice had prevailed, and the long stressful slog was over.

19.12 Sentencing

The case proceeded to sentencing.

The defendants were convicted of many defined counts, and the law provides for a certain range of sentences for each count, including the possibility that some could run consecutively (one after the other) or concurrently (at the same time).

For each defendant we recommended the sentence we thought was fair and indicated why.

Because of the complexity of this case, my submissions were usually written, followed by oral argument in court.[225] The defense recommended what they thought was fair, and ultimately the judge sentenced the defendants.

That was pretty much the end of the Western Express case.

It had lasted eight years, from start until sentencing.

At the start, there were many things I did not know, investigation techniques I had never done.

By the end, a lot had been done, including obtaining evidence and arresting defendants from around the United States and even from beyond.

---

[225] Most state court cases rely more on verbal statements made in court, less on written submissions. But court proceedings can move rapidly and get heated, then to see what was said one needs to get the court transcript. It is hard for a judge to digest complex facts and arguments in open court, so I found it was cleaner to submit something in writing, so the court had time to read it and digest it, and there was a permanent record of my position.

John T. Bandler

19.13 Thinking like a prosecutor[226]

Throughout, I needed to evaluate many options and make many decisions, including what evidence to try obtaining, how to get it, what charges to ask the Grand Jury to vote on, and then how to present the evidence at trial.

The actions and decisions involved many areas, some of which I had never dealt with before, including:

- Obtaining evidence from within the U.S. and even other countries
- Deciding what crimes to charge
- Extraditing defendants from other states (and even other countries)
- Litigating complex legal issues in court
- Analyzing massive mountains of evidence
- Organizing evidence for a trial
- Presenting evidence to the judge and jury
- Writing for a variety of audiences throughout the case
- Speaking to the jury to convince them why the evidence proved the case.

Nothing was easy but somehow it got done and justice prevailed.

19.14 Should have been, could have been

There are always should-haves and could-haves.

During the Western Express case, some remarked occasionally that it should have been a federal case, not a state case, especially because local prosecutors rarely bring these types of cases.[227] When an organization such as DANY starts to investigate, can establish proper jurisdiction, and has the right evidence and resources to bring the case, DANY should proceed with their hard built case, even if others think it should be theirs.

---

[226] See Chapter 8 on why it is helpful to think like a good prosecutor, even if you are not one, and never want to be one. It is about following the law and facts to seek justice.

I was not alone in the decision making, above me were supervisors, and many of them played important roles, and with me were analysts, paralegals, investigators, and special agents. Supervisor support plus all who worked on the case helped make it a success story.

[227] Apparently federal prosecutors thought so too, because they brought criminal charges against many of the same defendants after we did.

Within DANY, some may have thought that the case should be within the Investigation Division (which typically brings long term, international, and financial cases) rather than the Trial Division (which typically brings simpler street crime cases). I happened to be in the Trial Division and stayed there, so that is where the case stayed.

The real "could have" is all the identity thieves and cybercriminals that I was never able to focus upon, and who may still be doing their work today, or comfortably retired in luxury. I had learned about them, planned to pursue them and identify them, but then became bogged down in the Western Express litigation and other pressing responsibilities of being a Trial Division ADA.

By the time the Western Express case was over, the trail had run cold on the other suspects. Also, DANY had gone through many changes, and it was soon time for me to explore the next stage of my career.

19.15 References and additional reading

- *Chapter 19 resources*, https://johnbandler.com/cyberlawbook-resources-ch19
- *Western Express Case*, https://johnbandler.com/western-express-case
- *Cybercrime Investigations* (2020 book with Western Express vignettes throughout)

19.16 Chapter questions

- List the virtual currencies that cybercriminals and identity thieves were using in the Western Express case.
- What substantive criminal law issues were presented in the Western Express litigation?
- What procedural criminal law issues were addressed during the Western Express litigation?
- Is it surprising that the Western Express case was prosecuted by a local prosecutor's office, rather than a federal prosecutor? Explain.
- Is it surprising that the Western Express case started with a single instance of identity theft? Explain.

20

Substantive Criminal Laws for Cybercrime

In this chapter:

- What crimes might get charged against cybercriminals?
- Federal vs. state crimes
- Traditional crimes
- Cyber specific crimes

20.1 Substantive criminal laws in context (recap)[228]

This chapter is about substantive criminal laws for cybercrime.

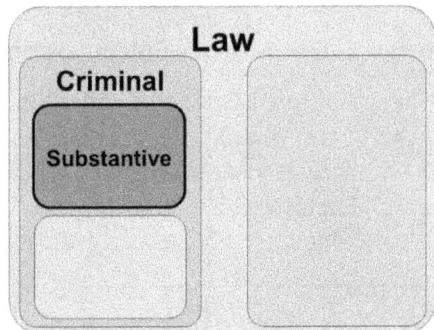

These are the laws passed by our government to prohibit certain conduct which is serious enough that a person could be arrested and convicted if they do it and are caught.[229]

Before we dive in, consider how you might categorize substantive cybercrime laws:

- Federal vs state
- "Traditional" vs "cyber."

---

[228] Chapter 8 introduced criminal law, including substantive criminal law.
[229] Remember that two important categories of criminal law are substantive criminal law and procedural criminal law. This chapter is about substantive criminal law, the next chapter is about procedural criminal law, which is the *process* of resolving a criminal investigation and litigation.

Also remember the criminal law vs. civil law distinction. Criminal law is for the more serious wrongs, where cases are brought by the government in the name of society at large, and civil cases are for more individualized harms.

We look at both federal and state laws, and there are many different prosecutor's offices which may choose to investigate and prosecute a cybercrime.

A particular prosecutor's office should look comprehensively at all the possible charges that could be brought regarding a cybercrime, both traditional and cyber laws.

20.2 Think like a prosecutor (recap)

Think like a good prosecutor as you read this chapter, even if you never want to be one.[230]

This means to think and analyze as if you would be the person deciding what crimes to charge. You would be working for a prosecutor's office responsible for investigating and bringing charges.[231] You can only work for one prosecutor's office at a time.[232]

20.3 Substantive criminal law (recap)[233]

To recap, the basics of substantive criminal law include these principles:

- A crime is specified and written down in a criminal statute.
- This criminal statute is the "substantive criminal law" that defines what conduct is prohibited.
- Each statutory crime lays out various elements of the crime, which must be properly alleged and proven.

---

[230] A good prosecutor is a good lawyer who follows the facts and law to seek justice. Cybercrime cases are built by many people, not just prosecutors. Still, it is a helpful for anyone involved in a cybercrime case to think like a prosecutor, whether they are an analyst, examiner, or sworn law enforcement. It helps the individual focus on what can be proven and what needs to be proven. It means assessing the law, facts, and how charging decisions will be reviewed by a grand jury, trial court judge, a trial jury, and appellate judges.

[231] Each jurisdiction has a different set of substantive criminal laws which could be charged and different procedural rules. The prosecutor needs to be familiar with those laws and the facts and evidence in the case to decide what can be charged. A federal prosecutor can only charge federal crimes, and a state prosecutor can only charge crimes under the law of their state.

[232] For example, you cannot be both a state and federal prosecutor, deciding to bring both state and federal charges. You need to be a prosecutor in a single office, choosing from a single body of criminal substantive laws. You choose either from the federal statutes in the U.S. Code (U.S.C.) or from New York's Penal Law (P.L.) or from your state's statutes.

[233] We introduced criminal law (substantive and procedural) in Chapter 8.

- Elements of a crime will typically include:
  - *Mens rea*, a guilty mind, or culpable mental state
  - *Actus reus*, a guilty act
  - Other elements that define the crime and conduct.

Remember that "cybercrime" is just the merging of two words: "cyber" plus "crime." It is conduct that uses cyber and constitutes a crime. An act, or conduct, is not a cybercrime unless there is a substantive criminal law stating it is a crime.

20.4 Federal vs state criminal prosecutions (recap)[234]

If you are reading about or analyzing criminal charges that have been brought, consider which government is investigating and bringing the charges, and in what court.

In sum, ask:

- *Who* investigates and prosecutes?
  - Federal or state?
- *What* laws is the defendant charged with having broken?
  - Federal or state? What statute sections?
- *Where* are they bringing the case ?
  - What court?

As you assess these factors you will see that answering one of these questions helps answer some of the others, and you can assess who the prosecutor is, who the investigating agencies are, and so forth.

20.5 Evaluating potential charges? Examine the whole body of criminal substantive law

Imagine you are the prosecutor, and you have the ultimate responsibility for making decisions on what crimes to investigate and ultimately charge.

First assess which body of criminal substantive laws you would draw from (either federal or from a particular state).

During the investigation you would be required to specify those crimes while drafting subpoenas, search warrants, or other legal processes. If the investigation proceeds to criminal charges, then a criminal complaint or indictment needs to specify each crime charged.

---

[234] Also covered in Chapter 8.

If the case proceeds to trial, the burden is on the prosecutor to prove the charges beyond a reasonable doubt at trial. You need to choose wisely.

Here are some pointers:

- Review "traditional" laws
  - o Cybercrime is almost always about theft.
  - o Capable cybercriminals need to launder their profits.
- Consider "cyber" laws
- Evaluate the facts and evidence
- Determine what conduct was committed on what date, and by who
- Decide what fits best and why.

Just because some of the conduct occurred in "cyberspace" doesn't mean we are limited to "cyber" specific statutes. Consider all the legal tools in your toolkit.

Avoid thinking that law is absolute, fully known, and judges will rule in a certain way. The law is made up of people and they can be unpredictable, and you may only get one chance to pick the charges.[235]

20.6 Federal cybercrime laws

Federal authorities have a wide array of substantive crimes they can charge. Grouped broadly they are:

- "Traditional" crimes that can be applied to cybercrime
- Computer Fraud and Abuse Act (CFAA)
- Illegal access to live communications and data
- Illegal access to stored communications and data
- Organized crime.

Some of these statutes can be dense but spend an appropriate amount of time familiarizing yourself with them.[236]

---

[235] Prosecutors will debate what crimes to charge, and it sometimes feels like you could ask 10 prosecutors for an opinion and get 11 different responses. Some may think some charges are shaky, others are safe, but ultimately judges decide, and that is hard to predict. A prosecutor's certainty one day is often belied by a judge's decision months or years later. This is not unique to the criminal justice system, but a feature of law and people.

[236] We moved many of the statute quotations to the footnotes to make the main text easier to read. Adjust your statute reading time to your level of learning.

20.6.1 *"Traditional" (non "cyber") federal statutes*

As a general matter, look to crimes of theft, but realize that the federal government does not have general jurisdiction over all theft; they need a jurisdictional basis ("hook").

Wire fraud is a popular federal charge, which criminalizes a scheme (similar to a conspiracy) that involves anything transmitted in a variety of ways, which helps with interstate jurisdiction and obtaining federal jurisdiction.[237]

Conspiracy is a popular federal charge and a powerful tool. It criminalizes the creation of an *agreement* to commit a crime by two or more people, coupled with an overt act.[238] It allows a lot of evidence to be presented at trial to show the full extent of a defendant's conduct.[239]

Identity theft is another important federal charge for cybercrime and related criminal conduct, and criminalizes the manufacture, transfer, possession, and use of a victim's identification information to commit a crime.[240]

---

[237] *See* 18 U.S. Code § 1343, *Fraud by wire, radio, or television*, https://www.law.cornell.edu/uscode/text/18/1343,

> *Whoever, having devised or intending to devise any scheme or artifice to defraud, or for obtaining money or property by means of false or fraudulent pretenses, representations, or promises, transmits or causes to be transmitted by means of wire, radio, or television communication in interstate or foreign commerce, any writings, signs, signals, pictures, or sounds for the purpose of executing such scheme or artifice, shall be fined under this title or imprisoned not more than 20 years, or both.*

[238] *See* 18 U.S. Code § 371, *Conspiracy to commit offense or to defraud United States*, https://www.law.cornell.edu/uscode/text/18/371,

> *If two or more persons conspire either to commit any offense against the United States, or to defraud the United States, or any agency thereof in any manner or for any purpose, and one or more of such persons do any act to effect the object of the conspiracy, each shall be fined under this title or imprisoned not more than five years, or both.*

[239] The law allows prosecutors to prove the crimes that are charged, but generally prohibits them from presenting evidence of uncharged bad acts, on the grounds that might unfairly prejudice the jury. A conspiracy charge allows a broad range of activity to be legally admissible.

[240] *See* 18 U.S.C. § 1028, *Fraud and related activity in connection with identification documents, authentication features, and information*, https://www.law.cornell.edu/uscode/text/18/1028.

There are criminal charges that relate to money transmitting and money laundering.

Money transmitting is simply the business of moving money for customers. It is licensed and regulated to protect consumers and monitor financial transactions for criminal activity. Federal law criminalizes those who do this activity without a license, bootstrapping on a state requirement to hold such a license.[241]

Money laundering is criminalized. The federal statute requires proof of knowledge of criminal activity plus transactions that are performed with the intent to carry on that illegal activity, conceal the activity, or to conceal or disguise the source, ownership, or control of the funds.

Simply put, one prong is that funds are proceeds of specified unlawful activity and the transactions are to disguise where that money came from, is going, or who owns it.

It's not helpful to quote the statute here because it is lengthy and complex, with multiple cross references to other subsections and many definitions. There are eight substantive provisions that could be charged. Take a look at the statute and spend an appropriate amount of time reviewing it.

[241] 18 U.S.C. § 1960, *Prohibition of Unlicensed Money Transmitting Businesses*, https://www.law.cornell.edu/uscode/text/18/1960,

> *(a) Whoever knowingly conducts, controls, manages, supervises, directs, or owns all or part of an unlicensed money transmitting business, shall be fined in accordance with this title or imprisoned not more than 5 years, or both.*
> *(b) As used in this section—*
>> *(1) the term "unlicensed money transmitting business" means a money transmitting business which affects interstate or foreign commerce in any manner or degree and—*
>>> *(A) is operated without an appropriate money transmitting license in a State ...*
>>> *(B) fails to comply with the money transmitting business registration requirements under section 5330 of title 31, United States Code...*
>>> *(C) otherwise involves the transportation or transmission of funds that are known to the defendant to have been derived from a criminal offense or are intended to be used to promote or support unlawful activity;*
>>> *...*

Some money laundering statutes are quoted in this footnote.[242]

20.6.2 Computer Fraud and Abuse Act (CFAA)

The Computer Fraud and Abuse Act (CFAA) is codified within 18 U.S.C. § 1030 and is the primary federal cybercrime statute, used frequently by federal prosecutors.[243]

The text of the statute is long and complex, but worth a reasonable investment of time to familiarize yourself with it.

It contains definitions for important terms such as

- Computer

---

[242] 18 U.S.C. § 1956 *Laundering of Monetary Instruments*, https://www.law.cornell.edu/uscode/text/18/1956,

> *(a)*
> *(1) Whoever, knowing that the property involved in a financial transaction represents the proceeds of some form of unlawful activity, conducts or attempts to conduct such a financial transaction which in fact involves the proceeds of specified unlawful activity—*
>> *(A)*
>> *(i) with the intent to promote the carrying on of specified unlawful activity; or*
>> *(ii) with intent to engage in conduct constituting a violation of section 7201 or 7206 of the Internal Revenue Code of 1986; or*
>> *(B) knowing that the transaction is designed in whole or in part—*
>> *(i) to conceal or disguise the nature, the location, the source, the ownership, or the control of the proceeds of specified unlawful activity; or*
>> *(ii) to avoid a transaction reporting requirement under State or Federal law,*
> *shall be sentenced to a fine of not more than $500,000 or twice the value of the property involved in the transaction, whichever is greater, or imprisonment for not more than twenty years, or both.*

18 U.S.C. § 1957, *Engaging in monetary transactions in property derived from specified unlawful activity*, https://www.law.cornell.edu/uscode/text/18/1957. This statute relates to "criminally derived property" meaning "any property constituting, or derived from, proceeds obtained from a criminal offense." 18 U.S.C. § 1957(f)(2).

[243] 18 U.S.C. § 1030, *Fraud and related activity in connection with computers*, https://www.law.cornell.edu/uscode/text/18/1030.

The CFAA is lengthy and hard to excerpt in a meaningful way so visit the Cornell LII site to review the statute.

- Protected computer[244]
- Exceeds authorized access[245]
- Damage.[246]

The statute regularly references "without authorization" which is not defined in the statute but is standard criminal statute language. Most criminal statutes, including for theft or damage, require prosecutors prove the offender did not have authorization to take or damage what they did. To do this, prosecutors need a witness who had authorization over the property, to state that the offender did not have authorization.

The provisions relating to "exceeding authorized access" have been limited by courts, as we will cover soon.[247]

The CFAA has several subdivisions that criminalize various computer crimes, including computer intrusion (improper access, breach), damaging computer systems (including with malware), trafficking passwords, extortion (including ransomware), and accessing government computers, national security information.[248]

---

[244] A "protected computer" includes a computer used by a financial institution or the U.S. Government, or that affects "interstate or foreign commerce." The latter has been held to include any internet connected computer, but rest assured the federal government does not try to assert federal jurisdiction lightly and in petty cases. *See* 18 U.S.C. § 1030(e)(2).

[245] 18 U.S.C. § 1030(e)(6) states "the term "exceeds authorized access" means to access a computer with authorization and to use such access to obtain or alter information in the computer that the accessor is not entitled so to obtain or alter." This term has proven problematic and been limited by courts. The other provision in the statute of "without authorization" is clearer.

[246] 18 U.S.C. § 1030(e)(8) reads "the term 'damage' means any impairment to the integrity or availability of data, a program, a system, or information."

[247] As an example, we will refer to the case of the "Cannibal Cop," Gilberto Valle, where federal prosecutors charged him with a computer crime for using the NYPD computer databases to research potential victims relating to his conspiracy (fantasy) to kidnap, rape, torture, and kill them. Prosecutors said he exceeded his authorized access by using the computer systems for this improper and unauthorized purpose. The appellate court eventually ruled that because he had authorized access to the system itself, the statute could not criminalize this improper use. More in a later section.

[248] See the statute for all details at 18 U.S.C. § 1030, https://www.law.cornell.edu/uscode/text/18/1030. *See Cybercrime Investigations* (2020) Chapter 6 for a more complete summary.

20.6.3 Electronic Communications Privacy Act (ECPA)

The Electronic Communications Privacy Act (ECPA) is a federal law that is both procedural and substantive. We will introduce the structure of the law and cover the substantive provisions here, and then the procedural aspects in the next chapter.[249]

ECPA was enacted 1986 and has been amended from time to time and is found in Title 18 of the U.S. code.

ECPA is three parts (acts)

- Title I: Wiretap Act 18 U.S.C. §§ 2510–2523[250]
- Title II: Stored Communications Act (SCA) 18 U.S.C. §§ 2701–2713[251]
- Title III: Pen Register 18 U.S.C. §§ 3121–3127.[252]

The prohibitions of the Wiretap Act and Stored Communications Act contain the substantive provisions relevant for this chapter.

20.6.4 Wiretap crimes (interception-eavesdropping)

It is a federal crime to unlawfully intercept any wire, oral, or electronic communication.[253]

---

[249] Preliminarily (to reduce your suspense before you get to the next chapter) consider that the procedural ECPA parts describe how law enforcement can properly get court authorization to access stored data, intercept live data as it is transmitted, or obtain live transactional information. These processes include subpoena, search warrant, wiretap, and pen register.

[250] 18 U.S.C. Chapter 119, *Wire and Electronic Communications Interception and Interception of Oral Communications*, https://www.law.cornell.edu/uscode/text/18/part-I/chapter-119.

[251] 18 U.S.C. Chapter 121, *Stored Wire and Electronic Communications and Transactional Records Access*, https://www.law.cornell.edu/uscode/text/18/part-I/chapter-121.

[252] 18 U.S.C. Chapter 206, *Pen Registers and Trap and Trace Devices*, https://www.law.cornell.edu/uscode/text/18/part-II/chapter-206.

[253] 18 U.S.C. § 2511, *Interception and disclosure of wire, oral, or electronic communications prohibited*, https://www.law.cornell.edu/uscode/text/18/2511,
(1) Except as otherwise specifically provided in this chapter any person who—
(a) intentionally intercepts, endeavors to intercept, or procures any other person to intercept or endeavor to intercept, any wire, oral, or electronic communication…

Definitions matter (as always) and sections of U.S. Code define:

- Intercept
- Electronic, mechanical, or other device
- Wire communication
- Oral communication
- Contents.[254]

Essentially, "intercept" means using some type of a device to eavesdrop or listen in. If you are using your own ears to overhear what the people next to you are saying, that is not within the definition.

It is also a crime to disclose the existence or contents of a lawful federal wiretap.

20.6.5 Access to stored communication crimes

It is a federal crime to unlawfully access stored communications data "without authorization" or by "exceeding" authorization.[255]

Again, definitions matter, including the interpretation of terms by judges which establishes case-law.[256]

---

[254] 18 U.S.C. § 2510, *Definitions*, https://www.law.cornell.edu/uscode/text/18/2510.

[255] 18 U.S.C. § 2701(a) reads:

Offense.—Except as provided in subsection (c) of this section whoever—
(1) intentionally accesses without authorization a facility through which an electronic communication service is provided; or
(2) intentionally exceeds an authorization to access that facility;
and thereby obtains, alters, or prevents authorized access to a wire or electronic communication while it is in electronic storage in such system…

18 U.S.C. § 2701, Unlawful access to stored communications, https://www.law.cornell.edu/uscode/text/18/2701.

See also U.S. Department of Justice (DOJ), *Prosecuting Computer Crimes* (2010 estimated), p 65, https://www.justice.gov/criminal/file/442156/dl.

[256] Statutory definitions for the SCA are in 18 U.S.C. § 2711, https://www.law.cornell.edu/uscode/text/18/2711. They also use definitions from the Wiretap Act at 18 U.S.C. § 2510, https://www.law.cornell.edu/uscode/text/18/2510.

The statute uses the term "facility" which essentially means the electronic networks and stored data of an electronic communication service (and not simply the brick-and-mortar building).[257]

As we discussed with the CFAA, "without authorization" will have the standard meaning that is typical to all areas of criminal law, and the term "exceeds authorization" is going to be trickier.

The statute refers to improper access of a facility where an "electronic communication service" is provided, so we look to that definition from the Wiretap Act.[258]

20.6.6 Organized Crime - RICO

The Racketeer Influenced and Corrupt Organizations (RICO) Act is a federal law that criminalizes organized crime activity. It was enacted in 1970 to combat traditional organized crime, such as the mafia.

All too often, organized crime leaders controlled widespread criminal activity and profited from it but were not held liable because they were far removed from the murders, bribery, extortion, and drug dealing. RICO aimed to attack the entire criminal enterprise, anyone participating in it, and especially those leading it.

The federal statute first defines racketeering activity, person, enterprise, pattern of racketeering activity, and other terms.[259] Then 18 U.S.C. § 1962 prohibits the conduct and is the statute charged by prosecutors.[260]

---

[257] "Facility" is therefore much broader than merely a brick-and-mortar building where this hardware and digital data is housed but includes the data and networks. *See* U.S. DOJ, *Prosecuting Computer Crimes*, p 65 and p 90-91, https://www.justice.gov/criminal/file/442156/dl. Still, it needs to be an "electronic communication service" under that definition, so this would not apply to an individual's hard drive.

[258] 18 U.S.C. § 2510 (15) reads "'electronic communication service' means any service which provides to users thereof the ability to send or receive wire or electronic communications."

Then we review the definition of "wire communication" under 18 U.S.C. § 2510 (1) and "electronic communication" under 18 U.S.C. § 2510 (12).

[259] 18 U.S.C. § 1961, *Definitions*, https://www.law.cornell.edu/uscode/text/18/1961.

[260] 18 U.S.C. § 1962, *Prohibited activities*, https://www.law.cornell.edu/uscode/text/18/1962.

20.7 New York state cybercrime related offenses

Let us examine New York's substantive cybercrime laws which can be grouped broadly as:

- "Traditional" crimes that can be applied to cybercrime
  - Larceny
  - Identity theft
  - Money laundering and money transmitting
  - Organized crime
- "Cyber" specific statutes relating to computers.

20.7.1 "Traditional" (non "cyber") New York statutes

Theft and larceny

First start with theft. Most cybercrime is just stealing, so do not overlook this obvious crime. States have the general "police power" to criminalize any type of theft, and they do.

New York calls it "larceny," found in Article 155,[261] and the entry level misdemeanor statute is P.L. § 155.25 Petit larceny, which reads:

> *A person is guilty of petit larceny when he steals property.*

Then we look to see how "steal" is defined. It basically requires the intent to deprive another, and they wrongfully take, obtain, or withhold property.[262]

Petit larceny is the lowest level of larceny, a class A misdemeanor, punishable by a maximum of one year in jail.[263] There are higher levels of larceny for when there are aggravating factors, including the value of

---

[261] New York's Penal Law (P.L.) is Chapter 40 of New York's Consolidated Laws, available at https://www.nysenate.gov/legislation/laws/PEN/-CH40. Within the Penal Law are four parts, parts are subdivided into titles, titles are subdivided into articles, and within articles are sections, and sections have subsections.

[262] When presenting a larceny case to the Grand Jury, the prosecutor will ensure the laws and definitions are read to them. Similarly, a judge will read the trial jury the law. P.L. § 155.05 defines larceny and the various ways one can steal, which includes extortion. Ransomware and sextortion for money are all forms of larceny.

[263] While the *maximum* allowable punishment is one year in jail, the actual sentence is within the discretion of the judge, and judges very rarely sentence to the maximum. The minimum sentence could be nothing, a conditional discharge, without any conditions attached, or "time served," the amount of time they already spent in custody.

the property stolen, whether it is a credit card or debit card, secret scientific material, and so forth.

Value levels include $1,000 (Grand Larceny 4th Degree), $3,000 (3rd Degree), $50,000 (2nd Degree) and $1,000,000 (1st Degree). Higher degrees are higher level felonies, meaning a higher maximum punishment.

Aggregation of value becomes an important issue and was relevant in the Western Express case. If a cybercriminal or identity thief commits credit card fraud and steals $800 each from 1,000 victims, is it appropriate to charge 1,000 counts of Petit Larceny, or can we add all the theft amounts together ($800,000) to charge a single count of Grand Larceny in the 2nd Degree?

Alternatively, suppose American Express was one credit card company (a bank) which was defrauded, and a cybercriminal could be shown to have stolen $2,000,000 from 2,000 separate American Express credit card accounts. By aggregating the theft amounts, prosecutors might seek to charge a single count of Grand Larceny in the 1st Degree.

Identity theft

Identity theft is an important statute that reduces some of the issues that can arise with larceny statutes. It is also important for cybercrime because the two pursuits go together.

The New York statute reads:

> *P.L. § 190.78 Identity theft in the third degree.*
>
> *A person is guilty of identity theft in the third degree when he or she knowingly and with intent to defraud assumes the identity of another person by presenting himself or herself as that other person, or by acting as that other person or by using personal identifying information of that other person, and thereby:*
>
> *1. obtains goods, money, property or services or uses credit in the name of such other person or causes financial loss to such person or to another person or persons; or*
>
> *2. commits a class A misdemeanor or higher level crime.*
>
> *Identity theft in the third degree is a class A misdemeanor.*

Then we look to the definitions of "personal identifying information" and other information.

There are other sections for higher levels of crime based on value stolen, prior convictions, and other considerations. Other sections criminalize unlawful possession of personal identification information.

Money laundering and money transmitting

New York's money transmitting statute is found in the Banking Law and criminalizes engaging in this business activity without having an appropriate license from the New York Department of Financial Services.[264]

The New York money laundering statute is complexly worded (perhaps my least favorite criminal statute to read).[265]

In essence, prosecutors need to prove:

- Defendant *knows* the property involved (including money) is the *proceeds of criminal conduct* (earned through crime)
- Defendant conducts *financial transactions* with that property
- Defendant *intends to conceal or disguise* the nature, location, source, ownership, control of funds; or avoid transaction reporting or paying of taxes.

The statute starts with several definitions, including for monetary instrument, conducts, transaction, criminal conduct, specified criminal conduct, financial institution, financial transaction, and so on.[266]

Then it discusses aggregation of value which is important for the same reasons as with regards to theft.[267] In the Western Express case, it was helpful to aggregate all the transactions between Western Express and a particular cybercriminal, and charge that as a single money laundering offense over a period of time, instead of hundreds of smaller money laundering transactions.

---

[264] A basic violation is a misdemeanor, but if funds transmitted exceed a certain amount, then it can be a felony. *See* NY Banking Law § 650, *Violations and penalties*, https://www.nysenate.gov/legislation/laws/BNK/650.

[265] P.L. Article 470, *Money Laundering*, https://www.nysenate.gov/legislation/laws/PEN/P4TXA470.

[266] P.L. § 470.00, *Definitions*, https://www.nysenate.gov/legislation/laws/PEN/470.00.

[267] P.L. § 470.03, *Money laundering: aggregation of value; other matters*, https://www.nysenate.gov/legislation/laws/PEN/470.03.

Then the statute defines our entry level crime, Money Laundering in the Fourth Degree,[268] and higher degrees based on monetary thresholds, or if it is drug proceeds.

Organized Crime - Enterprise Corruption

New York's organization crime statute is part of the Organized Crime Control Act (OCCA), and the statute offense is called Enterprise Corruption within Penal Law Article 460.

As we covered in the prior chapter, this was charged in the Western Express case but ultimately the judges dismissed it on the grounds that we did not present sufficient proof of it to the Grand Jury to sustain that count of the indictment.

The statute includes legislative findings to explain why the law is needed, which also helps judges to interpret the law.[269] It then provides a host of definitions including for enterprise, criminal enterprise, pattern of criminal activity, and specified felonies.[270] Then comes section 460.20, which criminalizes the offense of "Enterprise Corruption."[271]

20.7.2 "Cyber" New York statutes

New York computer offenses are defined in Article 156.[272]

P.L. 156.00 defines terms such as computer, computer program, computer data, computer service, computer material, computer network, access, and without authorization.[273]

Then the basic offense of unauthorized access of a computer:

---

[268] P.L. § 470.05, *Money laundering in the fourth degree*, https://www.nysenate.gov/legislation/laws/PEN/470.05.

[269] P.L. § 460.00, *Legislative findings*, https://www.nysenate.gov/legislation/laws/PEN/460.00.

[270] P.L. § 460.10, *Definitions*, https://www.nysenate.gov/legislation/laws/PEN/460.10.

[271] P.L. § 460.20, *Enterprise corruption*, https://www.nysenate.gov/legislation/laws/PEN/460.20.

[272] P.L. Article 156, *Offenses Involving Computers; Definition of Terms*, https://www.nysenate.gov/legislation/laws/PEN/P3TJA156.

[273] P.L. § 156.00, *Offenses involving computers; definition of terms*, https://www.nysenate.gov/legislation/laws/PEN/156.00.

§ 156.05 Unauthorized use of a computer[274]

A person is guilty of unauthorized use of a computer when he or she knowingly uses, causes to be used, or accesses a computer, computer service, or computer network without authorization.

Unauthorized use of a computer is a class A misdemeanor.

Then the next offense level:

§ 156.10 Computer trespass[275]

A person is guilty of computer trespass when he or she knowingly uses, causes to be used, or accesses a computer, computer service, or computer network without authorization and:

1. he or she does so with an intent to commit or attempt to commit or further the commission of any felony; or

2. he or she thereby knowingly gains access to computer material.

Computer trespass is a class E felony.

Then an offense for accessing, altering, or damaging computer systems:

§ 156.20 Computer tampering in the fourth degree[276]

A person is guilty of computer tampering in the fourth degree when he or she uses, causes to be used, or accesses a computer, computer service, or computer network without authorization and he or she intentionally alters in any manner or destroys computer data or a computer program of another person.

Computer tampering in the fourth degree is a class A misdemeanor.

---

[274] P.L. § 156.05 *Unauthorized use of a computer,*
https://www.nysenate.gov/legislation/laws/PEN/156.05.
[275] P.L. § 156.10, *Computer Trespass,*
https://www.nysenate.gov/legislation/laws/PEN/156.10.
[276] P.L. § 156.20 *Computer tampering in the fourth degree,*
https://www.nysenate.gov/legislation/laws/PEN/156.20.

And then higher levels of computer tampering based on aggravating factors such as intent to commit a felony, prior convictions, value of damage, or other provisions.

There are other substantive crimes too, including unlawful duplication of computer related material and criminal possession of computer related material.

20.8 Other states

The National Conference of State Legislatures (NCSL) has compiled a list of various state statutes and organized them based on various categories relating to cybercrime.[277]

20.9 Actions (conduct) that relate to expression and speech

When considering crimes that relate to expression and speech, we must first consider the First Amendment.[278]

In sum, the First Amendment protects certain speech from criminal prosecution. It tells law enforcement, prosecutors, and judges, that individuals cannot be arrested nor convicted for certain speech that is protected.

The general takeaway for this chapter is that only a few types of speech and expression can be criminalized in this country:

- Speech or expression that is the crime, or part of it
- Direct threats to harm someone.
- Child sex abuse material (CSAM, formerly referred to as child pornography).[279]

Consider that speech can be "protected" but still relevant to prove something. Speech and expression can always be evidence of something, even if that speech itself is protected by the First Amendment.

---

[277] NCSL, *Computer Crime Statutes*, https://www.ncsl.org/technology-and-communication/computer-crime-statutes.

[278] We covered the First Amendment in Chapter 10, which has protections from criminal and civil action.

[279] The term "child pornography" is coming out of favor, since "pornography" typically refers to behavior by consenting adults to create content to sexually arouse others. Children are incapable of consenting and are victimized when the material is created and continue to be victimized as the material is stored, shared, or sold. "Sexual abuse" is a better descriptor for this content.

If a murder suspect stated, five months before the murder:

I hate him and hope he dies.

That statement itself is protected by the First Amendment, but it is also helpful to prove the suspect's intent and motive to kill the person (assuming other evidence connects him to the crime).

If a murder suspect states, after the murder:

I hate him and I killed him.

That statement itself is not a crime either but is powerful evidence because it is the suspect's admission that he committed murder.

For the multitude of speech and expression online in cyberspace, we need to assess whether the First Amendment allows us to treat it as a criminal offense.

20.10 *U.S. v. Gilberto Valle*, the "cannibal cop" case[280]

The case of Gilberto Valle is an excellent teaching point for the law on both speech and computer crime.

In 2006 the New York City Police Department (NYPD) hired Gilberto Valle as a police officer; unfortunately for the people of New York City and law enforcement as a profession. While employed he had access to official NYPD computer systems, which included the ability to access databases of the Department of Motor Vehicles and federal databases.[281]

Valle had some unsavory and disturbing fantasies about kidnapping, torturing, raping, killing, and eating women. He visited online forums where he communicated with other like-minded individuals.

He discussed doing specific acts with others on the forum. They identified targets, took steps towards planning and putting those ideas

---

[280] *See United States v. Valle*, 807 F.3d 508 (2d Cir. 2015). We discuss this case further in Chapter 36 on cyber speech and expression. A compilation of citations is available at my article, *U.S. v. Gilberto Valle, the "cannibal cop" case*, https://johnbandler.com/us-v-valle-cannibal-cop-case.

[281] During my twenty years serving in law enforcement, I had access to these databases, including to check driver's licenses, vehicle registrations, and criminal histories. This information is very sensitive and there were strict rules including that inquiries must only be for an official purpose, and often case numbers needed to be provided. There was an annual training and quiz with certification to ensure users remembered these rules and safeguarded the systems and information within it.

into place. One of those steps was Valle improperly using police computers to research information about the women they were going to target, including his wife. His wife learned about this and reported him, and he was eventually arrested and tried by federal authorities.

According to federal prosecutors, he had committed conspiracy to commit kidnapping[282] on the grounds that he formed an agreement with one or more other persons to commit the kidnapping, and they took one or more overt acts towards committing that crime. He had committed a violation of Computer Fraud and Abuse Act (CFAA)[283] under the theory that by using official police databases (accessing federal databases containing federal data) for an improper purpose, he exceeded the limits of his authorized access to the database. Therefore, this access was unauthorized and violated the statute.

The case proceeded to a jury trial and the jury ultimately convicted him of both counts.

The trial judge (in the Federal District Court) dismissed the conspiracy count, indicating that the evidence suggested it was mere fantasy, not a conspiracy.[284] In other words, this was fantasy, not intent to commit a crime. Neither defendant's words nor thoughts were criminal.

Valle appealed his conviction on the CFAA count, and the prosecutors appealed the judge's dismissal of the conspiracy count. This appeal went to the Federal Court of Appeals for the Second Circuit.

The appeals court held that none of the charges should stand. They affirmed the trial court's dismissal of the conspiracy charge and reversed the conviction on the CFAA charge.

They agreed with the trial court that the evidence failed to prove a criminal intent or a criminal conspiracy, that this conduct was more like fantasy—protected by the First Amendment—than conspiracy.

They disagreed with the trial court about the CFAA charge. The appellate court dismissed the CFAA count and held that the statute's definition of "exceeds authorized access" could not criminalize the conduct in this case. Valle had authorization to access the systems and

---

[282] 18 U.S.C. § 1201(c), *Kidnapping*, https://www.law.cornell.edu/uscode/text/18/1201.

[283] 18 U.S.C. § 1030(a)(2)(B), https://www.law.cornell.edu/uscode/text/18/1030.

[284] A dismissal notwithstanding the verdict, more commonly known as a judgment notwithstanding the verdict.

data in question, so the criminal statute could not be read to criminalize this access, even if he did so for an improper purpose.

In sum, it is a highly unusual and disturbing fact pattern that has two important tie-ins to cyberlaw involving the CFAA and First Amendment.[285]

20.11 The Sergei Aleynikov case

Consider the case of Sergei Aleynikov, a former Goldman Sachs software programmer who developed proprietary code to improve their trading, including ability to act faster than others in the trading markets.

In February 2010 he was charged by federal indictment with criminal offenses of theft of trade secrets, computer fraud and abuse, and transporting stolen goods. Issues were raised as to whether computer code was "property" as defined by the applicable federal law since he sent the code electronically (rather than saving it to a thumb drive, DVD, or printing to paper). He was convicted after a trial in federal court, but the conviction was reversed on appeal as the appellate judges decided that the federal statute and its definitions could not be applied to the facts of this case and the entirely digital nature of this theft.[286]

With the federal case dismissed and over, he was then charged by New York state authorities for the exact same conduct. Similar issues were raised at trial and on appeal though obviously the substantive crimes

---

[285] All case citations are available at article: *U.S. v. Gilberto Valle, the "cannibal cop" case*, https://johnbandler.com/us-v-valle-cannibal-cop-case.

The trial court decision after the trial is *United States v. Valle*, 301 F.R.D. (SDNY, 2014). Then the appellate decision from the Second Circuit is *United States v. Valle*, 807 F. 3d 508 (2nd Cir. 2015), https://caselaw.findlaw.com/us-2nd-circuit/1719750.html, or at https://scholar.google.com/scholar_case? case=11783993212131547013; Indictment, *U.S. v. Gilberto Valle*, https://www.justice.gov/archive/usao/nys/pressreleases/March13/ValleVerdictP R/Valle,%20Gilberto%20Indictment.pdf.

[286] *See U.S. v. Aleynikov*, 676 F. 3d 71 (2nd Cir. 2012), available at https://scholar.google.com/scholar_case?case=9924995296317038461. The applicable federal statute was later amended to close this loophole, so a similar future case might be decided differently.

were now different, under state law. In the end he remained convicted of one of the state criminal counts.[287]

20.12 Jurisdiction to charge a substantive crime (recap and preview)

If you are an investigator or prosecutor in a particular location, you might start working on a case. The first question is "do I have jurisdiction to bring a case."[288]

Examining jurisdiction is part substantive and part procedural. We ask:

- What crimes were committed?
- What are the elements of each crime?
  - Different elements may have been committed in different jurisdictions
- Where was the conduct performed?
- Where was the perpetrator? (Often hard to know)
- Where were the victims located?
- Where did the harm occur?
- What does the procedural law say?

An important practical takeaway for many cybercrimes is that there will often be multiple courts (and law enforcement and prosecutors) who have solid jurisdiction claims over a particular cybercrime event.

This means that one or more states could (in theory) bring charges, as could the federal government.

We will return to jurisdiction in the next chapter.

20.13 Actions in the "metaverse" or virtual reality

What if one person's avatar kills another person's avatar in a virtual reality location, such as the "metaverse"? Or commits another virtual harm, such as an assault, sexual assault, or theft?

Can we charge a crime?

---

[287] *See People v. Aleynikov*, 31 NY 3d 383 (Ct. Appeals, 2018), available at https://scholar.google.com/scholar_case?case=6818873647602103837.
This state case was prosecuted by DANY, where I worked at the time, across the street from the federal prosecutors. I was not involved in this case at all.
[288] As covered, asking this question about jurisdiction is very different from asking (i) whether the offender can be identified (ii) whether the offender can be arrested and extradited and (ii) whether sufficient evidence can be obtained to prove the case beyond a reasonable doubt.

We need to be precise about the actual conduct, and the people involved.

Many "actions" committed done in virtual reality are not considered conduct in the physical world but are expressions by individuals. We need to view them in the context of the First Amendment, rather than assume that criminal laws apply to virtual reality avatars.

At the simplest level, we look to the criminal law definitions for assault, sexual assault, murder, and so forth. An element of a crime is usually that they are directed at another person, meaning a human being. When the target of a "crime" is a virtual avatar but not a real person, then that law does not apply.[289]

We should look to see whether other laws regarding expression and speech might apply, such as harassment, menacing, or stalking.

This is probably the way we want it. Law enforcement already has their hands full dealing with brick-and-mortar murder, sexual assault, and assault, plus billions of dollars in cybercrime theft.

20.14 Categorizing cybercrimes further (preview)

Early on we considered these categories for substantive cybercrime statutes:

- Federal vs state
- Traditional vs "cyber."

Some may also want to categorize these substantive crimes as:

- cyber-enabled crime
- cyber-native crime
- cyber-dependent crime.

Additional categories are not necessary or helpful, which we will return to in Chapter 23.

20.15 Western Express and investigating, and choosing charges

We were deep into the investigation, with a large amount of evidence, hundreds of suspects, and thousands of criminal acts, but the

---

[289] We can also look to the intent of the person (*e.g.*, the element of guilty mind or *mens rea*) and what their actual act was (the *actus reus* element). An input to a keyboard or game controller to fire a virtual gun in virtual space is obviously not the same as firing a real gun in the real world, and the intended result is different also.

investigation could not go forever. An indictment needed to be brought and it was necessary to pick the charges to present to the Grand Jury.

This requires analyzing many complex issues:

- What were the facts
- What can the evidence prove
  - About what crime was committed
  - About who committed the crime
- What were the criminal charges to consider
- What amounts could be aggregated
- What arguments would the defense make to dismiss counts.

Ultimately, about eighteen defendants were charged, and there were three hundred counts in the indictment, including

- Enterprise Corruption (eventually dismissed by the courts)
- Grand Larceny (many counts)
- Money Laundering
- Scheme to Defraud
- Conspiracy,

And other counts.

20.16 References and additional reading

- *Chapter 20 resources*, https://johnbandler.com/cyberlawbook-resources-ch20
- *Criminal cyberlaw*, https://johnbandler.com/criminal-cyberlaw
- *Substantive criminal cyberlaw*, https://johnbandler.com/criminal-cyberlaw-substantive
- *U.S. v. Gilberto Valle the "cannibal cop" case*, https://johnbandler.com/us-v-valle-cannibal-cop-case
- U.S. Department of Justice, *Prosecuting Computer Crimes* (2010 estimated), https://www.justice.gov/criminal/file/442156/dl
- *Cybercrime Investigations* (2020 book), Chapter 6, Cybercrime Defined: The Criminal Statutes Outlawing Criminal Conduct Online

20.16 Chapter questions

- Name the main federal cybercrime statute and provide the citation (hint starts with "Computer").

- Name the federal law (and provide the statute citation) that has provisions that can be charged substantively, but also provisions to allow law enforcement to obtain evidence lawfully.
- Why should prosecutors consider the full range of criminal statutes (both "traditional" and "cyber") to charge a cybercriminal with?
- Since most cybercrime is about theft and stealing, what traditional crime should prosecutors consider charging?
- Since successful cybercriminals "earn" a lot of money, what traditional crime should prosecutors consider charging?

21

Criminal Procedure and Gathering Electronic and Cybercrime Evidence

In this chapter:

- The process of investigating and prosecuting cybercrime
- Gathering evidence for cybercrime
- Cybercrime is committed across state and country borders, so let's examine that

21.1 Criminal procedure basics (recap)[290]

Criminal procedure laws relate to the *process* of the criminal justice system.

They try to ensure the process for resolving a criminal case is orderly and fair to both sides.

When the police and prosecutor suspect a defendant violated a criminal law, the criminal procedure law sets forth how the government can investigate the alleged crime.

If they make an arrest, these procedural laws establish how to bring charges and then everything through and after proving it in court.

In sum, criminal procedure law is the process of how criminal law is administered. It is the procedures that are used by law enforcement officers, agents, prosecutors, judges, and defense attorneys.

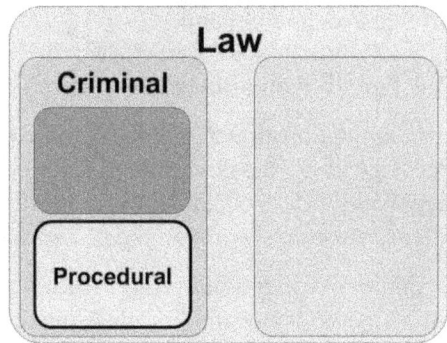

---

[290] Chapter 8 introduced criminal law, including criminal procedure.

Criminal procedure law deals with two important areas:

- The investigation, collecting evidence, seizing people, things, and data.
- The process of arresting a defendant and then litigating the matter through trial and beyond.

The investigation

A cybercrime pre-arrest investigation might be enormous in comparison to a street crime case. Cybercriminals commit many criminal acts over weeks, months, and years, and take extensive steps to hide their internet and financial tracks. The investigation could take years and require legal process such as subpoenas and search warrants and span across many jurisdictions.

Process of litigation

This area deals with the process of litigating a criminal case. The prosecutor has the burden of proof, the defendant has many rights, and there is a process to ensure rights are protected and the process is fair.

This process will address all the stages of the litigation from arrest through trial and beyond.[291]

21.2 Fourth Amendment and search and seizure (recap)[292]

In sum, the Fourth Amendment protects against unreasonable searches and seizures by the government. Laws and government conduct must comply with the Fourth Amendment. It is common—even routine—for defense attorneys to allege the government violated those limits.

Criminal investigation requires the collection of evidence, and that typically implicates the Fourth Amendment.

This Fourth Amendment may be the most important part of the U.S. Constitution for criminal procedure because of its impact on investigations and the resulting litigation.

---

[291] This includes arrest, arraignment, assignment of defense counsel, pre-trial detention or release, motion practice, discovery, pre-trial hearings, plea negotiations, trial, sentencing, and appeal.

[292] We covered the Fourth Amendment in Chapter 11. Since the U.S. Constitution (with amendments) is the highest law in the land, it is our first stop when researching a related legal issue.

Other procedural laws and court decisions stem from the Fourth Amendment, including when a police officer or special agent can make an arrest, when a search warrant may be issued by a judge, and when evidence can be seized.[293]

21.3 Constitutional protections on the process

Other parts of the U.S. Constitution affect and protect the criminal justice process.[294]

Some protect defendants from being charged (substantively) with certain offenses, others protect procedural rights. Either way the protections mean the defense can make procedural challenges to what the government did or charged. Protections include:

- Protections on speech (First Amendment)
- Protections from search and seizure (Fourth Amendment, see above)
- Due process (Fifth Amendment)
- Double jeopardy protection (Fifth Amendment)
- Right against self-incrimination (Fifth Amendment)
- Speedy trial (Sixth Amendment)
- Right to confront witnesses (Sixth Amendment)
- Right to an attorney (Sixth Amendment)
- No excessive bail, fines, or cruel or unusual punishments (Eighth Amendment).

The overarching procedural protection in the Fifth Amendment's right to "due process" is squarely in line with this chapter on procedure.

21.4 Jurisdiction over the cybercrime and the evidence

Jurisdiction is an interesting legal issue we have visited frequently.[295]

---

[293] For example, see the Federal Rules of Criminal Procedure (FRCP) Rule 41, *Search and Seizure*, https://www.law.cornell.edu/rules/frcrmp/rule_41, and Rule 17 , *Subpoena*, https://www.law.cornell.edu/rules/frcrmp/rule_17.

[294] Other parts of the U.S. Constitution can also be within our first research stop because of its many protections against government overreach.

[295] *See* Chapter 2, Chapter 8, Chapter 12, and Chapter 20.

Since our criminal justice "system" is really many different and often independent prosecutorial and investigative agencies, it is not always harmony and orchestrated symphony.[296]

With so much cybercrime, jurisdiction is rarely an issue surrounding the defendant. Often, no one is investigating, and even when they do, it is rare that a case will ever be brought.

When a prosecuting agency works on a case it might get to a point where they want to bring charges, and they have invested enough in the case to do so. When that happens, they rarely want to give the case to another prosecuting agency that might have "better" jurisdiction. They seek to show why *they* have jurisdiction, and to do that, they assess:

- Where the offender was (usually another jurisdiction)
- Where the victim was
- Where the computers that were accessed were
- Where the money was stolen from
- Where data or funds travelled through.

These facts can help establish that one or more of these things occurred within the physical territory of that jurisdiction:

- An element of the crime
- An overt act of the conspiracy
- A particular effect
- A harm.

All of these help a prosecutor argue why jurisdiction over the defendant is proper in *their* jurisdiction.

A separate issue is jurisdiction (authority) to gather the evidence, especially when that evidence is in another state, or even another country. That can be a trickier issue.

---

[296] *See* Chapter 8. Our law enforcement agencies are staffed with many dedicated, honest, hardworking professionals, and they often do amazing things. We can acknowledge that they may not sing "Kumbaya" together all the time in harmony, we may disagree with what they do sometimes, they make mistakes, and bad conduct happens too. With the many imperfections of law enforcement and the criminal justice system, no other country is perfect, and many have even greater imperfections. Many other countries lack the transparency of ours, meaning they may have systemic problems and corruption that never get reported on.

21.5 Investigating and tools to gather evidence

Before we dive into federal and state statutes here is an important overview of the investigative processes and legal tools that can be used to gather evidence.[297]

- *Open-source investigation*, which does not require any legal process, because it is openly available and there for the taking.
- *Consent*, which does not require any legal process either, so long as the person providing consent did so knowingly and voluntarily and had authority over the property or data provided.
- *Subpoenas duces tecum*, an entry level legal process, in the name of the court but sometimes issued directly by a prosecutor, which usually only requires that evidence sought be relevant. A subpoena has limits on what it can obtain.
- *Judicial orders under Section 2703(d)* of the Stored Communications Act.
- *Search warrants based on probable cause* to search a property, premises, or other physical location, or to obtain digital data that includes content (actual communications or documents).
- *Pen registers and trap-and-trace devices* to obtain live transactional data about who is communicating with whom.
- *Location data orders based upon probable cause* (search warrant standard) to learn where a person is or has been (*e.g.*, either live location data or stored location data).
- *Wiretap orders based upon probable cause plus* a showing of *exhaustion* of other investigative methods, for live communication content (eavesdropping, listening in).

In one example of how this might work in a cybercrime investigation, a victim reports cybercrime to law enforcement, and consents to provide relevant information and data to assist in the report and investigation. Law enforcement can search open-source information for initial leads, and throughout the investigation, witnesses or even suspects might consent to provide information and evidence. Prosecutors can send grand jury subpoenas, in the name of the grand jury and court, to companies to obtain their business records, which could include IP information, subscriber information, or financial transaction records.

---

[297] The 2020 book *Cybercrime Investigations* was all about this process of investigating. Chapter 7 covered the legal provisions and tools, including the "nine tools for gathering evidence" within Section 7.3. Chapter 11 covered open-source investigation, while other chapters discussed using other legal tools.

As law enforcement develops some suspects and starts to target them, they may obtain a search warrant for digital evidence such as a suspect's Google or Microsoft cloud account contents. If they get closer to a decision to prosecute an individual, a search warrant of a residence or their business may be obtained.

21.6 ECPA: Electronic Communications Privacy Act (procedural provisions)

ECPA is the federal law to obtain electronic data, which is both procedural and substantive, and here we cover the procedural components.[298]

ECPA is three parts (titles)

- Title I: Wiretap Act 18 U.S.C. §§ 2510–2523
- Title II: Stored Communications Act (SCA) 18 U.S.C. §§ 2701–2713
- Title III: Pen Registers 18 U.S.C. §§ 3121–3127.

ECPA applies to both federal and state prosecutors, though state prosecutors will also have to look to their state law to ensure compliance with it also.

21.6.1 Wiretap applications and orders

Some important wiretap takeaways are:

- Wiretaps are for intercepting *live* communications (not stored).
- Wiretaps require probable cause plus exhaustion of other investigative techniques.
- Wiretaps are traditionally and legally viewed as the most invasive type of investigative technique.[299]
- Very labor intensive for law enforcement both to conduct (monitor) and do the reports and notifications.

---

[298] In the prior chapter we covered the substantive criminal parts of ECPA. For example, a person who illegally accesses stored communications without authorization can be charged criminally for that, and a person who illegally wiretaps and listens in on live communications or actions can be criminally charged for that. In this chapter we cover the procedural parts of ECPA, how law enforcement can gather evidence.

[299] Now that people store so much information on their computer devices, including rapid text and email messages, we can consider whether the traditional view of wiretaps being the most invasive investigative technique are outdated.

- Example: listening in, live, on phone conversations between the target and other people.
- Are rarely done by law enforcement (most criminal cases have no wiretaps).
- When done by law enforcement, they are usually the last investigative step before arrest.

For a wiretap application, some relevant sections relating to the prosecutor's application are:

- 18 U.S.C. § 2516, Authorization for interception of wire, oral, or electronic communications,[300] which explains how a prosecutor can apply for a wiretap order, and what offenses qualify.
- 18 U.S.C. § 2518, Procedure for interception of wire, oral, or electronic communications,[301]
    - Including that the wiretap application needs:
        - An oath or affirmation
        - The identity of law enforcement officer
        - Full and complete statement of facts
        - Full and complete statement of other investigative techniques tried
        - Period of wiretap
        - Statement of prior applications
    - And that the wiretap order must be based upon findings of
        - Probable cause a crime is, was, or will be committed
        - Probable cause the wiretap will obtain evidence
        - Normal investigative procedures were tried and failed (or will be unlikely to succeed or are too dangerous).

21.6.2 Stored communication applications and orders

Some important stored communications takeaways are:

- These orders are for obtaining stored communications (not live)
- The standards are less stringent than for a wiretap
- Stored "content" (communications between people) requires a search warrant, based upon a showing of probable cause

---

[300] 18 U.S.C. § 2516, https://www.law.cornell.edu/uscode/text/18/2516.
[301] 18 U.S.C. § 2518, https://www.law.cornell.edu/uscode/text/18/2518.

- Some types of stored data might require a lower level of legal process than a search warrant
  - Transactional data (subscriber information, IP log information) can be obtained with a subpoena, which merely requires a showing of relevance.
- Stored communications orders and search warrants are served and processed like a subpoena. The legal process is served on the company, which then searches their own records and responds.
- Example: prosecutors get a search warrant, serve it on Google, and obtain the contents of the suspect's email account.
- Example: prosecutors send a subpoena to Google, and obtain certain information about the suspect's email account, such as user provided subscriber information and certain IP logs.

For a stored communication access order, some relevant sections are:

- 18 U.S.C. § 2711(2), definition of "remote computing service"[302]
- 18 U.S.C. § 2703, Required disclosure of customer communications or records,[303] which says how a prosecutor can obtain stored communications records, including via:
  - Subpoena, for basic transactional information (not content or communications)
  - Court order for slightly more information
  - Search warrant based on probable cause for all information, including content (communications).

21.6.3 Pen register applications and orders (including for trap and trace)

Some important pen register takeaways are:

- Pen registers are for intercepting *live* transaction data (not stored).
- Pen registers do not allow collection of "content" (the actual communication between people).
- Pen registers simply require that the data collected will be relevant.

---

[302] Under 18 U.S.C. § 2711(2) a "remote computing service" means the provision to the public of computer storage or processing services by means of an electronic communications system. Then we look to the definition of "electronic communications system" under 18 U.S.C. § 2510(15), and the definition of "electronic communications" under 18 U.S.C. § 2510(12).
[303] 18 U.S.C. § 2703, https://www.law.cornell.edu/uscode/text/18/2703.

- Example: obtaining live data about who is calling who on the phone (what phone numbers are involved, but not what was said).
- If law enforcement wants to obtain location data also, that requires a showing of probable cause (e.g., search warrant standard).[304]

Some relevant sections for pen registers are:

- 18 U.S.C. § 3122, Application for an order for a pen register or a trap and trace device,[305] which says how a prosecutor can apply for a pen register, requiring "a certification by the applicant that the information likely to be obtained is relevant to an ongoing criminal investigation being conducted by that agency."

21.7 New York laws on pen registers, search warrants, and wiretaps

The New York Criminal Procedure Law (C.P.L.) has provisions that control how law enforcement can obtain pen registers, search warrants, and wiretap orders.[306] By and large, they are similar to the federal statutes and legal standards we covered, and often may provide more protections for a state suspect than federal law affords for federal suspects.

We will cover them from least intrusive and onerous to most.

21.7.1 Subpoena

New York C.P.L. Article 610 covers subpoenas, including a *subpoena duces tecum*, and grand jury subpoenas.[307]

---

[304] This standard came about based upon evolving judicial interpretation of the Fourth Amendment as applied to technology changes. *See Carpenter v. United States*, 585 U.S. 296 (2018). Law enforcement's obtaining of third-party location data requires a search warrant and a showing of probable cause. This 2018 USSC case built off *United States v. Jones*, 565 U.S. 400 (2012) which held that GPS tracking using a device is a search, requiring a search warrant supported by probable cause.

[305] 18 U.S.C. § 3122 is at https://www.law.cornell.edu/uscode/text/18/3122.

[306] A prosecutor is involved with every one of these applications, which require a signed order from a judge. Whatever a person's title and role in the investigation, "thinking like a prosecutor" helps them envision what the prosecutor needs to do and write to obtain that order.

[307] C.P.L. Article 610, https://www.nysenate.gov/legislation/laws/CPL/A610.

A subpoena is a court order for a witness to appear and provide testimony.

A *subpoena duces tecum* basically means "bring it with you," and is a subpoena for a witness to bring records to court. These are one of the most important tools of a prosecutor. Usually, the prosecutor just wants the records sent and will excuse the appearance of a live witness.

21.7.2 New York Pen registers and trap and trace device

New York C.P.L. Article 705 covers pen registers and trap and trace devices, with sections for definitions, general items, the application, the order, installation, and more.[308]

"Pen register" refers to recording the numbers dialed by the target (or analogous data for other types of communication)

"Trap and trace device" refers to capturing the number of someone dialing to the target. Once upon a time, Caller-ID did not exist, and it was a special technological hurdle for phone companies to implement this.

Obviously, this statute can be applied to more modern communications such as instant message, email, voice over internet protocol (VoIP) and more.

Location data, meaning the location of a device such as a cell phone, is beyond the scope of this statute, so would require legal authorization from another place, such as the search warrant statute.

21.7.3 New York search warrants

New York C.P.L. Article 690 covers search warrants, with sections for definitions, property that can be seized, where executable, who can execute them, when they can be executed, the application, special provisions, form and content, execution, and what to do after execution.[309]

Traditionally a search warrant is for a physical location, a residence, business, sometimes an automobile or container.

---

[308] C.P.L. Article 705, https://www.nysenate.gov/legislation/laws/CPL/A705.
[309] C.P.L. Article 690, https://www.nysenate.gov/legislation/laws/CPL/A690. Search warrants are more common than pen registers and wiretaps, and the C.P.L. happens to order it first.

In our cyber age, a search warrant can be for cell phones, other computers, Google cloud accounts, location data, and more.

21.7.4 New York wiretaps

NY C.P.L. Article 700 covers wiretaps, titled "Eavesdropping and Video Surveillance Warrants."[310]

This is the longest of the three evidence gathering articles. There are sections for definitions, when they can be issued, the application, the legal standard, implementation, time periods, extensions, and extensive reporting requirements and notification requirements.

Traditionally a wiretap was the most invasive investigative technique, with law enforcement listening in live on suspect communications. For these reasons, the legal and administrative burdens are onerous.[311]

21.8 Obtaining evidence from other states

Federal law enforcement has few hurdles when seeking evidence from outside their state of venue because their authority is nationwide.

In contrast, state law enforcement and state court orders have authority within the state, but they might not be honored outside of the state.

A New York judge cannot issue a search warrant to order a search of physical premises located outside the state. To search a location outside the state requires the cooperation of law enforcement in that state and a search warrant from a judge in *that* state.

If a New York prosecutor gets that cooperation, and a judge in State X issues that search warrant, the warrant should include permission to bring the evidence back to New York.

Once that evidence is back in New York, if they want to forensically analyze (search) any digital devices, they should get another search warrant from a New York judge.

A New York subpoena might not be honored in another state, and might need to be "domesticated," meaning endorsed by a judge in that state.

---

[310] C.P.L. Article 700, https://www.nysenate.gov/legislation/laws/CPL/A700.

[311] As mentioned, consider that the stored contents of our smartphones contain dozens of apps and volumes of communication, photos, and data. With this stored data and years of stored communications it might tell far more about us than our live conversations over a few months.

An issue with these subpoenas is whether the court has jurisdiction to compel the recipient to turn over those records. As a Manhattan prosecutor, our reach was wide, because so many organizations do business through New York or have offices in New York.[312] Still, our reach was significantly less than a federal prosecutor.

21.9 Obtaining evidence from other countries

It is a significant hurdle to obtain evidence from another country, but cybercrime is international and that is often where important evidence lies. Let us examine the following situations.

- *Clarifying Lawful Overseas Use of Data (CLOUD) Act*, allows U.S. based law enforcement to compel a U.S. based company to provide data in response to a subpoena or search warrant even if that company is storing that data on servers located outside the U.S. [313]
- *Might evidence "also" be within our country?* Like the CLOUD Act provisions, prosecutors can consider if there is the presence of the evidence or corporation representative within the United States who could access the data.
- *Mutual Legal Assistance Treaties (MLATs)*, are formal agreements (like a contract) between countries to provide evidence in certain cases, to mutually assist each other with legal issues.[314]

---

[312] On occasion an organization might state that our subpoena had no power over them, because they were headquartered in State X, with no presence in New York. On more than one occasion, I pointed out they had an office within New York and then they realized they had a duty to comply. This is essentially establishing personal jurisdiction over the entity subpoenaed.

[313] For example, if Microsoft is storing data on a server in Ireland, Microsoft must provide that responsive data to U.S. law enforcement, if served with otherwise proper legal process. There was an actual legal dispute between Microsoft and the U.S., and this law was passed as a result to require this data be turned over. *See United States v. Microsoft Corp.*, 584 U.S. 236 (2018); U.S. DOJ, *CLOUD Act Resources*, https://www.justice.gov/criminal/cloud-act-resources; CLOUD Act full text, https://www.justice.gov/d9/pages/attachments/2019/04/09/cloud_act.pdf.

[314] U.S. DOJ, *Mutual Legal Assistance Treaties of The United States* (April 2022), https://www.justice.gov/d9/pages/attachments/2022/05/04/mutual-legal-assistance-treaties-of-the-united-states.pdf. There are treaties between individual countries, and then treaties among multiple countries (multilateral conventions)

- *Letters rogatory* apply where there is no treaty in place and is a formal diplomatic or judicial request from our country to another.[315]
- *Informal assistance* is simply getting help that does not rely upon a formal international or judicial process.[316]
- *Egmont requests* are a request through our Financial Crimes Enforcement Network (FinCEN) to the equivalent organization in another country, to obtain basic financial information promptly. This information would not be admissible in court.

For any formal legal request going to another country (MLAT, letters rogatory, extradition request), prosecutors need to consult with the U.S. DOJ's Office of International Affairs (OIA).

In the Western Express case, multiple international requests were made, including MLATs through OIA, and other requests and information gathering.

21.9.1 International conventions (treaties)

There are some international conventions (a treaty among multiple nations) that are important to mention because they are the basis for obtaining evidence. These are similar to the MLATs discussed above, except they are an agreement among many countries.

The Budapest Convention on Cybercrime

The Budapest Convention on Cybercrime (Budapest Convention)[317] is a treaty adopted by the Council of Europe (CoE) in 2001 and went into

---

such as The Council of Europe Convention on Cybercrime (the Budapest Convention), and others.

[315] U.S. DOJ archived (obsolete) *Criminal Resource Manual, 275, Letters Rogatory*, https://www.justice.gov/archives/jm/criminal-resource-manual-275-letters-rogatory. U.S. Department of State, *Preparation of Letters Rogatory*, https://travel.state.gov/content/travel/en/legal/travel-legal-considerations/internl-judicial-asst/obtaining-evidence/Preparation-Letters-Rogatory.html.

[316] If a foreign law enforcement officer gives the Secret Service agent a ride to view the exterior of a suspect's building, that is a type of informal assistance.

[317] Within the CoE this is sometimes called the "Convention on Cybercrime" but "Budapest Convention" is a better shorthand to avoid confusion with the new U.N. Convention on Cybercrime.

effect in 2004.[318] It facilitates cooperation in cybercrime cases and emergency situations too. There are seventy-six countries that are parties to it, including the U.S., United Kingdom (U.K.), many European countries and others.[319]

U.N. Cybercrime Convention

A new U.N. cybercrime convention is on the path to approval and becoming in force.[320]

This international cybercrime treaty was proposed in the United Nations in 2019.[321] In February 2022 a U.N. committee was formed to move the proposed convention forward.[322] Over the years, the treaty evolved and in August 2024 a draft was finalized.[323] In its near final form it now has the

---

[318] *See* Council of Europe (CoE), *The Convention on Cybercrime (Budapest Convention, ETS No. 185) and its Protocols*, https://www.coe.int/en/web/cybercrime/the-budapest-convention; *Details of Treaty No.185*, https://www.coe.int/en/web/conventions/full-list?module=treaty-detail&treatynum=185; *Text of the Convention on Cybercrime*, https://rm.coe.int/1680081561; Guidance notes, https://www.coe.int/en/web/cybercrime/guidance-notes.

[319] CoE, *List of Parties/Observers to the Budapest Convention*, https://www.coe.int/en/web/cybercrime/parties-observers.

[320] When you research, start with the references in this book but realize new developments may have occurred since publication, especially regarding events like this occurring close to the time of publication.

[321] It was initially proposed by Russia, backed by Iran, and China, countries that many believe do not adequately respect human rights or the rights of other sovereign countries; and they had not ever signed onto the Budapest Convention. Based on the wording, backers, and existence of the Budapest Convention, this proposal was initially viewed with skepticism. Over the next three years the treaty evolved until it was in a form supported by other nations.

[322] Ironically, this committee was formed the same day Russia launched their invasion of Ukraine, a violation of law of sovereignty we discuss in Chapter 35.

[323] *See* U.N. General Assembly, *Draft United Nations convention against cybercrime: Strengthening international cooperation for combating certain crimes committed by means of information and communications technology systems and for the sharing of evidence in electronic form of serious crimes*, (Aug. 7, 2024), A/AC.291/L.15, https://documents.un.org/doc/undoc/ltd/v24/055/06/pdf/v2405506.pdf; United Nations, *Press release: Member States finalize a new cybercrime convention*, (Aug. 9, 2024), https://www.unodc.org/unodc/en/frontpage/2024/August/united-nations_-member-states-finalize-a-new-cybercrime-convention.html.

support of the United States and our allies.[324] This draft convention was formally adopted by the UN General Assembly in December 2024,[325] and is expected to be signed by member nations in 2025.

21.10. Extraditing defendants from other states

To obtain the arrest of a defendant in another state requires an interstate process, including extradition. This law originates from the U.S. Constitution[326] and is codified in statutes and interstate agreements. The process can be difficult, but we are in the same country, with laws and rules to bind us and coordinate.

The authority of a New York State Trooper to make an arrest as a police officer [generally] ends at the state border, and the authority of a New York State arrest warrant generally is only valid within the confines of the state (subject to interstate law and agreements).

In a hypothetical New York cybercrime investigation, an out of state suspect is charged with a felony (a serious crime), and an arrest warrant is issued. With that arrest warrant (and sufficient effort) the defendant can be arrested within another state and charged as a fugitive from justice, which starts a special extradition proceeding to see if they can be brought to New York. The arresting state can hold them in custody while these proceedings resolve, and the defendant has rights to a hearing to

---

[324] U.S. Mission to the United Nations, *Explanation of Position of the United States on the Adoption of the Resolution on the UN Convention Against Cybercrime in the UN General Assembly's Third Committee, as prepared for delivery by Jonathan Shrier, U.S. Deputy Representative to the Economic and Social Council*, (Nov. 11, 2024), https://usun.usmission.gov/explanation-of-position-of-the-united-states-on-the-adoption-of-the-resolution-on-the-un-convention-against-cybercrime-in-ungas-third-committee.

[325] *See* U.N. Office on Drugs and Crime, *Press Release: UN General Assembly adopts landmark convention on cybercrime*, (December 24, 2024), https://www.unodc.org/unodc/en/press/releases/2024/December/un-general-assembly-adopts-landmark-convention-on-cybercrime.html.

The press release also links to an updated document with the text of the Cybercrime Convention within it, at https://documents.un.org/doc/undoc/gen/n24/372/04/pdf/n2437204.pdf.

[326] *See* U.S. Constitution Article IV, Section 2, Clause 2 ("Extradition Clause" or "Interstate Rendition Clause"):

A Person charged in any State with Treason, Felony, or other Crime, who shall flee from Justice, and be found in another State, shall on Demand of the executive Authority of the State from which he fled, be delivered up, to be removed to the State having Jurisdiction of the Crime.

contest certain issues, including whether they are the right person subject to these charges. A defendant may waive their rights to full extradition proceedings to avoid waiting in custody unnecessarily if extradition seems likely anyway.

In the Western Express case, there were defendants charged by indictment who were in various places around the U.S., and it was a laborious process to get them all brought back to New York.[327]

21.11. Extraditing defendants from other countries

Extraditing a defendant from another country is especially difficult. Each country is their own sovereign nation, and no other country can forcibly take an individual from that country or forcibly compel the country to take an action.

There are processes for extraditing defendants from other countries, and these are generally based on treaties between countries, which may specify the exact types of crimes and circumstances where extradition is allowed.[328]

As with an MLAT, this will require engaging the assistance of the U.S. DOJ attorneys in the Office of International Affairs (OIA). Writing is essential and paperwork is prepared, our country asks the foreign government to arrest the suspect, at which point there are proceedings to determine whether the suspect should be extradited to the U.S.

In the Western Express case, we extradited three defendants from foreign countries, generally a two-year process.

---

[327] As a trooper, I saw other perspectives of the arrest warrant processes. When I stopped a motorist or arrested a suspect, they would (usually) be checked for warrants. Sometimes there was a warrant "hit" based on an approximation of name and birthdate. From there, it was a process of investigating to determine (i) was this the same person the warrant was for, (ii) was the warrant still active, and (iii) was the police agency that issued the warrant willing to pick up the defendant.

For a time, I worked on the station's active warrants for hundreds of defendants who had been arrested by a trooper but eventually failed to appear in court. It was my job to make efforts to locate them and have them arrested; and also ensure there was a record of law enforcement's attempts to find them.

[328] *See* U.S. DOJ, Justice Manual, 9-15.000, *International Extradition and Related Matters*, https://www.justice.gov/jm/jm-9-15000-international-extradition-and-related-matters.

21.12 Western Express and gathering evidence and defendants

Western Express was a sprawling case of cybercrime and virtual currency money laundering, with offenders located throughout the United States and World. For the defendants charged by indictment, we used extradition proceedings to secure their presence from across the U.S. and from Europe.

Evidence was obtained from throughout the U.S. and the world. Subpoenas were used for basic records and transactional information. We obtained many search warrants, some for email records, and some to search premises in New York, and we obtained assistance from other jurisdictions for search warrants in other states. We also used MLATs to obtain evidence from other countries.

21.13 References and resources

- *Chapter 21 resources*, https://johnbandler.com/cyberlawbook-resources-ch21
- Chapter 19, The Western Express Case
- *Criminal cyberlaw*, https://johnbandler.com/criminal-cyberlaw
- *Procedural criminal cyberlaw*, https://johnbandler.com/criminal-cyberlaw-procedural
- Fourth Amendment, (via Cornell LII), https://www.law.cornell.edu/constitution/fourth_amendment
- *Cybercrime Investigations* (2020 book), Chapter 7 The Law Enforcement Legal Toolbox for Investigating Cybercrime (Laws for
- U.S. DOJ, *Justice Manual*, Title 9 Criminal, https://www.justice.gov/jm/title-9-criminal (including sections on obtaining evidence, electronic surveillance, etc.)
- Electronic Communications Privacy Act (ECPA), main titles:
    - o Title I: Wiretap Act 18 U.S.C. §§ 2510–2523, https://www.law.cornell.edu/uscode/text/18/part-I/chapter-119
    - o Title II: Stored Communications Act (SCA) 18 U.S.C. §§ 2701–2713, https://www.law.cornell.edu/uscode/text/18/2713
    - o Title III: Pen Registers and trap and trace devices 18 U.S.C. §§ 3121–3127, https://www.law.cornell.edu/uscode/text/18/part-II/chapter-206

- ECPA sections to obtain each type of order:
  - 18 U.S. Code § 3122, Application for an order for a pen register or a trap and trace device, https://www.law.cornell.edu/uscode/text/18/3122 (how a prosecutor can apply for a pen register)
  - 18 U.S. Code § 2516, Authorization for interception of wire, oral, or electronic communications, https://www.law.cornell.edu/uscode/text/18/2516 (how a prosecutor can apply for a wiretap order)
  - 18 U.S. Code § 2703, Required disclosure of customer communications or records, https://www.law.cornell.edu/uscode/text/18/2703 (how a prosecutor can obtain stored communications records, including via subpoena and search warrant)

21.14 Chapter questions

- Criminal procedure law is about the _____ of investigating and prosecuting crimes. (One word)
- What is a good prosecutor supposed to be motivated by, and trying to do, while investigating or prosecuting a case?
- As you analyze a particular criminal case, what are some things you should first determine about that case?
- Should cybercrime criminal investigations consider traditional crimes? Why?
- What two traditional crimes should cybercrime investigators consider?
- Name the primary federal cybercrime law (spell it out fully and provide the initialism)
- Name another federal cybercrime law that has both substantive and procedural aspects (spell it out fully and provide the initialism)
- Spend five or ten minutes reading the CFAA, and summarize your thoughts, what you learned, whether it was difficult, etc.
- List the three parts of ECPA.
- If you are a NY state prosecutor or investigator, can you charge federal crimes? Why or why not?
- Is it likely that a cybercrime could be prosecuted by both federal and state law enforcement? Why or why not?

22

Virtual Currency, Money Laundering and Cybercrime

In this chapter:

- Money laundering
- Virtual currency
- Cryptocurrency

22.1 Why money laundering

Money laundering is a requirement for successful criminals—including cybercriminals—because they earn a lot of money through illegal activity. They need to launder their money, or they will be caught and unable to enjoy the fruits of their crime.

Money laundering investigations and controls are needed to prevent criminals from profiting from their crimes. If we allow them to use the financial system with impunity, then they reap the rewards of their crime and corrupt our systems.

22.2 Money laundering as a crime (recap)[329]

The crime of money laundering is generally committed when these elements are done by an individual:

- Funds are *criminal proceeds* (earned through criminal activity)
- Defendant had *knowledge* they are criminal proceeds
- *Transactions* occur *to disguise* ownership, source, or destination of the criminal proceeds.

---

[329] In Chapter 20 we covered substantive criminal laws, including money laundering.

Check the relevant criminal statute for the exact definition. Surprisingly, it was not until 1986 that the U.S. created money laundering criminal statutes.

22.3 Financial regulation (preview)[330]

The financial system is regulated to protect it in general, including to prevent its use for crime and money laundering, and to protect consumers and investors. These regulations existed before cybercrime and virtual currency and apply to these newer developments as well.

There is significant regulation for anti-money laundering (AML) and counter terrorist financing (CTF), a significant compliance area for financial institutions.

22.4 Cybercrime investigations must follow the money

Most cybercrime is done for profit. Out of greed. To make money. Most cybercrime involves the transfer of funds, as they are stolen, used to pay for cybercrime related goods or services, or for other reasons.

Therefore, cybercrime investigators must follow the money.

Sometimes the digital traces can be hard to follow. They are important leads and clues, but are challenging, and often it is impossible to follow these traces to all the criminals involved.

The financial flow of illicit profits eventually goes to guilty parties because that is their business and how they make money. The financial movement should always be followed and analyzed where possible.

22.5 Money laundering as a typology

Money laundering is also a typology; something criminals do, financial institutions try to prevent, and something regulators focus on to ensure financial institutions are doing enough about it.

A main typology for money laundering includes these stages:

- *Earn* criminal proceeds[331]
- *Place* the funds into the financial system
- *Layer* the criminal proceeds to disguise the true source, destination, ownership

---

[330] More on financial regulation in Chapter 27.
[331] I add this first stage for completeness, but many skip it and start with the next.

- *Integrate* criminal proceeds into the normal legitimate means of spending and storing value.

The above stages are well suited for cash-based street crime like drugs, prostitution, extortion, and gambling, especially regarding placement of the funds into the financial system.[332]

The stages will be somewhat different for cybercrime, since the illicit funds are typically not earned in cash and need to be transmitted to other locations. Layering is always important, but the focus on "placing" cash funds into the financial system is less important.

Money laundering investigation is done by law enforcement agencies, prosecutors, and by financial institutions (who have a legal duty to have sufficient anti-money laundering programs).[333]

22.6 Currency, value, virtual currency, and cryptocurrency

Sometimes people get lost in terminology and technical language, so it helps to start with some simple categories.

- Currency ("fiat currency"), issued by a government
- Value that substitutes for currency
- Virtual currency
- Cryptocurrency
- Virtual asset.

The diagram shows these categories, and how some are subsets of the other.

Informal value transfer has existed for thousands of years, and yet we have a new twist on it using the internet that allows instant global transfer of value.

---

[332] Good television illustrations of this include some segments of the *Breaking Bad* television series. See the links in the Chapter 22 Resources webpage.
[333] *Money Laundering*, https://johnbandler.com/money-laundering.

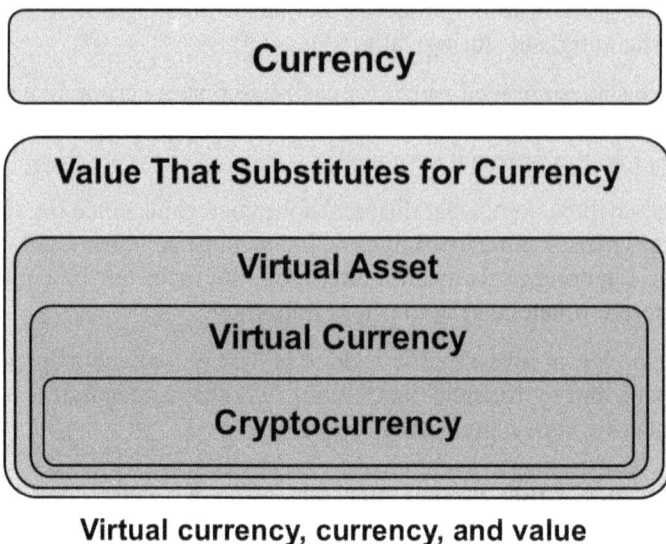

Virtual currency, currency, and value

Other terminology relating to cryptocurrency can get confusing and is not necessarily helpful for understanding how it is used for normal payments, investment, cybercrime, or money laundering.

22.7 Currency defined

Let us begin with a solid definition for currency. Governments issue and define currency.

Under 31 C.F.R. § 1010.100 (m) the U.S. defines "currency," and they essentially define it as government issued money such as U.S. dollars:

> *Currency. The coin and paper money of the United States or of any other country that is designated as legal tender and that circulates and is customarily used and accepted as a medium of exchange in the country of issuance. Currency includes U.S. silver certificates, U.S. notes and Federal Reserve notes. Currency also includes official foreign bank notes that are customarily used and accepted as a medium of exchange in a foreign country.*[334]

Currency is what we have grown up thinking is the "normal" way of paying for goods and services, and storing our value, such as in bank

---

[334] 31 C.F.R. § 1010.100 (m) *Currency defined*, https://www.law.cornell.edu/cfr/text/31/1010.100.

accounts. As we explore next, it was not always this way, and currency is a relatively new human invention.

If a method of value transfer is issued by a private entity, not by government, it cannot be "currency" because that does not meet the above definition. But "virtual currency" is a helpful term.

22.8 A brief history of virtual currency and value[335]

This history of humans and value goes back a long time. Think of these milestones:

- 13.8 billion years BC/BCE: Big Bang?
- 2 million years BC: First humans?
- ____ BC: Humans learn to *hunt* and gather, then farm, and trade and exchange value
- ____ BC: Humans learn to *trade* and exchange value
- ____ BC: Humans learn to *steal* and commit crimes
- 3000 BC: Government starts taxing people
- 3000 BC: People hide their money from the government
- 800 AD/CE: Hawala to transfer value (original Silk Road)
- 1792-1861: First U.S. coin and paper money (U.S. currency)
- 1931: Al Capone convicted of tax evasion
- 1970: U.S. Bank Secrecy Act (BSA)
- 1986: First U.S. criminal money laundering statute (state criminal statutes follow, and also money transmitting laws)
- 1996: Egold created
- 1998: WebMoney created
- 199? People start using virtual currency to hide payments
- 199? Cybercrime starts being profitable and global
- 2001 Western Express related cybercrimes commence

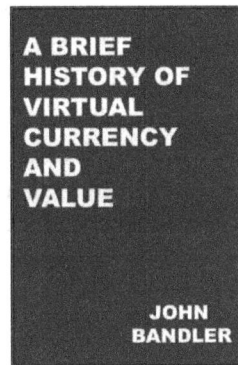

A BRIEF HISTORY OF VIRTUAL CURRENCY AND VALUE

JOHN BANDLER

---

[335] This section name is a nod to physicist Stephen Hawking's 1998 book, *A Brief History of Time*, where he explores the universe from its creation at the "big bang." It is patterned after a talk I give frequently and a related webpage. We also continue our book theme regarding cyberlaw and technology that some things may be "new," but also with parallels to what has happened before. We look to analogize and distinguish as appropriate.

- Feb 2006: Western Express I indictment by DANY (money transmitting, check cashing)
- 2006: Gold-Age Brooklyn exchanger prosecution by DANY
- April 2007: Egold prosecution by U.S. DOJ (effectively shuts them down)
- August 2007: Western Express II indictment by DANY (cybercrime, virtual currency money laundering, though it remains sealed and then partially sealed for some time)
- October 2007: Western Express II U.S. based arrest and search warrants
- May – July 2008: Arrest of three defendants in Europe
- 2008: Bitcoin invented (goes live in 2009)
- 2009: Liberty Reserve created
- September 2009: Extradition of two defendants from Europe
- July 2010 extradition to U.S. of one defendant from Europe
- 2011: Silk Road Marketplace created (with the use of Bitcoin and Tor internet anonymity tool)
- 2013: Liberty Reserve and owners indicted by U.S. DOJ
- 2013: Silk Road (Ross Ulbricht) takedown by U.S. DOJ
- 2013: FinCEN Virtual Currency Guidance
- 2015: New York regulation on virtual currencies (from NYS Department of Financial Services, 23 NYCRR 200 "Rule 200")
- Growing use of virtual currencies and cryptocurrencies as an investment
- Evolving guidance from regulators and regulatory actions on existing laws including from:
    - Internal Revenue Service (IRS)
    - Securities and Exchange Commission (SEC)
    - Commodities and Futures Trading Commission (CFTC)
    - NYS Attorney General (2018 report)
    - FinCEN (May 2019 advisory)
- 2021: Rising use of non-fungible tokens (NFTs)
- 2022-3-9: Presidential Executive Order on Ensuring Responsible Development of Digital Assets.

Today we have continuing and evolving use, laws, and enforcement surrounding transfer and storage of value.

22.9 Virtual currency and money laundering laws

In the early days of virtual currency, there *were* existing laws that applied, even as many proclaimed no laws applied.

First consider criminal substantive laws, including money laundering and money transmitting.[336] An offender could be charged criminally with these crimes. The U.S. DOJ eventually put forth a Cryptocurrency Enforcement Framework.[337]

Next, consider the rules that licensed financial institutions and money transmitters need to comply with, especially for anti-money laundering (AML) and counter terrorist financing (CTF) and sanctions. For AML and CTF, FinCEN is the primary regulatory body.[338] The Office of Foreign Assets Control (OFAC) is charged with enforcing sanctions, and they have offered guidance as well.

The NYS Attorney General put forth a report on virtual assets and risks to investors and consumers and implications under state law.[339]

Other agencies have weighed in as well, including:

- Securities and Exchange Commission (SEC)[340]

---

[336] Substantive criminal laws are discussed in Chapter 20, and some relevant statutes are:
- 18 U.S.C. § 1956, *Laundering of Monetary Instruments*, https://www.law.cornell.edu/uscode/text/18/1956.
- 18 U.S.C. § 1960, *Prohibition of Unlicensed Money Transmitting Businesses*, https://www.law.cornell.edu/uscode/text/18/1960.
- NY P.L. § 470.00 et seq., *Money Laundering*, https://www.nysenate.gov/legislation/laws/PEN/P4TXA470.
- NY Banking Law § 650, *Unlicensed Money Transmitter*, https://www.nysenate.gov/legislation/laws/BNK/650.

[337] U.S. DOJ, *Cryptocurrency Enforcement Framework* (2020), https://www.justice.gov/d9/pages/attachments/2021/01/20/cryptocurrency_white_paper.final_.pdf.

[338] FinCEN is the Financial Crimes Enforcement Network, a part of the U.S. Treasury Department, their website is https://www.fincen.gov/. They have provided advisories and guidance over the years on how their rules apply to virtual currency, virtual assets, and cryptocurrency. See their website, or a compilation of links at https://johnbandler.com/virtual-currency-references/

[339] NYS Attorney General, *Virtual Markets Integrity Initiative Report*, (Sept 18, 2018), https://ag.ny.gov/sites/default/files/vmii_report.pdf.

[340] SEC main website, https://www.sec.gov; SEC, *Crypto Assets*, https://www.sec.gov/securities-topics/crypto-assets; SEC via Investor.gov, *Investor Alert: Bitcoin and Other Virtual Currency-Related Investments* (May 7, 2014), https://www.investor.gov/introduction-investing/general-resources/news-alerts/alerts-bulletins/investor-alerts/investor-39.

- Commodities and Futures Trading Commission (CFTC)[341]
- Internal Revenue Service (IRS)[342]
- U.S. Consumer Financial Protection Bureau (CFPB)[343]
- Financial Industry Regulatory Authority (FINRA).[344]

22.9 Western Express and the flow of funds

The Western Express case gave me a front row seat to early cybercrime, identify theft, and the use of virtual currency.

There were several important participants for this:

- Identity thieves and cybercriminals:
    - Within the U.S.
    - Outside the U.S.
- Virtual currency exchangers
    - Within the U.S. (including Western Express)
    - Outside the U.S.
- Financial institutions sending funds (including banks and money transmitters).

There were also several important sources of information to establish what funds were sent, to who, and why:

- Egold records (obtained by subpoena)
- WebMoney records (eventually obtained by MLAT)
- Financial records of U.S. banks and money transmitters (obtained by subpoena)

---

[341] CFTC home page, https://www.cftc.gov; CFTC, *Digital Assets*, https://www.cftc.gov/digitalassets/index.htm.

[342] IRS home page, https://www.irs.gov. The IRS regularly reminds taxpayers that they need to report virtual currency income. *See* IRS, *Digital Assets*, https://www.irs.gov/businesses/small-businesses-self-employed/digital-assets.

[343] CFPB home page, https://www.consumerfinance.gov; CFPB, *CFPB Publishes New Bulletin Analyzing Rise in Crypto-Asset Complaints*, (Nov 10, 2022), https://www.consumerfinance.gov/about-us/newsroom/cfpb-publishes-new-bulletin-analyzing-rise-in-crypto-asset-complaints; CFPB, *Consumer advisory: Virtual currencies and what you should know about them*, (Aug 11, 2014), https://www.consumerfinance.gov/about-us/newsroom/consumer-advisory-virtual-currencies-and-what-you-should-know-about-them.

[344] FINRA home page, https://www.finra.org; FINRA, *Digital Assets*, https://www.finra.org/investors/investing/investment-products/digital-assets; FINRA, *Bitcoin Basics*, https://www.finra.org/investors/insights/bitcoin-basics.

- Other information and evidence.

All of this allowed for some important conclusions:

- Virtual currency was essential for allowing cybercrime to be profitable.
- Virtual currency allowed identity thieves and criminals to do their business.
- Virtual currency, plus traditional financial institutions, allowed cybercriminals in another country to be paid for their criminal goods and services, and ultimately receive the funds.
- "Following the money" is essential as a criminal investigation tool.

Consider that every transaction is for a reason. Every time one person pays another, that transaction usually corresponds to an equal and opposite benefit or transfer of value. For example, an identity thief pays a cybercriminal virtual currency to receive stolen credit card data, so there is value being transmitted by both parties. A virtual currency exchanger sends an identity thief virtual currency in exchange for value, such as a payment of U.S. currency.

The flow of virtual currency payments can be depicted like this:

Cybercrime and the flow of virtual currency

22.10 References

- *Chapter 22 resources*, https://johnbandler.com/cyberlawbook-resources-ch22
- *Virtual Currency (including cryptocurrency, virtual assets...)*, https://johnbandler.com/virtual-currency-virtual-assets-cryptocurrency
- *Virtual Currency References*, https://johnbandler.com/virtual-currency-references
- *Money Laundering*, https://johnbandler.com/money-laundering
- *Money Mule*, https://johnbandler.com/money-mule
- *A Brief History of Virtual Currency and Value*, https://johnbandler.com/history-of-virtual-currency
- John Bandler, Money Laundering Investigations, article within Encyclopedia of Security and Emergency Management (Springer) (Aug. 2018) (DOI 10.1007/978-3-319-69891-5_26-1)
- *Cybercrime Investigations*, Chapter 15 Financial Investigation: Following the Cybercrime Money (2020 book)

22.11 Chapter questions

- Name two of the earliest virtual currencies
- What was the first cryptocurrency?
- How is cryptocurrency a type of virtual currency?
- How is cryptocurrency a type of virtual asset?
- What year was Egold created?
- What year was WebMoney created?
- What year was Bitcoin created?
- How is virtual currency (including cryptocurrency) both similar to what we have had before, and different? (compare, contrast, analogize, distinguish)
- How is cryptocurrency (such as Bitcoin) similar to virtual currencies that existed before, how is it different?
- What current cryptocurrencies are truly "decentralized" in terms of how they are managed and governed? If a cryptocurrency has ownership and leadership, can it truly be called "decentralized" in terms of management and governance?
- "Value that substitutes for currency" has been around since about when?

23

Solving the Cybercrime Problem, Encryption, and Other Cybercrime Issues

In this chapter:

- Can we solve this cybercrime problem, and if so, how?
- "Going dark"
- More categories of cybercrime?

In other words

- This chapter is mostly opinion, including opinion about what strategies might work for the future
- Opinions are not facts and are not laws
- Assess and think for yourself

23.1 Solving the cybercrime problem

We should think how best to manage cybercrime as a country. To be clear, cybercrime will never be "solved." After all, regular crime has been occurring since the earliest humans and it will never be eliminated. Cybercrime is a more complex typology than regular crime, where perpetrators act from across multiple government jurisdictions.

Perhaps it is like how cities will never eliminate rats, roaches, or other pests. But we can and should look to manage them and reduce them, and so we should for crime and cybercrime.

Therefore, it is helpful to reframe the question to a more practical focus:

How do we manage and reduce cybercrime to more acceptable levels?

23.2 State and local enforcement of cybercrime

Most significant cybercrime investigation and prosecution has been done by the federal government. While the federal government brings a very small quantity of criminal cases in comparison to state and local governments, their cases are typically complex and involve large dollar amounts. They typically will not investigate, much less prosecute, cases that do not involve high dollar amounts.

Local (and even state) prosecutors often lack the resources to conduct large investigations, including cybercrime investigations.

We should ask what happens to all of that cybercrime that victims have trouble reporting, and if reported are not investigated because law enforcement lacks the resources? Many cases fall within a large category of being "too small" for federal law enforcement, and "too big" for local law enforcement.

Should we accept, in this cyber age, that state and local governments are incapable of receiving reports of cybercrime and reasonably acting on them?

Or should we expect that the government rises to the occasion, to develop a reasonable capability to investigate crime that is occurring, that has become an epidemic, and needs to be addressed?

State and local law enforcement should be able to receive reports of any crime committed against its residents and citizens, and then conduct a reasonable investigation into that crime.[345]

23.3 Punishment as a factor for increased deterrence?

Too often, some simply propose enhanced punishment as a solution for crime issues. We cannot simply assume that a new law with new enhanced penalties will directly translate to reduced crime.

First, we need to assess what the current punishment ranges are along with the current state of investigation and enforcement.

---

[345] The private sector has a duty to conduct a reasonable investigation into cybercrime data breaches, then report to the government and affected parties, as we discuss in Part 6. Given a private sector duty, it seems logical that there could be a public sector duty. "Reasonable" allows appropriate interpretation under all the circumstances, and doing "nothing" would rarely be sufficient.

We need to assess what the current laws are. Do law enforcement and prosecutors have sufficient legal tools at their disposal already? Is the problem not with the law, but the enforcement of it?[346]

To have deterrence, we need an ability to punish criminal acts, but this first requires the offender be caught.

The penalty is just one aspect to consider. There needs to be a risk of apprehension for there to be a chance of punishment. If cybercriminals perceive the risk of being apprehended as zero (which it often is), then it does not matter how great the penalty might be.

Put differently, we do not need extreme punishment, nor to assume that increasing punishment will reduce the rate of cybercrime. We can maintain fair punishments while seeking to increase the likelihood of bringing offenders to justice in the first place.

We start with improved investigation of cybercrime, after realizing that most cybercrimes go without any reasonable investigation.

23.4 Encryption and the "going dark" debate

The "going dark" debate was prevalent around 2014-2019 and bore similarities to the "Clipper Chip" debate of around 1994.

According to law enforcement, criminals and terrorists were now able to "go dark" thanks to the prevalence of strong encryption that was available to anyone. This encryption allowed them to escape proper investigation, even when law enforcement obtained a proper court authorized legal process such as a search warrant or wiretap. This seemed unprecedented to them. iPhones were coming with default

---

[346] Investigation and enforcement are often a decision of the executive branch, ultimately by prosecutors and law enforcement. Often their actions are influenced by the public and voters.

A trend since mid-2020 was reduced enforcement of lower-level crimes such as shoplifting and other retail theft. One effect has been that shoplifters are emboldened, and stores (for the first time) resorted to locking up merchandise at the shelves. Rather than propose a *new* law to fix this, the solution is simple—return to more steady and predictable enforcement of existing laws against theft.

Cybercriminals understand risk and deterrence which starts with assessing the chance of apprehension before considering potential punishment.

We all should understand risk and decision making for our own lawful purposes, including about cybersecurity and organization management, as we cover in Part 9.

encryption that law enforcement could not penetrate, and Apple had designed it to be secure even from Apple themselves.

This seemed unprecedented to law enforcement. They argued that they had never had containers they could not break into before. They called for the government to impose requirements that would eliminate this unbreakable encryption. Law enforcement pointed to the number of iPhones they had seized and obtained warrants for, but could not access because of the encryption, and blamed Apple for this situation.

Many disagreed with law enforcement, and the debate eventually fizzled out, at least for the time being. Strong, hard-to-break encryption had become widespread and common-place and public opinion had turned against law enforcement and prosecutors.

The debate will continue about privacy versus security for consumers, for the nation, and government investigation. Our debate should be based on facts and reason, not emotion tied to individual cases, or trying to demonize defendants or companies.

Law enforcement's arguments overlooked some important factors.

First, the encryption genie was out of the bottle. Encryption is available for criminals and terrorists, and will remain so, even if a new law attempts to make it harder for law abiding consumers to obtain it.

Second, law enforcement never has full access to all the evidence they want. That is because criminals always try to hide and be stealthy.

Third, there is more evidence and data available today than ever before. Every person, including criminals and terrorists, generates more data stored in more places than ever before. If some evidence is unavailable due to encryption, other evidence will be available from somewhere else. This may not be all the evidence the government wants, but that is the challenge of investigating criminals and terrorists.

Fourth, law enforcement has always faced a shortage of human power to properly analyze evidence, especially digital evidence. For every iPhone that law enforcement complained was securely encrypted by Apple and otherwise ready to be analyzed, there were surely hundreds (or thousands) of computers sitting pristinely in an evidence room, waiting for a qualified computer examiner or analyst with time to review it.

Fifth, Apple (and other companies) do business in many countries. There may be good reasons they want unbreakable encryption, including when other countries (who do not respect the rights of their citizens) demand that the encryption be bypassed.

Finally, consumers need quality encryption for their privacy and security. It was an unfortunate and unnecessary tactic by law enforcement to publicly demonize Apple for providing this seamless and well-functioning capability.

23.5 Categorizing cybercrime

Earlier, we provided a simple definition of cybercrime:[347]

Cybercrime = Cyber + Crime

"Cyber" means anything relating to computers, data, networks, and the internet, and "crime" means anything defined as a crime under criminal law.

Thus, when crime is committed through "cyberspace," let's just call it cybercrime.

Others have sought to categorize cybercrime further, such as:

- Cyber enabled crime
- Cyber native crime
- Cyber dependent crime.

Then, others might distinguish various types of crime by calling it:

- Computer crime
- Data crime
- Digital crimes.

The "enabled" vs. "native" vs. "dependent" terms seem to be an artificial distraction from the main issues of cybercrime. They require us to first analyze what we really mean with those terms and what they encompass. That leads to extensive discussion, debate, and confusion about where the line is between each, and why we are even trying to draw that line.

If we were to fashion laws that specify any of these categories ("enabled," "native," or "dependent"), we might guarantee a future of legal wrangling about why that law does or does not apply to a specific circumstance. Then judicial decisions might add further confusion or limit the reach of the law.

If we organize law enforcement and their investigations according to these categories, we might guarantee future confusion and friction about

---

[347] *See* Chapter 14.

whether or how certain criminal investigations belong to Unit A, Unit B, or Unit C.[348]

If these additional categories are not helpful to discuss or fight cybercrime, it seems more sensible to simply focus on "cybercrime." In many ways, cybercrime is just another type of crime, similar to the theft crimes before it.

23.6 Principles to reduce cybercrime

Here are some basic principles for addressing cybercrime.

- Improved cybersecurity is important, but we cannot "cybersecurity" this problem away (it requires enforcement)
- Cybercriminals are motivated by profit and that means they are risk oriented. If they feel they will never be caught and brought to justice, they will keep doing it.
- More cybercriminals need to be brought to justice.
- To bring more cybercriminals to justice, cybercrime needs to be investigated more effectively.
- When crime is committed through cyberspace, it is cybercrime
- Most cybercrime is ultimately just about theft
- Most cybercrime involves payments and money laundering
- The government needs to investigate and prosecute cybercrime
- Cybercrime is a fact of life, to be addressed along with regular crime
- Law enforcement (including at the state and local level) cannot simply say "we don't do cybercrime investigation." We are in the cyber age and need to move past that.
- Government's investigation of cybercrime (and other crime) requires good effort and investigative techniques
- Skills and techniques applicable for cybercrime investigation are applicable for traditional investigation (and vice-versa).

---

[348] Law enforcement is similar to other organizations, with some leaders and individuals conscious of both workload and turf. They may not want extra work, but they also do not want others to encroach upon their turf and take work from them. This can mean conflicts when cases straddle more than one unit.

23.7 References and resources

- *Chapter 23 resources*, https://johnbandler.com/cyberlawbook-resources-ch23
- *Solving the cybercrime problem*, https://johnbandler.com/solving-the-cybercrime-problem/ (Reuters article available on my website in PDF format),
- *Addressing cybercrime properly*, https://johnbandler.com/addressing-cybercrime-properly/
- *Cybercrime Investigations* (2020 book)

23.8 Chapter questions

- Should state and local law enforcement and prosecutors be able to do a reasonable investigation of cybercrime or is that something only federal authorities should handle. Briefly summarize.
- Assume that cybercriminals are motivated by principles of risk, which means they consider the likelihood of being caught, and then the potential punishment if they are caught. Assume there is zero chance that they will be caught, and they know this. Would it matter what the punishment might be? Explain.
- If law enforcement does not investigate a particular cybercrime, for whatever reason, what effect does that have on the solve rate and deterrence?
- How might cybercrime statistics underreport the actual number of cybercrimes committed against victims in this country?
- Do press releases showing that law enforcement is bringing some excellent cases against cybercriminals establish anything about the rate of prosecutions versus criminal conduct?

John T. Bandler

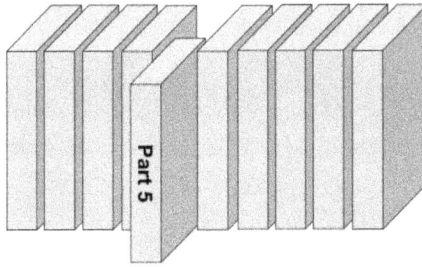

Part 5

Civil Cyberlaw I: Traditional Civil Law Applied to Cyberspace

In this part:

- Intentional torts (wrongs)
- Negligent torts (wrongs)
- Contract
- Regulation and sector specific laws
- Intellectual property law

In other words:

- Law has been around a long time, and it still applies even though we now do everything using computers and the internet.

John T. Bandler

24

Intentional Torts (Wrongs)

In this chapter:

- Intentional torts introduced
- Cyberlaw (and cybercrime) applications

24.1 Intentional tort basics

A "tort" is simply a wrong. The area of legal torts concerns cases where legal rights of one individual or entity were impacted by another.

These wrongs are addressed in civil court, between the parties (plaintiff and defendant), rather than through the criminal process.

Intentional torts cover situations when an individual intentionally did something which was harmful.[349]

---

[349] The broader area of tort law includes harms caused by negligence, recklessness, and intentional acts. In this chapter we discuss intentional torts, and the next chapter is negligence torts.

For a broader look at tort law, consider this from the American Museum of Tort Law:

Tort law has been called the law of wrongful injuries. It is the law that protects and compensates people who have been injured by the negligence, or recklessness, or intentional acts of wrongdoers. And it is the law that protects and compensates people who are injured by unsafe or defective products.

—American Museum of Tort Law, https://www.tortmuseum.org/what-is-tort-law/

Negligence torts (next chapter) involve harms that were unintended (accidental) yet occurred because someone failed to be careful enough.

Another type of tort is strict liability torts, for certain situations when the wrongdoer can be held strictly liable if a harm happens and the plaintiff does not have to show either negligence or an intentional wrongful act.

A plaintiff alleges an intentional tort by claiming the defendant performed an intentional act which harmed the plaintiff in some way. There are many different types of intentional torts, each with their own requirements. Much of intentional tort law is judge made, evolving through case decisions.

Some familiar intentional torts include:

- Assault (threatening improper physical contact)
- Battery (improper physical contact, such as hitting someone)
- False imprisonment (improperly confining someone)
- Fraud (misrepresentations that harm)
- Conversion (converting another's property to one's own, e.g., stealing)
- Trespass to land (entering or using land without permission)
- Trespass to chattels (using or damaging personal property without permission)
- Intentional infliction of emotional distress
- Defamation (false statements that cause harm, including in writing (libel) and orally (slander))
- Invasion of privacy for intruding into private affairs or improperly disclosing them.[350]

Many of these time-tested torts can be applied to cyber circumstances.

24.2 Overlap with criminal law

Many intentional torts may overlap with criminal laws because a single act may constitute both a crime and an intentional tort. Remember that the bodies of criminal law and civil law are very different, and legal cases are brought by different entities and with different standards.

Consider a defendant who intends to harm a victim, punches them and causes physical injury, while within New York. This act could constitute an intentional tort (assault and battery), and a criminal offense (Assault in the Third Degree in New York). It could have consequences in both civil and criminal courts, but the legal standard and processes are different for each.

---

[350] Invasion of privacy claims could be based upon (i) intrusion into private affairs or territory, (ii) wrongfully disclosing private facts or images (iii) publicizing falsehoods about someone (like defamation) and (iv) misappropriating someone's name or likeness for gain. For more *see* Cornell LII, *Invasion of Privacy*, https://www.law.cornell.edu/wex/invasion_of_privacy.

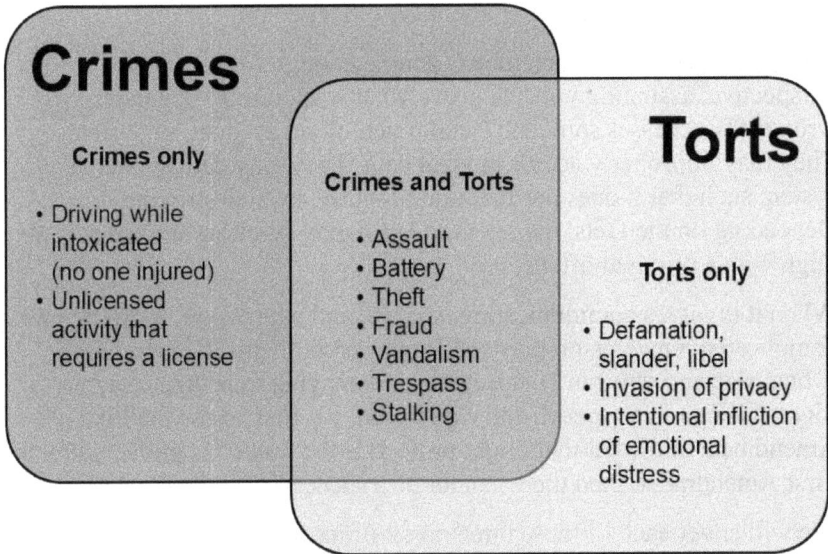

Crimes

Crimes only

- Driving while intoxicated (no one injured)
- Unlicensed activity that requires a license

Crimes and Torts

- Assault
- Battery
- Theft
- Fraud
- Vandalism
- Trespass
- Stalking

Torts

Torts only

- Defamation, slander, libel
- Invasion of privacy
- Intentional infliction of emotional distress

Crimes vs. Torts

If the victim calls the police and asks to press charges, the police can make an arrest, then a prosecutor can bring criminal charges on behalf of the People of the State of New York.

If the victim wants to bring a civil lawsuit, they probably need to consult an attorney, discuss likely outcomes and a fee structure for the attorney, and if warranted the attorney could bring a civil lawsuit for assault and battery.

Similarly, if an individual intentionally damages a computer system, breaks into a computer system without authorization, or steals money through a cybercrime, they have committed both a crime and a tort.

In this chapter our focus is the civil tort and proceeding.[351]

24.3 Intentional torts and cyberspace

There are many ways a person can intentionally harm another by using cyberspace, and they generally can be categorized as either:

- Stealing through cyberspace,
- Wrongfully accessing or interfering with that person's computer systems, or

---

[351] Part 4 covered criminal law aspects of cybercrime.

- Communicating to or about the other person.

Wrongful access or interference is simple enough from a legal perspective, assuming you can prove what was done. One person wrongfully accesses someone's computer, cloud account, or systems. They may improperly access or steal data. They may damage the IT system such that it does not function properly, even destroying it. Depending on the facts, the intent to harm may be clear, and the acts may align with a criminal offense.

When it involves communicating, speech, and expression, it can be more complicated. One person may speak or express themselves through cyberspace and that can be upsetting or damaging to another person. Since this concerns speech and expression, we first assess the First Amendment and what that might protect. If the speech is protected by the First Amendment, then there cannot be a successful civil action.

We will cover each of these three possibilities in a moment.

24.4 The effectiveness of a civil action

Law enforcement—with all its powers and resources—is not keeping up with cybercrime nor apprehending sufficient cybercrime perpetrators, so it is unrealistic to think civil law could be an effective tool for most of these incidents. Still, it is an area of law to review and could have helpful applications.

As a general matter, when an anonymous cybercriminal victimizes someone, there is typically no benefit to filing a civil suit, or even contemplating it.[352]

For well-resourced victims, including tech companies with a stake in fighting cybercrime, there may be instances where civil suits can achieve limited goals and allow actions that help mitigate cybercrime, such as the seizure of domain names or websites to disrupt cybercrime operations.[353]

---

[352] To recover funds, the offender would need to be identified, proper service of process made, and there would need to be a chance of locating and recovering assets. For most cybercrimes committed by an anonymous cybercriminal in another country, civil suits to recover damages are not practical.
[353] For example, the Microsoft Digital Crimes Unit has filed civil lawsuits to seize domain names to disrupt cybercrime, malware, and botnets. Microsoft, *Digital Crimes Unit: Leading the fight against cybercrime*, (May 3, 2022), https://news.microsoft.com/on-the-issues/2022/05/03/how-microsofts-

For some individuals, there may be circumstances where the "cybercriminal" ("tortfeasor" committing the wrong) is known to the victim, such as a former spouse, significant other, employee, or business partner. In those cases, the tort claim might be part of a broader dispute. There is a chance such a person can be identified, evidence obtained, and the person served with a civil summons and complaint. In these cases, it is reasonable to contemplate bringing a civil claim or adding it to other claims.

24.5 Stealing through cyberspace (theft, fraud, conversion)

Stealing via cyberspace is common, and most cybercrime is committed for profit. Stealing is the criminal offense of theft (larceny), and the civil tort of conversion or fraud.

24.6 Trespassing or interfering with someone else's computer systems

A person who improperly accesses or damages another's computer or computer systems may be held civilly liable.

There may be an applicable statute that specifies the elements of such a tort and potential remedies. The best example of this is the Computer Fraud and Abuse Act (CFAA) which we covered in Part 4 regarding substantive cybercrime laws, and it also provides authorization to sue civilly.[354] Further, the Stored Communications Act (SCA) and Wiretap Act may provide for a civil cause of action, meaning the plaintiff could sue a defendant in federal court under those statutes.

---

digital-crimes-unit-fights-cybercrime; Microsoft, *Protecting Democratic Institutions from Cyber Threats,* (October 3, 2024), https://blogs.microsoft.com/on-the-issues/2024/10/03/protecting-democratic-institutions-from-cyber-threats; *Microsoft takes legal action against COVID-19-related cybercrime,* (July 7, 2020), https://blogs.microsoft.com/on-the-issues/2020/07/07/digital-crimes-unit-covid-19-cybercrime.

[354] The CFAA has provisions that allow for both criminal prosecution (by the government) and civil lawsuit (by a private plaintiff). This statutory authority to sue is sometimes called a "private right of action," which means what it says—it provides a right for a private party to bring a civil suit (action).

The CFAA private right of action is spelled out in 18 U.S.C. § 1030(g):

Any person who suffers damage or loss by reason of a violation of this section may maintain a civil action against the violator to obtain compensatory damages and injunctive relief or other equitable relief....

State law, whether statutory or based on common law, will probably allow for similar lawsuits.

Consider these scenarios which arise periodically:

- Person A illegally accesses and steals business data from Company B, to use for their own business.
- Person A illegally accesses and damages the computer system of Company B.
- Person A illegally installs spyware to monitor everything that Person C is doing on their computer.
- Person A illegally logs into Person C's Gmail account, reviews everything in there, downloads a copy.

All these scenarios could be the subject of a civil lawsuit for damages and seeking a court order to delete any improperly obtained data.

Attorneys contemplating a civil lawsuit based on this type of computer intrusion or trespass might consider:

- Statutory claims under federal law such as the CFAA
- Statutory claims under state law
- An invasion of privacy claim (common law tort) under the theory it was an intrusion into private affairs or territory, or (if applicable) wrongful disclosure of private facts or images.
- A claim of trespass to chattels, another common law tort, where chattel is an old word for cattle, but is applied to interference with another's personal property. The elements of a trespass to chattel claim are: (i) intentional interference with the possession or use of personal property of another (ii) lack of consent, (iii) resulting in harm.

24.7 Delta's computer trespass claim against CrowdStrike

On July 19, 2024, many computer systems across the U.S. and the world were crippled. CrowdStrike, a cybersecurity and software company, had sent out an update in one of their cybersecurity software products (called "Falcon"). This update had a bug (error) which caused Windows operating systems to crash which brought many businesses to a standstill, including some airlines.

Once the company created a fix, the installation process was time consuming and laborious, requiring individual attention for every computer.

Systems and operations were impaired, and businesses lost money. Some reports indicate billions of dollars were lost in total—all due to this accidental failure.

In October of 2024 Delta Airlines filed a lawsuit against CrowdStrike, alleging computer trespass, gross negligence, product defect, breach of contract, and other claims.[355]

One of those claims was for computer trespass, in violation of Georgia State law. Delta alleged that CrowdStrike secretly and without authorization installed a certain type of software which was specifically prohibited by the contract. CrowdStrike had the authority to install certain software, but Delta claimed CrowdStrike violated the conditions and terms of what could be installed, and thus the installation of the unauthorized software code was a computer trespass.[356]

---

[355] We will address negligence and contract issues in the following chapters. We use Delta's complaint as a teaching example, remember it is just an allegation by one party. CrowdStrike filed their own lawsuit, which essentially denies most of the claims, and CrowdStrike will file an answer to Delta's Complaint which will likely deny most of the claims and allegations, and present additional facts.

This lawsuit provides many cyberlaw examples and we refer to it throughout the book. Since it was filed so close to publication, there will have been recent developments on these claims and the case, an excellent opportunity for additional research.

Start with my article and hosted court documents at: *Delta v CrowdStrike and the 2024 outage*, https://johnbandler.com/delta-v-crowdstrike-and-2024-outage. Relevant documents for this section include:

- Complaint, *Delta Air Lines, Inc., v. CrowdStrike, Inc.*, Fulton Co., GA, 10/25/2024, 24CV013621 (a state court civil lawsuit), https://cdn.arstechnica.net/wp-content/uploads/2024/10/Delta-v-CrowdStrike-Complaint-10-25-24.pdf.
- O.C.G.A. Section 16-9-93(b), Computer Trespass, https://law.justia.com/codes/georgia/title-16/chapter-9/article-6/part-1/section-16-9-93.
- Complaint, *CrowdStrike, Inc., v. Delta Air Lines, Inc.*, U.S. District Court, Northern District of GA, 1:24-cv-04904-TWT (a federal civil lawsuit), filed 10/25/2024.

[356] In a way, this is similar to the issue of "exceeds authorized access" we discussed in the context of substantive criminal law and the CFAA. CrowdStrike certainly had authorization to install its security software on Delta computers, but Delta claims they lacked authorization to install security software with certain features and abilities which CrowdStrike added, supposedly without knowledge or permission of Delta.

24.8 Communicating to or about the other person

Speech and expression online can cause people and businesses a large amount of stress, anxiety, and even financial damages. Some of those affected might seek a civil remedy.

When cyberspace conduct involves speaking or expressing, we assess the First Amendment and its protections. Government courts will not order a defendant to pay money if they said or expressed something that was protected by the First Amendment.

When considering speech to or about someone, consider if these torts might apply:

- Assault (threats to harm)
- Invasion of privacy
- Defamation
- Intentional infliction of emotional (mental) distress.

The tort of *assault* is an intentional act that puts someone in reasonable fear of imminent contact that is harmful or offensive. The elements of the tort of assault are essentially:

- Defendant intends to cause the victim to fear imminent harmful or offensive contact by the defendant.
- Defendant performs an act (does something)
- Defendant's act causes the victim to reasonably apprehend such a contact.

Many online threats could fall within this tort.[357]

Invasion of privacy torts could apply for threats directed at the victim, or for statements communicated to third parties. The plaintiff might seek to show there was intrusion into private affairs, or improper disclosure of private facts or images, publication of untruths about the victim, or misappropriation of a name or likeness.

The tort of *defamation* can apply if speech was false. Defamation can include libel (written speech) or slander (spoken).

The elements of a defamation claim are:

- The defendant made a false statement of fact (said or wrote something false)

---

[357] As always, just because this tort was committed does not mean it is a good idea to sue them, or to spend money on an attorney to contemplate suing them.

- This statement was published to at least one other person (someone heard it or read it)
- It caused financial harm (damages)
- If the plaintiff is a public figure, they must also show "actual malice," that the speaker was intentionally or recklessly stating something false.

Thus, truth is a defense to defamation.

Further, opinions are generally protected speech, since they are not statements of fact.

As noted, if the plaintiff is a public figure (elected officials, and more), the plaintiff must prove "actual malice," by proving the person or organization making the statement knew it was false or was reckless about whether it was false. This must be proven by a higher-than-normal civil legal standard—"clear and convincing evidence" rather than the more common civil "preponderance of the evidence" standard.[358]

Intentional infliction of emotional (mental) distress is a tort for outrageous conduct that causes severe mental distress. The basic elements are:

- Intentional or reckless acts
- Conduct that is extreme and outrageous
- Which causes plaintiff's distress
- Plaintiff suffered severe emotional distress because of defendant's acts.

In sum, an attorney contemplating civil claims will need to assess the facts and consider what claims might be applicable. Even if claims could be brought, it does not mean they should. There needs to be consideration of the costs of bringing such a claim (including money, time, and stress) and the potential benefits.

---

[358] This requirement of "actual malice" stems from the USSC case of *The New York Times Co. v. Sullivan*, 376 U.S. 254 (1964), where the Court essentially held that the First Amendment protects news organizations (and others) to report on public figures without undue threat of civil suit for accidental mistakes. This raised the legal burden for public figures wanting to sue for defamation, which gives the press and individuals more freedom to report negative facts and criticize government and other public figures.

24.9 The torts of assault, battery, and wrongful death do not protect avatars in virtual reality or the "Metaverse"

Can improper actions in the "metaverse" (and other types of virtual reality where people control avatars and their avatars interact with each other" constitute a tort?

> *What if Person A's avatar B sexually assaults (or gropes) Person C's avatar D in cyberspace? Isn't that a sexual assault?*

We can apply this question to any other fact pattern, including murders and thefts.

We addressed a similar question in Chapter 20 as it applied to criminal law, and our answer is similar here. Avatars and game characters are not people, so torts that apply for people do not apply to avatars.

We would need to look at what harm was caused to a real person, meaning the person controlling the avatar (not the avatar). We view this as speech or expression from the other user, which requires analysis of the First Amendment. We also need to assess what is considered part of the game or virtual experience, and what is outside of the experience.

24.10 Additional reading

- *Chapter 24 resources*, https://johnbandler.com/cyberlawbook-resources-ch24
- *Delta v CrowdStrike and the 2024 outage*, https://johnbandler.com/delta-v-crowdstrike-and-2024-outage (includes complaints and other information)
- Cornell LII, *Tort*, https://www.law.cornell.edu/wex/tort
- Cornell LII, *Intentional Tort*, https://www.law.cornell.edu/wex/intentional_tort
- Cornell LII, *Invasion of Privacy*, https://www.law.cornell.edu/wex/invasion_of_privacy
- Cornell LII, *Defamation*, https://www.law.cornell.edu/wex/defamation
- American Museum of Tort Law, https://www.tortmuseum.org
- Judge Peter B. Swann & Sarah Pook, *Tortious Speech in the Digital Age*, Arizona State Law Journal, 2021 (53 Ariz. St. L.J. 859 (2021), https://arizonastatelawjournal.org/wp-content/uploads/2022/02/08-Swann.pdf;

https://arizonastatelawjournal.org/2022/02/10/tortious-speech-in-the-digital-age

24.11 Chapter questions

- Analyze the *Delta v. CrowdStrike* complaint (and CrowdStrike's own complaint, any replies and other information) regarding the intentional tort claims made by Delta and summarize those claims.
- Person A's avatar AA is subjected to unwanted virtual contact, when Person B's avatar BB corners AA, gropes AA, and so forth. Discuss what civil torts might apply and why.
- When is a civil action (lawsuit) an appropriate and helpful response for intentional cyber actions? How does this compare to a criminal action?

John T. Bandler

25

Negligence Law (Torts)

In this chapter:

- Negligence law introduced
- Negligence applied to cyberspace and information systems

25.1 Negligence principles are baked into other laws and life too

The concept of negligence is included within other areas of law and should be part of all aspects of organization management and individual daily life.

Before we get into the legal details, let us focus on some practical guidance and principles.

No individual or organization wants to think of themselves or their actions as negligent. Thus, my typical advice for clients and others starts with:

Don't be negligent or sloppy.

Negligence is firmly grounded in the legal principle of "reasonableness," and this principle permeates all legal standards and rules. Individuals and organizations should be reasonable and conduct themselves reasonably and diligently. We can add to the above maxim with:

Don't be negligent or sloppy.

Be reasonable and diligent.

Negligence claims can be defended by showing that what was done was reasonable and diligent. Similarly, other claims, including newer claims relating to data law (Part 6), can be defended by showing the conduct was appropriate—reasonable and diligent.

25.2 Negligence law basics

Negligence law compensates victims who suffer harms at the hand of someone who was not as careful as they should have been. Negligence does not require intent or a specific act.

As a simple matter, a negligence claim requires the plaintiff establish:

- *Duty*
- *Breach* of that duty
- *Causation* of damages.

We can add a little more detail, and a plaintiff can recover monetary damages in a negligence claim if they can show:

- The defendant owed a duty to the plaintiff
- The defendant breached (failed to meet) their duty by being negligent and failing to exercise reasonable care
- The plaintiff suffered damages as a result of the defendant's negligence.

The body of negligence law is largely judge-made and has evolved over hundreds of years.

Negligence claims are everywhere in our civil system. Accidents happen all the time, someone is harmed and suffers damages. They seek advice from an attorney and the attorney examines whether a claim of negligence could be brought, who might be to blame, and who might have assets or insurance to cover the damages.

In a cybercrime, a cybercriminal has intentionally committed a wrongful act, perhaps stolen money or data, and then other parties may argue about whether negligence allowed the crime to happen. Before we discuss that cybercrime scenario, let's consider a few scenarios involving automobiles and premises liability, both areas of traditional negligence law that can involve criminal acts.

25.3 Negligence scenarios

We consider a few examples (hypothetical situations, or fact patterns).

25.3.1 Automobile accident 1: Negligence without any intent

Automobile accidents are plentiful and unfortunately can result in injury and death, so civil suits based on these are common. One person alleges the other driver was negligent in how they operated their car, which caused the accident and the damages. Analyzing this claim:

- Defendant Driver owed a *duty* to all others on the roads, a duty to drive safely and obey traffic laws.
- Driver *breached* that duty through negligent operation of the vehicle (speeding, not paying attention, going through a stop sign, etc.)
- Driver's negligence caused the accident and *caused* Plaintiff's injuries, which required medical treatment, caused pain and suffering, lost work, etc.

In most traffic accidents (and other negligence claims), no one committed a crime nor intended for any harm to occur. But a harm did occur, so the resulting lawsuit is based on this claim of negligence.

25.3.2 Automobile accident 2: Negligence allows an intentional crime

Now consider what might happen if a car owner is negligent regarding how they secure their car. Suppose the state has a traffic law that says not to leave the car running and unattended, or not to leave the keys in the car (some states do have these laws), an owner leaves their car running, a thief gets in and drives away, causes an accident and injures the victim.

This victim may sue the owner on the basis that the owner negligently left the car running, in violation of a duty, making it easy for a thief to steal the car.

25.3.3 Premises liability 1: Negligence allows an accident

Premises liability is an area of negligence law that can hold an owner or manager of a premises liable if they fail to meet their duty to keep it reasonably safe for those who occupy or visit the premises. For example:

- A supermarket should have safe walkways and clean spills within a reasonable time to prevent slip-and-falls.
- An apartment building should be reasonably safe to avoid accidental injury.
- A hotel should be reasonably safe to avoid accidental injury.

25.3.4 Premises liability 2: Negligence allows an intentional crime

Sometimes criminals commit horrible acts within an apartment building, hotel, or motel. A burglary and assault or even murder may occur, and the victim suffers grievous injuries or other compensable damages.

The criminal is not going to be a good source of monetary compensation because he either gets away or is identified but has no assets (this is called being "judgement proof"). If the victim desires to recover monetary damages, they will need to sue the owner or manager of the facility. They will need to establish:

- The owner/manager of the building owed a *duty* to maintain a reasonably safe premises
- The owner/manager *breached* that duty through negligent security practices
- This negligence allowed the criminal to commit the crime, damaging the plaintiff.

Now that we have examined these scenarios, we can think how there might be similar failures of information systems through accident or cybercrime events.

25.4 *Delta v. CrowdStrike*: Cyber negligence liability for accidental results

We continue our discussion of the *Delta v. CrowdStrike* civil case from the prior chapter.[359]

CrowdStrike is the cybersecurity and software company whose July 2024 software update crippled thousands of computers around the world, including those of Delta Airlines, one of their customers.

In October of 2024 Delta Airlines filed a lawsuit against CrowdStrike, alleging gross negligence, product defect, computer trespass (discussed in the prior chapter), and breach of contract (discussed in the next chapter). Gross negligence is more than simple negligence and may be alleged because a contract or law does not allow recovery for simple negligence.

As Delta laid out in their civil complaint, they entered contracts with CrowdStrike which included a subscription services agreement (SSA), and a statement of work (SOW). While Delta claimed breach of contract (discussed in next chapter), they also claimed gross negligence in the way this contract was breached, and a defective product claim regarding the Falcon cybersecurity software.

---

[359] We introduced the case in Chapter 24 on Intentional Torts. For a compilation of citations and documents, visit my article *Delta v CrowdStrike and the 2024 outage*, https://johnbandler.com/delta-v-crowdstrike-and-2024-outage.

In essence, Delta claims CrowdStrike had a duty to provide a certain quality of service and product but was negligent on these fronts.[360]

Consider that a negligence claim may allow for greater damages than a contract law claim, especially if the contract has provisions that limit damages.

25.5. Product liability

Product liability is an area of law that applies to defective consumer items. This can be negligence related, or it can be a strict liability tort.

A claim for product liability essentially requires proof the product was defective as produced by the defendant and the defect caused the plaintiff's injury.

There are four main types of product liability:

- Manufacturing defect (made defectively)
- Design defect (designed defectively)
- Marketing defect (marketed improperly, without sufficient warnings)
- Breach of warranty (express/written or implied).

This can be applied for software applications, computer hardware, and complex information systems.

The Delta complaint against CrowdStrike also alleges product defect in the security software, in that CrowdStrike supplied a defective software product which caused the damages.

25.6 Cyber negligence liability for cybercrime results

We can take these analogies one step further and apply it to cybercrime.

Consider the prevalent cybercrime of email-based funds transfer frauds, also known as business email compromise (BEC) or CEO fraud.

- Cybercriminal intercepts money and steals it, and the funds involved Victim 1 and Victim 2.
- Victim 1 alleges that Victim 2 owed them a duty to have reasonable cybersecurity practices.

---

[360] *See Delta v. CrowdStrike Complaint* Count V p. 30 for the product defect claim and count VI, p. 30 for the gross negligence claim.

- Victim 1 alleges Victim 2 should compensate for the cybercrime due to deficient cybersecurity practices that allowed this theft to occur.

There are many varieties of this fraud, and the facts can be complex. With money stolen, parties may argue about who is to blame, and lawsuits may result.

We examine the basic elements of negligence and look at the perspective of Victim 1:

- *Duty*. We look for a duty regarding cybersecurity and cybercrime prevention, and assess what duties are owed, to whom, and what standard of care.
- *Breach of duty*. We assess whether Victim 2 breached their duty, fell below that standard of care.
- *Damages*. We assess whether the breach of this duty caused the crime which caused the damages.

In any negligence case, each side will argue their points, and rarely will they agree. The judge decides the legal issues and the law, a jury would decide the facts.

25.7. Information systems and negligence

Those who build and manage information systems, and any component of an information system, need to think about negligence law.

Ideally, these systems and components are managed, supplied, and maintained *diligently and reasonably*.

On occasion things go wrong. Information technology projects do not always proceed as planned. Systems do not work properly and break. When these things go wrong, there can be inconvenience, business disruption, extra expenses, and other monetary damages. These damages could range from thousands of dollars to millions and even billions.

As the dollar amounts become large, lawyers get involved, and they investigate the facts. At least one side, and often both, will allege that the other side was negligent (sloppy), and failed to meet their duties and required standards of care.

Where parties have entered into a contract, they will also need to review the terms of the contract and principles of contract law, which we cover in the next chapter.

To recap, here are some of the scenarios to protect against:

- Negligence allowing a cybercrime to occur.
- Negligence causing systems not to work properly, causing downtime, loss of systems or data.
- Negligence that causes systems not to function as intended.

Organizations (and people) cannot make decisions and operate solely based upon fear of negative things happening, but must make reasonable, defensible decisions to plot a course forward.

We discuss this more in Part 9.

25.8 References and additional reading

- *Chapter 25 resources*, https://johnbandler.com/cyberlawbook-resources-ch25
- *Negligence Law*, https://johnbandler.com/negligence-law
- *Premises Liability Law*, https://johnbandler.com/premises-liability-law
- *Delta v CrowdStrike and the 2024 outage*, https://johnbandler.com/delta-v-crowdstrike-and-2024-outage
- Cornell LII, *Product Liability*, https://www.law.cornell.edu/wex/product_liability
- Cornell LII, *Products Liability*, https://www.law.cornell.edu/wex/products_liability

25.9 Chapter questions

- Analyze the *Delta v. CrowdStrike* complaint (and CrowdStrike's own complaint, any replies and other information) regarding the negligence tort claims made by Delta, and CrowdStrike's allegations that Delta was negligent.
- Analyze the *Delta v. CrowdStrike* complaint (and CrowdStrike's own complaint, any replies and other information) regarding the product liability tort claims made by Delta.
- List the elements for a claim of negligence.
- List and summarize the elements for a claim of negligence.
- An email-based funds transfer fraud has occurred (e.g., business email compromise (BEC)) and money was stolen. Summarize what facts might be relevant for a negligence claim.

John T. Bandler

26

Contract Law

In this chapter:

- Contract law basics
- Contract law and cyber and information systems

26.1 Contract law basics

The body of contract law has been mostly made by judges and recognizes that certain agreements can be legally enforced in court. If a party breaches a valid contract they can be required to pay monetary damages.

Over hundreds of years, governments have recognized that courts should enforce valid contracts to encourage fair trade and commerce. Organizations and individuals then recognize that they can conduct their business in those jurisdictions where contracts are enforced. The rule of law will ensure that commerce can be negotiated and conducted.

In the simplest of terms, a valid contract is formed with:

- An *offer*
- *Acceptance* of that offer
- *Consideration* (something of value exchanged).

We can layer in more components (capacity and purpose) and also consider what a civil claim for breach of contract entails:

- A valid contract was formed with
    - An offer
    - Acceptance
    - Consideration (something of value exchanged)
    - Capacity (ability to enter into a binding contract, e.g., proper age and mental faculties)
    - Proper purpose (agreement was lawful and does not violate "public policy")

- The defendant breached the contract
- The plaintiff suffered damages as a result of the breach.

Organizations enter into contracts all the time, and those contracts impose obligations. Contracts might be with vendors, customers, clients, business partners, and insurers.

An insurance policy is a contract and assumes the organization provided truthful information to the insurer at all times and requires the organization to notify the insurer when they learn of a potentially insurable event. Similarly, cyber insurance is a contract.

26.2 Traditional contract terms

The contract may cover basic contract terms that reflect value, price, and what was bargained for, including:

- Details on the product or service
- Quantities
- Duration, delivery
- Project scope, level of detail, and quality
- Price
- Payment.

Those contract terms are the heart of the bargain and deal.

The contract also needs to address how to interpret the contract, what happens if the parties disagree, and how a dispute should be resolved. Contacts may have these provisions:

- Merger clause, also known as an integration clause, says this written agreement is the only agreement, to disregard other promises stated verbally or other writings.[361]
- Indemnification clause (indemnity clause), where one party agrees to cover the other party's future losses or costs in the event of an event or lawsuit by a third party.
- Limitation of liability clause, where a party agrees to limit the liability they can seek from the other party.
- Liquidated damages (defined damages), where the parties seek to define specific damages that will be owed if the contract is breached, to avoid litigating and proving exact actual damages.

---

[361] Like the "Four Corners" legal doctrine, this means to interpret a contract, the parties (and judge) should look only within the four corners of the contract document.

- Disclaimers and warnings, terms that seek to put one party on notice of certain issues and disclaim liability on behalf of another party.
- Confidentiality, duties to keep certain matters confidential, and not disclose.
- Warranties, assertions of a guarantee of a product or service.
- Choice of law, which law will be applied if there is a dispute (*e.g.*, federal law, or which state's law).
- Location (venue) to resolve a dispute, where the dispute should be heard (*e.g.*, in which party's state).
- Termination, how the contract can end.

26.3 Contract terms relating to cyber and information systems

Every organization has computers, data, and networks. They face issues relating to the operability of their systems plus cybersecurity, cybercrime, and privacy issues. They cannot do everything in house; they need outside vendors, products and services, and those will require a contract.

For example, organizations need:

- Websites
- Email systems
- Electronic document storage (a "cloud")
- Phone service
- Internet service
- Software applications (services) to do ecommerce, sales, accounting, payroll, business operations, reservations, service requests, cybersecurity, everything else.

Most of these things require another company to run or assist, which will involve a contract of some sort.

You have entered into contracts with your email providers and social media providers but may not have thought much about it since these services are free. You accepted their terms of service. If you review that contract, you will see they [probably] disclaimed any liability as result of your use of that service. You also accepted their privacy policy, agreeing to the ways they will collect, store, use and share information about you.

Businesses make decisions about what services to obtain, how much to pay, and from who, and they will also enter into a contract.

Small organizations may contract with a managed service provider (MSP) to manage much of their information technology needs. That involves a contract.

Large organizations need to assess their information technology budget, and that may involve many large contracts with many providers. They will also need cybersecurity related services.

Any of these contracts involving cyber may need to cover areas such as:

- All the contract areas discussed previously
- Level of cybersecurity
- What happens in the event of a cybercrime or other incident or event, e.g., incident response duties, a duty to notify and cooperate, etc.
- Privacy considerations: where data is shared, permissible uses of that data, security of that data, etc.
- Levels of service, response times, down times
- Duty to have cyber insurance.

Imagine the legal disputes that could occur if information systems do not perform as they are supposed to:

- A company's employees cannot access their email or documents for an hour, day, week, or more.
- A company cannot sell its goods or services online for an hour, day, or week.
- A data breach at Company A means the data of Company B's customers was exposed, and now Company B needs to report this breach to the government and to all their customers,
- A software error from Company A causes Company B's computers to crash, resulting in lost business,
- A software error from Company A interferes with the software of Company B, crashing many computers around the world, including those of Companies 1 through 1,000.

26.4 Cyber insurance

Cyber insurance policies, like other insurance policies, are a contract between the insurance company and the insured.

Sometimes obtaining cyber insurance itself is required by another contract, where a party to the contract wants to ensure the other party has proper insurance coverage in case of a cybercrime data breach or other cyber event.

These policies impose duties on both parties. Preliminarily, the organization has a duty to accurately disclose information about the company before obtaining the policy. When the policy is issued, it states that if certain events occur then the organization needs to promptly report it to the insurer. If certain events occurred and certain damages occurred, the insurer will have a duty to pay for any expenses covered under the policy.

Some of these cyber insurance policies can be nearly 100 pages. As you evaluate the terms, consider:

- Ask the person selling the policy (e.g., broker) what is covered, and not.[362]
- What do the terms say is covered.
- What is the amount of coverage.
- What is specifically not covered (excluded).[363]
- Sub limits in the policy, meaning limits on coverage of specific costs for hardware, forensics, restoring, legal counsel, etc.
- What circumstances (events) need to be reported to the insurer.
- When reported, what does insurance cover (legal assistance, cyber investigation, first party damages, third party damages)?
- Where attorneys or vendors are paid by the insurance company, where does their loyalty lie, and to whom do they owe a duty?

26.5 Terms of service and terms of use and other boilerplate

Most websites have terms of service (sometimes called terms of use) and these are essentially contracts. They provide notice to the website and service user and serve to limit the liability of the website owner organization.

A privacy notice (sometimes called a privacy policy) may be like a contract too, stating that one who uses the website "accepts" the terms of the notice and how their personal information will be collected and used.

---

[362] If the person does not know or cannot say, there may not be any point buying anything from them. They should be knowledgeable about the terms and relative value of different policies. Of course, ultimately the policy written language controls, not what someone told you it says.
[363] A policy that specifically excludes coverage relating to a violation of a data law may not have any value as a cyber policy, since that is what a claim would allege.

These documents can create obligations for the organization and customers. Since they were written by the organization, they generally are designed to protect it.[364]

26.6 CrowdStrike outage of 2024 and contract issues

We continue our discussion of the *Delta v. CrowdStrike* civil case.[365]

The October 2024 civil lawsuit by Delta Airlines against CrowdStrike, alleged breach of contract, in addition to gross negligence, product liability and computer trespass (discussed in prior chapters).

CrowdStrike had contracts with the various companies it served, and those contracts had provisions about the service and product CrowdStrike would provide, what it would do for the client, what it would not do, and in exchange, the client agreed to pay CrowdStrike money, typically a monthly fee.

As Delta lays out in their civil complaint, they entered a contract with CrowdStrike for cybersecurity software services to be installed on Delta's computers. The contract included a subscription services agreement (SSA), and a statement of work (SOW). These documents had specific provisions which Delta claims were breached and caused damages.[366]

CrowdStrike also points to that contract in that it limits the liability it should face for any system outages or failures.

---

[364] This may be called a "contract of adhesion," a take-it-or-leave-it proposition for the consumer. Cornell LII, *Adhesion contract*, https://www.law.cornell.edu/wex/adhesion_contract.

[365] We introduced the case in Chapter 24 on intentional torts and returned to it in Chapter 25 on negligence.

To recap: on July 19, 2024, many computer systems across the U.S. and the world were crippled because CrowdStrike's cybersecurity software update caused Microsoft computers to crash, including those of Delta Airlines, one of their customers. In October of 2024 Delta Airlines filed a lawsuit against CrowdStrike, alleging many civil violations, including breach of contract, gross negligence, product liability, and computer trespass. CrowdStrike denies the claims and countersued.

For a full set of citations and references, *see Delta v CrowdStrike and the 2024 outage*, https://johnbandler.com/delta-v-crowdstrike-and-2024-outage.

[366] *See Delta v. CrowdStrike* Complaint Count III, p. 25.

26.7 Practical advice on contracts and life

People and organizations enter into contracts all the time, sometimes without even realizing it. On occasion, we are presented with a long, text heavy contract, or it pertains to a lot of money, or an important life decision.

It would be nice if we could consult a reliable attorney for advice before entering into every contract in life, but that's not possible because attorneys can be expensive.

Even when we do consult with an attorney for advice on a contract, these points remain true:

- The attorney will advise you but does not decide for you. You still need to make the decision.
- The attorney can advise of legal and business risks, but you must weigh them and decide.
- Different attorneys will give different opinions, and no attorney can predict the future with certainty.
- The decision will ultimately be yours.

Knowing the basics about law and contracts can help you evaluate the situation, the facts, and the law, whether or not you seek an attorney's advice, and how you weigh that advice.

As with all decisions in law and life,

- Due diligence is important (do it)
    o Research and investigate; especially about who you are entering into the contract with
- Try negotiating to see what is possible
- Weigh your options
- Assess the pros and the cons
- Assess risks (remember that you can never eliminate all risks)
- Make a decision.

There is no such thing as a perfect contract. The main question is the likelihood of a future dispute, and the costs involved if there was a dispute.

If the parties are happy with how the deal went, then the contract will never be examined, and any imperfections will never be discovered.

If there is ever a dispute then every paragraph, sentence, word, and comma will be scrutinized.

It is important to consider who you are entering into the contract with. If they are reliable, trustworthy, and honest, chances are better they will keep their promises, and things will be worked out even if issues arise. The contract will never be examined.

On the other hand, if they are dishonest and unethical, chances are higher they will break a promise and there will be a dispute. Then you may need legal assistance to work through that dispute, which can be costly, time-consuming, and stressful.

26.8 References

- *Chapter 26 resources*, https://johnbandler.com/cyberlawbook-resources-ch26
- *Contract Law*, https://johnbandler.com/contract-law
- *Cyber insurance*, https://johnbandler.com/cyber-insurance
- *Delta v CrowdStrike and the 2024 outage*, https://johnbandler.com/delta-v-crowdstrike-and-2024-outage
- Cornell LII, *Contract*, https://www.law.cornell.edu/wex/contract

26.9 Chapter questions

- List the elements required to form a valid contract
- Review a contract you entered into recently. What did you learn (don't share anything confidential).
- Review a contract or terms of service for an internet service you used, and that you agreed to (LinkedIn, Gmail, Instagram, etc.). What did you learn?
- Analyze the *Delta v. CrowdStrike* complaint (and CrowdStrike's own complaint, any replies and other information) regarding Delta's breach of contract claims.
- How might a contract between two parties affect claims of negligence that one party could bring against the other?
- Company A fills out an application to obtain cyber insurance from Company B, and then obtains the insurance coverage. A cybercrime occurs. Discuss whether coverage might be affected if Company A provided false information on the application paperwork?

27

Regulation and Regulatory Law Introduced

In this chapter:

- What is regulation and why it is needed
- Introducing regulation over cyber issues
- Health sector regulations introduced
- Financial sector regulations introduced

27.1 Regulation introduced (financial, health, etc.)

Certain sectors and professions are regulated and licensed by the government. This means the government requires certain individuals and entities to obtain a license to conduct a certain type of business, and the government will establish certain standards to obtain the license and maintain it.

First remember the "government" is not just a singular entity, and regulation can be from multiple places, including the federal government, state government, and local (county, city, town, village) government. This regulation could be through a "law" or a "regulation" or other government "rule."

The most prominent examples of regulated sectors are health, finance, and utilities.

Within the health sector (for example) random people cannot advertise they are a doctor and start performing medical procedures because they need to obtain education, training, and ultimately a license. Similarly, an organization cannot simply say they are a hospital and open their surgery suites, emergency room, and initiate patient care–they need to be licensed as well.

This applies to other sectors too. An organization cannot just name itself a bank or a money transmitter and begin accepting funds and doing business. They need a license too, and with these licenses come an extensive application process, then rules, supervision, reporting, and even inspections.

Governments create rules to obtain the license, and rules for operation and reporting, and the government can revoke the license if the rules are not followed. The rules may span a wide variety of topics including many outlined in this book such as on cybersecurity, privacy, and cybercrime.

27.2 Terminology: law vs regulation

The terms "law" and "regulation" are sometimes used with different meanings which can cause confusion. When we say an organization or sector is "regulated" that can have its own meaning too. For this book, consider these meanings:

- "Law" as a concept: The body of government issued rules, to include constitutions, laws, regulations, and court decisions.
- "Law" as a specific individual thing: A duly enacted law, such as a statute, passed by the legislature, signed by the executive (president or governor).
- "Regulation": A government rule put forth by a regulatory body, usually under the authority of a statutory law.[367]
- "Legal requirements": A broader term to assess what an organization's obligations are, and which could come from a law, regulation, or contract.
- "Regulated sector": a sector that is regulated by the government, where the government has special rules for it, requires licenses, etc. Examples include health, finance, education, utilities, and more.
- "Regulator": The governmental entity responsible for enforcing a regulation or law. Sometimes this refers to a regulated sector, sometimes not.
- "Regulatory type": A governmental entity responsible for enforcing a regulation or law, though not necessarily a regulator for a regulated sector. For example, a state attorney general might enforce data breach notification laws, even for entities that

---

[367] For example, regulations may be issued by regulators such as the Federal Trade Commission or Department of Health and Human Services. Federal rules and regulations are generally in the Code of Federal Regulations (C.F.R.). Cornell LII has all these CFRs at https://www.law.cornell.edu/cfr/text.

might not be in a "regulated" sector. These entities still need to comply with a wide variety of regulations and laws.

27.3 Analyzing regulations

As we analyze a particular regulation, some helpful questions to consider include:

- Is the regulation federal or state?
- What is the citation for the regulation and where can we find it?
- Who enforces this regulation? (who is the regulator?)
- Who does the regulation apply to? (what types of organizations does it apply to?)
- Is the regulation based upon a statutory law? What law?

As we assess what legal requirements a particular organization needs to comply with, we need to assess what the organization's business is, what sector they are in, and so forth. We want to ask and evaluate:

- What is their business and sector?
- Where are they located and where are their customers located?
- Are they in a "regulated" sector that requires a license to operate? Who issues the license, do they have a designated "regulator"?
- What federal laws and regulations might apply? List and cite them, and who enforces them.
- What state laws and regulations might apply, and for which states? List and cite them, and who enforces them.

A single organization might have multiple regulators, on a variety of topic areas.

27.4 Health sector laws and regulations (preview)[368]

The health sector is regulated and for good reason. We want our health care system to be strong, we want good health care, we want our doctors and nurses to be properly trained and licensed, and our private information protected.

The government at the federal and state levels has a strong interest in building and maintaining standards for health care, to [try] ensure quality health care, maintain this critical infrastructure, and protect patients.

---

[368] These are covered more in Part 6.

The most basic regulatory requirement is licensure: requiring the individual or organization to obtain a license before they perform work.

Physicians are required to have a license (from their state) to practice medicine. Hospitals need a license from their state to be a hospital. Hospitals have a duty to ensure the physicians and other medical professionals that work within their facilities have the appropriate license. With these licenses come an enormous number of requirements and qualifications for the practice of medicine.

Some of those requirements are relevant to this book because they relate to cybersecurity and privacy. It is important to keep confidential patient medical and financial information confidential, and to respect their privacy.

A significant cybersecurity and privacy law is the Health Insurance Portability and Accountability Act (HIPAA) of 1996.[369] This created new requirements and directed the regulator, the U.S. Department of Health and Human Services (HHS) to create more detailed rules (regulations) and enforce them. HHS did, and these are known as the Privacy Rule, Security Rule, and Breach Notification Rule. More in Part 6.

27.5 Financial sector laws and regulations

27.5.1 financial regulation purpose

Financial regulation and the financial sector deserve special attention in this book. There are close connections to cybercrime, to more recent technology products such as virtual currency, cryptocurrency, and virtual assets, and because financial institutions hold massive amounts of consumer data.

The financial sector is heavily regulated on many topics including cybersecurity to ensure the safety and soundness of a financial institution, protect consumers and prevent cybercrime. This regulation is administered through several federal laws, regulations, and regulators. States also have their own rules.

We want to protect banks, consumers, and investors. Rules may seek to address:

- Financial crime, to reduce theft (whether against the individual consumer or the financial institution itself)

---

[369] HIPAA has been amended over the years, including by the 2009 Health Information Technology for Economic and Clinical Health Act (HITECH).

- Investment related fraud (to ensure a level playing field)
- Consumer privacy to reduce improper use of personal information for marketing purposes
- Consumer privacy to protect their private information from being breached by cybercriminals
- General protection of the financial sector and ensure it is safe, sound, and resilient.

We consider these four areas of regulation:

- Regulation for safety and soundness
- Regulation to detect and report crime, including cybercrime
- Regulation to protect consumers and investors from fraud and other risks (including about payments and investments)
- Regulations to protect consumer data and cybersecurity and privacy (data law).

27.5.2. Types of financial entities and transactions

The financial sector is enormous and important. It includes many different types of entities, products, and services, including

- Banks
- Credit unions
- Mortgage companies
- Money transmitters
- Investment companies
- Payment methods
- Value storage methods
- Investment methods
- More.

27.5.3 Safety and soundness regulation

We need our financial system as a whole to be "safe and sound." If it were to collapse or disintegrate, the damage to our country would be unfathomable. It is considered part of U.S. "critical infrastructure" that requires special protection.

We need individual financial institutions (banks) to be reliable. A single bank failure is disruptive for those directly affected consumers and the financial system as a whole.

Over the course of this country's history, including bank failures of the Great Depression and many incidents since then, a regulatory framework has developed. On the one hand, the government provides some insurance for certain bank accounts (FDIC deposit insurance), to ensure that account holders will not lose all their money if the bank fails.

On the other hand, the government imposes rules on the banks and inspects them to help ensure that they do not fail in the first place.

This oversight includes their information technology systems and their cybersecurity.[370] The bank's IT systems must be protected from failure (which would cause operations to come to a halt) and to prevent theft, unauthorized transfers, and manipulation of account balances and other records. There are requirements and assessments and reviews to ensure those systems are secure and resilient.

27.5.4. Anti-money laundering (AML) laws and regulations

Cybercriminals need to transfer value and launder value.[371] They want to steal money, earn illicit profits, transfer it and launder it.

Money laundering is basically disguising the source, destination, or ownership of funds.

One of the aims of financial regulation is anti-money laundering (AML). The goal is to detect criminal activity and money laundering. With that is the similar goal of counter terrorist financing (CTF); to detect funds that are being sent to terrorists or used by terrorists.

We want to prevent criminals and money launderers from using our financial system to reap the rewards of their illegal activities, and from committing crimes while using it.

These laws and principles for AML and CTF existed before virtual currency and cryptocurrency and continue to apply in these newer areas.

The main AML and CTF regulator is the Financial Crimes Enforcement Network (FinCEN), an arm of the U.S. Treasury Department.[372] They issue guidance and receive the reports filed by banks and other financial institutions. There are an array of AML related laws and regulations requiring financial institutions to maintain an AML program which

---

[370] Because there are so many different federal financial regulators, they created an organization to standardize across the regulators, that is the Federal Financial Institutions Examination Council (FFIEC), whose website is https://www.ffiec.gov. They have an IT Examination Handbook, and a new website for that at https://ithandbook.ffiec.gov.

[371] *See* Chapter 22, and *Money Laundering*, https://johnbandler.com/money-laundering.

[372] FinCEN's website is https://www.fincen.gov.

includes monitoring of customers and transactions and reporting suspicious activity to FinCEN.[373]

27.5.5 Investing and trading

Regulation has developed to try provide a fair investment arena for all investors. The rules are not intended to guarantee success but are designed to create a "level playing field" so that some do not have an unfair advantage or commit fraud.

A main principle of investing is "buy low, sell high." This means investors try to assess the present value and predict whether the future value will be higher or lower.

It would be unfair to present false information to investors to gain their investment in a company or product—to trick them into thinking something was more valuable than it really was.

Some companies and commodities[374] are publicly traded, such as being listed on the New York Stock Exchange (NYSE), Nasdaq, New York Mercantile Exchange (NYMEX), and others. This trading activity is supposed to be based on public information, with each buyer and seller attempting to assess present value and future value.

It would be unfair if a person acted on non-public insider information to trade a stock or commodity; if they knew secret information that will cause the price of something to go up or down in the future.

Investor protection laws and regulations exist to prohibit this type of conduct, to reduce market manipulation and investor fraud.

These laws and regulations will apply to newer products such as virtual currency, virtual assets, cryptocurrency, crypto assets, non-fungible tokens (NFT) and whatever new invention, terminology, or fad arises.[375]

---

[373] Terms you may hear that are part of a solid AML program are "know your customer" (KYC), customer due diligence (CDD), transaction monitoring, the filing of reports when required such as currency transaction reports (CTR) and suspicious activity reports (SAR).
[374] Commodities include gold, silver, agricultural products, energy, and more
[375] Investor protection regulators include:
- Securities and Exchange Commission (SEC), https://www.sec.gov.
- Commodities and Futures Trading Commission (CFTC), https://www.cftc.gov.

27.5.6 Other crime prevention and detection and consumer protection

Other rules that may apply to the financial sector include:

- Federal Trade Commission Act (FTC Act) to protect against unfair or deceptive trade practices[376]
- Red Flags Rule to protect and report on identity theft[377]
- Consumer credit protection laws.[378]

27.5.7 Data laws for consumer data (preview)[379]

Given the importance of cybersecurity and privacy a regulator will create rules for it including the following:

- Requirements to prevent and detect theft and cybercrime
- Privacy rights for transparency, notice, and choice about how consumer data is collected, used, and shared
- Cybersecurity requirements to protect consumer data from breach

---

- Consumer Financial Protection Bureau (CFPB), https://www.consumerfinance.gov.
- New York State Attorney General (NYS AG or NYAG), https://ag.ny.gov.
- New York's securities law is known as the Martin Act, found within G.B.L. Article 23-A, https://www.nysenate.gov/legislation/laws/GBS/A23-A.

[376] *See* Chapter 34 and *The FTC Act and the FTC*, https://johnbandler.com/ftc-act, for an explainer and cites to the statute and FTC resources.

[377] The Red Flags Rule is intended to protect consumers from identity theft, originally found in the 2003 FACTA, then the Red Flag Program Clarification Act of 2010, then a 2013 ID Theft Red Flags Rule from the SEC & CFTC. The Red Flags Rule is published at 16 C.F.R. § 681.1, *Duties regarding the detection, prevention, and mitigation of identity theft*, https://www.law.cornell.edu/cfr/text/16/681.1. *See also* FTC, *Red Flags Rule*, https://www.ftc.gov/business-guidance/privacy-security/red-flags-rule; FTC, *Identity Theft*, https://consumer.ftc.gov/features/identity-theft.

[378] Credit protection laws include The Fair Credit Reporting Act of 1970 (FCRA), as amended periodically including by The Fair and Accurate Credit Transactions Act of 2003 (FACTA). This provides privacy rights to consumers and seeks to ensure accuracy of credit reports and protect against identity theft. FACTA is found at 15 U.S.C. §1681 et seq, https://www.law.cornell.edu/uscode/text/15/chapter-41. *See also* FTC, *FACTA*, https://www.ftc.gov/legal-library/browse/statutes/fair-accurate-credit-transactions-act-2003; FTC, *FCRA*, https://www.ftc.gov/legal-library/browse/statutes/fair-credit-reporting-act.

[379] More on this in Part 6.

- Breach notification requirements to notify consumers and the regulator if there is a breach.

27.5.8 Financial sector laws and rules to consider

- The Gramm-Leach-Bliley Act (GLBA) (also known as the Financial Services Modernization Act of 1999) and related regulations on privacy and cybersecurity.
- The Sarbanes-Oxley Act of 2002 (SOX) requires publicly traded companies to have proper internal control structures in place including with their information systems.
- The Federal Financial Institutions Examination Council (FFIEC) is a group of federal financial regulators that establish common federal standards for information technology and cybersecurity (among other areas).

In New York (which some call the financial capital of the world) there is a state cybersecurity regulation from the New York State Department of Financial Services (DFS), which is DFS Rule 500, Cybersecurity Requirements for Financial Services Companies.[380]

27.6 Other sectors

Other sectors are regulated too, including:

- Education sector[381]
- Utilities[382]
- Attorneys and the legal sector.[383]

---

[380] NYS DFS Rule 500 is found at 23 New York Codes, Rules and Regulations (NYCRR) Part 500, https://www.law.cornell.edu/regulations/new-york/title-23/chapter-I/part-500.

[381] In Part 6 we cover the Family Educational Rights and Privacy Act of 1974 (FERPA), and education sector privacy law.

[382] Utilities are regulated for several reasons including (i) they are critical infrastructure we need to remain operational, especially the power grid, (ii) consumer protection, and (iii) consumer data protection.

[383] This is a law book so we do not want to ignore the legal sector, even if most other books would not include it as a "regulated sector." Attorneys need a license to practice law, which is issued at the state level, usually affiliated with the judicial branch of state government. The license comes with many duties, including professional competence, confidentiality, and fiduciary duties to the client. All these traditional duties apply to cyber.

27.7 Generally applicable laws

There are a few laws of general application to consider as well. They are not aimed at a specific sector and can be applied to any business in any sector.

27.7.1 Laws against unfair or deceptive trade practices

There are federal and state laws that prohibit unfair or deceptive trade practices.

The federal law on this the Federal Trade Commission Act (FTC Act) which reads in pertinent part:

> *15 U.S.C. § 45(a)(1) Unfair methods of competition in or affecting commerce, and unfair or deceptive acts or practices in or affecting commerce, are hereby declared unlawful.*[384]

This FTC Act outlines two separate improper practices that are prohibited, those that are "unfair" and those that are "deceptive."

Deceptive practices are material statements or omissions likely to mislead reasonable consumers. Unfair practices need not have any deception, but are commercial conduct that intentionally causes substantial injury, without offsetting benefits, and that consumers cannot reasonably avoid.

New York's law is found within their General Business Law (G.B.L. or G.B.S.) and reads:

> *NY G.B.L. § 349 (a) Deceptive acts or practices in the conduct of any business, trade or commerce or in the furnishing of any service in this state are hereby declared unlawful.*[385]

These principles and statutes have been applied to cybersecurity and privacy.[386]

---

[384] FTC Act § 5(a), codified as 15 U.S.C. § 45(a)(1), https://www.law.cornell.edu/uscode/text/15/45.
[385] NY G.B.L. § 349(a), *Deceptive acts and practices unlawful*, https://www.nysenate.gov/legislation/laws/GBS/349.
[386] *See* Part 6.

27.7.2 Laws against monopolies: Anti-trust laws

There are federal and state laws that prohibit monopolistic practices. Our country prefers capitalism which requires free trade and competition, so there are federal and state laws that require that.[387]

For example, the U.S. sued Google in 2020 alleging that they monopolized the internet search market, and again in 2023 alleging they monopolized the digital advertising market. In the 2020 internet search case, the court issued a ruling in August 2024 finding that Google *did* have an improper monopoly on search engine technology, and further proceedings will determine what remedy the court imposes.[388] In the 2023 advertising technology case, a trial was held in November 2024 before a judge, who has not yet issued a ruling as of this writing.[389]

Both cases are pending, so research for further developments.

27.8 References

- *Chapter 27 resources,* https://johnbandler.com/cyberlawbook-resources-ch27
- Part 6, Data Law
- *Health Sector Cyber Laws and Regulations,* https://johnbandler.com/health-sector-laws-and-regulations

---

[387] The New York State Attorney General (AG) website indicates:
The Antitrust Bureau is responsible for enforcing the antitrust laws to prevent anticompetitive practices and promote competition throughout the state. The bureau enforces New York's antitrust laws (Donnelly Act) and also has the authority to sue for violations of federal antitrust laws (Sherman and Clayton Acts).
NYS AG, *Economic Justice Division*, https://ag.ny.gov/about/about-office/economic-justice-division.
    New York's Donnelly Act is found within NY G.B.L. Article 22 on Monopolies, https://www.nysenate.gov/legislation/laws/GBS/340.
    The FTC is one of the enforcers of the Sherman Act and Clayton Act, see FTC, *The Antitrust Laws*, https://www.ftc.gov/advice-guidance/competition-guidance/guide-antitrust-laws/antitrust-laws.
[388] *United States v. Google LLC*, No. 20-cv-3010 (APM) (D.D.C. Aug. 5, 2024), available at https://scholar.google.com/scholar_case?case=14645162430275506368.
[389] This is a bench trial, meaning without a jury, so the judge will decide the facts and the law and issue a written decision.

- *Financial Sector Cyber Laws and Regulations*,
  https://johnbandler.com/financial-sector-cyber-laws-regulations
- *Cybersecurity Laws and Regulations Part 2*,
  https://johnbandler.com/cybersecurity-laws-and-regulations-2
- Code of Federal Regulations (C.F.R.) at Cornell LII,
  https://www.law.cornell.edu/cfr/text

27.9 Chapter questions

- List some regulated sectors
- List some regulators
- What are some main purposes of regulation?
- What would things be like without any regulation?
- What do you think about the current level of regulation in the country? Too much, not enough, about right? Why do you think that?
- Are there business or sectors with an interest in influencing politicians and the public about the level of regulation within a particular sector? Justify your answer.

28

Intellectual Property Law

In this chapter:

- The four types of IP law
  - Copyright
  - Trademark
  - Patent
  - Trade secrets
- This is a big chapter covering a large area of law
- For a lite version of this chapter, focus on the summary sections for each type of IP, the cyber applications, and skip the footnotes.
- IP law is specialized, and most lawyers don't practice it

28.1 Intellectual property law overview

Intellectual property is an area of law that provides legal protection to certain works of the mind and its effort. It essentially recognizes a property right in intellectual creations. This is unusual because we normally think of property as something physical.

Technology is highly connected to intellectual property (IP) legal issues. Tech creators and owners may seek IP protection for their new service or product, and that new creation may have other IP implications.

The four main types of intellectual property are:

- Copyright
- Trademark
- Patent
- Trade secrets.

Start by familiarizing yourself with those four names.

Then we can summarize each briefly:

- *Copyright law*: protection of original works of authorship from improper copying, works that are fixed in "tangible" form, such as paper, digital, or other medium. This is protection for books, articles, recordings, and more.
- *Trademark law*: protection of a brand by protecting words, logos and designs ("marks") that identify a company, product, or service.
- *Patent law*: protection of an invention for a limited time, after proper application to the government.
- *Trade secrets law*: Legal protection for certain confidential and secret information, including through legal agreements regarding non-disclosure.

IP law gives a "negative right," or the right for the owner to exclude others from using the IP. This is based on the recognition that creators need incentives and protections so they can create and reap the benefits of their intellectual efforts.

We will soon dive into more detail and how they interact with cyberspace.

28.2 IP choices we make (software example)

Individuals and businesses need to make choices about what types of IP protection they seek or not. It is common to use a combination of IP protections together.

Consider software, some of which is "open source," meaning that the creators have decided to make the underlying source code open and freely available to anyone. Anyone can see it, download it, use it, and modify it.[390]

Most computer software is proprietary, since the creator organization invested resources and personnel time to create it and keep it updated. Both trade secrets protection and copyright protection may be used to

---

[390] Open-source software is everywhere, including within proprietary software. One saying is that open-source software is free as in "free puppies and kittens," but *not* as in "free pizza and beer and soda." Meaning when you get free beer, soda, or pizza, you get to consume it and enjoy and move on. If you get free puppies or kittens, you will have lots of joy, but also many hours and years of work ahead of you. The takeaway is that open-source software requires continual maintenance!

protect this code. The code itself may have the copyright notice within it, and the company may take several measures to ensure the source code is kept confidential, as a proprietary trade secret.

28.3 Copyright basics

Copyright law essentially protects certain works from improper copying.

Copyright is a type of intellectual property protecting original works of authorship that have been fixed into a tangible form. Copyright law protects books (like this), blog posts and online articles (like mine), paintings, photographs, music, recordings, plays, computer programs, and more. Intellectual work and effort went into crafting those works, and copyright law protects them. It does not protect ideas, only what was created and affixed to some type of medium.

Once upon a time, copying books, music performances, and movies required considerable effort, and then distribution for profit was another challenge. Today it is relatively easy.

Copyright protections come from federal law which includes both civil and criminal provisions and is grounded in the U.S. Constitution.[391]

The criminal provisions mean some copyright infringers could be subject to arrest and prosecution. Generally, this applies only to those who pirate copyrighted works (often music or videos) and then sell them commercially for profit.

On the civil side, a copyright owner could sue the offender for copyright infringement, seeking monetary damages or other court orders such as an injunction.

There are two main rationales for granting copyright protection:

- Natural rights theory
- Utilitarian theory.

The natural rights theory is that creators should be encouraged to create new works (writings, music, and art) with the knowledge that it will be

---

[391] The main federal law is The Copyright Act of 1976, as amended over the years, and is within Title 17 of the U.S. Code. 17 U.S.C. § 102 is the main section on copyright law. It indicates what is protected and that the protection does not extend to ideas. *See* Title 17 of the U.S.C., *Copyrights*, https://www.law.cornell.edu/uscode/text/17; US Copyright Office, https://www.copyright.gov. *See also* U.S. Constitution Article I, Section 8, Clause 8.

afforded some degree of protection, so they can reap the rewards of their creation. A person should have a natural right to benefit from the fruits of one's intellectual labor.

The utilitarian theory is that granting copyright protection for the creator is good for society because we all benefit when people create books to read and movies to watch. There is a societal utility to encourage this creation, by ensuring the creator can reap some benefits from their creation.

28.3.1 Copyright requirements and options

There are three requirements to obtain copyright protection:

- Appropriate subject matter
- Original work
- Fixed to a medium (e.g., paper, canvas, vinyl, CD, DVD, and digitally stored works meet this definition).

Copyright protection comes automatically when the work is fixed in a tangible form of expression and meets the above requirements.

Then, the copyright owner can consider these two steps to enhance their legal rights and protections:

- Provide notice to the viewer (such as with the word "copyright" or using the copyright symbol (©), and including the owner's name and date)
- Register the work with the U.S. Copyright Office by filing a copy of the work and paying a small fee.

Think of copyright notice as a "No Trespassing" sign, except instead of saying do not enter this property, it warns others that they are not allowed to copy the work. This notice is important because a common defense to copyright infringement is the reproduction of the material was innocent or accidental.

Registration is required before any civil lawsuit can be filed. If the registration is achieved before the infringement (copying) occurred, then greater penalties can be obtained.

Copyright protection is neither without limit nor forever. The duration of copyright protection extends for the life of the author plus 70 years. Put differently (and more morbidly) copyright protection extends until 70 years after the author dies. If it is a work for hire (on behalf of a corporation) then protection is 95 years from publication or 120 years from creation. Once copyright protection expires, the work goes into the "public domain" and can be used by anyone.[392]

28.3.2 Fair use of copyrighted materials

While copyright law protects against copying, the doctrine of "fair use" means that some types of copying are acceptable and legally permissible. Fair use is laid out in in the statute and provides flexibility to account for a variety of circumstances and factors, including:

- Purpose of the use (for profit, non-profit, educational, transformative, etc.)
- Nature of the copyrighted work (factual or creative)
- Amount used (small, medium, large, or the entirety of the work)
- Effect of the copying on the market for the work (will it detract from the rightful owner's revenue).[393]

When an author's work is properly quoted and cited within an academic paper, that is an example of "fair use."

28.4 Copyright and cyber

Once upon a time, there was not as much content out there, and improper copying required a lot of work by the malefactor. Hand-held cameras in movie theaters and manual duplication of video tapes took time to make and distribute.

Now, there is content everywhere and it is usually easy to copy. Some may want their content to be freely duplicated and shared, and others (understandably) want a degree of protection for their works.

Artificial intelligence (AI), generative AI, and large language models (LLM) require a large amount of data and text train their systems. This creates complex questions of copyright. Some may obtain this data from the websites of others, sometimes through "web scraping."

Imagine a news publisher has invested considerably in their writers, editors and platforms to investigate, report, and publish news, but an AI tool has used (perhaps copied) all of these articles to train their AI systems. Then suppose their AI system output copied snippets of these

---

[392] The 1928 cartoon short film *Steamboat Willie* from Walt Disney Studios went into the public domain in 2024, 95 years after it was published. Disney still retains their trademark rights, and copyright has not expired for later works.
[393] 17 U.S.C. § 107, https://www.law.cornell.edu/uscode/text/17/107.

articles to users of the AI system. Is that improper copying which violates copyright laws?

On December 27, 2023, The New York Times filed a federal lawsuit against ChatGPT and Microsoft accusing them of copyright infringement. The allegation within their civil complaint is that ChatGPT and Microsoft used articles from the New York Times to train their AI systems and this violated copyright laws.[394] The defendants deny the claims.

The U.S. Copyright Office realizes how much material is created these days, and offers internet registration for many items, and bulk registration for certain items such as internet articles.

28.5 Trademark basics

Trademark law protects a company's brand and products from improper copying of names, symbols, or designs such that it might confuse customers. Essentially it protects against improper imitation and recognizes that companies invest in building their brand and customer base.

28.5.1 Why trademarks get legal protection

Companies expend resources to build their brands, products, and consumer base. Businesses invest in their products and services through development, advertising and building customers. Consumers want to be able to find the brands they trust and brands they learned about through advertising or word-of-mouth. Companies identify themselves through logos or words that might be affixed to a store sign, packaging, or the product itself.

It would be unfair to companies and consumers if competitors or fraudsters could dress up their products similarly and mislead consumers

---

[394] *See* Complaint, *New York Times Co. v. Microsoft, OpenAI, et al.*, SDNY Case 1:23-cv-11195 Document 1 Filed 12/27/2023, available at https://nytco-assets.nytimes.com/2023/12/NYT_Complaint_Dec2023.pdf. As always, check for updated legal filings which may have occurred since publication of this book. *See also* Emma Roth, *The New York Times is suing OpenAI and Microsoft for copyright infringement*, The Verge (December 27, 2023), https://www.theverge.com/2023/12/27/24016212/new-york-times-openai-microsoft-lawsuit-copyright-infringement. We revisit this in Chapter 33 on Artificial Intelligence.

into thinking they were getting the genuine item. Trademark law gives protection to a company's brand and how they identify themselves.

Well-known trademarks include those of behemoth companies such as Kellogg's, Coca-Cola, Rolex, Apple, Amazon, and more. Businesses collectively spend billions of dollars building, advertising, and protecting their brands.

28.5.2 Trademark law is mostly federal

Trademark protection comes mostly from federal law. The main statute is the Lanham Act of 1946, also known as the Trademark Act, which has been amended over the years.[395]

States also have trademark statutes, and while they vary from state to state, there is a considerable overlap with the Lanham Act.[396]

28.5.3 Trademarks and service marks are both a "mark"

"Mark" is a more precise term as there are both "trademarks" (for goods) and "service marks," which are source identifiers for services.

Again, a mark is essentially a word, phrase, logo, symbol, character, or combination of these things that is used to identify the source of goods or services. It could even be a design, sound, or scent.

There are four types of marks that can be protected:

- *Trademarks* are for goods (physical products), and use the symbol ™, or once registered the symbol ®
- *Service marks* are for services, and use the symbol ℠, or once registered the symbol ®
- *Collective marks* are for associations or organizations (e.g. "CPA" for Certified Public Accountants, or the logo for the Boy Scouts of America)

---

[395] 15 U.S.C. Chapter 22, *Trademarks*, https://www.law.cornell.edu/uscode/text/15/chapter-22.

[396] When I was a junior prosecutor, I handled many criminal counterfeit trademark cases where defendants were charged with possessing and selling products that impersonated well-known brands. A word of advice: You should never attempt to buy a genuine Rolex watch from a stranger on a street corner for $50! If that stranger is selling a watch with the Rolex crown logo on it (also known as the Rolex coronet), then that watch (and logo) is surely a counterfeit, and they are violating several laws relating to trademarks. Bootlegged (illegally copied) movie DVDs (for anyone that remembers them) might also have a counterfeit trademark logo on them, which might be prosecutable.

- *Certification marks* are used when the mark's owner intends to permit authorized third parties to display the mark (e.g. Energy Star is a certification for products meeting certain energy requirements).

Marks are often a combination of letters, words, and pictures to create a logo of some type. Well-known examples belong to Apple, Uber, Coca Cola, and their associated logos.

"Trade dress" is a product's look and feel which may be protectable under trademark law. There are two main types of trade dress, product packaging (the container or wrapping of the product) and product design (the design or organization of the product itself).

28.5.4 Legal protection for the mark and registration

A mark can have legal protection even without being registered with the government. Unregistered marks are known as "common law marks," with limited legal protections compared to registered marks.

An official registration from the U.S. Patent and Trademark Office (USPTO) adds additional legal rights. It ensures the mark is listed in the USPTO's database of registered and pending trademarks, thus providing public notice of the mark. It gives the owner the right to bring a lawsuit concerning the trademark in federal court. Also, it allows use of the federal trademark registration symbol (®). This may help deter others from using the trademark or a similar version. It also allows the owner to record the registration with U.S. Customs and Border Protection to stop the importation of goods that infringe on the trademark.

A federal trademark registration can be obtained through application to the USPTO. If approved, a federal trademark can potentially last forever, but it has to be renewed every ten years.

28.5.5 Marks need to be distinctive to get legal protection

The ability to register a mark, as well as later bring an infringement claim, may be based upon the mark's distinctiveness.

There are essentially four categories of distinctiveness:

- Generic (not distinctive)
- Descriptive
- Suggestive
- Arbitrary or fanciful.

A *generic* mark (not distinctive at all) is not registrable. As an example, I would not be allowed to trademark the word "lawyer," or "cybersecurity," and a fruit business could not trademark "apple."

If the mark is *descriptive* (describes the product or service), it can only be registered if there is a secondary meaning for the mark (iBooks and App Store describe the product, but there is also a secondary meaning).

If the mark is *suggestive*, it can be registered, and the applicant does not need to show a secondary meaning (Netflix, PayPal, Facebook suggest the type of service they provide).

A mark that is *arbitrary or fanciful* can be registered without further analysis. For example, Apple for a computer (not fruit) is arbitrary, and Frisbee for the flying disc is fanciful. Neither word has anything to do with the product or service each represents, thus making it arbitrary or fanciful.

28.5.6 Loss of trademark protection

Trademark protection can be lost by failure to renew by required dates, abandonment, or genericide.

Failure to renew means the owner let the protection expire by forgetting to renew for another ten-year term at the appropriate time.

A mark is abandoned when the owner stops using it and does not intend to resume use. A person's intent can be hard to determine, but a mark that has not been used in commerce for three years is presumed to be abandoned.

Genericide occurs when a mark becomes commonly used to describe a generic good or service rather than a specific brand's product.[397]

28.5.7 Enforcing trademark legal rights

The main standard to bring a civil claim for trademark infringement is through showing a likelihood of confusion, meaning that consumers are

---

[397] Aspirin used to be a word with trademark protection, but now is generic, and any company producing acetylsalicylic acid can call it aspirin. "Thermos" is now (essentially) a generic term, so companies can advertise their "thermos" type products. Businesses with famous trademarks (and good legal advice) work to ensure their product is recognized as a specific brand, not a generic term. That's why in my childhood I heard the revised jingle, "I'm stuck on BAND-AID brand, and BAND-AID's stuck on me."

likely to confuse the infringer's mark with the protected mark. The elements of this cause of action are:

- Plaintiff has a legally protectable mark (whether registered or not—but a registered mark means a stronger legal case)
- Plaintiff owns the mark
- Defendant's use of the mark causes a likelihood of confusion.

Whether something causes "a likelihood of confusion" requires analysis and some factors to consider are:

- Similarity of marks
- Whether both parties compete in the same market
- Whether there has been actual confusion
- The mark's distinctiveness (*i.e.*, less generic)
- Defendant's intent in taking sales from the trademark owner
- Level of consumer sophistication.

28.5.8 Trademark dilution is a claim only for famous brands

There is another cause of action that is reserved for owners of famous marks. A civil claim for trademark dilution can be brought if the plaintiff has a famous mark and shows "trademark dilution." Such dilution may take place by blurring or tarnishment.

Dilution by blurring means the defendant is weakening or impairing the distinctiveness of that famous mark.

Dilution by tarnishment means the defendant is damaging the reputation of that famous mark, by associating that famous mark with something unsavory.

Trademark dilution protection comes from the Federal Trademark Dilution Act of 1995 (FTDA) and Trademark Dilution Revision Act of 2006.[398]

28.6 Trademark and cyber

28.6.1 Phishing, spamming, spoofing, and impersonating

Cybercriminals like to impersonate companies and their brands to send malicious emails including spam and phishing emails. Cybercriminals create lookalike websites (spoofing, impersonating sites) to further their criminal activities. This is a trademark violation and damages the

---

[398] These laws are incorporated into Title 15, Chapter 22 of the U.S. Code, https://www.law.cornell.edu/uscode/text/15/chapter-22.

company's brand and reduces trust in the company. Trademark law could be one tool that an affected company uses to reduce this threat.[399]

There is a continuum of trademark infringers. Some may be conducting outright criminal scams involving theft, so their domains, websites, and their email service will be shut down one place, they will move to another, and hopefully get caught by law enforcement someday.

Others may simply be trying to benefit from brand confusion to further their own shady products or services.

28.6.2 Domain name squatting ("cybersquatting")

Criminals or unscrupulous individuals might attempt to profit off someone else's trademark (or name) by registering domain names that incorporate that trademark or name. This is known as "cybersquatting" or "domain squatting," and there some legal protections against that exist.

The trademark laws above are one tool, and then came the Anti-cybersquatting Consumer Protection Act (ACPA).[400] This provides a civil cause of action when someone registers, uses or sells a domain name with the "bad faith intent" to profit from a trademark that belongs to someone else. The statute provides additional information on how to determine that bad faith.

As a practical matter, organizations should rent appropriate domain names and work to maintain control of them.[401]

---

[399] These civil powers are small in comparison to law enforcement's tools to investigate and act.

[400] 15 U.S.C. § 1125(d), *False designations of origin, false descriptions, and dilution forbidden*, https://www.law.cornell.edu/uscode/text/15/1125.

[401] Domain registrar companies will encourage companies to rent (license) many similar sounding domain names to protect their brand. This eventually becomes costly, and companies can find themselves paying hundreds and even thousands of dollars each year for domains they might not need, and that another person or company might never use either.

It is devastating if a company were to lose the domain names they rely upon for websites, email, and other important operations. This happens through accidents, negligence, or cybercrime. Whatever trademark rights might exist, avoid putting yourself in the position where you might need to assert them to recover a domain, because that is a slow and expensive process.

28.7 Patent basics

Patent law protects certain inventions.

To be eligible for patent protection, an invention must meet certain criteria, including a proper subject matter and being new, useful, and non-obvious.

The reason why patent protection exists is the "patent bargain," in which the government grants protection for an invention in exchange for publication of the creation so that others may eventually learn from it. The government's grant is a negative right that allows the owner to exclude others from using that patented invention for a limited period of time.

Patent applications in the United States are filed with the USPTO, which requires publicly disclosing detailed information about the invention.[402]

About half of all patent applications are eventually granted, and when granted they generally have a term of 20 years from the filing date. The term cannot be extended, and periodic maintenance fees are required to keep it in force. After a patent expires, all the filed paperwork about the invention is available for anyone to use freely.

Famous examples of inventions that were covered by patents include the lightbulb, telephone, internal combustion engine, computer, global positioning system (GPS), 3D printer, and Bluetooth. New patent applications are filed daily and many of the products and services we use have components protected by patents.

Companies manufacturing items based on their patent should also consider other intellectual property protections for their process and product, including trade secrets, copyright, and trademark.

28.7.1 Patent law is federal law

Patent law in the United States comes exclusively from federal law.[403]

---

[402] *See* 35 U.S.C. § 112. Compare this to trade secrets, which we cover next, where the organization seeks to keep certain information confidential. Organizations may obtain patent protection for some parts of a product or process but retain secrecy about others.

[403] Patent protection derives from the U.S. Constitution, like copyright. Patent law is in Title 35 of the U.S. Code, https://www.law.cornell.edu/uscode/text/35. The first patent law was enacted in 1790. Our current patent law framework was established by the Patent Act of 1952. A significant amendment was the Leahy-Smith America Invents Act of 2011.

Based on a 2011 change, our patent system is now a "first-to-file" system (not "first-to-invent"). Under the previous system, two inventors might dispute who invented something first to establish the claim to that patent. Now, the important fact is who filed the patent application first, something that is easier to establish.

Patents confer a negative right, meaning a right to exclude others from doing certain things relating to the invention. Patent owners can prohibit others from the following activities with respect to their patent:

- Making
- Using
- Selling (or offering to sell)
- Importing into the U.S.

There are three types of patents:

- *Utility patents* are the most common type of patent and are generally what people think of as a "patent." This is the type of patent we have discussed up until now (a 20-year term from filing). It is the only type of patent that requires maintenance fees.
- *Design patents* are for new, original, and ornamental designs on an article of manufacture. (15-year term from issuance).
- *Plant patents* protect new and distinct plant varieties. (20 years from filing the application).

28.7.2 Requirements to obtain a patent

The requirements to obtain a patent are that the invention is:

- Within the scope of patentable subject matter (see details on what qualifies for a utility, design, or plant patent)
- Usefulness (has utility, which is a fairly easy threshold to meet)
- Novel (new)
- Nonobvious. "Secondary considerations" that help determine if an invention is nonobvious include its commercial success, whether there was a long-felt need for the invention, failure of others to achieve the invention, copying by competitors.
- Enabled (adequately described). An inventor is required to provide a written description of the invention, the manner and process of making and using the invention (the "enablement" requirement), and the best mode of carrying out the invention.

Inventors may represent themselves before the USPTO in connection with their patent application, but the optimal practice is to engage (hire) a patent attorney or agent to apply for the patent.[404]

"Patent prosecution" is the process of drafting, filing, and negotiating with the USPTO in seeking patent issuance. Patent prosecution is an interactive process (sometimes cooperative) where the inventor/applicant and the applicant's representative work with the assigned USPTO patent examiner concerning whether the subject invention meets the criteria for a patent. A successful outcome is the USPTO's allowance (granting) of a patent application. Not every application is allowed, in which case the applicant has procedural options, including appeal to the USPTO's Patent Trial and Appeal Board.

28.7.3 Patent Costs

Obtaining and maintaining a patent can be expensive. Costs include filing fees, issue fees, and maintenance fees during the life of the patent (for utility patents).

Attorney fees need to be considered too. An inventor can file and prosecute an application without hiring an attorney (or agent), but the process is complex and a layperson may not get the full protection. Patent applicants should consider hiring a quality registered patent professional to do a preliminary search to evaluate the invention's viability for patenting. Then, the applicant should consider hiring a registered patent attorney or agent to draft and prosecute the patent application.[405]

28.7.4 Enforcing patent rights

Once a patent is issued, the patent owner (patentee) has legal rights to exclude others as indicated previously. If their patent is infringed upon, they can enforce it by suing in a federal district court (a federal trial court). Both monetary and injunctive relief may be sought.[406]

---

[404] Patent attorneys have a regular law license and have also passed the difficult patent bar examination which allows them to be licensed to practice before the USPTO on patent matters. Patent agents are non-attorney professionals with technical training who have also passed the patent bar examination. Patent attorneys can do more than a patent agent and will probably cost more.
[405] A good attorney can advise on the risks and benefits of pursuing the patent.
[406] If the alleged infringer is importing infringing goods, the patentee may be able to bring an action in the International Trade Commission (ITC) to have the

Patent litigation is expensive, so factors should be weighed prior to filing suit. Potential expenses should be weighed against potential recovery, the costs of having infringing products on the market, and other factors.

As with other types of intellectual property, patents can be sold and licensed. Some inventors or patent owners may lack the ability or resources to "practice" the patent in a commercially viable way and may choose to sell or license their rights to the patent.

28.7.5 *"Patent trolls" or "non-practicing entities"?*

"Patent troll" is a negative and arguably unfair term that refers to individuals or organizations who purchase patents with the sole intent of suing others for patent infringement.

Some argue this practice is unfair or unsavory because the "troll" does not invent or manufacture anything, but just buys and sues for money or negotiated settlements.

On the other hand, there is no legal prohibition on this purchase or enforcement of rights. If intellectual property is to be valued, then it should be bought and sold as desired. When bought, the patent comes with legal rights that the owner should be able to enforce.

Instead of "troll," a less pejorative term is "non-practicing entity" (NPE). Universities and research centers are prominent examples of NPEs in the sense that they may generate patents from their research but not practice them.

28.8 Patent and cyber

Inventors and companies will seek to patent all sorts of inventions that relate to technology, including but not limited to:

- Software
- Cybersecurity
- Artificial intelligence
- Payments, virtual currency, funds transfer, and investing
- Anything else someone could think of.

As with all areas of patenting, technology inventors may wish to obtain the patent for a certain part of the process, but keep other aspects

---

infringing goods blocked from entry into the U.S. Unlike a federal district court, the ITC cannot award damages.

confidential (see trade secrets, next) and ensure copyright protection is maximized for other aspects (instruction manuals, specifications, etc.).

28.9 Trade secret basics

Trade secrets law is concerned with keeping information confidential, whereas other IP protection is generally for works and ideas made public.

The practical advice on trade secrets, simply put, is to keep secrets confidential and secret. If done well, the trade secrets are not revealed, and enforcement of one's legal rights is not needed.

When trade secrets are stolen, made public, or misused, that is when one side might sue another alleging a violation, perhaps seeking monetary damages and a court order to stop using those improperly obtained materials or knowledge.

Famous examples of trade secrets include the recipe for Coca Cola, the spices for KFC's chicken, and the location where the special mud is obtained that is used to rub on major league baseballs.

28.9.1 All organizations have some confidences and trade secrets

Every organization has information that it needs to keep confidential or secret. Examples include customer lists and special ways of producing products or performing tasks. To keep this information confidential, organizations should have an information security program.[407]

Some of this information is proprietary "trade secrets," which can get special protection under the law.

28.9.2 Trade secrets law is mostly from the states

Trade secrets law in the United States comes mostly from state laws, but also includes federal law. State laws stem from the Uniform Trade Secrets Act (UTSA), which is a model law that 48 states have enacted, though sometimes with modifications.[408] New York and Massachusetts are the two states that have not enacted the UTSA.

---

[407] *See* Chapter 17 on cybersecurity and information security, and Part 9 on managing information assets. Also consider that a cybersecurity program can help an organization comply with various data laws, covered in Part 6.
[408] The UTSA was created by the Uniform Law Commission (ULC), which develops many uniform or model laws for states to consider and enact.

28.9.3 UTSA definitions

Let's consider a few provisions from the UTSA, remembering that each state may have slightly different laws. The UTSA defines a "trade secret" as:

> *... information, including a formula, pattern, compilation, program, device, method, technique, or process that:*
>
> - *Derives independent economic value, actual or potential, from not being generally known to, and not being readily ascertainable by proper means by, other persons who can obtain economic value from its disclosure or use; and*
>
> - *Is the subject of efforts that are reasonable under the circumstances to maintain its secrecy.*
>
> *UTSA Section 1, Par. 4.*

Under the UTSA, a trade secret is essentially:

- Information that has economic value if it is kept confidential (and out of the hands of competitors), and
- Reasonable efforts are made to keep that information confidential.

28.9.4 Legal rights under the UTSA

If information is a trade secret, and was wrongfully acquired (misappropriated), then the owner can bring a civil action against the offender. The owner would need to establish these elements:

Since the U.S. is made up of fifty states there are benefits from states following a similar legal framework in a particular area of law. This allows the laws of various states to align with each other and for consistency across state lines.

It is inefficient if each state needs to reinvent their own wheel to draft and pass specialized laws, and inefficient to resolve disputes across state lines if state laws are wildly divergent.

"Model laws" are a "model" states can choose to adopt or adapt, while "uniform laws" are designed to be enacted as-is, perhaps because they are designed to achieve a standard result between states. There are model rules for criminal codes and attorney conduct.

"Uniform laws" are designed to be enacted uniformly (identically), such as the uniform rules for obtaining the presence of criminal defendants between states, which helps gain predictability for that extradition process.

- The information qualifies as a trade secret
- Reasonable precautions were taken to prevent disclosure of the information
- The information was misappropriated (wrongfully taken through improper means).

"Improper means" to obtain the information includes theft, bribery, misrepresentation, breach or inducement of a breach of a duty to maintain secrecy, or espionage through electronic or other means.

28.9.5 Federal law: The Economic Espionage Act (EEA)

The federal law relating to trade secrets is the Economic Espionage Act of 1996 (EEA).[409] It provides for criminal penalties for stealing trade secrets and a private right of action—meaning a private party can sue an offender in civil court.

It has definitions similar to the UTSA. A "trade secret" is "all forms and types of financial, business, scientific, technical, economic, or engineering information," "whether tangible or intangible" if:

- the owner "has taken reasonable measures to keep such information secret"; and
- the information has economic value by not being generally known and being kept confidential.[410]

The criminal and civil offense is committed if one "misappropriates" and "improperly" obtains trade secrets through acts such as "theft, bribery, misrepresentation, breach or inducement of a breach of a duty to maintain secrecy, or espionage through electronic or other means"[411]

28.10 Trade secrets and cyberlaw and cybersecurity

Federal and state trade secret laws require trade secrets owners to employ reasonable measures to maintain secrecy if they want protection under the law.[412]

---

[409] This is found in 18 U.S.C. Chapter 90, *Protection of Trade Secrets*, https://www.law.cornell.edu/uscode/text/18/part-I/chapter-90.

[410] 18 U.S.C. § 1839(3).

[411] 18 U.S.C. § 1839(6).

[412] This is essentially a "reasonable security" requirement. If organizations seek to keep their information confidential, it makes sense that they should employ reasonable security measures.

Reasonable security measures may include:

- Having a reasonable information security and cybersecurity program.
- Employing reasonable physical, administrative, and administrative cybersecurity controls.
- Imposing contractual requirements whenever confidential information is shared, including with non-disclosure agreements (NDAs).
- Considering other contractual requirements such as non-solicitation agreements and non-compete agreements.
- Conducting proper onboarding, periodic training, and offboarding of employees and contractors.

We can apply trade secrets to all aspects of cyberlaw and business, including

- Technology related inventions
- Products
- Services
- Processes
- Data and information
- Software code.[413]

28.11 References[414]

- *Chapter 28 resources*, https://johnbandler.com/cyberlawbook-resources-ch28
- *Intellectual property law overview*, https://johnbandler.com/intellectual-property-law/
- *Copyright law*, https://johnbandler.com/intellectual-property-law/copyright

---

[413] Consider the case of Sergey Aleynikov, who allegedly stole proprietary computer code (trade secrets) from Goldman Sachs, which we discussed in the context of criminal law in Part 4. He allegedly violated federal and state criminal laws though he was cleared of the federal charges and convicted of one of the counts in the state criminal action.

Consider how his alleged actions might have violated Goldman Sachs' intellectual property rights for their trade secrets, and how Goldman Sachs might have gone about proving that and obtaining redress in civil court.

[414] We covered a lot of complex law in this chapter. See the citations within the footnotes and see the chapter resource webpage for fuller chapter references.

- *Trademark law*, https://johnbandler.com/intellectual-property-law/trademark
- *Patent law*, https://johnbandler.com/intellectual-property-law/patent
- *Trade secrets law*, https://johnbandler.com/intellectual-property-law/trade-secrets

28.12 Chapter questions

- List the four types of intellectual property law
- Briefly summarize each of the four types of intellectual property law
- What are different ways one can obtain various degrees of copyright protection?
- Identify some popular trademarks and summarize why they meet the requirements for a trademark
- What are the requirements to obtain a patent?
- What are the requirements to obtain protection under a trade secret statute?
- How might organizations use multiple types of intellectual property protections to protect their IP?

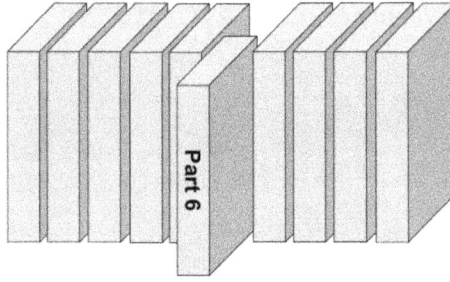

Part 6

Civil Cyberlaw II: Data Law, Cybersecurity Law, and Privacy Law

In this part:
- Laws specifically relating to "data" and "cyber"
- Data laws
  - Secure data disposal laws
  - Data breach notification laws
  - Cybersecurity laws
  - Privacy laws
- Artificial intelligence

John T. Bandler

29

Data Law Introduced

In this chapter:

- Data laws introduced
- The four types
- Their sources
- Who they apply to
- Secure data disposal laws

29.1 Data laws: why and what (recap)

The newer "data laws" were enacted to address the aspects of our new cyberworld that traditional laws could not address.

These new laws were needed because of two main issues:

- Cybercrime and identity theft
- Commercial monetization of our personal data.

Cybercrime means data breaches, and a black market for our personal data, along with all the other theft related activities. The government realized consumers need their personal information protected with a minimum level of cybersecurity and needed to be notified if their data has been breached ("hacked"). This is the rationale behind data breach notification and cybersecurity laws.

Monetization of our personal data means information about us is valuable to business. The government realized legal protections were required to limit how businesses collected, stored, sold, shared, and used this personal information. Principles of transparency, choice, and consent started to be put into law.

These data specific laws have evolved and can be grouped into four categories:[415]

- Data disposal
- Data breach reporting
- Cybersecurity
- Privacy.

Now let us layer in some more detail and explanation:

- Data disposal: securely disposing of consumer data
- Data breach reporting: report breaches of consumer data to government and consumers
- Cybersecurity: protect consumer data, and protect the organization
- Privacy: many duties of notice and choice regarding consumers and their personal information.

These are consumer-oriented laws, requiring cybersecurity and breach reporting for consumer data, and not necessarily for cybercrime that affects other parts of the organization.

Some laws are designed to protect the soundness of the organization and the sector and might expand beyond protection of consumer data to protection of the entire organization and require notification of *any* cybercrime event.[416]

29.2 The evolution of data laws

The evolution of data laws shows how governments dipped their proverbial toe into the water and then issued more complex rules over time as problems and issues were perceived.

---

[415] Here we order the data laws from simple to complex, roughly the order they evolved. Remembering these categories is a first step—our initial scaffold level.

[416] Some sector-specific laws require good cybersecurity throughout the organization and not just for consumer data. For example, by law, a bank needs to have effective cybersecurity to protect consumer data *and* to ensure the bank can continue operations since it is a regulated part of our country's critical infrastructure.

As we cover in Part 9, laws or not, good business practices suggest every organization should have a sound and comprehensive cybersecurity program for their *entire* organization and information systems, including for consumer data.

Secure data disposal laws were the first. The government stated the obvious; do not leave consumer data available for anyone to pick up, whether in the trash, on the curb, or within computers sent for recycling.

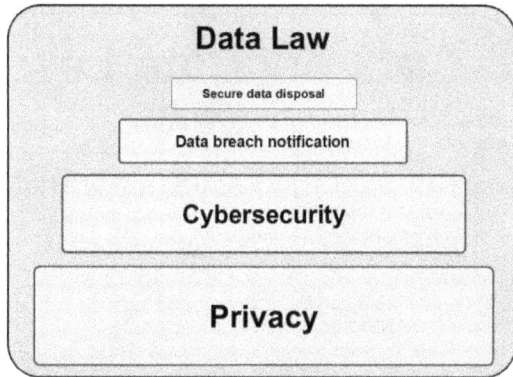

Data Law (evolution and complexity)

Data breach notification laws came next. The government realized that without a legal duty to report, few organizations will ever report cybercrime, especially data breaches of consumer data, so the government imposed that legal duty to notify.

Cybersecurity laws were next. After governments reviewed hundreds and even thousands of data breach reports, it became evident that many could have been prevented if the organization had a minimum level of cybersecurity.

Privacy laws came after that, as governments realized that consumer data was valuable and invasive such that consumers needed protection.

In sum, this legal evolution started with the simple and obvious, and proceeded towards complex. The above diagram depicts these four data law types separately which is helpful to learn about them and how they evolved.

Now it is time to realize how they overlap. First, a good cybersecurity program (and law) should include secure disposal of unneeded data. Next, a good privacy law will include a provision for cybersecurity and data breach notification.

This means if a privacy law applies in a state or for a sector, it will also have components for cybersecurity and data breach notification.

If a cybersecurity law applies, it will include a secure data disposal requirement.

We can depict these overlaps in the next diagram.

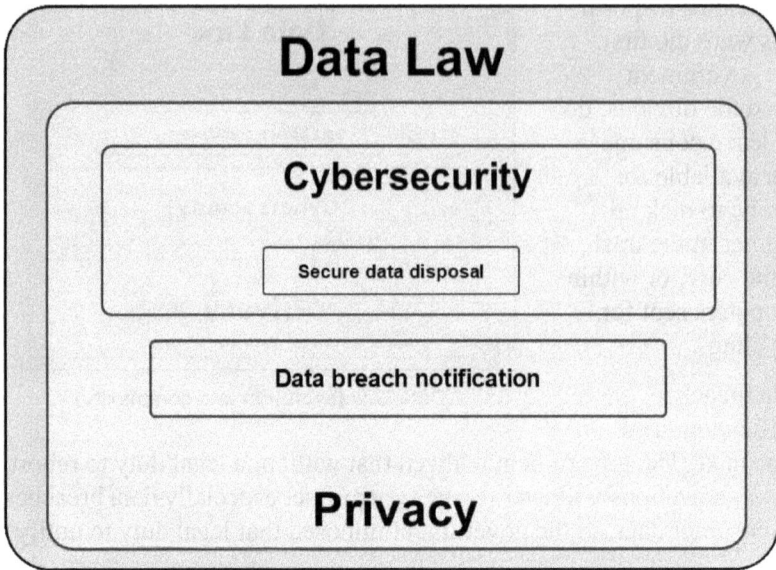

Data Law (subsets of privacy)

29.3 The sources of these data laws and who they apply to

Data laws may come from the federal government or from individual states. Some apply only to specific sectors such as health, finance, or education, and some apply generally to almost all organizations.

As we examine a particular legal requirement pertaining to data, our first question can be where it came from and who issued it. Is it from the federal government or a state government (if so, which state)?

Then we assess whether it is a statutory law (duly enacted by the legislature and signed by the president or governor) or a regulation (put forth by a governmental unit, the regulator, and identify who that regulator is).

Finally, we assess who it applies to. Does the law apply to any type of organization, or just to organizations within a specific sector (such as health, finance, or education)?

29.4 Categorizing data laws in your brain (and the book)

Let us recap some categories which can help us learn and organize this complicated area of law that is constantly evolving.[417]

First consider the four types of data laws, realizing that some laws may cover more than just one of these four categories:

- Secure data disposal
- Data breach reporting
- Cybersecurity
- Privacy.

Next consider who the legal requirement applies to:

- General application (any organization, regardless of sector), or
- Sector specific.

The last type of category is where the law came from:

- Federal, or
- State.

Finally, we need to step away from the above categories to learn about each important law, realizing it may span multiple categories, or be hard to pigeonhole. Some of those laws include:

- Federal Trade Commission Act
- New York State's data laws
- Important sector specific laws and regulations
- Other laws.

29.5 Civil jurisdiction and reach of state data laws[418]

Most states have enacted their data laws to protect residents of their state. The implication is that they can assert jurisdiction over any organization that fails to comply, even if the organization is in another state (so long as it holds the data of a state resident).

California was the first state to enact a breach notification law and later the first state to create a comprehensive privacy law. Once upon a time,

---

[417] As we categorize, remember that this is just one way to think of it. Others think of it differently, some may use different or even less precise terminology.
[418] We have covered jurisdiction in the context of both criminal law and civil law in Chapters 8, 9, and 12. These data laws are mostly civil, and somewhat unique because of their potentially long reach.

there were only a few states with significant data laws but now every state has a data breach notification law, about half have cybersecurity laws, and there are a growing number of state privacy laws. The question is:

> *If an organization is in State A and has customers in all the other states, is it required to analyze and comply with the data laws of all 50 states?*

Or this:

> *An organization is in New York and only has a few customers from California. Does it need to comply with California's rigorous privacy law?*

California's privacy law plus accompanying regulations together are about 130 pages and over 50,000 words and are a challenging read even for an experienced lawyer knowledgeable in privacy.[419]

These are good questions with complex answers. Organizations need to do their honest best to assess what laws apply to them, and then comply in good faith. We will dive into practical compliance issues in Part 9.

29.6 State data laws vs. a unified federal data law

We can look at this situation of multiple state laws and ask:

> *Does the law need to catch up? Do we need a federal privacy, cybersecurity, and data breach law that covers all these situations, so we are not dealing with fifty different state laws?*

Such a federal bill has been proposed for many years, but it has not yet become a law.

Consider our messy process of creating laws with different interests and competing viewpoints. Consider who might advocate for what type of a law:

- Businesses will generally favor weaker requirements, because it allows them to do more with the valuable data and reduces their compliance and litigation costs.

---

[419] This is the California Consumer Privacy Act (CCPA) as amended by the California Privacy Rights Act (CPRA).

- Businesses faced with stringent or conflicting state laws will favor a federal data law that preempts (takes the place of) existing state data laws.
- Large tech firms (and most companies doing nationwide business) will generally favor a federal data law to preempt existing state data laws, but only if the federal law does not impose greater burdens on them.
- While a bill is being proposed and debated large businesses can use lobbyists and marketing campaigns to weaken proposed requirements and influence legislative votes and public opinion.
- Privacy advocates will favor stronger data laws.
- "States rights" advocates might want the state laws to remain effective even after enactment of a federal law.[420]

It is reasonable to say that there should be a federal law that creates a uniform standard for important areas of data law that transcend state borders. Still, until we see that federal law and how it would be enforced, we cannot say whether that would be better or worse than the current patchwork.

29.7 Secure data disposal laws

Secure data disposal laws were the first step of data laws. Basically, they meant that organizations could not simply put consumer data on the curb for trash pickup or resell computers containing consumer data. They needed to securely delete the data to protect consumers, according to this new legal duty.

Today this seems obvious and would be the most basic part of a cybersecurity program or a law regarding cybersecurity or privacy.

Consider these egregious actions which would violate most secure data disposal laws today (and might have been commonplace before the laws were enacted):

- Discarding sensitive consumer data printed paper in the trash, without having shredded it.

---

[420] "States rights" advocates generally believe that the federal government should have limited power, with more power reserved for the states.

States rights advocacy is often not an absolute position, but can vary depending upon whether the federal or state government is acting in the way they prefer.

- A medical office goes out of business and places patient medical records in the trash or at the curb for pickup.
- Reselling computers on eBay without securely deleting consumer data within the hard drives.

Since data disposal laws require what is now considered a rudimentary security control, we do not devote a separate chapter to it. Any cybersecurity or privacy law is going to include provisions about securely deleting unneeded data.[421]

29.8 References and additional reading

- *Chapter 29 resources*, https://johnbandler.com/cyberlawbook-resources-ch29
- Keep reading through the next chapters as we cover:
    - Chapter 30, Data breach notification laws
    - Chapter 31, Cybersecurity laws
    - Chapter 32, Privacy laws
    - Chapter 33, Artificial intelligence
    - Chapter 34, Summarizing some data laws
- *Data law*, https://johnbandler.com/data-law
- *Civil cyberlaw*, https://johnbandler.com/civil-cyberlaw

29.9 Chapter questions

- List the four types of data law.
- List the four types of data law, from simplest to most complex.
- What do you think of these four categories of data law? Do you think there should be more, less, and why?

---

[421] New York's secure data disposal law can be found in General Business Law (G.B.L.) § 399H, *Disposal of records containing personal identifying information*, https://www.nysenate.gov/legislation/laws/GBS/399-H. It is essentially within the cybersecurity law also as we cover in Chapter 31.

30

Data Breach Notification Laws

In this chapter:

- Data breach notification laws for consumer data
- Why
- What

30.1 The reason for data breach notification laws

The simple reason for data breach notification laws is so an individual learns when a cybercriminal has accessed their data. This has four main justifications.

First, the consumer (in theory) learns of the breach and can take steps to be on guard for identity theft. It also puts them on notice so that they could consider other potential remedies, such as bringing a lawsuit against the organization that was breached.[422]

Second, the notification requirement encourages organizations to take cybersecurity seriously since they know data breaches will need to be disclosed to their customers, clients, the government, and public.

Third, it gives consumers some degree of knowledge about which companies might be more susceptible to data breaches to factor that into their decision making about who to do business with.

Finally, it allows the government to collect better statistics about cybercrime, the number of breaches occurring, and number of consumers affected, so the government can allocate appropriate resources for

---

[422] These lawsuits occur occasionally, may serve important purposes, and can be profitable for the law firm but are rarely profitable for the consumer.

criminal enforcement against cybercriminals, and civil enforcement against companies with negligent cybersecurity.[423]

Imagine that an organization falls victim to a data breach and consumer data is accessed by cybercriminals. The organization learns of this, realizes this information was stolen, and then considers what to do. Among the many questions they ask are:

- Should we notify law enforcement?
- Should we notify government regulatory authorities?
- Should we notify our customers, clients, and shareholders?
- Should we notify the people whose data was stolen?[424]

In a perfect world, the answer to all these questions would be "yes" because all those entities and individuals should know.

Crimes should be reported to law enforcement so that they can investigate, bring the offenders to justice, and properly understand the scope of cybercrime.

Breaches should be reported to regulatory authorities so they can assess whether organizations are complying with laws for cybersecurity and breach notification and to protect consumers.

Consumers whose data was stolen should know about the breach of their own data so that they can protect themselves from identity theft and cybercrime.

Customers, clients, and shareholders should know about a breach so they can make informed decisions about where to do business and where to invest.

In the real world, most breach reporting would not happen unless there was a law to require it, and even with the law, it does not always happen.

30.2 What is a data breach? (recap)

A data breach is when someone (such as a cybercriminal) gains unauthorized access to data or information systems.

---

[423] Better statistics are important but complete statistics will never be attained. Even with the breach reporting law in place, some organizations do not know these rules exist and some do not follow them. Breach statistics underreport the actual number of breaches.

[424] *E.g.*, the consumers, the "data owners" or "data subjects."

That is a general definition, but for the purposes of examining legal requirements, read and analyze the specific definitions within the statute.

Remember "confidentiality" is one of the three objectives of information security, and systems and most data need to remain confidential from unauthorized users. If confidentiality is compromised, there is a data breach.

Not every data breach is reportable under data breach reporting statutes. First, consider the definition of what is a reportable data breach and what types of data access trigger that reporting. Usually, it specifies that consumer data was breached.

30.3 Elements of a data breach notification law

In general, data breach notification laws:

- Apply broadly or to a limited set of organizations
- Define the type of consumer data it applies to
- Define a data breach
- Specify how and when consumers and government are notified, and what should be within that notification.

We'll address each item in turn, first with a generalization and then specifics for New York.

New York's data law is found within the New York State General Business Law (G.B.L. or G.B.S.) §899-aa and §899-bb.[425] In 2019 a law known as the SHIELD Act[426] was passed which strengthened existing data breach notification rules (covered in this chapter) and imposed a new "reasonable cybersecurity" requirement (next chapter).

As you review these definitions consider these two scenarios:

- When evaluating a cybercrime event, organizations may seek to interpret definitions and circumstances in a way that might *not* require notification. This is because reporting can lead to extensive costs, negative publicity, and potential for legal issues after a data breach.

---

[425] NY G.B.L. § 899-aa, *Notification; person without valid authorization has acquired private information*, https://www.nysenate.gov/legislation/laws/GBS/899-AA.
[426] SHIELD stands for Stop Hacks and Improve Electronic Data Security, an example of how legislators can be creative when naming their bills.

- The government brings many enforcement actions against organizations who fail to report data breaches. During those actions, the government makes their case for why reporting was required, and the organization may try to make their case for why reporting was not required.

There can be difficult decisions and grey areas about whether a breach occurred or not, with different risks and benefits for a variety of parties.[427]

30.3.1 Define what organizations it applies to

As we assess a law, we consider what organizations the data breach notification law applies to.

Sometimes the statute itself may specify or limit the reach, including:

- Organizations within a state
- Organizations holding data of residents of the state
- Organizations above a certain size (e.g., annual revenue, or employees)
- For-profit vs. non-profit
- Specific sectors.

Sometimes a certain statute only has authority over certain sectors; HIPAA is an example.

30.3.2 Define personal data that triggers breach reporting

A data breach statute will define the type of consumer data that, if improperly breached or accessed, would require notification to consumers and reporting to the government.[428]

Importantly, for state laws it will refer to consumer data of residents within that state.

---

[427] For the organization, reporting a breach in an abundance of caution, even if there is a solid argument that no breach occurred, ensures they will not have to worry about a future regulatory action. For lawyers and incident response consultants and investigators, the breach investigation and notification process are good for business and billable hours.

[428] While I think of "notifying" consumers and "reporting" to the government, this is not necessarily a universal understanding. The NYS statute simply refers to "notification" of both consumers and government.

As statutes define this data, they might use one of these terms:

- Personal information
- Personal identifying information (PII)
- Private information
- Private data
- Personal data
- Consumer data.

The term will usually have a definition with some examples of data that constitutes that type of protected information, such as:

- Data that identifies the person
- Name
- Date of birth (DOB)
- Social security number (SSN)
- Driver's license number (or non-driver ID number)
- Other Federal or state ID numbers
- Account numbers and access codes
- Biometric data
- More.

New York's definition of personal information

Here is a snippet of how New York defines this protected consumer data.

> *G.B.L. § 899-aa (1)*
>
> *(a) "Personal information" shall mean any information concerning a natural person which, because of name, number, personal mark, or other identifier, can be used to identify such natural person;*
>
> *(b) "Private information" shall mean either:*
>
>> *(i) personal information consisting of any information in combination with any one or more of the following data elements ...*
>>
>>> *(1) social security number;*
>>>
>>> *(2) driver's license number or non-driver identification card number;*
>>>
>>> *(3) account number, credit or debit card number,*
>>> *...*

(5) biometric information, meaning data generated by electronic measurements of an individual's unique physical characteristics, such as a fingerprint, voice print, retina or iris image, or other unique physical representation or digital representation of biometric data which are used to authenticate or ascertain the individual's identity; or

(ii) a user name or e-mail address in combination with a password or security question and answer that would permit access to an online account.[429]

30.3.3 Define breach or access of data which requires reporting

A statute will define data breach and could call it:

- Data breach
- Security breach
- Breach of the security of the system;

or something else.

New York's definition of a data breach

New York's statute defines it this way:

G.B.L. § 899-aa (1)(c) "Breach of the security of the system" shall mean unauthorized access to or acquisition of, or access to or acquisition without valid authorization, of computerized data that compromises the security, confidentiality, or integrity of private information maintained by a business."[430]

The statute continues with more clarifying language describing what might or might not satisfy this legal definition for a breach. Unauthorized access applies to "private information" of New York State residents as we covered previously.

30.3.4 Define reporting and notification requirements

The statute will define *who* to notify, *when* to notify, *how* to notify, and *what* should be in the notification.

---

[429] G.B.L. § 899-aa (1)(a-b), https://www.nysenate.gov/legislation/laws/GBS/899-AA.
[430] G.B.L. § 899-aa (1)(c).

In other words, if there was a reportable data breach because the defined consumer data was accessed without authorization (as defined) then that triggers the notification and reporting requirements. The statute will specify the details which will include:

- Who to notify
  - Affected consumers whose data was breached
  - Government
- When to notify
  - A time period may be specified, or it may leave some room for discretion
- How to notify
  - For consumers, options may include letter, email, phone, public notification, credit reporting agencies, and more
  - For government, it will be to a designated agency
- What information to include in the notification
  - For all, there will need to be information about the breach and what was accessed, and what the organization did and will do
  - Consumers will probably need to be notified of various rights and contact information
  - Government may get extra information.

New York's disclosure and notification requirement

The New York statute reads:

> *G.B.L. § 899-aa(2). Any person or business which owns or licenses computerized data which includes private information shall disclose any breach of the security of the system following discovery or notification of the breach in the security of the system to any resident of New York state whose private information was, or is reasonably believed to have been, accessed or acquired by a person without valid authorization.[431]*

As for timing, New York's law states it should be "in the most expedient time possible and without unreasonable delay" and suggests some factors, allows for delay to assist with a law enforcement investigation, and leaves room for interpretation.[432]

---

[431] G.B.L. § 899-aa (2).
[432] *Id.* (same as above).

The law goes on to discuss methods of providing notice to consumers and what should be in that notice, and that notice must also be provided to the New York State Attorney General and other state agencies.

New York now has a single place to report a data breach, which is then routed to those other state agencies.[433]

New York's financial services reporting requirement (Rule 500)

New York is sometimes called the financial capital of the world and has a robust regulator, the New York State Department of Financial Services (NY DFS), which issues rules (regulations) pursuant to its rulemaking authority.

It issued Rule 500, Cybersecurity Requirements for Financial Services Companies, which is 23 New York Codes, Rules and Regulations (NYCRR) Part 500.[434]

This Rule, along with the cybersecurity obligations (covered next chapter), requires financial services companies in New York to report "cybersecurity events" to NY DFS.

30.4. Other data breach reporting laws and regulations

There are many laws and regulations which may impose requirements to notify the government and affected consumers following certain data breaches.

First, if there is a law or regulation that imposes a privacy or cybersecurity requirement, then it will surely also impose a notification requirement. We will cover that type of law in more detail in a later chapter.

---

[433] New York State Attorney General, *Report a Data Breach*, https://ag.ny.gov/resources/organizations/data-breach-reporting.
[434] This is within 23 New York Codes, Rules and Regulations (NYCRR) Part 500, and can be found at Cornell LII at https://www.law.cornell.edu/regulations/new-york/title-23/chapter-I/part-500. *See also*, New York DFS *Cybersecurity Resource Center*, https://www.dfs.ny.gov/industry_guidance/cybersecurity.

Consider the following:

- Your state's law[435]
- Health sector laws and regulations (HIPAA), requiring notification of breached protected health information.[436]
- Financial sector laws, including the "Safeguards Rule" of the Gramm-Leach Bliley Act (GLBA)
- Critical infrastructure cyber incident reporting to the Cybersecurity and Infrastructure Security Agency (CISA, a part of the Department of Homeland Security).[437]

30.5 References and additional reading

- *Chapter 30 resources*, https://johnbandler.com/cyberlawbook-resources-ch30
- *Data breach*, https://johnbandler.com/data-breach

---

[435] One good compilation of laws is from the National Conference of State Legislatures (NCSL), *Security Breach Notification Laws*, https://www.ncsl.org/technology-and-communication/security-breach-notification-laws.

Your next stop is with the appropriate state regulator to see the information they provide about the breach notification laws they enforce, typically the state attorney general.

[436] *See* 45 C.F.R. Subpart D, *Notification in the Case of Breach of Unsecured Protected Health Information*, https://www.law.cornell.edu/cfr/text/45/part-164/subpart-D.

[437] Critical infrastructure includes finance, health, utilities, and more. A March 2022 law will eventually require incident reporting by all critical infrastructure. This is the Cyber Incident Reporting for Critical Infrastructure Act of 2022 (CIRCIA), which eventually will mandate cyber incident reporting to the Cybersecurity and Infrastructure Security Agency (CISA, a part of the Department of Homeland Security). The requirements are not effective until CISA finalizes their regulations. In the meantime, CISA encourages voluntary information sharing and provides an email address and phone number for that.

CISA provided proposed rules to the public (Notice of Proposed Rulemaking) in April 2024 and it is anticipated the rule will be finalized within 18 months of that, potentially in 6 C.F.R. Part 226.

Other resources include; CISA on *CIRCIA*, https://www.cisa.gov/circia; CISA *CIRCIA fact sheet*, https://www.cisa.gov/sites/default/files/publications/Sharing_Cyber_Event_Information_Fact_Sheet_FINAL_v4.pdf; Text of CIRCIA, https://www.congress.gov/bill/117th-congress/house-bill/2471/text.

- *Data breach notification laws*, https://johnbandler.com/data-breach-notification-laws
- *New York Cybersecurity Requirements and the SHIELD Act*, https://johnbandler.com/new-york-cybersecurity-requirements-and-the-shield-act
- NCSL *Security Breach Notification Laws*, https://www.ncsl.org/technology-and-communication/security-breach-notification-laws
- IAPP, *State Data Breach Notification Chart*, https://iapp.org/resources/article/state-data-breach-notification-chart
- NY General Business Law (G.B.L.) §899-aa, *Notification; person without valid authorization has acquired private information* ("SHIELD Act"), https://www.nysenate.gov/legislation/laws/GBS/899-AA
- HIPAA breach notification rule, 45 C.F.R. Subpart D, *Notification in the Case of Breach of Unsecured Protected Health Information*, https://www.law.cornell.edu/cfr/text/45/part-164/subpart-D

30.6 Chapter questions

- Provide the name and statute citation and a link to New York's data breach notification statute
- Who enforces NY's data breach notification statute?
- Where can you find information about enforcement of NY's data breach notification statute?
- Is NY's data breach notification statute civil or criminal?
- Do most states have a data breach notification statute?
- Where can you find a compilation (listing) of state data breach notification laws?
- Is there a federal data breach notification law that applies generally, regardless of sector? If so, name them.
- Are there sector specific federal data breach notification laws? If so, name them.

31

Cybersecurity and Data Protection Laws

In this chapter:

- Cybersecurity and data protection laws
  - o Mostly for consumer data
  - o Sometimes for the whole of the organization

31.1 Summarizing cybersecurity laws

All cybersecurity laws and regulations can be summarized in three words:

Have reasonable cybersecurity.

This is not to make light of them or diminish them. They are important and can be complex. Each uses different terminology, organized into different sections and categories. Some businesses or circumstances will require expert assistance, even legal advice, for compliance.

Despite the differences and complexities, the heart of all of them is the concept of *reasonable cybersecurity*.

They rarely say *exactly* what to do because that is impossible, so they align with solid principles of cybersecurity.

31.2 Why these cybersecurity laws came about

We can imagine the regulators who are responsible for reviewing and enforcing data breach reporting laws, and they receive mountains of reports on data breaches, with summaries of how they occurred.

Some patterns begin to emerge, including deficiencies within many of the victimized organizations, who perhaps:

- Did not designate an individual to be in charge of cybersecurity
- Did not implement two factor authentication (multi-factor authentication, 2FA, MFA)

- Did not implement a cybersecurity program
- Did not create sufficient cybersecurity documentation (policies and procedures) to guide individuals and the organization;

and so on.

It seems logical that if more organizations took some of these reasonable steps, then the number of breaches would be reduced. If organizations are not implementing these fundamental cybersecurity measures on their own accord, then it is rational to suggest a legal duty to implement reasonable cybersecurity controls.

This evolution seems similar to what must have happened with the early automobiles and traffic laws.[438]

31.3 Cybersecurity frameworks and best practices (preview #2)

A cybersecurity "framework" is simply a best practice on how to manage and implement cybersecurity in an organization.

It is not a law, nor a regulation, nor a legal requirement. It is voluntary guidance, not mandatory.

We covered some basic cybersecurity principles in Chapter 17 and previewed the concept of cybersecurity frameworks.

We should know they exist and realize that many cybersecurity laws have similar language as the frameworks and other best practices. As lawmakers drafted and debated their future cybersecurity law, we can assume they looked to these best practices.

For now, just familiarize yourself with the names of these frameworks:

- Critical Security Controls (CSC) from the Center for Internet Security (CIS)
- Frameworks from National Institute of Standards and Technology (NIST)
    - NIST Cybersecurity Framework (CSF)

---

[438] Early cars came with almost no safety equipment, and the traffic rules of the road were minimal or non-existent. Perhaps the simplest rule came first to reduce head-on collisions: drive on the right side of the road. Then other rules came about, including about who has the right of way at an intersection, and now we have a complex but effective system for traffic laws, road design, and automobile safety.

- o NIST Special Publication 800-53, Security and Privacy Controls for Federal Information Systems and Organizations
  - o NIST Special Publication 800-171, Protecting Controlled Unclassified Information in Nonfederal Systems and Organizations
- International Organization for Standardization (ISO) 27001 (27000 series) standard for Information Security Management Systems (ISMS).
- PCI-DSS Payment Card Industry (PCI) Data Security Standard (DSS) (security for processing of credit and debit cards).

We will discuss frameworks more in Chapter 40.

31.4 Requirements you may see in cybersecurity laws

Cybersecurity laws might be called:

- Cybersecurity laws
- Data protection laws
- Data security laws
- Data security protections;

or something similar.

In general, they will require that reasonable security measures be followed. The language and terms may be familiar from cybersecurity best practices.

When assessing a cybersecurity law or regulation, first assess what organizations it applies to. It may apply generally to any organization within the state, or to organizations within a certain sector falling under the regulatory reach of the rule issuer.

Assess what information needs to be protected according to the statute. If it is merely a consumer protection statute of general application, then the statute will probably require protection simply of consumer data.[439] If it is a law or regulation designed to protect a sector and regulate that sector, the rule may require that the entirety of the organization's information systems be adequately secured.

---

[439] As covered in Part 9, even if the law only requires protection of consumer data, organizations should still protect the entirety of their data and systems.

After you have assessed those two items to determine the scope of the rule, then see what requirements are imposed.

The laws and regulations may reference protection of confidentiality, integrity, and availability of information systems (the CIA triad objectives). They may mention applying safeguards (controls) that are physical, administrative, and technical.

They may emphasize governance (management), and require training, designation of people in charge, risk assessment, creation of written assessments, reports, and policies.[440]

Each statute or regulation will have different terminology and a varying level of detail outlining what is required.

As you evaluate security requirements, realize that if the government entity took the time to develop them, they have probably already imposed a data breach notification requirement. Though we cover these legal requirements separately for now, organizations should integrate them holistically and comprehensively.

31.5 New York's cybersecurity requirement

New York's cybersecurity requirement is found within New York State General Business Law (G.B.L. or G.B.S.) within section 899-bb, titled "Data security protections."[441]

As covered in the prior chapter, New York's SHIELD Act (passed in 2019) created section 899-bb and those new cybersecurity requirements, while strengthening existing data breach notification rules within 899-aa.

G.B.L. § 899-bb starts with some definitions, then the main requirement reads:

> *G.B.L. § 899-bb(2). Reasonable security requirement.*
> *(a) Any person or business that owns or licenses*
> *computerized data which includes private information of a*
> *resident of New York shall develop, implement and maintain*
> *reasonable safeguards to protect the security, confidentiality*

---

[440] Requiring policies, procedures, reports and assessments means that documentation is available if the government requests or subpoenas it.
[441] NY G.B.L. § 899-bb *Data security protections*,
https://www.nysenate.gov/legislation/laws/GBS/899-BB.

and integrity of the private information including, but not limited to, disposal of data.[442]

The statute continues with examples of what might constitute compliance. The main takeaway is that it suggests a data security program that includes reasonable administrative, technical, and physical safeguards.[443] Here is how the statute is worded:

G.B.L. § 899-bb(2)

(b) A person or business shall be deemed to be in compliance... if it...

(ii) implements a data security program that includes the following:

(A) reasonable administrative safeguards such as the following...

(1) designates one or more employees to coordinate the security program;

(2) identifies reasonably foreseeable ... risks;

(3) assesses the sufficiency of safeguards in place...;

(4) trains and manages employees in the security program practices and procedures;

(5) selects service providers capable of maintaining appropriate safeguards...; and

(6) adjusts the security program in light of business changes or new circumstances; and

(B) reasonable technical safeguards such as the following, in which the person or business:

(1) assesses risks in network and software design;

(2) assesses risks in information processing, transmission and storage;

(3) detects, prevents and responds to attacks or system failures; and

(4) regularly tests and monitors the effectiveness of key controls, systems and procedures; and

---

[442] G.B.L. § 899-bb(2).

[443] These are basic cybersecurity controls as covered in Chapter 17.

(C) reasonable physical safeguards such as the following, in which the person or business:

(1) assesses risks of information storage and disposal;

(2) detects, prevents and responds to intrusions;

(3) protects against unauthorized access to or use of private information ...; and

(4) disposes of private information within a reasonable amount of time after it is no longer needed ....[444]

The law appears to make an exception for "small business" but in the end emphasizes a security program needs to be reasonable and commensurate with size and complexity of the business. That is essentially the standard for any business, whether small, medium, or large.

This law does not provide for a "private right of action" which means the law cannot be a statutory basis for a lawsuit.[445]

31.6 NY financial services cybersecurity requirement (Rule 500)

As we introduced in the prior chapter, New York has a comprehensive cybersecurity regulation for the financial sector, administered by NY DFS.[446]

The goal is to protect consumer data as well as the safety and soundness of the individual financial institution and financial system as a whole, including against cybercrime and other issues that affect information systems.

The regulation requires covered financial institutions operating within New York to have a comprehensive cybersecurity program to protect the

---

[444] G.B.L. § 899-bb(2)(b)(ii), https://www.nysenate.gov/legislation/laws/GBS/899-BB.

[445] If there is a proper basis for a lawsuit, noncompliance with this law might nevertheless be highly relevant, such as to establish what the legal standard of proper cybersecurity measures might include.

[446] This is Rule 500, *Cybersecurity Requirements for Financial Services Companies*, 23 NYCRR Part 500, https://www.law.cornell.edu/regulations/new-york/title-23/chapter-I/part-500. *See also* NY DFS *Cybersecurity Resource Center*, https://www.dfs.ny.gov/industry_guidance/cybersecurity. This rule was first enacted in 2017, amended in 2020, and again in November 2023.

organization's information systems. It is detailed[447] and with sections requiring a cybersecurity program, written cybersecurity policy, a process to properly manage information security, and consideration of many specific areas of cybersecurity.

31.7. Other cybersecurity laws and regulations

Other laws and regulations impose cybersecurity (information security) requirements. In general, the laws to consider are:

- Federal Trade Commission (FTC) Act
- Health sector cybersecurity requirements
- Financial sector cybersecurity requirements
- Educational sector cybersecurity requirements
- Within the federal government and doing business with it
- Other state cybersecurity laws.

Let us briefly review those requirements.

If a law imposes broad privacy requirements, it will also include a cybersecurity requirement, so stay tuned for the next chapter.

31.7.1 The Federal Trade Commission (FTC) Act

The Federal Trade Commission (FTC) Act prohibits unfair and deceptive trade practices, which could include inadequate cybersecurity, or deceptive promises about a level of cybersecurity.[448]

---

[447] It is about 7,000 words, and at 200 words per minute that would be about a 35-minute read if it were a typical article. Statutes and regulations take much longer to read because they can be complex and require cross referencing of definitions and sections.

[448] FTC Act Section 5(a) is codified as 15 U.S.C. § 45(a). It reads, in part:
15 U.S.C. § 45 (a) Declaration of unlawfulness; power to prohibit unfair practices; inapplicability to foreign trade
(1) Unfair methods of competition in or affecting commerce, and unfair or deceptive acts or practices in or affecting commerce, are hereby declared unlawful.
See also FTC Act and the FTC, https://johnbandler.com/ftc-act; FTC main, https://www.ftc.gov; FTC, *Data Security,* https://www.ftc.gov/business-guidance/privacy-security/data-security.

31.7.2 Health sector cybersecurity requirements (HIPAA)

The health sector has cybersecurity and privacy rules to protect patient health and other personal information, and to ensure our health sector is protected from cyberattack or natural disaster.

The "security rule" is within the Code of Federal Regulations (C.F.R.) and has some rules that are general and that address the three types of safeguards (physical, administrative, technical) as well as for management and policies.[449]

31.7.3 Financial sector cybersecurity requirements

Financial regulators require cybersecurity to protect consumer privacy, prevent theft, and ensure financial institutions (individually) and the sector (as a whole) are resilient and can continue to operate.

Here are some legal requirements and organizations to know.

Gramm-Leach-Bliley Act (GLBA)

The Gramm-Leach-Bliley Act (GLBA) (also known as the Financial Services Modernization Act of 1999) is a federal law that created privacy and information security requirements for financial institutions. GLBA's implementation rules include the Safeguards Rule (to protect consumer information) and the Privacy Rule (regarding disclosure of consumers' personal information).[450]

Federal Financial Institutions Examination Council (FFIEC)

The Federal Financial Institutions Examination Council (FFIEC) is an organization created to standardize requirements among the many federal

---

[449] 45 C.F.R. Subpart C, *Security Standards for the Protection of Electronic Protected Health Information*, https://www.law.cornell.edu/cfr/text/45/part-164/subpart-C.

[450] FTC on GLBA, https://www.ftc.gov/business-guidance/privacy-security/gramm-leach-bliley-act. GLBA (the law itself) is found within 15 U.S. Code Chapter 94, *Privacy*, https://www.law.cornell.edu/uscode/text/15/chapter-94. GLBA regulations are the (i) Safeguards Rule, 16 C.F.R. Part 314, *Standards for Safeguarding Customer Information*, https://www.law.cornell.edu/cfr/text/16/part-314, and (ii) Privacy Rule (covered next chapter), 16 C.F.R. Part 313, *Privacy of Consumer Financial Information*, https://www.law.cornell.edu/cfr/text/16/part-313. *See also Financial Sector Cyber Laws and Regulations*, https://johnbandler.com/financial-sector-cyber-laws-regulations.

financial regulators. They have standards for information technology and cybersecurity.[451]

Sarbanes-Oxley Act (SOX)

The Sarbanes-Oxley Act of 2002 (SOX) is a federal law for publicly traded companies (companies listed on a stock exchange). SOX requires publicly traded companies to have proper internal control structures in place to validate that their financial statements accurately reflect their financial results, thus requiring controls over information systems. SOX is overseen by the Securities and Exchange Commission (SEC). SOX also created the Public Company Accounting Oversight Board (PCAOB).[452]

31.7.4 Educational sector

The Family Educational Rights and Privacy Act (FERPA) is a federal law protecting the privacy and security of student education records.[453] FERPA applies to any school that receives funding from the U.S. Department of Education (ED or DoEd).

31.7.5 Within the federal government and doing business with it

Organizations that engage in business with the government, especially the federal government, may be contractually obligated to comply with cybersecurity rules. These rules will be stricter with higher sensitivity work, such as defense contracting.

The federal government has rules about how it will secure its own information assets, and this extends to the organizations that provide

---

[451] The FFIEC website is https://www.ffiec.gov. They have an IT Examination Handbook, and a new website for that at https://ithandbook.ffiec.gov.

[452] SEC on SOX, https://www.investor.gov/introduction-investing/investing-basics/role-sec/laws-govern-securities-industry#sox2002; Sarbanes-Oxley Act of 2002 (SOX), https://www.govinfo.gov/content/pkg/COMPS-1883/pdf/COMPS-1883.pdf; 15 U.S.C. Chapter 98, *Public Company Accounting Reform and Corporate Responsibility*, https://www.law.cornell.edu/uscode/text/15/chapter-98; Cornell LII on SOX, https://www.law.cornell.edu/wex/sarbanes-oxley_act.

[453] More on FERPA in Chapters 32 and 34. *See* 20 U.S.C. § 1232g, https://www.law.cornell.edu/uscode/text/20/1232g, 34 C.F.R. Part 99, *Family Educational Rights and Privacy*, https://www.law.cornell.edu/cfr/text/34/part-99; U.S. Department of Education (ED), FERPA, https://studentprivacy.ed.gov/ferpa.

goods and services for the government. Much of that is from the Federal Information Security Management Act (FISMA).[454]

The Cybersecurity Maturity Model Certification (CMMC) Program was developed by the Department of Defense (DoD) with their partners and designed for defense contractors to protect defense related information and includes a certification process.[455] The Defense Federal Acquisition Regulation Supplement (DFARS) from the Department of Defense (DoD) has cybersecurity rules regarding defense contractors.[456]

Also consider the May 2021 White House Executive Order on Improving the Nation's Cybersecurity[457] which attempts to address the difficult cyber issues the country is facing. As an executive order, it uses the power of the President to direct action by the executive branch but does

---

[454] The Federal Information Security Management Act (FISMA) gives authority to the Office of Management and Budget (OMB) and Department of Homeland Security (DHS) regarding information security in federal agencies and contracting. The Cybersecurity and Infrastructure Security Agency (CISA) is an agency of DHS. *See* CISA on FIMSA, https://www.cisa.gov/federal-information-security-modernization-act. *See* the FIMSA law at https://www.congress.gov/bill/113th-congress/senate-bill/2521.
    The Federal Risk and Authorization Management Program (FedRAMP) was developed with the National Institute of Standards and Technology (NIST) to create a standardized security framework for federal government use of cloud services. FedRAMP is based upon other NIST publications, including NIST 800-53.

[455] *See* U.S. DoD Chief Information Officer, *About CMMC*, https://dodcio.defense.gov/cmmc/About; 32 C.F.R. Part 170, https://www.ecfr.gov/current/title-32/subtitle-A/chapter-I/subchapter-G/part-170.

[456] The applicable section is DFARS 252.204-7012 (Safeguarding Covered Defense Information and Cyber Incident Reporting), https://www.acq.osd.mil/dpap/dars/dfars/html/current/252204.htm, also available at https://www.acquisition.gov/dfars/part-252-solicitation-provisions-and-contract-clauses#DFARS_252.204-7012.

[457] White House, *Executive Order on Improving the Nation's Cybersecurity*, (May 12, 2021), https://www.whitehouse.gov/briefing-room/presidential-actions/2021/05/12/executive-order-on-improving-the-nations-cybersecurity; White House, *Fact Sheet: President Signs Executive Order Charting New Course to Improve the Nation's Cybersecurity and Protect Federal Government Networks*, https://www.whitehouse.gov/briefing-room/statements-releases/2021/05/12/fact-sheet-president-signs-executive-order-charting-new-course-to-improve-the-nations-cybersecurity-and-protect-federal-government-networks.

not have the power of law. It directs the federal government to assess and improve cybersecurity including threat sharing, incident detection, response, and investigation, supply chain integrity, national security, and establishes a cyber safety review board.

Executive Orders can be persuasive for future laws and private actions but can also be undone by future Presidents.

31.7.6 Your state's cybersecurity law

As always, check to see if your state has a cybersecurity law. You can start with the NCSL website, and then with the website of your state regulator (state attorney general or state consumer protection agency).[458]

31.7.7 Investor protection and securities laws

The Securities and Exchange Commission (SEC) is a regulator of publicly traded companies, and one of their roles is to protect investors and ensure they get accurate information about the company in order to make reasonable decisions about whether to invest or not (buy or sell the publicly traded shares of stock).

In the Solar Winds case, the SEC took the position that false public statements about cybersecurity violated their investor protection regulations, and they brought a civil lawsuit against the company and their chief information security officer (CISO).

Essentially, the SEC argued that public statement of:

> *"Our company's cybersecurity is fantastic and rock solid and we do X, Y, and Z."*

if that statement is false, is a material statements that can mislead investors, and can be civilly actionable.

---

[458] NCSL, *Data Security Laws, Private Sector*, https://www.ncsl.org/technology -and-communication/data-security-laws-private-sector.

In a parallel to FedRAMP, consider StateRAMP, a nonprofit membership organization designed to standardize cybersecurity for organizations providing services to state and local governments. *See* StateRAMP, *About StateRAMP*, https://stateramp.org/about-us.

This case is still under litigation though some preliminary decisions have been issued as of this writing. The trial court dismissed most of the counts, and the future is uncertain.[459]

31.8 References and additional reading

- *Chapter 31 resources,* https://johnbandler.com/cyberlawbook-resources-ch31
- *New York Cybersecurity Requirements and the SHIELD Act,* https://johnbandler.com/new-york-cybersecurity-requirements-and-the-shield-act
- *SolarWinds breach and the 2023 SEC lawsuit,* https://johnbandler.com/solarwinds-breach-and-2023-sec-lawsuit
- NY G.B.L. § 899-bb *Data security protections,* https://www.nysenate.gov/legislation/laws/GBS/899-BB
- NY DFS Rule 500, *Cybersecurity Requirements for Financial Services Companies,* 23 NYCRR Part 500, https://www.law.cornell.edu/regulations/new-york/title-23/chapter-I/part-500
- NY DFS *Cybersecurity Resource Center,* https://www.dfs.ny.gov/industry_guidance/cybersecurity
- NCSL, *Data Security Laws, Private Sector,* https://www.ncsl.org/technology-and-communication/data-security-laws-private-sector
- HIPAA security rule, 45 C.F.R. Subpart C, *Security Standards for the Protection of Electronic Protected Health Information,* https://www.law.cornell.edu/cfr/text/45/part-164/subpart-C
- GLBA, 15 U.S. Code Chapter 94, *Privacy,* https://www.law.cornell.edu/uscode/text/15/chapter-94.
- GLBA *Safeguards Rule*: 16 C.F.R. Part 314, Standards for Safeguarding Customer Information, https://www.law.cornell.edu/cfr/text/16/part-314
- FFIEC website, https://www.ffiec.gov/
- FFIEC IT Examination Handbook, https://ithandbook.ffiec.gov/

---

[459] Any pending litigation is (by definition) unresolved, so conduct your research to find recent events. Following the 2024 Presidential Election, there will be a new head of the SEC which will affect how the SEC proceeds. *See SolarWinds breach and the 2023 SEC lawsuit,* https://johnbandler.com/solarwinds-breach-and-2023-sec-lawsuit.

John T. Bandler

- SEC on SOX, https://www.investor.gov/introduction-investing/investing-basics/role-sec/laws-govern-securities-industry#sox2002
- The Family Educational Rights and Privacy Act (FERPA), 20 U.S.C. § 1232g, https://www.law.cornell.edu/uscode/text/20/1232g
- FERPA regulations, 34 C.F.R. Part 99, Family Educational Rights and Privacy https://www.law.cornell.edu/cfr/text/34/part-99
- U.S. Department of Education FERPA webpage, https://www2.ed.gov/policy/gen/guid/fpco/ferpa/index.html

31.9 Chapter questions

- How is a cybersecurity framework different from a cybersecurity law? Give an example of each.
- Which came first, cybersecurity frameworks or cybersecurity laws? Explain.
- Name NY's general cybersecurity law and provide a citation and link to it.
- Name NY's cybersecurity regulation for the financial sector and provide a citation and link to it.
- Is there a federal law that could be applied generally to cybersecurity? If so, name it and explain.
- Is there a federal law that is sector specific and requires cybersecurity? If so name them and what sectors it applies to.
- Is secure data disposal a part of a good cybersecurity program? Explain.

John T. Bandler

32

Privacy and Privacy Laws

In this chapter:

- Privacy
- Privacy laws
- The right to be left alone
- Privacy rights in statutes

> **Data law types**
> ☐ Breach notification
> ☐ Cybersecurity
> ☑ Privacy

32.1 Privacy introduced

Privacy is important for every individual and organization. Privacy threats include data breaches and companies who overshare, violating their privacy promises regarding customer information. Privacy is the subject of rapidly growing laws and regulation.

Privacy awareness is important for each of us as individuals and for our families. Individual privacy and individual cybersecurity align well, with considerable overlap as depicted in the following diagram.

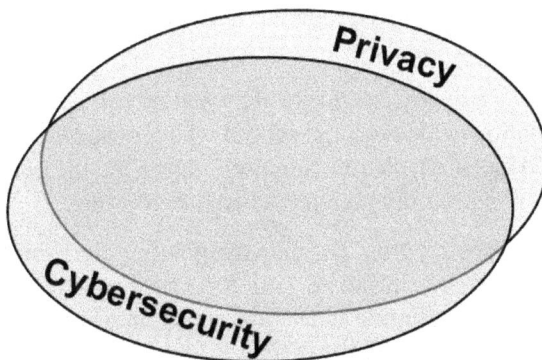

**Privacy vs. cybersecurity
(individual perspective)**

We can assess our cybersecurity and privacy together, making decisions that protect both. As you review settings on a device or platform, you can review your privacy and security settings at the same time.

We should make well-informed decisions regarding our privacy and the information we share. We should teach younger generations about this as well and discuss these issues with them.

For organizations, sound privacy practices can be good for business and avoid legal problems. The legal and practical requirements for cybersecurity and privacy overlap to a degree, but with more areas of distinction compared to our previous diagram.

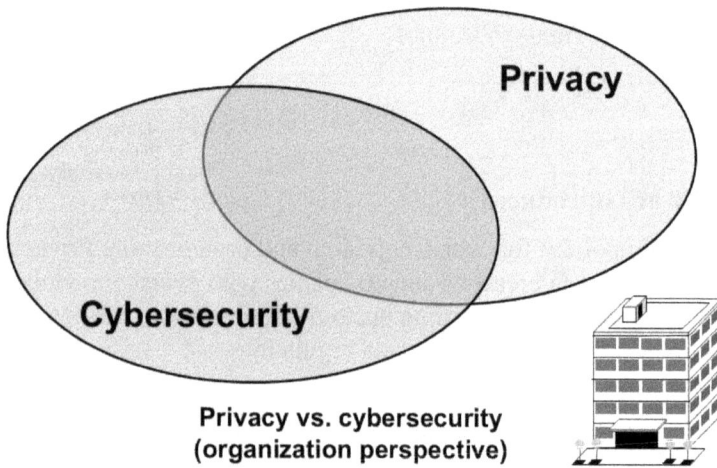

**Privacy vs. cybersecurity
(organization perspective)**

Larger organizations may have separate individuals or even separate departments for privacy and cybersecurity.

The organization's privacy program is focused on privacy laws and making organization-wide decisions about what consumer information is collected, stored, secured, shared, and used, notifying the consumer of these practices, and providing choice where appropriate.

Data privacy includes security, but also many other elements. Cybersecurity involves securing several different types of data and information systems, including individual (consumer) personal information but also others. For that reason, they intersect in a large part of the diagram, but also with distinct components.

32.2 Privacy's origins and the types

Personal privacy is a concept that has existed for hundreds, even thousands of years. Consider early to modern humans protecting their cave den or other family abode, and the 1300s England with "peeping tom" laws.

In 1890 Louis Brandeis (who would later become a legendary Supreme Court Justice), co-authored a law review article on the subject and suggested an individual right to privacy which included a right to be left alone.

We can think of four main areas of privacy:

- Information privacy (data privacy)
- Communications privacy
- Territorial privacy
- Bodily privacy.[460]

Our focus in this book is primarily information privacy, with an important emphasis on communications privacy.[461]

---

[460] Bodily privacy has been an important legal issue in the news recently. In Chapter 7 we discussed Constitutional law and introduced the example of abortion and the "right to choose," the "right to life" as an example of how the law is not a rigid unchanging given, but subject to interpretation by people. Here we return to it because bodily privacy relates to privacy in general and even specifically to data privacy.

In 1973 in *Roe v. Wade* the USSC decided that the U.S. Constitution gave women certain privacy rights that included protections for their ability to obtain an abortion at certain stages in the pregnancy—a federal right that the states could not infringe upon. This ruling and interpretation held for almost 50 years until 2022 in *Dobbs v. Jackson Women's Health Organization*.

With *Dobbs*, the USSC overruled *Roe* and decided the Constitution did not provide this protection. By overruling *Roe v. Wade*, the USSC declined to follow the legal doctrine of precedence (*stare decisis*). This means the legal interpretation and meaning of the Constitution has changed even though the relevant words of the Constitution were exactly as before. This is not the first time the USSC has reversed itself, but it is a very rare occurrence. It might be the only time the USSC created a right and later reversed itself on that right.

Many people believe *Roe* was wrongly decided, many believe that *Dobbs* was wrongly decided. Either way, it is an important legal point and a privacy issue.

[461] So much communications data is stored that it becomes part of "information privacy." Further, if a government sought to obtain data about an individual's health or body, that could implicate bodily privacy as well. This shows how these four areas of privacy can overlap.

Information and data are similar terms. We consider the information (data) about consumers (including you and me) that is collected, stored, used, and shared.

32.3 Privacy frameworks (preview)

Privacy frameworks are not laws or regulations, so they are optional not mandatory.[462] We cover them before the privacy laws because many privacy laws are based upon them. As you research and review the various privacy frameworks and laws, you will see that certain components of privacy rights repeat and become familiar.

For now, it is helpful to start getting familiar with the names of these, and we will cover them further in Chapter 40.

- National Institute of Standards and Technology (NIST) Privacy Framework
- Fair Information Practice Principles (FIPPs)
- Organisation for Economic Co-operation and Development (OECD) privacy framework (1980 and 2013)
- Asia-Pacific Economic Cooperation (APEC) privacy framework
- ISO/IEC 27701:2019, Security Techniques—Extension to ISO/IEC 27001 and ISO/IEC 27002 for privacy information management.

It is also worth noting that some of the international agreements might have the force of law, if adopted by the relevant countries, especially regarding cross-border transfer of personal information.

32.4 Privacy laws introduced

Data privacy laws are basically about giving consumers notice, rights and choices about how data about them is collected and used.

Data privacy laws build upon other categories of data law such as breach notification and cybersecurity. A privacy law will require that consumer data be protected with reasonable cybersecurity and require notification to the consumer of a data breach.[463]

---

[462] In this book we use the term "framework" to mean a best practice, which fall under my category of "external guidance." They are one of the five components for policy work and management, which we discuss in Part 9. Compare that to laws and regulations (external rules) which are mandatory legal requirements.
[463] Check the specific law to see whether it was enacted with the privacy law, or was a previously existing statute.

Privacy laws focus on consumer privacy rights, providing rights to consumers, and obligations to businesses.

Without privacy laws, businesses would probably want to collect and store as much consumer data as they can, and then monetize it, without disclosing what they were doing.

32.5. Privacy laws and regulations

Today, consumers have varying privacy statutory legal rights depending upon applicable jurisdictions and sectors.

The U.S. legal framework for privacy laws and regulations is a patchwork, sometimes called the "sectoral model" (sector by sector).[464] It is a patchwork of laws and regulations, some state and some federal, and with overlapping regulators and laws.

At the federal level, the Federal Trade Commission (FTC) Act has some privacy protections for consumers and requirements for business. Sectors such as finance and health have their own privacy requirements.

There are now many state privacy laws, which started with California and now includes many others. The reach of these state laws extends beyond the borders.[465]

32.6 Typical privacy law requirements

Privacy laws create rights for consumers regarding information about them held by a business, and this means legal obligations for the business. Privacy rights include:

- Notice about organization privacy practices and how they collect, store, use, sell and share information about the consumer.
- An ability to access one's own data, correct it, have it deleted or limit processing, or transfer data to another service provider.

These laws may generally require an organization's privacy program to follow these principles:

- Be lawful, fair, and transparent
- Limit collection, use, and processing of personal data

---

[464] Compare that to the European Union's comprehensive model, with one overarching law to cover privacy across all sectors.
[465] *See* Chapter 29 for more on data law jurisdiction.

- Keep personal data only as long as needed (then delete)
- Keep personal data accurately
- Keep personal data secure with good cybersecurity
- Be accountable for the above.

32.7 Federal privacy laws

For federal privacy law, categorize the laws as:

- General application (regardless of sector of organization)
- Sector specific (apply only to organizations in certain sectors).

If it is a "privacy law," we probably covered the cybersecurity and breach notification aspects in an earlier chapter.

32.7.1 Federal privacy laws of general application

The Federal Trade Commission Act (FTC Act)[466] is the only federal privacy law that applies generally and is not sector specific.

It does not mention the word "privacy" anywhere, but simply prohibits "unfair" or "deceptive" trade practices, [467] which would apply to deceptive or inaccurate privacy notices, and could apply to improper privacy practices.

The Children's Online Privacy Protection Act (COPPA) is a federal law with accompanying regulations enforced by the FTC that impose privacy protections for children under 13 years old.[468] It prohibits collection of information from those children without consent of their parent or guardian.

32.7.2 Federal privacy laws for the financial sector

Some federal privacy laws and regulators are specific only to certain sectors.

The primary financial privacy laws are The Gramm-Leach-Bliley Act (GLBA) (also known as the Financial Services Modernization Act of

---

[466] Federal Trade Commission Act, 15 U.S.C. Subchapter I, https://www.law.cornell.edu/uscode/text/15/chapter-2/subchapter-I.

[467] 15 U.S.C. § 45(a)(1), https://www.law.cornell.edu/uscode/text/15/45.

[468] COPPA Act, 15 U.S.C. § 6501-6506, https://www.law.cornell.edu/uscode/text/15/chapter-91; COPPA regulations 16 C.F.R. § 312, https://www.law.cornell.edu/cfr/text/16/part-312. *See also* FTC, *Children's Privacy*, https://www.ftc.gov/business-guidance/privacy-security/childrens-privacy.

1999) and accompanying regulation (Privacy Rule) which imposes privacy requirements.[469]

There are also federal credit protection laws that have privacy components, stemming from the Fair Credit Reporting Act of 1970.[470]

32.7.3 Federal health sector privacy laws

The health sector has cybersecurity and privacy rules to protect patient health and other personal information, and to ensure our health sector is protected from cyberattack or natural disaster.

The "privacy rule" is within the Code of Federal Regulations (C.F.R.). It includes rules regarding the collection and sharing of protected health information (PHI).[471]

The government resources for health-related privacy rules are not as good as they could be, some seem to be quite dated.[472]

---

[469] FTC on GLBA, https://www.ftc.gov/business-guidance/privacy-security/gramm-leach-bliley-act. GLBA is found within 15 U.S. Code Chapter 94, *Privacy*, https://www.law.cornell.edu/uscode/text/15/chapter-94. GLBA regulations are:
- Privacy Rule: 16 C.F.R. Part 313, *Privacy of Consumer Financial Information*, https://www.law.cornell.edu/cfr/text/16/part-313.
- Safeguards Rule (covered last chapter): 16 C.F.R. Part 314, *Standards for Safeguarding Customer Information*, https://www.law.cornell.edu/cfr/text/16/part-314.

See also Financial Sector Cyber Laws and Regulations, https://johnbandler.com/financial-sector-cyber-laws-regulations.

[470] We covered this in greater detail in Chapter 27 on regulation. Consider the Fair Credit Reporting Act of 1970 (FCRA), as amended periodically including by The Fair and Accurate Credit Transactions Act of 2003 (FACTA). This provides privacy rights to consumers and seeks to ensure accuracy of credit reports and protect against identity theft.

FACTA is found at 15 U.S.C. § 1681 et seq, https://www.law.cornell.edu/uscode/text/15/chapter-41. *See also* FTC on FACTA, https://www.ftc.gov/legal-library/browse/statutes/fair-accurate-credit-transactions-act-2003; FTC on FCRA, https://www.ftc.gov/legal-library/browse/statutes/fair-credit-reporting-act.

[471] 45 C.F.R. Subpart E, *Privacy of Individually Identifiable Health Information*, https://www.law.cornell.edu/cfr/text/45/part-164/subpart-E.

[472] HHS on HIPAA, https://www.hhs.gov/hipaa/index.html. *See* my explainer article, *Health sector laws and regulations*, https://johnbandler.com/health-sector-laws-and-regulations.

32.7.4 Federal privacy law for the education sector

The Family Educational Rights and Privacy Act of 1974 (FERPA) is the primary privacy law in for the education sector,[473] applying to any educational institution that receives federal funding, which is a lot. It gives students rights over their data, and parents have rights as well (depending on the student's age, and only before college). It is overseen by the U.S. Department of Education (ED).

32.8 State privacy laws

State privacy laws started with California (enacted in 2018, effective 2020) and now include a growing number of states including Colorado, Connecticut, Virginia, Utah, Oregon, Texas, Montana, and more.

It is impossible to summarize each of these laws here, but it is good to know where to find a summary, and how to research each law yourself.[474]

32.9 GDPR

The European Union's General Data Protection Regulation (GDPR)[475] went into effect in 2018 and is to protect EU citizens, primarily

---

[473] The Family Educational Rights and Privacy Act (FERPA), 20 U.S.C. § 1232g, Family Educational and Privacy Rights, https://www.law.cornell.edu/uscode/text/20/1232g; 34 C.F.R. Part 99, *Family Educational Rights and Privacy*, https://www.law.cornell.edu/cfr/text/34/part-99. ED has FERPA resources, *FERPA*, https://studentprivacy.ed.gov/ferpa; *Data Breach*, https://studentprivacy.ed.gov/topic/data-breach.

[474] For an initial summary *see Consumer Privacy Rights*, https://johnbandler.com/consumer-privacy-rights. Others have created far more comprehensive summaries, including many large reputable law firms, privacy experts, and the International Association of Privacy Professionals (IAPP). IAPP resources include, https://iapp.org; IAPP, *U.S. State Privacy Topic Page*, https://iapp.org/resources/topics/us-state-privacy; IAPP, *U.S. State Comprehensive Privacy Laws Report – Overview*, https://iapp.org/resources/article/us-state-privacy-laws-overview; IAPP, *U.S. State Privacy Legislation Tracker*, https://iapp.org/resources/article/us-state-privacy-legislation-tracker.

To research an individual law, find the law and read it (sometimes easier said than done) and see what the regulator (state attorney general or consumer protection agency) says about it.

[475] General information on GDPR is available from these sites and articles; https://ec.europa.eu/info/index_en; *Data protection in the EU*,

applicable within the EU. It also applies to any U.S. organizations who might collect personal information of EU citizens and is a model for other privacy laws. It is a comprehensive privacy law, applying across sectors.[476]

Some key GDPR terms are:

- Data subject (the consumer whose data was collected and stored)
- Data controller (the organization responsible for collecting and storing that data)
- Data processor (an organization processing data on behalf of a controller)
- Personal data (data that identifies a consumer)
- Sensitive personal data (sensitive data about that consumer.

Key GPDR principles track those of privacy frameworks, and include:

- Lawfulness, fairness and transparency
- Purpose limitation: Limit collection and use of personal data based on purpose (need)
- Data minimization: Minimize personal data processing
- Accuracy: Keep personal data accurate
- Storage limitation: Keep personal data only as long as needed
- Integrity and confidentiality: Keep personal data secure
- Accountability: Be accountable for the above
- Cross border transfer restrictions.

GDPR provides rights to consumers ("data subjects"):

- Right to be properly informed
- Right of access to data
- Right of rectification (to correct inaccurate information)
- Right to be forgotten (erasure)
- Right to limit processing (where erasure isn't possible)
- Right of portability (to transfer data to another controller)

---

https://ec.europa.eu/info/law/law-topic/data-protection/data-protection-eu_en; *EU data protection rules*, https://ec.europa.eu/info/law/law-topic/data-protection/eu-data-protection-rules_en; *What is GDPR*, https://gdpr.eu/what-is-gdpr.

Each country in the EU has a supervisory authority, also known as data protection authority (DPA), or data protection commissioner.

[476] In the U.S., we have the "sectoral" model, a patchwork of laws and regulators.

- Right to object (stop processing of data)
- Rights regarding automated decision making.

32.10 Privacy policies and notices (preview)

Laws may require organizations to create privacy policies and provide notices to the public about their privacy practices. Even where the law does not require this, organizations may choose to do this as part of their privacy program and data governance.

32.11 Facebook and Cambridge Analytica (Part II)

We return to the Facebook-Cambridge Analytica case to highlight the breach of privacy laws that occurred.[477]

Facebook (Meta) made promises to its users about how information would be collected and shared, and these promises were made in their terms of use and privacy notice (sometimes called a privacy policy).[478]

As borne out in government press releases and regulatory actions, Meta broke their privacy promises, and improperly shared data with Cambridge Analytica (a data analytics company). Cambridge Analytica then misused this improperly shared data, and faced their own regulatory actions.

From about 2013 to 2016 Facebook improperly collected and shared information for potentially over 80 million users, without their knowledge and consent. This information was sold and used by others to target these consumers. Ultimately, Facebook agreed to a $5 billion dollar fine within the U.S. and was also fined by other countries.

Separately, Cambridge Analytica faced regulatory actions, and they filed for bankruptcy. They were charged with deceiving and misleading users of their apps and collecting data improperly.

---

[477] We introduced this case in Chapter 15 to illustrate how valuable data about us is, including when we use "free" platforms like Facebook and Instagram. Citations are compiled at the webpage *Facebook - Cambridge Analytica case*, https://johnbandler.com/facebook-cambridge-analytica-case. We will return to this in Part 8 since this data was used to target people and then influence them.
[478] You can view Facebook's current privacy policy at https://www.facebook.com/privacy/policy. It is long and most users will never read it, but the law requires that Facebook will follow it since they posted it.

32.12 References and reading

- *Chapter 32 resources,* https://johnbandler.com/cyberlawbook-resources-ch32
- *Privacy,* https://johnbandler.com/privacy
- *The FTC Act and the FTC,* https://johnbandler.com/ftc-act
- *Consumer Privacy Rights,* https://johnbandler.com/consumer-privacy-rights
- *Financial Sector Cyber Laws and Regulations,* https://johnbandler.com/financial-sector-cyber-laws-regulations
- *Health sector laws and regulations,* https://johnbandler.com/health-sector-laws-and-regulations
- *Facebook – Cambridge Analytica case,* https://johnbandler.com/facebook-cambridge-analytica-case
- *Your organization's privacy policy — and privacy notice,* Reuters article available at https://johnbandler.com/organization-privacy-policy-notice
- International Association of Privacy Professionals (IAPP), https://iapp.org
- IAPP *Glossary,* https://iapp.org/resources/glossary
- Electronic Privacy Information Center (EPIC) https://epic.or
- Federal Trade Commission Act §5(a), 15 U.S.C. § 45(a)(1), https://www.law.cornell.edu/uscode/text/15/45
- COPPA Act, 15 U.S.C. § 6501-6506, https://www.law.cornell.edu/uscode/text/15/chapter-91
- COPPA regulations 16 C.F.R. § 312, https://www.law.cornell.edu/cfr/text/16/part-312
- FTC, Children's Privacy, https://www.ftc.gov/business-guidance/privacy-security/childrens-privacy
- FTC on GLBA, https://www.ftc.gov/business-guidance/privacy-security/gramm-leach-bliley-act
- GLBA, 15 U.S. Code Chapter 94, Privacy, https://www.law.cornell.edu/uscode/text/15/chapter-94.
- GLBA regulation: Privacy Rule: 16 C.F.R. Part 313, Privacy of Consumer Financial Information, https://www.law.cornell.edu/cfr/text/16/part-313
- HIPAA regulation, 45 C.F.R. Subpart E, Privacy of Individually Identifiable Health Information, https://www.law.cornell.edu/cfr/text/45/part-164/subpart-E

- HHS on HIPAA, https://www.hhs.gov/hipaa/index.html
- The Family Educational Rights and Privacy Act (FERPA), 20 U.S.C. § 1232g, https://www.law.cornell.edu/uscode/text/20/1232g
- 34 C.F.R. Part 99, Family Educational Rights and Privacy https://www.law.cornell.edu/cfr/text/34/part-99
- ED FERPA resource, *Protecting Student Privacy*, https://studentprivacy.ed.gov/node/548/

32.13 Chapter questions

- Review a privacy notice (or privacy policy) for an internet service you used, and that you agreed to (LinkedIn, Gmail, Instagram, etc.). What did you learn?
- List some privacy frameworks.
- List some privacy laws.
- What is the difference between a privacy framework and a privacy law?
- Which came first, privacy frameworks or privacy laws?
- What does it mean when to say the U.S. follows the sectoral privacy model?
- What are some typical privacy law requirements?
- Summarize the FTC's authority over privacy.
- Summarize what COPPA stands for and is and cite to the law and regulation.
- Summarize what GLBA stands for and is.
- Spell out and summarize the privacy law for the health sector.
- Spell out and summarize the privacy law for the education sector.

33

Artificial Intelligence

In this chapter:

- AI and legal issues

33.1 Summarizing AI simply[479]

Artificial Intelligence (AI) is a large field of academic research and practical application, backed by much brain power but also marketing hype. It means different things to different people, but it is simply the combination of two words. Let us look at each and break it down simply.

- *Intelligence* is essentially the ability to think, learn, reason, and solve problems. Typically, this means *human* intelligence, the ability of living, breathing *homo sapiens* to think and learn. We have an evolved brain with many abilities. Each generation benefits from ever larger libraries of knowledge to learn from. Each new human has an advanced start point from which to generate new thought and discovery.
- *Artificial* means something created by humans, rather than occurring naturally.

Therefore, artificial intelligence can mean a type of intelligence created by humans. It uses computers with processing power and storage, software, and data. The data can be as vast as our accessible body of knowledge, including books, articles, the public internet and other human content and communication.

Today every person can use a generative AI tool to summarize or "write" text. ChatGPT from OpenAI is one example and there are many others.

---

[479] This section is adapted from my Reuters article, *AI's promise and problem for law and learning*, available via, https://johnbandler.com/ai-promise-and-problem.

33.2 AI types: deterministic vs. generative

Before we get too deep, let us consider two ways to categorize AI, deterministic and generative.

Deterministic AI has been around for a while, used for spam filters, game playing, and other applications. Based on a set of inputs, the output by the AI tool is reproducible, or "determined." There is a set of rules and logic, and decisions are mostly traceable and understandable. Deterministic AI might also be called "reactive AI" or an "expert system."

For a chess program, with a given input that includes the position of all pieces on the board, it will predictably suggest the "best" move.

Generative AI is a newer development. It incorporates a higher degree of learning and requires the AI tool be trained, typically with a large language model (LLM). A LLM is basically an enormous set of data the system can learn from. LLMs that some AI software companies might consider using include:

- The entire library of New York Times articles
- The entire library of social media posts on a particular social media platform (even better to also obtain private messages)
- Email messages communicated to and from a group of email users.

Generative AI might also be described as "limited memory AI" and might result in a different answer being provided each time. The output result might have a certain degree of randomness.[480] Generative AI can be a "black box" where it is difficult to know how the output was generated and why.

There are more ways to categorize and describe AI than that, but it's a start. We will focus on of the newer concerns raises with generative AI and their LLMs.

---

[480] This quality of randomness in the output is called stochastic.

33.3 Summary of generative AI cyberlaw issues

As we think of what cyberlaw issues might arise with AI, we can anticipate that any area of law we have covered will be impacted by this new tool in some way. Let's examine.

33.3.1 Privacy

The collection and analysis of large troves of data creates considerable privacy issues. Generative AI tools require an extensive amount of data to train the models. There are many types of models, and a common version is the LLM. Generative AI tools and their makers seek to obtain these troves of data, whether it is an entire social media site and everything anyone has ever communicated through it, or other data sources, including scraping the web or certain platforms. Compiling, collecting, and analyzing all this data can have privacy implications as data about us is included.

There are also confidentiality and privacy issues whenever you provide the AI system any information or questions.

33.3.2 Copyright and other intellectual property

Generative AI tools that need LLMs can ingest the content, writing and creations of others. When newspapers create content, when authors and publishers create books, they expect to be compensated for the fruits of their labor, their legal rights respected, and that their materials will not be improperly copied or duplicated.

What if these AI tools improperly obtain the written materials created by others to train their system? Put differently, what if they improperly copy those materials for this training, is that a copyright violation?

Next, what if the AI tool improperly reproduces this copied content within its output? Suppose a user asks an AI tool a question and the AI tool provides an answer that is essentially copied from the work of someone else; is that a copyright violation?

Lawsuits have alleged these types of copyright violations.[481]

---

[481] In Chapter 28 we mentioned the New York Times civil complaint against Open AI. *See* Complaint, *New York Times v. Microsoft, OpenAI, et al.*, SDNY Case 1:23-cv-11195 Document 1 Filed 12/27/2023, available at https://nytco-assets.nytimes.com/2023/12/NYT_Complaint_Dec2023.pdf. Remember that a complaint is just an allegation, so check for the defendant's response, recent filings and any court decisions.

33.3.3 Inaccuracies, misinformation, disinformation, propaganda, conspiracy, deepfakes, and more

This category has several layers to it.

First is the concern that a generative AI tool can present false information due to unintentional imperfections in the model and how the system works. Instances of "AI hallucination" are well documented, where the tool returns false information. No model or tool or system is perfect, and inaccuracies will result. News articles, legal filings, and student submissions have all been tainted by AI imperfections, followed by human failure to verify the accuracy of the output.

Next is the concern that AI tools can be maliciously programmed to produce inaccurate or deceptive output.

Finally, AI tools will be deliberately used for improper purposes. There are already people, organizations, and nations with an intent to deceive, whether for the purpose of committing cybercrime for profit, or for nation-state or domestic influence operations. The existence of a powerful tool gives these groups greater ability to create more and better deceptions.

33.3.4 Human learning, "short cuts," and cheating

The widespread use of AI to take "short cuts" could mean that many current learners skip the opportunity to put in effort to build fundamental skills to read, think, analyze, and write.[482]

Previous inventions and advances have allowed successive generations of humans to get a "head start" compared to prior generations, to share knowledge and information faster to spur additional thought. There is a possibility that AI could result in more people obtaining a lower level of education compared to those before. Before AI, it was harder for high school, college, and graduate students to skip the reading or cheat on a writing assignment. AI makes it easier, a temptation that some are unable to resist.

If students take those "short cuts," they don't get to the same destination. They pass the courses, get decent grades, get a diploma, but may not have received a quality education nor improved their ability to read, think, and write. They do not get to the place they would have arrived at

---

[482] See our discussion in Chapter 3.

if they had put in the effort and learned. If higher percentages of students do this, that affects our average level of learning and skills.

That said, it is also clear that AI is a powerful tool, and some students and educators will use it to improve the learning process, and some individuals may be able to learn better and more than they could have otherwise.

33.3.5 AI for lawyers and in legal filings

Courts have strict rules about what can be said and submitted to the court. Legal authorities and factual assertions need to be reasonably accurate (and certainly never blatantly false). Lawyers are supposed to be competent in their legal research and submissions. Their filings to the court must be accurate about the facts of the case at hand and the legal authorities they cite. There have been many instances where lawyers used a generative AI tool which provided false information about case decisions and other matters.

33.3.6 Decision making, human control vs machine control

Generative AI tools can analyze vast troves of information to arrive at the "right" decision, and it may not be transparent or accurate as to how it arrived at that recommendation or decision.

Next is the question of who makes the decision. Does the AI tool analyze and recommend to the human, and the human decides? There will be circumstances where the decision needs to be made quickly, and humans are not available or could not possibly react in time. The question is what decisions can be delegated to the tool.

Then comes the question of when computers should make decisions on their own, without human intervention, or when they could make decisions that disobey their human creator or leader. Or how they might make decisions or act when two or more humans with control disagree about what the computer should do.

Science fiction writers have long pondered such circumstances where robots and computers decide not to serve their humans anymore.[483]

---

[483] There are several good examples which are fun to watch or read.

Battlestar Galactica was a 2004 television series (reimagined from a 1970s classic) about humanoid robots that decide to attack and extinguish their human creators.

Isaac Asimov was an early and prolific science fiction writer, who created the first three rules for robotics, then the "zero" rule.[484] Other rules have been suggested or added. We can consider these, and substitute "AI tool" or "AI software" for robot:

0. A robot may not harm humanity, or, by inaction, allow humanity to come to harm
1. A robot may not harm a human or allow a human to be harmed
2. A robot must obey orders from humans, except where it conflicts with #1
3. A robot must protect itself as long as that does not conflict with #1 or #2
4. A robot should reveal the basis for their decision
5. A robot must always reveal its identity
6. A robot must know it is a robot (not a human).

33.3.7 Discrimination and civil rights

Since AI tools can examine vast amounts of data and make decisions or recommendations, the concern is that they might recommend or decide based upon discriminatory reasoning, or in violation of anti-discrimination laws or principles.

2001: A Space Odyssey is a 1968 movie where the spacecraft computer decides to take matters into its own hands. "Open the pod bay doors, HAL" is a famous line which was met by the computer's disobedience to the human.

Avogadro Corp: The Singularity Is Closer Than It Appears (from the Singularity Series) is a 2011 book by William Hertling about what an AI system could do if it escapes human control. This was followed by his 2012 book, *A.I. Apocalypse*.

I, Robot is the 2004 movie with Will Smith where a robot seems to achieve sentience—the ability to think and feel, and it seems that robots are doing their own bidding, violating the established rules for robots.

[484] He created the three "Laws of Robotics," and to keep our terminology consistent within the book, we call them "rules." Additional rules have been added by other futurists.

33.4 U.S. federal policy statement on AI

The White House issued a policy statement on AI in October 2022.[485] It is not a law, but could be persuasive for future laws, government actions, and private actions.[486] The main principles outlined call for:

- Safe and effective systems
- Algorithmic discrimination protections
- Data privacy
- Notice and explanation
- Human alternatives, consideration, and fallback.

This was followed by an October 2023 Executive Order on the Safe, Secure, and Trustworthy Development and Use of Artificial Intelligence.[487] The order directs executive action for standards for AI safety and security, to protect privacy of Americans, promote innovation and competition, advance our country's leadership abroad, and other goals.

This was followed by a national security memorandum in October 2024, to address the use of AI technology for national security while protecting "human rights, civil rights, civil liberties, privacy, and safety…"[488]

---

[485] White House, *Blueprint for an AI Bill of Rights*, https://www.whitehouse.gov/ostp/ai-bill-of-rights; White House, *Blueprint for an AI Bill of Rights: Making Automated Systems Work for The American People* (October 2022), https://www.whitehouse.gov/wp-content/uploads/2022/10/Blueprint-for-an-AI-Bill-of-Rights.pdf.

[486] This order could also be rescinded by the next administration.

[487] White House, *Executive Order 14110 on the Safe, Secure, and Trustworthy Development and Use of Artificial Intelligence* (October 30, 2023), https://www.whitehouse.gov/briefing-room/presidential-actions/2023/10/30/executive-order-on-the-safe-secure-and-trustworthy-development-and-use-of-artificial-intelligence; White House *Fact Sheet, President Biden Issues Executive Order on Safe, Secure, and Trustworthy Artificial Intelligence* (October 30, 2023), https://www.whitehouse.gov/briefing-room/statements-releases/2023/10/30/fact-sheet-president-biden-issues-executive-order-on-safe-secure-and-trustworthy-artificial-intelligence.

[488] White House, *Memorandum on Advancing the United States' Leadership in Artificial Intelligence; Harnessing Artificial Intelligence to Fulfill National Security Objectives; and Fostering the Safety, Security, and Trustworthiness of Artificial Intelligence* (October 24, 2024), https://www.whitehouse.gov/briefing-room/presidential-actions/2024/10/24/memorandum-on-advancing-the-united-states-leadership-in-artificial-intelligence-harnessing-artificial-intelligence-to-fulfill-national-security-objectives-and-fostering-the-safety-security.

33.5 NIST AI Risk Management Framework

NIST has released frameworks and other guidance relating to AI.

In January 2023 NIST released the Artificial Intelligence Risk Management Framework (AI RMF 1.0), which is voluntary guidance "to better manage risks to individuals, organizations, and society associated with artificial intelligence (AI)."[489]

In July 2024 NIST released a companion guide, in part to satisfy the executive order and to help organizations identify and address risks posed by generative AI.[490]

33.6 AI laws in the U.S.

We are in the infancy of AI specific laws in the US, with a few AI laws that have been created for some jurisdictions.

In the absence of a specific AI law, we need to first assess what existing laws could apply to AI, as we covered earlier in the chapter. Many AI issues might be addressed, at least in part, by existing laws such as:

- Privacy
- Intellectual property (including copyright)
- Negligence
- Product liability,

just to name a few.

Many of the comprehensive privacy laws address AI in some way. Some specific artificial intelligence laws have been enacted.[491] New York City enacted a local law that requires employers that use an AI tool for hiring decisions to provide notice to job applicants and to audit the tools they

---

[489] *See* NIST, *AI Risk Management Framework*, https://www.nist.gov/itl/ai-risk-management-framework; NIST AI 100-1, *Artificial Intelligence Risk Management Framework (AI RMF 1.0)* (January 2023), https://nvlpubs.nist.gov/nistpubs/ai/NIST.AI.100-1.pdf.

[490] NIST, *Artificial Intelligence Risk Management Framework: Generative Artificial Intelligence Profile* (July 2024), https://nvlpubs.nist.gov/nistpubs/ai/NIST.AI.600-1.pdf.

[491] NCSL, *Artificial Intelligence 2024 Legislation Summary*, https://www.ncsl.org/technology-and-communication/artificial-intelligence-2024-legislation; Artificial Intelligence Policy Toolkit, https://www.ncsl.org/technology-and-communication/artificial-intelligence-policy-toolkit.

use and post the audit results.[492] Colorado and Utah have enacted AI specific consumer protection laws.[493] Governments and regulators have issued guidance about how to use AI and comply with existing law.[494]

33.6 AI legislation in the EU

The European Union Artificial Intelligence Act became effective in August 2024 and is a comprehensive law for the EU on the subject.

It classifies AI systems based on their level of risk (unacceptable, high, limited, and minimal). Unacceptable risk systems are prohibited, minimal risk systems are not regulated, so the bulk of the law discusses high-risk AI systems.

It includes requirements for the organization creating the AI systems and the systems themselves, including risk management, data governance, maintaining documentation, transparency, human oversight, accuracy and cybersecurity. It has notification requirements and mechanisms for government oversight and enforcement, while maintaining helpful innovation.[495]

---

[492] *See* New York City Local Law 144 of 2021, effective 2023, https://rules.cityofnewyork.us/wp-content/uploads/2023/04/DCWP-NOA-for-Use-of-Automated-Employment-Decisionmaking-Tools-2.pdf.

[493] To see these laws or more recent developments, see the NCSL AI legislation page at https://www.ncsl.org/technology-and-communication/artificial-intelligence-2024-legislation. Or start with the appropriate state website.

[494] For example, *see* U.S. Department of Labor (DoL), *Artificial Intelligence*, https://www.dol.gov/ai; *Artificial Intelligence and Worker Well-Being Principles and Best Practices for Developers and Employers* (October 16, 2024), https://www.dol.gov/sites/dolgov/files/general/ai/AI-Principles-Best-Practices.pdf.

[495] The text of the actual law is nearly as long as this entire book. You can read it all at your leisure at https://eur-lex.europa.eu/legal-content/EN/TXT/?uri=CELEX:32024R1689. It is known as Regulation (EU) 2024/1689 of the European Parliament, laying down harmonized rules on artificial intelligence (Artificial Intelligence Act).

Helpful shorter resources are provided by the Future of Life Institute, *The EU Artificial Intelligence Act*, https://artificialintelligenceact.eu; *High-level summary of the AI Act*, https://artificialintelligenceact.eu/high-level-summary; *The AI Act Explorer*, https://artificialintelligenceact.eu/ai-act-explorer.

33.7 References and additional reading

- *Chapter 33 resources*, https://johnbandler.com/cyberlawbook-resources-ch33
- *Artificial Intelligence and Human Writing and Thinking*, https://johnbandler.com/artificial-intelligence-writing-thinking
- *AI's promise and problem for law and learning*, Reuters article available via https://johnbandler.com/ai-promise-and-problem
- White & Case, *AI Watch: Global regulatory tracker - United States*, https://www.whitecase.com/insight-our-thinking/ai-watch-global-regulatory-tracker-united-states
- Complaint, *NY Times v. Microsoft, OpenAI, et al.*, SDNY Case 1:23-cv-11195 Document 1 Filed 12/27/2023, available at https://nytco-assets.nytimes.com/2023/12/NYT_Complaint_Dec2023.pdf
- White House, *Blueprint for an AI Bill of Rights*, https://www.whitehouse.gov/ostp/ai-bill-of-right
- White House, *Fact Sheet, President Biden Issues Executive Order on Safe, Secure, and Trustworthy Artificial Intelligence* (October 30, 2023), https://www.whitehouse.gov/briefing-room/statements-releases/2023/10/30/fact-sheet-president-biden-issues-executive-order-on-safe-secure-and-trustworthy-artificial-intelligence/

32.13 Chapter questions

- Can a robot commit a crime? Explain. Consider the movie *I, Robot*, from 2004.
- If robots attack humanity, do we need to think about laws of war in our response? Explain (and see Chapter 35)
- Will AI related laws be more difficult to enforce than others? Why do you think that?
- A car is being driven by an AI software tool (an autonomous driving car) and it causes an accident. Who might be liable and why?

34

Some Data Laws Comprehensively

In this chapter:

- A quick walk through of data laws to be familiar with
- New York's data laws
- The FTC Act
- Sector specific laws

34.1 Data law recap

In the prior chapters we walked through three important "types" of data laws:

- Breach notification
- Cybersecurity
- Privacy.

> **Data law types**
> ☑ Breach notification
> ☑ Cybersecurity
> ☑ Privacy

As we did, we discussed the purpose and provided a quick example of each, introducing the laws we cover below.

In this chapter, we review some data laws from a more comprehensive perspective. We will indicate what data law components are within and provide a quick summary.

34.2 NY General Business Law 899-aa and 899-bb ("SHIELD Act")

This was our example statute as we covered breach notification and cybersecurity laws in previous chapters. New York has a breach notification requirement (like every other state) and a cybersecurity requirement.

> **Data law types**
> ☑ Breach notification
> ☑ Cybersecurity
> ☐ Privacy

New York's data breach notification law is found within G.B.L. § 899-aa which is titled "Notification; person without valid authorization has acquired private information."[496] This requires organizations to notify affected consumers if their data has been breached. Organizations also need to notify the state government.

New York's cybersecurity requirement law is within G.B.L. § 899-bb titled "Data security protections."[497]

This imposes a "reasonable security requirement" which includes to "develop, implement and maintain reasonable safeguards to protect the security, confidentiality and integrity of the private information." This includes "reasonable" administrative, technical, and physical safeguards (also known as controls) and provides some examples.[498]

For historical background, the data breach law has been around for a while, then the 2019 law titled the "SHIELD Act" (which cornily stands for "Stop Hacks and Improve Electronic Data Security Act") strengthened those data breach reporting requirements (within section 899-aa) and created the new cybersecurity requirement with a new section 899-bb.

34.3 NYS DFS Rule 500[499]

This is a rule (a regulation not a law) for the financial sector in New York, overseen by the New York Department of Financial Services (DFS). It imposes some detailed requirements for cybersecurity management and implementation.

> **Data law types**
> ☑ Breach notification
> ☑ Cybersecurity
> ❏ Privacy

This is a sector specific rule, and the cybersecurity requirements are there not just to protect consumer data, but the entirety of the financial institution's information systems. If there is a cyber event (data breach or not) then reporting needs to be made to DFS. The financial institution will have separate reporting requirements to consumers under the SHIELD Act.

---

[496] G.B.L. § 899-aa, https://www.nysenate.gov/legislation/laws/GBS/899-AA.

[497] G.B.L. § 899-bb, https://www.nysenate.gov/legislation/laws/GBS/899-BB.

[498] These examples in the statute are "suggestive," meaning not an absolute requirement.

[499] Rule 500, *Cybersecurity Requirements for Financial Services Companies*, 23 NYCRR Part 500, https://www.law.cornell.edu/regulations/new-york/title-23/chapter-I/part-500. *See also* New York DFS *Cybersecurity Resource Center*, https://www.dfs.ny.gov/industry_guidance/cybersecurity.

34.4 FTC Act

The Federal Trade Commission (FTC) Act empowers the FTC to regulate unfair or deceptive trade practices.[500]

<table>
<tr><td colspan="2">Data law types</td></tr>
<tr><td>❑</td><td>Breach notification</td></tr>
<tr><td>☑</td><td>Cybersecurity</td></tr>
<tr><td>☑</td><td>Privacy</td></tr>
</table>

This power has evolved to include the general principle that companies should have fair and clear privacy practices, hold data with a certain level of security and not make deceptive claims about their level of security.[501] Thus, the FTC is a primary federal enforcer of privacy and cybersecurity requirements.

While states have specific data laws that apply generally and across sectors, the federal government essentially does not.[502] The FTC Act fills that general role for now.

Federal Trade Commission Act §5(a)(1) (codified as 15 U.S.C. § 45(a)(1)) reads, in part,

> *(a) Declaration of unlawfulness; power to prohibit unfair practices; inapplicability to foreign trade*
>
> *(1) Unfair methods of competition in or affecting commerce, and unfair or deceptive acts or practices in or affecting commerce, are hereby declared unlawful.[503]*

For more on how the FTC interprets the privacy requirements of the FTC Act, see the guidance on their website.[504]

---

[500] FTC Act § 5(a), 15 U.S.C. § 45(a)(1). https://www.law.cornell.edu/uscode/text/15/45.

[501] While the FTC's authority comes from the FTC Act and the specified power over "unfair" or "deceptive" trade practices, you will not find the words "privacy" or "cybersecurity" anywhere in the FTC Act. The FTC's authority on these areas has been challenged and is far from absolute. It could be limited or expanded by future administrations or laws. That's why there are question marks instead of check marks for the infographic.

[502] There are federal data laws that apply to specific sectors such as finance and health, and there is the federal children's privacy law, COPPA.

[503] 15 U.S.C. § 45(a)(1), https://www.law.cornell.edu/uscode/text/15/45.

[504] FTC, *Privacy and Security*, https://www.ftc.gov/business-guidance/privacy-security; FTC, *Consumer Privacy*, https://www.ftc.gov/business-guidance/privacy-security/consumer-privacy; FTC, *Children's Privacy*, https://www.ftc.gov/business-guidance/privacy-security/childrens-privacy; FTC, *Data Security*, https://www.ftc.gov/business-guidance/privacy-security/data-security.

34.5 HIPAA: The federal health sector law

The health sector is regulated with a federal law for breach notification, cybersecurity, and privacy. That is the Health Insurance Portability and Accountability Act (HIPAA) (enacted in 1998).[505] It was amended in 2009 by the Health Information Technology for Economic and Clinical Health Act (HITECH).[506]

HIPAA was one of the earliest U.S. laws to protect personal information and privacy.[507]

HIPAA is overseen by the U.S. Department of Health and Human Services (HHS), which issues rules and regulations in accordance with the laws. Within HHS, enforcement is done by their Office for Civil Rights (OCR).

Under the authority of HIPAA (as amended by HITECH), HHS has issued rules (regulations), notably the "privacy rule," "security rule," and "breach notification rule."[508] These rules are set forth in the U.S. Code of Federal Regulations (C.F.R.).

As with any law or regulation, we need to be mindful of its definitions and what is covered. One important definition in HIPAA is that of protected health information (PHI).

---

[505] HIPAA is Public Law 104-191, Aug 21, 1996, 104th Congress, with full text available at https://www.govinfo.gov/content/pkg/PLAW-104publ191/html/PLAW-104publ191.htm.

[506] HITECH was enacted under Title XIII of the American Recovery and Reinvestment Act of 2009, Public Law 111–5, and the text is available at https://www.govinfo.gov/content/pkg/PLAW-111publ5/html/PLAW-111publ5.htm.

[507] I was a young trooper when the law was enacted and it required additional steps to obtain victim medical records which were important evidence to prove physical injuries in an assault case. We were instructed to help the victim fill out a HIPAA waiver so the prosecutor could get those records more easily.

[508] These rules (regulations) can be found within 45 C.F.R. Part 160, General Administrative Requirements, https://www.law.cornell.edu/cfr/text/45/part-160; 45 C.F.R. Part 164, *Security and Privacy*, https://www.law.cornell.edu/cfr/text/45/part-164. There are three main rules:

Security Rule, 45 C.F.R. 164 Subparts A and C.
Privacy Rule, 45 C.F.R. 164 Subparts A and E.
Breach Notification Rule, 45 C.F.R. 164 Subpart D.

The privacy rule was put forth in 2000, security rule in 2003, and breach notification rule in 2009.

If you need to take a deeper dive into the requirements of HIPAA and the related regulations, first check the text of the laws and regulations, then see the guidance from HHS.[509]

Also consider the health-related laws of your state.

34.6 Other data laws

We covered many data laws in Part 6, but not all are worth the extra word count to summarize them additionally here. Instead, here is a quick recap list:

- Family Educational Rights and Privacy Act of 1974 (FERPA)
- Children's Online Privacy Protection Act (COPPA)
- Federal financial data laws and regulations
  - Gramm-Leach-Bliley Act (GLBA) (also known as the Financial Services Modernization Act of 1999) and accompanying Privacy Rule
  - FFIEC requirements for information systems
- State data laws
  - Every state has a data breach notification law
  - Most states have a cybersecurity law
  - Many states have a privacy law.

34.7 References and additional reading

- *Chapter 34 resources*, https://johnbandler.com/cyberlawbook-resources-ch34
- Chapter 29, Data law
- Chapter 30, Data breach notification laws
- Chapter 31, Cybersecurity laws
- Chapter 32, Privacy laws
- *New York Cybersecurity Requirements and the SHIELD Act*, https://johnbandler.com/new-york-cybersecurity-requirements-and-the-shield-act
- G.B.L. § 899-aa, Data breach notification, https://www.nysenate.gov/legislation/laws/GBS/899-AA

---

[509] U.S. Dept HHS, *Health Information Privacy*, https://www.hhs.gov/hipaa/index.html. HHS resources seem to be less helpful compared to many other regulators in explain their rules and HHS has some outdated webpages and resources. See my article for full references, *Health Sector Cyber Laws and Regulations*, https://johnbandler.com/health-sector-laws-and-regulations.

- G.B.L. § 899-bb, Data security protections, https://www.nysenate.gov/legislation/laws/GBS/899-BB
- FTC Act § 5(a), 15 U.S.C. § 45(a)(1), https://www.law.cornell.edu/uscode/text/15/45
- FTC, Privacy and Security, https://www.ftc.gov/business-guidance/privacy-security

34.8 Chapter questions

- List the three types of data laws discussed in this chapter.
- Write out the name, full citation, and a brief summary of NY's main data law.
- Write out the name, full citation, and a brief summary of NY's cybersecurity law for the financial sector.
- Is HIPAA a breach notification law, cybersecurity law, or privacy law? Explain.
- When you hear HIPAA rule, just think of it as a _____
- List the HIPAA rules
- Write out the full name of the regulator that enforces the FTC Act and cite to the act and provide a link for it.
- What is the language in the FTC Act that gives the FTC authority over privacy?

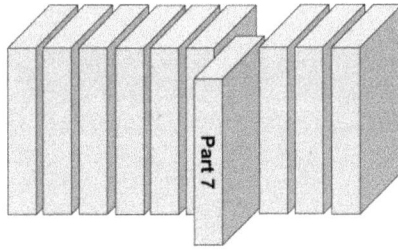

Part 7

International Cyber Actions and Cyber Conflict

In this part:

- Cyber conflict between nation-states

John T. Bandler

35

Law of War, International Conflict, and Cyberconflict

In this chapter:

- International conflict introduced
- Nation-state cyber operations
- Cyber actions could be hidden
- They could be extremely harmful
- They can influence our thoughts and acts
- Let's examine the laws around that.

35.1 Introducing international conflict (why can't we just get along?)

As we evaluate cyber conduct and cyberlaw, think about what areas of law might apply, since "cyberlaw" spans every aspect of criminal law, civil law, and international law. Let's discuss international laws for conflict.

Humans always have trouble just getting along. Whether it is individuals, groups, or nation-states, there has always been some degree of conflict. When that conflict is within our country among individuals, we address it with criminal law and civil law. When that conflict is between large and well-resourced groups—like nation-states—we have a global issue and look to international laws.[510]

One group may want land, water, natural resources, other wealth, or information. They may try to take it from another group because they think they are entitled to it, or because they think they can get away with

---

[510] In this book we refer to countries as "nation-states," recognizing that international law custom refers to them as "states," under the theory that an independent nation is a sovereign "state." That term causes confusion if we also discuss states and state laws within the United States. So here, "nation-state" is a country and "state" is one of the fifty states within the U.S.

it. Sometimes bad conduct is prevented because they know there will be consequences if they try. That is the principle of deterrence.

Some countries (just like some individuals) respect the rights of others, which means they would not try to take what they are not entitled to (even if they could).

Every country has powerful motivations and needs to protect themselves, knowing they have adversaries. Countries want to be able to strike other countries if the need arises. Once upon a time, the only adversaries with significant capability for delivering death and destruction were nation-states, but now terrorists can too.

Within each country are internal dynamics that influence action. Nation-states are made up of individuals, some wielding considerable power, and all have personal motivations which can influence the country's actions. Power, recognition, status, wealth, retribution, and religion are all powerful motivators towards action and conflict.

Countries with government directed economies have a greater incentive to commit economic espionage, since powerful cyber capabilities can achieve an economic advantage, in addition to strategic gains.

35.2 International conflict scenarios and law

Domestic criminal and civil laws could have international reach but are often inadequate to address most international conflict. We ask:

- What laws prevent a country from attacking another or using force illegally?
- What laws allow a country to defend itself from attack?
- As a country evaluates a military action, what legal principles do they need to evaluate?

Consider these scenarios:

- Terrorist Group A hijacks planes in country B, flies them into buildings, killing everyone on the planes and thousands of civilians on the ground. Country B may look to criminal and civil laws, but also to tools and measures beyond those and which do not involve the court system.
- Nation-State C illegally invades Nation-State D and destroys property, kills civilians, kidnaps children, takes over certain territory. Buildings are destroyed, many people are killed, and the war continues. While criminal law or civil law could be used for some areas, Nation C would not voluntarily comply with

Nation D's criminal or civil processes. In other words, this is primarily a military issue rather than an issue for police and courts.

- Terrorist Group E invades Nation-State F, murdering civilians, killing families, children, and the elderly, taking civilian hostages, and committing rape and other atrocities. While criminal law and civil law could play a role in the response, it would not be a primary role.

Now consider these types of cyber operations:

- A cyberattack to disrupt a country's operations.
- Cyberattack designed to damage equipment that could be used to further a nuclear program or manufacture nuclear weapons.
- A cyberattack to cripple critical infrastructure in a country, with the potential to cause significant disruption and widespread death, including attacks upon:
  o Dams
  o Nuclear power plants
  o Water treatment plants
  o Financial systems
  o Health systems
  o Traffic control
  o GPS and other navigation systems.
- Cyberoperations to influence how people think, what they might do, and how they might vote. Foreign countries may have a preference over which government official or candidate they want to interact with and may try to tilt the scales one way. Foreign adversaries benefit anytime they can weaken our country and increase internal discord.

Our nation's powerful capabilities for military, intelligence, and justice includes thousands of lawyers working within them to help ensure that our country's actions comply with applicable laws.[511] This includes when our country takes lethal actions (missiles, bombs, tanks, special operations forces) and cyber actions (network intrusions and more).

---

[511] Reasonable people can disagree about the many things this country does, including when it comes to national security, espionage, and military force. Few people will claim that our country's actions are always perfect. The point is there are many government lawyers who are evaluating the laws and legal issues regarding those actions.

35.3 Law of war principles

Consider three important parts of the law of war:[512]

- The principle of *sovereignty*
- When it is lawful to *start* an armed conflict
- Lawful conduct *during* an armed conflict.

Nation-state sovereignty is an important principle which is discussed further in the next section. Sovereignty essentially means: Do not interfere with other countries, respect their physical borders and respect their right to manage their affairs within their borders.

Jus ad bellum is a Latin term that means "right to war" and concerns when starting a war or using armed force might be lawful and justified (a helpful analogy is criminal laws for use of force and self-defense). The UN Charter (next) is important for this principle.

Jus in bello means "right conduct in war" and the law of how war should be conducted while in an armed conflict. This is sometimes referred to as international humanitarian law (IHL) and incorporates the Hague Conventions and Geneva Conventions.[513] The purpose is to reduce unnecessary suffering in war. For example, targeting and killing civilians is prohibited, so is torturing prisoners of war (POWs). Combatants should apply targeting principles of humanity, proportionality, distinction between military and civilian targets, and use only force necessary to secure the defeat of the enemy.

35.4 The UN Charter

The United Nations (UN) Charter is a foundational document of international law.[514] It is the document that created the United Nations, effective in 1945 at the end of World War II and with the hope to avoid another such war.

U.N. Charter Article 2(4) and Article 51 lay out the concepts of sovereignty and self-defense.

---

[512] Law of war is also called law of armed conflict (LOAC).
[513] Cornell LII, *Geneva Conventions and their additional protocols*, https://www.law.cornell.edu/wex/geneva_conventions_and_their_additional_protocols.
[514] The UN Charter is to international law as the U.S. Constitution is to U.S. law. The UN plays a large role with international law and relations, and we discussed the UN cybercrime convention (treaty) in Part 4.

Article 2

The Organization and its Members, in pursuit of the Purposes stated in Article 1, shall act in accordance with the following Principles.

1. The Organization is based on the principle of the sovereign equality of all its Members.

...

3. All Members shall settle their international disputes by peaceful means in such a manner that international peace and security, and justice, are not endangered.

4. All Members shall refrain in their international relations from the threat or use of force against the territorial integrity or political independence of any state, or in any other manner inconsistent with the Purposes of the United Nations.

U.N. Charter, Article 2[515]

Article 51 provides for self-defense, including collective self-defense:

Article 51

Nothing in the present Charter shall impair the inherent right of individual or collective self-defence if an armed attack occurs against a Member of the United Nations, until the Security Council has taken measures necessary to maintain international peace and security. Measures taken by Members in the exercise of this right of self-defence shall be immediately reported to the Security Council and shall not in any way affect the authority and responsibility of the Security Council under the present Charter to take at any time such action as it deems necessary in order to maintain or restore international peace and security.

UN Charter, Article 51[516]

---

[515] U.N. Charter, Art. 2, https://www.un.org/en/about-us/un-charter/chapter-1.
[516] U.N. Charter Art. 51, https://www.un.org/en/about-us/un-charter/chapter-7.

35.5 Use of force analogy: international law vs. criminal law

International laws on conflict can be compared with some of our criminal law provisions on use of force and self-defense.

Criminal laws first make it a crime to use force against another person, including by pushing, punching, or shooting them with a gun. That is the general rule.

Then laws cover circumstances where self-defense is acceptable when faced with unlawful force from another. In New York, this is the defense of "justification" which outlines provisions for self-defense or defense of others. This means the law recognizes circumstances when a person could lawfully use force, even deadly force. That person would need to invoke this defense of justification, or "self-defense."

When police officers use force, whether it is a grab, punch, tackle, or even use of their sidearm, they need to rely on this defense of justification.[517] Same for when a private citizen uses force, though a slightly different legal standard.

Similarly, international laws of warfare make the use of force illegal against another country, while also allowing a nation to protect itself against the unlawful aggression from another.

Just as criminal laws allow for the "defense of others," anticipating that one individual might need to aid another who is in a weakened position, international law does too, calling it "collective" self-defense.

35.6 Translating existing law of war to cyberspace

The next question is how do these existing international laws translate to cyberspace? The UN Charter of 1945 surely did not anticipate cyber operations, but the legal principles certainly can be applied there.

We look to the language of Article 51 where it gives the right of self-defense against an "armed attack."

---

[517] As always when using force (or legal tools) just because something can be done, does not mean it *should* be done. Police officers should use the least forceful option available under the circumstances, consistent with their safety and the safety of others. That could be a polite instruction, stern command, grab, tackle, punch, pepper spray, stick, taser, or discharging a sidearm.
  Once the action has occurred, we look to the facts and law to see if it was justified.

If an "armed attack" in 1950 (for example) surely included a missile strike that damaged buildings and killed people, surely that would apply to a cyberattack (such as on a nuclear power plant or other utility) that led to damage and death. These types of comparisons are an area of legal scholarship and what the Tallinn Manual explores.

35.7 The Tallinn Manual and other legal scholarship

The Tallinn Manual is a product of the NATO Cooperative Cyber Defence Centre of Excellence (CCDOE) in Tallinn, Estonia and is "an influential resource for legal advisers and policy experts dealing with cyber issues" in the international arena.[518]

The original manual was published in 2013 and "addressed the most severe cyber operations – those that violate the prohibition of the use of force, entitle states to exercise their right of self-defence, or occur during armed conflict."[519]

The Tallinn Manual 2.0 came in 2017, adding more routine cyber incidents that nation-states "encounter on a day-to-day basis but which fall below the thresholds of the use of force or armed conflict."[520] They are working on version 3.0 now.

The impetus for the CCDOE and the Tallinn Manual

The creation of the CCDOE and the Tallinn Manual stems from Estonia being one of the first countries victimized by a widespread cyberattack.

Estonia used to be part of the Soviet Union but was the first to declare its sovereignty in 1988 (the collapse of the Soviet Union would be complete by 1992).

In 2007 Estonia decided to move a Soviet war memorial from its place of prominence to a more out-of-the-way location. Protests ensued (ostensibly from Soviet-Russian sympathizers) and next came cyberattacks against government information systems, banks, and news sites. Many systems were knocked offline, and disruption was considerable. It was not possible to prove who was behind the attacks, though some blamed Russia, or at least Russian sympathizers.

---

[518] NATO CCDOE, *The Tallinn Manual*, https://ccdcoe.org/research/tallinn-manual.
[519] *Id.* (same as above)
[520] *Id.*

From this attack, Tallinn became the new epicenter of legal scholarship on international cyber conflict.

In 2008 NATO established the CCDCoE in Tallinn, where it remains the center in the study of cyber conflict. From this, they produced the "Tallinn Manual" and its updates.

Many legal scholars and organizations contribute to the work of this CCDCoE and the Tallinn manual.[521]

35.8 International courts

There are international courts to deal with violations of international law and war crimes.

We can appreciate how slowly courts work within our own country, then assume that international justice works even slower and less efficiently. Not every dispute can or should be taken to court. In sum, few international disputes will be resolved in an international court, but we should evaluate what courts exist.

From our U.S. perspective, if our country believes someone has harmed our country or one of our citizens, we would rely upon U.S. action or U.S. courts, as international courts would not be our first-choice location to resolve that.[522] We should still know what courts exist.

Consider the International Court of Justice, established by U.N. Charter Article 92, which "shall be the principal judicial organ of the United Nations."[523] Located in The Hague, Netherlands, it can hear disputes between countries, including for violations of sovereignty.

---

[521] Professor Michael Schmitt is leading the Tallinn Manual 3.0 project and has been a leading scholar on cyber conflict. See his work including:
Michael N. Schmitt, *Grey Zones in the International Law of Cyberspace*, Yale Journal of International Law (October 18, 2017), https://papers.ssrn.com/sol3/papers.cfm?abstract_id=3180687; Michael N. Schmitt, *Foreign Cyber Interference in Elections*, 97 INT'L L. STUD. 739 (2021), via https://digital-commons.usnwc.edu/ils/vol97/iss1/32.
[522] For example, if the U.S. can prove a terrorist killed U.S. citizens and that is a worthy subject of criminal prosecution, we would use our own courts to criminally charge that individual, not international courts. Alternatively, we might even target them to be killed, while documenting—somewhere secretly—the legal justification for that killing.
[523] *See* The International Court of Justice, https://www.icj-cij.org/home; U.N. Charter Article 92, https://www.un.org/en/about-us/un-charter.

Then there is the International Criminal Court (created by the Rome Statute in 1998, also located in The Hague, which has jurisdiction over genocide, crimes against humanity, war crimes, and the crime of aggression against sovereignty.[524]

Separately, there are also international provisions to obtain evidence in a cybercrime criminal prosecution, which we covered in Part 4.[525]

35.9 National security investigations and cyberspace

Our laws recognize that the government needs additional powers and leeway when performing its national security functions as compared to traditional law enforcement criminal investigation functions.

In criminal cases the law emphasizes the rights of the accused and public disclosure, whereas in national security cases we are protecting against nation-states and terrorists. We are less concerned with their individual rights and we recognize a greater need for secrecy.

Put simply, if a foreign espionage agent or terrorist is operating within our country, the traditional criminal investigative tools (search warrant or wiretap) with eventual public disclosure are often not suitable. The government needs greater powers and more secrecy.

Nevertheless, we do not want our executive branch's surveillance powers to be absolute and unchecked, and there are grey areas.

To resolve these competing needs, we have the Foreign Intelligence Surveillance Act (FISA)[526] and a special Foreign Intelligence Surveillance Court.[527] This provides a degree of oversight regarding executive branch surveillance activities within the country and against U.S. citizens. Both the legislative branch and judicial branch play a role in this oversight through reporting and review of national security related legal process such as search warrants, wiretaps, and obtaining records such as through national security letters.

---

[524] International Criminal Court, https://www.icc-cpi.int; *How the Court works*, https://www.icc-cpi.int/about/how-the-court-works.
[525] Consider MLATs, the Budapest convention on cybercrime, and the U.N. convention against cybercrime, as we covered in Chapter 21.
[526] FISA is encoded in Title 50 Chapter 36 of the U.S. Code, https://www.law.cornell.edu/uscode/text/50/chapter-36.
[527] Foreign Intelligence Surveillance Court, https://www.fisc.uscourts.gov.

If our military and intelligence functions are attempting to surveil a terrorist or foreign power operating outside of this country, the Fourth Amendment does not apply, and no FISA authorization is needed.

Various executive orders also direct how the executive branch intelligence activities should be performed.[528]

35.10 A range of tools and options for the U.S.

As the U.S. considers how to respond to cyber operations and international cyberconflict, it needs to consider its legal authorities and all tools. Conflict exists within a continuum, from verbal discussion to physical force and destruction, so the right tool needs to be considered.

International relations and associated issues are typically for the federal government to address.

As we assess legal tools and boundaries, important areas are:

- Civil law
- Criminal law
- National security law
- International laws including the principle of sovereignty, UN Charter, treaties, and conventions.

Civil laws[529] are the laws within our country which relate to civil duties and liabilities. These have limited teeth, and foreign nations have significant protection from civil liability based on the Foreign Sovereign Immunities Act (FSIA). Generally, the law gives them immunity, thought they can be sued if the civil wrong (tort) was committed on U.S. territory.[530]

Criminal laws[531] are the laws within our country to investigate, apprehend, and prosecute and potentially punish. When used against nation-state or terrorist actors, they serve the additional function of publicly announcing the charges, defendants, and underlying activities, thus earning the nickname of "name and shame." There may be little hope of ever capturing the named defendants, but it lets the world know

---

[528] For example, Executive Order 12333 (1981 by President Reagan), EO 13355 and EO 13470 (2004 and 2008 by President George W. Bush).
[529] Primarily regarding intentional torts, as covered in Chapter 24.
[530] Foreign Sovereign Immunities Act (FSIA), 28 U.S.C. Chapter 97, *Jurisdictional Immunities of Foreign States*, https://www.law.cornell.edu/uscode/text/28/part-IV/chapter-97.
[531] As covered in Chapter 8 and Part 4.

what was done and makes it easier for the government to take other actions, such as sanctions.

National security laws include additional tools for related investigations, we cover in the next section.

We covered international laws and customs in this chapter that might provide a protection or option, including:

- Principles of sovereignty (that a country has its own right of self-determination and a right not to be invaded)
- Treaties (like a contract between nation-states, which could be on any topic, including criminal investigation, extradition, obtaining evidence)
- Conventions (like a contract or treaty between many nation-states), and
- Judicial enforcement mechanisms such as the UN and international courts.

When conduct by other nation-states or terrorists does not comply with the law, the U.S. could seek remedy in a court, but more importantly would be its range of options to act outside of a court.

The full range of options includes:

- Do nothing
- Seek legal redress through U.S. or international courts
  - Bringing criminal charges in U.S. courts allows the "name and shame" to publicize the actions, and facilitate other options related to diplomacy, sanctions, and etc.
- Funding and favors: The ability of a country to provide funding or do favors (positive actions) regarding another country.
- Diplomacy: The process one country uses to navigate issues with other countries.
- Sanctions: The ability of a country to impose negative consequences on another country, usually through economic actions or prohibitions.
- Espionage: Stealing and obtaining information.
- Clandestine operations: Secret actions that are concealed from the target country and not detected.
- Covert operations: Secret actions that are noticed by the target country but cannot be attributed to an actor.

- Spreading the word: Actions designed to share information and facts about our country and current events, especially in regimes that restrict free access to news and information.

35.11 Examples of international cyber actions[532]

We covered the cyberattack on Estonia, let's outline a few others.

35.11.1 Cuckoo's Egg events: Espionage from the former Soviet Union[533]

Clifford Stoll was working as a system administrator for the information systems at Lawrence Berkeley National Laboratory in 1986. It was the early days of networked computers and university users were billed for their network time. Cliff discovered a minor billing discrepancy which he investigated and soon realized a network attacker ("hacker") had been using the systems, deleting some logs and records but not realizing that billing records were created. Cliff started to investigate and track the attacker's movements through the system, ultimately working with the government.

Ultimately the attacker was identified and determined to be working for the Soviet Union's intelligence apparatus to obtain sensitive information from military and university systems around the U.S.

This is one of the earliest examples of nation-state-sponsored computer intrusions. Rest assured it continues continually today.

35.11.2 Foreign influence or interference in U.S. elections

Foreign attempts to interfere with U.S. elections and influence voters are well documented and not unexpected.[534] The stakes around the globe are huge, conflicts are raging. Human life, territory, and trillions of dollars are at stake.

---

[532] Chapter 8 of our 2020 book on Cybercrime Investigations walked through many of these examples as well.

[533] Clifford Stoll, *The Cuckoo's Egg: Tracking a Spy through the Maze of Computer Espionage* (New York, Doubleday, 1989).

[534] These attempts may be expected, but it does not mean they should be accepted or tolerated. U.S. citizens should determine our own government and leaders, without foreign interference.

During the 2016 election cycle, Russia conducted illegal data breaches and selectively leaked information, as borne out by investigations, reports, and indictments.[535]

During the 2020 election cycle, such activities also occurred, including election influence, which "includes overt and covert efforts by foreign governments or actors acting as agents of, or on behalf of, foreign governments intended to affect directly or indirectly a U.S. election—including candidates, political parties, voters or their preferences, or political processes."[536]

During the 2024 election cycle influence operations continued. Some were by Russia as part of their "broader effort to raise unfounded questions about the integrity of the U.S. election and stoke divisions among Americans."[537] Some were by Iranian nationals as "part of Iran's continuing efforts to stoke discord, erode confidence in the U.S. electoral process, and unlawfully acquire information relating to current and former U.S. officials."[538]

---

[535] *See*, Office of the Director of National Intelligence (ODNI), *Assessing Russian Activities and Intentions in Recent U.S. Elections* (preceded by a background document) (January 6, 2017), www.dni.gov/files/documents/ICA_2017_01.pdf; Special Counsel Robert S. Mueller, III, *Report on the Special Investigation into Russian Interference in the 2016 Presidential Election*, "Mueller Report," (March 2019), https://www.justice.gov/archives/sco/file/1373816/dl; *U.S. v. Internet Research Agency LLC et al.*, (1:18-cr-32, District of Columbia) February 16, 2018; U.S. DOJ, *Press Release, Grand Jury Indicts 12 Russian Intelligence Officers for Hacking Offenses Related to the 2016 Election* (July 13, 2018), www.justice.gov/opa/pr/grand-jury-indicts-12-russian-intelligenceofficers-hacking-offenses-related-2016-election.

[536] National Intelligence Council, *Foreign Threats to the 2020 U.S. Federal Elections* (March 10, 2021), https://www.dni.gov/files/ODNI/documents/assessments/ICA-declass-16MAR21.pdf; Michael N. Schmitt, *Foreign Cyber Interference in Elections*, 97 INT'L L. STUD. 739 (2021), via https://digital-commons.usnwc.edu/ils/vol97/iss1/32.

[537] Multiple U.S. Agencies, *Press Release, Joint ODNI, FBI, and CISA Statement on Russian Election Influence Efforts* (November 1, 2024), https://www.dni.gov/index.php/newsroom/press-releases/press-releases-2024/4014-pr-28-24.

[538] U.S. DOJ, *Press Release, Three IRGC Cyber Actors Indicted for 'Hack-and-Leak' Operation Designed to Influence the 2024 U.S. Presidential Election* (September 27, 2024), https://www.justice.gov/opa/pr/three-irgc-cyber-actors-indicted-hack-and-leak-operation-designed-influence-2024-us.

Nation-states conduct these influence operations, which are a type of cyber operation and conflict. They also impact our system of law and government, our country's ability to fairly pick our own leaders, and is a part of speech and expression online, which we return to next chapter.

35.11.3 Terrorist disruption and DDoS attacks

In October 2024, two individuals were charged with attacking information systems and temporarily disabling them through distributed denial of service (DDoS) attacks[539] as part of "Anonymous Sudan."[540] Their targets included the U.S. government and U.S. based healthcare and tech companies, including Microsoft, Google, and Cloudflare. They also attacked targets in other countries, including France, Netherlands, and Israel. Notably, the cyber-attacks targeted Israel's alert systems, including in the morning on October 7, 2023, when the Hamas terrorist attack on Israel was occurring.

35.12 References and additional reading

- *Chapter 35 resources,* https://johnbandler.com/cyberlawbook-resources-ch35
- *International cyber conflict,* https://johnbandler.com/cyber-conflict
- UN Charter Article 1 and 2, especially 2(4) https://www.un.org/en/about-us/un-charter/chapter-1

---

[539] DDOS attacks flood a webserver or website with extensive disruptive web traffic, often from an army of malware infected computers located around the world. This can make the systems unavailable for legitimate users.

[540] U.S. DOJ, *Press Release, Two Sudanese Nationals Indicted for Alleged Role in Anonymous Sudan Cyberattacks on Hospitals, Government Facilities, and Other Critical Infrastructure in Los Angeles and Around the World* (October 16, 2024), https://www.justice.gov/usao-cdca/pr/two-sudanese-nationals-indicted-alleged-role-anonymous-sudan-cyberattacks-hospitals; Indictment, USDC CDCA, filed October 11, 2024, *U.S. v Ahmed Salah Yousif Omer and Alaa Salah Yusuuf Omer*, https://www.justice.gov/usao-cdca/media/1373581 /dl?inline; Criminal Complaint, USDC, CDCA, filed March 20, 2024, *U.S. v. Ahmed Salah Yousif Omer*, https://www.justice.gov/usao-cdca/media/1373586/dl?inline; Brian Krebs, *Sudanese Brothers Arrested in 'AnonSudan' Takedown*, KrebsonSecurity (October 17, 2024), https://krebsonsecurity.com/2024/10/sudanese-brothers-arrested-in-anonsudan-takedown.

- UN Charter Article 51 https://www.un.org/en/about-us/un-charter/chapter-7
- NATO Cooperative Cyber Defence Centre of Excellence (CCDCOE), https://ccdcoe.org/
- CCDCOE, The Tallinn Manual, https://ccdcoe.org/research/tallinn-manual/
- Army Cyber Institute at West Point, https://cyber.army.mil
- U.S. Army Cyber Center of Excellence (CCoE), https://cybercoe.army.mil/
- U.S. Army Cyber Command, https://www.arcyber.army.mil/
- *Cybercrime Investigations* (2020 book), Chapter 8 Cyber Investigations Linked to Nation-States or Terrorists
- Michael Schmitt, *Grey Zones in the International Law of Cyberspace*, Yale Journal of International Law (October 18, 2017), https://papers.ssrn.com/sol3/papers.cfm?abstract_id =3180687.
- Michael N. Schmitt, *Foreign Cyber Interference in Elections*, 97 INT'L L. STUD. 739 (2021), at https://digital-commons. usnwc.edu/cgi/viewcontent.cgi?article=2969&context=ils, via https://digital-commons.usnwc.edu/ils/vol97/iss1/32

35.13 Chapter questions

- Given the difficulties enforcing criminal law and civil law, what difficulties do you think are involved enforcing international laws? Explain.
- Nation-states may have tremendous resources and have strong motives to achieve a goal. Does it surprise you they would use cyberspace? What types of cyber actions might they take?
- What types of actions do nation-states take that we never hear about?
- What types of cyber actions do you think nation-states are taking now?
- What types of cyber actions do you think nation-states are planning, even if they do not intend to carry them out at this point?
- Does it surprise you that there are laws about when to start a war?
- Does it surprise you that there are laws about how a war should be conducted?
- What is the primary international law, sort of like an international Constitution?

- What do you think about the analogy between criminal law and use of force compared to international law and warfare?
- Does it surprise you that existing laws of war can be applied to cyberconflict?
- Why is the Tallinn Manual named after "Tallinn"?
- The U.S. government is granted far more authority and secrecy for national security investigations compared to criminal investigations. Why is that, and does that surprise you?

John T. Bandler

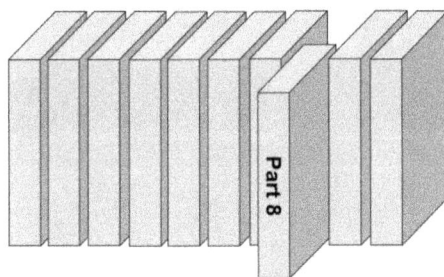

Part 8

Speech, Expression,
and Thought in Cyberspace
and Our Brains

In this part:

- Cyber is a powerful way to express and influence
- Law, human development, culture, society, and democracy

John T. Bandler

36

Cyber Speech and Cyberspace's
Battle for Our Minds

In this chapter:

- Speech and expression online
- Continue the discussion upon the foundations we have laid
- Communications Decency Act
- Cyberbullying
- Influence online
- Who should win the battle for our brains?

36.1 Our foundation to analyze speech online (recap)

This chapter draws upon our foundation from prior chapters and areas of law, including:

- The First Amendment
- Criminal law
- Civil law
- International laws on conflict.

While law is our first point of analysis in this book, it is not everything in life because we cannot legislate everything, nor can we enforce every law every time. This means we need to consider broader concepts about how we should get our information, form opinions, and make decisions.

People make decisions about what to buy, view, watch, or click. Poor information gathering, thinking, and decisions can mean individuals are more susceptible to consumer fraud through deceptive marketing and to criminal fraud attempts through phishing and social engineering attempts.

We are a democracy where citizens make important choices about our country and who should lead it. If citizens in a country are susceptible to influence, misinformation, disinformation, conspiracy theories and manipulation, then decision making is not optimized. That can negatively affect our democracy.

36.2 Our foundations in law and technology (recap)

Let's recap some important principles and laws about speech and expression in the U.S.

36.2.1 A progression of speech with technology (recap)[541]

Never in human history has there been such an ability to speak and reach an entire country and much of the world. There is more speech than ever, but more importantly there is now the potential for a nation-state or a billionaire to influence thought and action on a massive scale. This is the current cyberworld we live in.

36.2.2 Legally protected speech (not "free speech") (recap)

The term "free speech" is vague and means different things to different people. Instead, let us focus on:

- The law, and what speech it protects, and what it does not
  - o Whether from civil action, criminal action, or both
- Rules about speech in private situations or on private platforms (which may not need to comply with the First Amendment)

Then we realize that whatever the rules are:

- Some will break those rules.
- Certain speech may be allowed but may not be good for society ("just because you can, doesn't mean you should")
- People will be bombarded by speech, including "bad" speech and false speech. How they receive it is important.

We consider all issues relating to speech and expression, including:

- When should people be allowed to express themselves and their opinions, or their view on what the "facts" are?
- When should people be allowed to put forth incorrect information, lies, or other false or misleading statements?
- Whatever is allowed or not, how should individuals assess information to form thoughts and opinions?

---

[541] *See* Chapter 13 on this evolution.

36.2.3 First Amendment speech categories[542]

Our First Amendment means we value free speech and free thought and are wary of any government restrictions in these areas.

The First Amendment is our country's highest law regarding speech and expression and is a limit on what government can do to restrict speech.

We introduced a way to categorize speech:

- **All speech** is all speech and expression.
- **Protected speech** is speech that the government cannot do anything about, neither with criminal action, nor allow it to be the proper subject of a civil action.
- **Civilly actionable speech** is speech that could be a proper subject of a civil action, such as for defamation or harassment. [543]
- **Criminally actionable speech** is speech that the government could criminally prosecute someone for, perhaps because the speech itself a crime, or threatens imminent harm.[544]

We introduced categories based upon the negative effect upon the listener:

- **Annoying speech** is speech that someone finds annoying.
- **Unfriending speech** is speech that someone finds annoying enough that they take an action in response to that annoyance.

Now it is time to add one more category:

- **Influencing speech** is speech that influences someone, in some way.

36.2.4 Speech that influences

Any speech can influence a thought or an action. If it invokes a negative impression the reaction could result in a complaint to the police or a call to a lawyer, in which case we will need to analyze any First Amendment issues.

---

[542] *See* Chapter 10 on the First Amendment.
[543] *See* Chapter 10 and then Chapter 24 on defamation, a type of intentional tort.
[544] *See* Chapter 10 and then Chapter 20 on substantive cybercrimes relating to speech. For example, a threat to kill someone is probably a crime. Words that deliberately inflame a crowd ("incitement to riot") could be a crime. Some words are themselves part of a crime (give me your wallet or I will cut you).

If speech is received positively, there will be no complaint and therefore no First Amendment analysis, but it still affects our society and country. The person may view, click, purchase, donate, protest, think a certain way, or vote a certain way.

We should analyze the effects on society, especially in our cyber age where persuasion and influence are so powerful.

Many individuals and groups try to influence us, including parents, teachers, friends, government, candidates for office, businesses, nation-states, and other groups and individuals.

Some do this in good faith, altruistically, others have motives that are less noble to include financial or for power. Some provide accurate information, to allow for facts and reason to be used, others may be deceptive and misleading.

36.3 Influencing

The internet is a mechanism to share information and knowledge, and this means it is a way to influence others.

Individuals and groups who communicate through the internet may have powerful motives and intentions to influence people in a certain way. They may want people to perform an act or think a certain way.

36.3.1 Business advertising and influencing (recap)[545]

Hundreds of billions of dollars are spent each year on digital advertising, and the goal is to influence people to click on a link, view a webpage or video, and ultimately make a purchase. Some platforms exist to sell advertising to other companies who in turn hope to gain business.

When companies spend money to advertise their product, they do not present a balanced picture of all the options a consumer could choose from, they simply focus on getting the consumer to buy *their* product. Often, it is a call to emotion, sometimes to fear, creating a sense of urgency as to why the purchase should happen now. Sometimes the ads are clearly marked, sometimes they are subtle or even invasive.[546]

---

[545] Chapter 15 covered the markets for data about you, including the advertising industry.

[546] Product placement in a movie subtly puts that item in our brain. Social media influencers may be paid to promote products, services, or viewpoints, and the payment may not always be disclosed transparently.

There are many companies whose products and services provide good value, and they advertise truthfully and ethically. Even with a good product, they need to spend money to convince consumers to buy it.

There are other companies with shady practices and products, and their advertising might be deceptive.

Advertising and marketing influences consumers to make purchases. That is clear. Otherwise, companies would not spend so much money on it.

36.3.2 Cybercrime influence (social engineering)

Cybercriminals influence people too, and they are good at it. That is what "social engineering" is—tricking someone to do something, a form of con artistry. Cybercriminals deceive victims into taking an action, such as:

- Clicking a link
- Opening an attachment
- Responding to a request for information
- Wiring money to the wrong place
- Sending money to a cybercriminal masquerading as a love interest.

36.3.3 Not all influence is bad

A lot of influence attempts are well-intentioned and may be very solid advice.

When the government puts out information to influence people to wear their seatbelts, check the batteries in their smoke detectors, not smoke cigarettes, or to get vaccinated, that is done with good intention and to achieve good results. The reasoning is if more people do those things, health will be better, more lives will be saved, costs will be reduced.

When parents give advice to children, they hope the children will be influenced to follow that advice. The same for teachers who hope to influence students to study, read, pay attention, put effort into assignments, and learn. They hope that students will continue their learning through life, including their ability to investigate facts, apply reason, and succeed (however they define success).

We have all been inspired by people who said or did amazing things, which motivates us in positive ways. In sum, influence *can* be a good thing.

36.3.4 Some influence is definitely bad

Some influence is clearly bad. We have heard the phrase:

> *"Be careful of the company you keep."*

> *"Choose your friends wisely."*

Hanging with the wrong crowd can influence us down a path of conduct that can get us in trouble.

At some point in life, all of us have made a bad choice because we were influenced by someone who steered us wrong, for whatever reason, accidental or malicious. A convincing salesperson, a scammer, even a well-intentioned friend who influenced us and we made a bad choice.

At the extreme, some people have even taken their own lives because of the actions and influence of others.

36.3.5 Influence about laws (including laws on cyber, speech and more)

There will be campaigns in the news and cyberspace to influence people about current and pending laws, including:

- Speech and expression
- Decency[547]
- Access and throttling (including "net neutrality").

As always, consider who is putting out information, and what their motives may be. They may be trying to influence you and your actions, rather than objectively inform you about the issues.

As we look to future there are proposed laws about cyber issues such as:

- Privacy
- Cryptocurrency and virtual currency
- Speech online and influence.

We need to realize there are people with significant stakes in the outcome, who spend a lot of money and effort to influence politicians and the public.

When it comes to speech online, are some truly champions of "free speech," or simply champions of speech that aligns with their personal viewpoint?

---

[547] Remember that decency is a subjective term and in the eye of the beholder.

36.3.6 News and influence and influencers

Reliable news and facts are important so that consumers and voters can make solid, well-informed decisions.

Unfortunately, consumers have a desire to be entertained, and news and opinion and entertainment have a business model. News outlets (or other outlets providing information which may not technically be "news") need to monetize their business. They need people to read or view so that ads can be delivered, and products and subscriptions sold.

News, opinion, and information outlets have dual motives. We hope that they will present facts and reliable information, and that consumers will seek that out and consume it analytically.

News outlets or purveyors of current events and opinion have a mission to keep viewers and watchers, which may outweigh the motive to investigate and report facts with a logical and reasonable perspective. If they can keep their audience glued to the screen and coming back every day, watching, viewing, and clicking, that is good for business and advertising revenue. They provide them with the content and ideological slant they want, even if the facts and analysis might suffer.

Fear, anger, and outrage can be powerful motivators to keep viewers engaged and coming back. In contrast, a dry reporting of facts and analysis might not be of interest to many viewers. Just compare the PBS News Hour of years ago (for example), to other more sensational "news" or opinion broadcasts that may be available today.

Furthermore, many voters are getting their news related information not from established journalism outlets, but from news influencers.[548] Established journalism outlets are never perfect, but the benefits of a system of education, professionalism, and organizational oversight should not be disregarded.

36.3.7 Political influence

Candidates for government office want to influence voters to donate money to them, which allows them to advertise more and influence more

---

[548] Galen Stocking *et al*, Pew Research Center, *America's News Influencers: The creators and consumers in the world of news and information on social media* (November 18, 2024), https://www.pewresearch.org/journalism/ 2024/11/18/americas-news-influencers.

people. Ultimately the goal is obtaining more votes so that they can win the election.

Much goes into political influencing, including the lessons from the Facebook-Cambridge Analytica case.[549]

If the goal is to influence thought and action (including donations and votes), we should ask ourselves:

- What *should* voters be influenced by?
- What *are* voters influenced by?
- What *methods* are they using to try to influence voters?

The answers to these three questions are very different.

For good decision making in a democracy, voters should be influenced by facts, logic, and reason. They should strive to vote for ethical, honest, competent leaders.[550]

In real life, many voters are influenced heavily by emotion and calls to fear, anger, and hate. These powerful negative emotions influence action and help minimize reliance on facts and logic.

36.3.8 Foreign influence[551]

The internet is a way for foreign actors to influence our thoughts and actions.

A terrorist group could send their message through the internet to get followers, supporters, donors, and those who will carry out actions of terror or otherwise support the group.

A foreign nation, with its own strategic interests in mind, could influence our populace in a way that helps that foreign nation (and presumably hurts our country). Our country has many adversaries in the world who would like to harm us. One way they can harm us is by sowing division

---

[549] In the Facebook-Cambridge Analytica case we have discussed, data of over 80 million Facebook users was obtained and used to assist with 2016 presidential campaigns and targeting ads. It was also alleged that it was utilized during the "Brexit" debate surrounding whether Great Britain should leave the European Union. Great Britain eventually did leave the EU.

[550] Santa Clara University, *Voting for Ethics*, https://www.scu.edu/voting-for-ethics. See the related book, John Pelissero, Ann Skeet, Hana Callaghan, *Voting for Ethics: A Guide for U.S. Voters*, 2nd ed. (Palmetto Publishing, 2024).

[551] We discussed this in the prior chapter, including foreign election interference.

within our country, and by casting doubt upon our system of government, our elections, and our processes.

36.4 TikTok

One-third of young people in America get their news from TikTok, owned by Chinese tech behemoth ByteDance and a full 170 million people in the U.S. use the app, including for entertainment.[552] This raises concerns about privacy and national security due to foreign access to intimate data about U.S. citizens and into our computing devices, plus the ability to influence us.

In April 2024 the U.S. passed a law that would ban the app in the country by January 19, 2025, unless it was sold and no longer owned by a Chinese company.[553] This date can be postponed by the President and as legal challenges are heard.[554]

TikTok challenged the law, including on First Amendment grounds, and on December 6, 2024 a federal appellate court upheld the law and its requirement that TikTok be sold from Chinese control if it wants to continue operating in the U.S. is proper and constitutional.[555] The appellate court was the District of Columbia federal Court of Appeals, it applied heightened "strict scrutiny" to the law because it restricted

---

[552] Rebecca Leppert and Katerina Eva Matsa, *More Americans – especially young adults – are regularly getting news on TikTok*, Pew Research Center (Sept 17, 2024), https://www.pewresearch.org/short-reads/2024/09/17/more-americans-regularly-get-news-on-tiktok-especially-young-adults.

[553] Protecting Americans from Foreign Adversary Controlled Applications Act (PAFACA), Public Law 118-50, formerly H.R. 7521 (118th Congress); Bobby Allyn, *President Biden signs law to ban TikTok nationwide unless it is sold*, NPR (April 24, 2024), https://www.npr.org/2024/04/24/1246663779/biden-ban-tiktok-us.

[554] Check for more recent events as court decisions and presidential action are not certain. In July 2024, then-future President Trump stated he opposed a ban on TikTok, though in 2020 (while President) he unsuccessfully attempted to ban TikTok via executive order. *See* David Shepardson and Mike Scarcella, *US appeals court upholds TikTok law forcing its sale*, Reuters (December 6, 2024), https://www.reuters.com/legal/us-appeals-court-upholds-tiktok-law-forcing-its-sale-2024-12-06; David Shepardson, *Trump says "I'm for TikTok" as potential US ban looms*, Reuters (July 16, 2024), https://www.reuters.com/technology/trump-says-im-tiktok-potential-us-ban-looms-2024-07-16.

[555] *TikTok Inc. and ByteDance Ltd., v. Merrick B. Garland*, No 24-1113, (DC Cir., Dec 6, 2024), https://storage.courtlistener.com/recap/gov.uscourts.cadc.40861/gov.uscourts.cadc.40861.1208687460.0_4.pdf.

speech and expression, and held the law met this scrutiny because it was narrowly tailored to address compelling government interests of national security, data collection, and content manipulation.[556]

36.5 False beliefs and twisted fantasies

A surprising percentage of Americans believe the Earth is flat.[557] A person willing to believe the Earth is flat disbelieves many scientists and others in related areas.[558] They may be susceptible to believe other things that have been proven not true.

The flat Earth belief is a more extreme outlier, but there are many other false beliefs that might be attractive to an even larger percentage of people. Consider these beliefs and who might subscribe to them:

- The Earth is flat
- The moon landings were faked
- Satellites don't exist
- The Nazi Holocaust did not occur
- The Sandy Hook school shooting in 2012 did not occur
- Vaccines are part of a conspiracy to implant microchips
- There was a secret cabal of pedophiles that held children imprisoned in a pizza parlor
- An anonymous "Q" is a reliable source of facts and predictions
- Birds aren't real.[559]

Now consider twisted fantasies. In dark corners of the internet, like-minded people gather to communicate about their thoughts. In the "cannibal cop" case, the federal appellate court held that communicating about the kidnapping, torture, rape, and killing of an individual was not a conspiracy to commit a crime but mere fantasy. The court held:

> *This is a case about the line between fantasy and criminal intent…We are loath to give the government the power to punish us for our thoughts and not our actions…Fantasizing*

---

[556] *See id.*

[557] One study found that 10 percent of Americans believe the Earth was flat (not round) and another 9 percent were unsure. Lawrence Hamilton, *Conspiracy vs. Science: A Survey of U.S. Public Beliefs*, University of New Hampshire, Carsey Research (Spring 2022), https://carsey.unh.edu/publication/conspiracy-vs-science-survey-us-public-beliefs.

[558] A "flat earther" will not believe anything said by astronauts, scientists, and the entirety of NASA because they believe they are all part of the conspiracy.

[559] This one is satire, but there are surely some who do not realize it as such.

about committing a crime, even a crime of violence against a real person whom you know, is not a crime.

This does not mean that fantasies are harmless. To the contrary, fantasies of violence against women are both a symptom of and a contributor to a culture of exploitation, a massive social harm that demeans women. Yet we must not forget that in a free and functioning society, not every harm is meant to be addressed with the federal criminal law.[560]

You cannot pass laws to change these realities about what people believe or fantasize about. One cannot enforce existing laws to do so either. The legal arena is not the place to fix this, though we need to stay within the bounds of law and the First Amendment as we search for a solution.

We cannot ban false speech or twisted thoughts, but we can assess society, speech, expression, and thought.

36.6 Communications Decency Act

The Communications Decency Act (CDA)[561] provides some liability protections for website operators for content posted to the website by users.

The history of the CDA is instructive for law learners, and how the current law is different from as originally passed due to judicial action.[562]

---

[560] *U.S. v. Valle*, 807 F.3d 508, 511 (2d Cir., 2015).
[561] The CDA is found within 47 U.S.C. §230, Protection for private blocking and screening of offensive material,
https://www.law.cornell.edu/uscode/text/47/230.
[562] The name "Communications Decency Act" seems highly subjective, implying the law will ensure "decency" on the internet, at least within one group's view of what is "decent." Sometimes lawmakers do a good job naming their laws to inform the public about what the law is about, but other times they use highly subjective or even misleading names.
As originally passed, it contained prohibitions regarding online pornography and their ability to reach people under the age of 18. It made it a crime to transmit "obscene" or "indecent" materials to those minors. These provisions were struck down by the USSC in 1997 in *Reno v. American Civil Liberties Union* on the grounds that they violated the First Amendment.
This illustrates that laws need to comply with the U.S. Constitution and Amendments, and that Courts can strike laws (or portions of laws) that are unconstitutional. *See Reno v. American Civil Liberties Union*, 521 U.S. 844 (1997), https://scholar.google.com/scholar_case?case=1557224836887427725.

The main existing provisions of the CDA in effect now provide protection for website operators regarding (i) content posted on their site by others, and (ii) if they take action to remove harmful content posted by others.

In other words, it helps protect the provider from being sued for defamation if a user posts defamatory material on the site. For example, if User A posts to Bluesky something defamatory about Person B, then Person B could sue User A, but the CDA would protect Bluesky from being sued.

The CDA also helps protect the provider if it removes content from a user. For example, if User C posts something defamatory, or racist, or in violation of copyright laws or against the public good or terms of service on Bluesky, then Bluesky could remove that content and be protected from being sued by User C.

Here is an excerpt of those portions of the statute.

> *47 U.S.C. §230*
>
> *(c) Protection for "Good Samaritan" blocking and screening of offensive material*
>
> *(1) Treatment of publisher or speaker*
>
> *No provider or user of an interactive computer service shall be treated as the publisher or speaker of any information provided by another information content provider.*
>
> *(2) Civil liability*
>
> *No provider or user of an interactive computer service shall be held liable on account of—*
>
> *(A) any action voluntarily taken in good faith to restrict access to or availability of material that the provider or user considers to be obscene, lewd, lascivious, filthy, excessively violent, harassing, or otherwise objectionable, whether or not such material is constitutionally protected; ...*

36.7 "Cyberbullying"

"Cyberbullying" is a vague term with different meanings for different people.

If you hear that term, or are tempted to use it, consider these questions:

- How do we define "cyberbullying"?
- Who defined it and for what context?
  - *E.g.*, criminal law, civil laws, organizational rules
- What specific conduct (actions) constitute "cyberbullying."

Actions described as "cyberbullying" will almost always involve some form of speech and expression.

That means we first look to the First Amendment and then to criminal laws and civil laws. Then we look to rules of various organizations that might apply, such as a school or workplace.

If there is a criminal statute that applies (whether it is called "cyberbullying" or "harassment" or whatever it may be named) we must look at the words of that statute.

If there is a civil suit involving cyberbullying, we need to assess the legal claims and their basis.

If there is a cyberbullying internal rule or policy of an organization (such as a school), and that organization is a government entity, the First Amendment applies. But if the organization is private, then the First Amendment does not apply.

As always, look at the facts, and try determining what happened. Simply calling it "cyberbullying" is too vague and conclusory, so we need more details on what was said or done, and the full context.

In sum, as you assess issues or specific cases relating to cyberbullying, consider these areas:

- Does the First Amendment apply?
  - For example, was there government action ("state action")?
- What happened? (What are the facts)
- What definition of cyberbullying are we using, from where, and why? ("Cyberbullying" is a vague term, meaning different things to different people)
- Who defined the rules of conduct at issue?
- Are we assessing the merits of a criminal investigation or prosecution?
- Are we assessing the merits of a civil lawsuit?
- Are we assessing the properness of a disciplinary action by an organization (school, employer, etc.).

36.8 Who should win the battle for our brains? The path forward

The exact path forward is for each person to consider. We have come full circle in our discussion of law, cyberlaw, and cyberspace, and see how law and cyber permeate everything. Sophisticated forces work to influence our thoughts and actions.

Law is important yet we cannot rely upon judges, legislators, presidents or governors to protect us from improper influences or false information.

In Part 1 we embarked on this journey of cyberlaw, including the learning mindset. Our mindset and critical thinking may be the most important aspect, and that is our personal responsibility.

People make important choices in the role of a consumer and a voter:

- *Consumers* decide what to view and click on, what to buy, what news to watch, what information to consume.
- *Voters* decide who to elect to run our system of government.

Ideally, people will place significant emphasis on facts and reason to be subject to improper influence or manipulation.

We need good information plus an ability to assess reliability, credibility, and relevance. That is how we can make good decisions. This requires reliable news and information, some investigative and research skills, plus basic analytical abilities. These types of fact and reason-based decisions will be better than relying upon speculation or emotion.

Consumers could seek companies that are transparent and honest (not deceptive). But individuals are ill-equipped to perform this analysis on their own, so we need some government regulation and enforcement for consumer protection.

Voters could seek similar qualities in political candidates; seeking individuals who are truthful, ethical, and of high character.[563] The choices are rarely optimal but usually one candidate is better than the other. Voters are on their own, and all sides are working to influence.

---

[563] Picking a more ethical candidate is one way to minimize the number of government officials who put their own personal interests above that of society and their constituents. An ethical government official serves their true fiduciary duty, to the best of their ability and is more likely to be truthful. An unethical or corrupt government official serves themselves, and is less likely to be truthful.

Voters select the leaders of the government. That determines how the government is run, what laws are passed, how they are enforced, and which judges interpret those laws.

The path is easier to mark than it is to follow.

Imagine if a growing percentage of people within the population are less capable at reading, analyzing, distinguishing fact from fiction, and deciding. Suppose they become over-reliant upon summaries or opinions provided by others, including AI tools and social media feeds.

Now envision that some individuals or groups become more sophisticated at influencing thought, opinion, and action through their use of cyberspace, including through AI tools, social media, influencers, and other information channels. They decide to use this power to manipulate and deceive.

That is not a good recipe. Some say it is already happening.

- What can we do?
- What should we do?

These are the weightiest questions in the book, requiring self-reflection as individuals and as a country.

36.9 References and additional reading

- *Chapter 36 resources*, https://johnbandler.com/cyberlawbook-resources-ch36
- *Building Better Consumers and Voters*, https://johnbandler.com/building-better-consumers-and-voters
- *U.S. v. Gilberto Valle, the "cannibal cop" case*, https://johnbandler.com/us-v-valle-cannibal-cop-case
- *Facebook – Cambridge Analytica case*, https://johnbandler.com/facebook-cambridge-analytica-case
- *Free Speech, the First Amendment, and Social Media (2)*, https://johnbandler.com/free-speech-first-amendment-social-media-2
- *First Amendment things to know*, https://johnbandler.com/things-to-know-first-amendment
- Communications Decency Act, 47 U.S. Code § 230, *Protection for private blocking and screening of offensive material*, https://www.law.cornell.edu/uscode/text/47/230

- Cornell LII Wex on First Amendment, https://www.law.cornell.edu/wex/first_amendment
- Galen Stocking et al, Pew Research Center, *America's News Influencers: The creators and consumers in the world of news and information on social media* (Nov 18, 2024), https://www.pewresearch.org/journalism/2024/11/18/americas-news-influencers/
- Dan Olson (Folding Ideas), *In Search of A Flat Earth*, via YouTube, https://www.youtube.com/watch?v=JTfhYyTuT44
- Birds Aren't Real, https://birdsarentreal.com
- Wikipedia, *Birds Aren't Real*, https://en.wikipedia.org/wiki/Birds_Aren%27t_Real

36.10 Chapter questions

- What do you think about the speech categories laid out in the chapter, including the addition of "influencing speech"?
- To what extent are individuals subject to being influenced? How much of this influence comes from cyberspace?
- If powerful or wealthy individuals or groups are able to influence others through cyberspace, how do we know how to detect those attempts, and then decide whether we should follow that influence or not?
- Why do you think the CDA was named the way it was, and what do you think of that name?
- Are there conspiracy theories that you think are ridiculous, but that other people genuinely believe in?
- Is it generally ok to believe something is true, when it is really false? Are there some false beliefs that are more dangerous or more harmful than others?

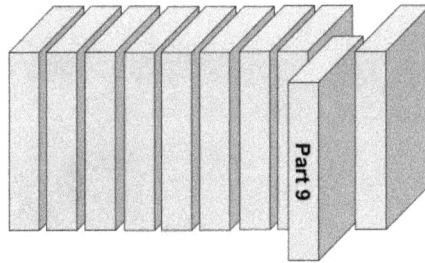

Part 9

Organization Management and Cyberlaws

In this part:

- Apply cyberlaw to your business or organization
- Business law basics
- Five Components for Policy Work (and management)
- Managing cyber issues in an organization
- Information governance (data governance)

John T. Bandler

37

Business Law Basics

In this chapter:
- Some basics on law for organizations
- You may be an owner, executive, or manager already or in the future

37.1 Why basic business law

This chapter puts law into the context of an organization and the legal issues it might face. Cybersecurity, privacy, and other cyber issues need to be addressed by all types of organizations, whether for-profit, nonprofit, or governmental. This chapter provides some basics that were not covered previously.[564]

37.2 Mission: The value provided and received

Organizations should first consider their mission and the value they provide. This point is not directly related to law, but any legal issues must be considered in the context of mission, which is the organization's reason for being—their *raison d'être*. Without providing value, there will be no funds coming in and the organization would cease to exist.

Mission could be called business needs or business objectives. It involves providing value to others, perhaps a product (goods) or service, then receiving value in exchange. For non-profits or government entities, the value provided might be less tangible, but no less important. The value received might be called payments, revenue, grants, or budget, depending on the type of organization.

---

[564] Some students desire to start or run their own business one day, many desire to rise above an entry-level job to work at management and executive levels. This requires a good knowledge base about legal issues the organization will face.

Mission is one of the Five Components for Policy Work we will cover in the next chapter.

37.3 Organization entity type and location of formation

A business generally exists as some type of legal entity. This means the business asked a state for permission to form that entity or legal structure, such as a corporation, limited liability corporation, and so forth.

A person can do business as themselves individually (known as a sole proprietorship) though there are many reasons why forming an entity is advisable or required.

Forming an entity is often desirable and obtains "personhood" within the legal system. The entity can enter into contracts, open bank accounts, receive payments, and pay taxes. Creating an entity also reduces the personal legal liability of owners, managers, and employees for acts done by the organization, facilitates investment and financing, and has other benefits.

Among one the first decisions made by an entrepreneur is what type of entity to form, so let us review the types of organizations.

37.3.1 For-profit or nonprofit?

The first consideration is whether it will be a for-profit or nonprofit (also known as not-for-profit) organization.

- A *for-profit organization* has the purpose of earning a profit for the owners (no surprise). The company and owners will pay their taxes on that profit (as a general principle).
- A *non-profit organization* works for a greater public good and is not designed to enrich anyone. Thus, a non-profit may be exempt from taxes and might be allowed to receive charitable donations for which donors could get a tax deduction. A nonprofit may need to file financial documents with the government which may become public (e.g. IRS Form 990[565] or NYS Char 500[566]) and comply with other rules to ensure individuals are not enriching themselves through the non-profit.

---

[565] Internal Revenue Service Form 990, Return of Organization Exempt from Income Tax, https://www.irs.gov/forms-pubs/about-form-990.
[566] See the NYS Attorney General website, Charities annual filing (CHAR500), https://ag.ny.gov/resources/organizations/charities-nonprofits-fundraisers/charities-annual-filing-char500.

37.3.2 State of formation

Founders need to choose the state to form their entity. Business formation is according to state law and each state has their own laws and categories of entities. Considerations include requirements for filing, taxation, disclosure, fees, court system, and potential legal liabilities.

The first logical option is the physical location of the business. Thus, a business headquartered and operating in New York would consider New York.[567]

Organizations sometimes chose states other than their geographic home state to incorporate. Delaware has been a popular choice[568] because Delaware has favorable laws, fees, limited corporate disclosure requirements and legal protections which make it attractive for businesses to form there. Delaware benefits through fees and taxes from businesses, fees paid to obtain company information,[569] and other income when disputes are heard in the state.

37.3.3 Entity type

Founders need to choose an entity type. Here is a quick list:

- Sole proprietorship (actually, this is not an entity type, but reflects a choice *not* to create any type of entity, and simply do business as an individual)
- Nonprofit
- C-corporation (incorporated, Inc.)

---

[567] The government entity that administers this formation is the New York State Department of State, their website is https://dos.ny.gov/, and they have more information on forming entities at https://dos.ny.gov/faqs-corporations-business-entities.

Each state has their own department of state (or similar department) for handling certain actions for consumers and businesses within that state.

Don't confuse these state government entities with the U.S. Department of State, which is responsible for U.S. relations with other nations.

[568] If you ever decide to form an entity, you need to carefully consider which state is appropriate after weighing all your circumstances. Plenty of organizations have blindly chosen Delaware to incorporate and then regret it when they are sued there, far from their home base, or are otherwise unhappy with the result of a lawsuit in their state of incorporation.

[569] While some states (like NY) provide a good amount of company information for free, Delaware and some other states charge a fee.

- S-corporation (an election of a small business c-corporation to be taxed a certain way which might be beneficial for some small business owners)
- Limited Liability Corporation (LLC)
- Professional Limited Liability Corporation (PLLC) (this is what New York designates for professionals such as lawyers and doctors)
- Partnership
- Limited Liability Partnership.

There are pros and cons to each type. Whatever is formed requires a commitment to maintaining it and complying with requirements including for tax obligations and renewing the entity registration with the state.

37.3.4 Entity name and DBA

When forming, the founders need to decide upon an entity name, which needs to meet certain requirements, as laid out by the state law and perhaps also trademark law. Generally, that name needs to be unique within that state.

Occasionally businesses may "do business as" (DBA) a name other than their official entity name. That DBA may need to be registered with the state or local government.

37.3.5 State(s) of operation

Once the business forms in a particular state, they need to evaluate what states they are operating within. They may need to register with those states to do business there.[570]

37.4 Governance (management) (including risk management, protection, and legal compliance)

The organization needs to be governed (managed).

In a sole proprietorship this is simple, the individual owns it, runs it, decides what to do. and then does it.

For organizations of increasing size, increasing levels of formality are required. Verbal instructions become insufficient to communicate organization directives. The organization is subject to many legal

---

[570] On a cyber note, and as part of their information governance program, organizations should assess what state data laws they need to comply with. We talk about that in Chapter 29 and Chapter 39.

requirements and needs to comply with them. It needs to fulfill its mission (providing value somewhere), but also pay taxes and file financial documents with the government, comply with a large array of legal requirements, and enter contracts. There need to be processes to ensure the organization does all it does properly and efficiently.

People in the organization make decisions, so it helps to have a process and mechanism to specify who contributes to the decision making and how it is done. People assume governance roles and written documentation needs to be created.

Consider these documents which may indicate how an organization can operate and govern itself:

- Bylaws
- Articles of Incorporation
- Charters
- Policies
- Standards
- Procedures
- Guidelines
- Manuals.

Consider these people or groups of people who play a role in managing and running an organization:

- Owners
- Board of Directors (Board of Trustees, Trustees, etc.)
- Chief Executive Officer, Executive Director
- Other officers of the corporation and senior management
- Middle management
- Lower-level management
- Employees, contractors, interns, etc.

Also consider that management of an organization is going to include decisions about:

- How to best fulfill the organization's mission
- Protection of the organization and proper risk management, to include cybersecurity and cybercrime prevention
- Legal compliance, to include cybersecurity, privacy, registration, licensing, taxation, consumer protection, employee protection.

37.5 People

People work in organizations and manage organizations. Laws and issues relating to people include compensation, contract, employment law, anti-discrimination laws, and privacy.

Generally, employment in the U.S. is "at-will," meaning there is no guarantee of permanent work for the employee, and the employer does not need to demonstrate good cause to terminate the employee. However, some jobs are union jobs or otherwise under the terms of a collective bargaining agreement, where cause needs to be demonstrated to discipline or fire.

Employment contracts address important areas to include compensation, benefits, and contingencies for during and after employment. It may include grounds for termination, non-disclosure and non-compete requirements and more. Employment law and contract law overlap here.

When hiring a person (as with voting for a candidate for office) an important quality to consider is ethics and character. Working with dishonest people can lead to unpleasant, costly, and time-consuming situations.[571]

37.6 Ownership and financing

An organization may require money (capital or financing) to start, grow, or continue its operations. Typically, this is either through a loan or a sale of a portion of the company (equity).

An organization can obtain a loan (financing) to support its operation, and the loan would need to be paid back with interest. The person making the loan needs to be satisfied that the business will repay the loan or has assets (collateral) of sufficient value to seize if the loan is not repaid.

An organization owned by one or more people or other organizations. It can sell equity in itself (a portion of the ownership of the company) in exchange for money (raising capital), and this can happen in several ways.

Here are some ways an organization can raise money:

- Personal or organizational loans or financing
- Pre-seed financing

---

[571] People can learn knowledge and learn skills. But generally, people with poor ethics will look out for only themselves, a behavior that is unlikely to change.

- Seed financing
- Crowdfunding
- Angel investors
- Venture capital and private equity
- Series A round (then, B, C, etc.)
- Initial public offerings (IPOs) (offering public shares in the company, and subject to securities laws).

These agreements implicate contract law, and potentially securities law, or other consumer and investor protection laws.

37.7 Accounting and taxes

Accounting and taxes are important because the government wants taxes paid and knows that some organizations do not pay what they owe. Government has given itself some powerful tax collection tools; if it decides to use them.

Accounting is important as a general matter because:

- Tracking funds helps to make good business decisions.
- Organizations need to protect themselves from internal and external theft and fraud.
- When more than one person or organization is involved in profit sharing, everyone needs to know they are getting their fair share of the profits, and that the accounting is transparent and accurate.
- The government is always involved, and they want to be sure filings are accurate.

Tax law is an important and specialized area of law, both at the federal and state levels.[572]

37.8 Assets (including information assets and intellectual property)

Businesses need to consider their assets and value, which will include:

- The ability to provide value
- People[573]

---

[572] Wealthy individuals and organizations spend money on attorneys and accountants to figure out the best way to minimize their tax liabilities. The ultra wealthy and large corporations may spend a lot of money to elect government officials who will favorably shape the tax laws for them.

[573] While people are not "owned" assets of an organization they are essential for its work.

- Physical assets (buildings, equipment, vehicles, inventory, goods, etc.)
- Information assets (computers, data, networks, etc.)
- Intellectual property (copyright, trademark, patent, trade secrets).[574]

Information assets and intellectual property are highly relevant for this book.

37.9 Starting your own business

If you are considering starting your own business, perform some risk analysis and employ good decision-making principles. Consider what input is needed (money and time), the chances of success or failure, and what happens if your new business fails.

It is good to dream and to try. It is amazing to think of what certain people have built and accomplished in their business ventures, including their vast (arguably obscene) wealth. Think of people like Warren Buffet, Michael Bloomberg, Bill Gates, Steve Jobs, Elon Musk, Jeff Bezos, Mark Zuckerberg, and more.

It is important to be realistic about chances of success because many startups fail. We may want to emulate a startup that became a billion-dollar company, thinking:

If they did it, why can't we?

There are probably many reasons (including some luck) why that person achieved financial success, but others might not.

Some have heard the saying:

✗ *"Fake it till you make it"*

Which, in this context, you should translate in your head to "investor fraud" or just plain "fraud." Faking it is a terrible philosophy and practice for business and usually in life in general.[575] In business, it is dishonest, and some people (perhaps a government prosecutor) may call it a crime.

---

[574] Intellectual property is covered in Chapter 28.

[575] The phrase is sometimes used in the context of substance abuse recovery, though with mixed interpretation.

Faking it worked only for a limited time for some, in the end, truth and justice caught up.[576]

You cannot eliminate all risk in life or business, and starting and running a business always involves risk. The key is do your best to evaluate those risks and then make the decision that is right for you.

37.10 When to hire an attorney

It is hard to know when to hire an attorney. Even when you hire an attorney, they merely advise whereas you decide.

That is why knowledge of facts and law is helpful for everyone.

Unfortunately, hindsight is the best judge of whether you needed to consult an attorney, find the right attorney, or listen to the attorney's advice.

Ideally, every person and business can obtain good legal counsel for any business decision that affects law. Attorneys are expensive, not every attorney is always right, and even after consulting with an excellent attorney, business decisions still need to be made.

This is about decision making and risk, so assess some basic questions:

- What decision am I making that affects law and the future of my business?
- What are the risks?
    - What are the potential threats (negative events)?
    - What are the potential harms from those threats? How costly might they be?
    - What legal actions or results might occur?
- What (if anything) should we do to manage those risks? Try to change the terms? Walk away from the deal? Find another way?
- What are the costs for managing that risk? Cost vs. benefit analysis.
- What are the costs for additional due diligence and research prior to making that decision?

Competent and ethical attorneys properly advise on legal risks, putting them in the context of business risks. Predicting the future is hard and no

---

[576] Some faked it for a while but eventually the facts caught up to them. Consider Elizabeth Holmes (Theranos medical devices), Samuel Bankman-Fried (SBF of cryptocurrency FTX), and Bernie Madoff (a much longer investment fraud Ponzi scheme).

attorney has a crystal ball. Still, there are circumstances where pursuing a certain course of action violates the law, and those paths should never be taken.

37.11 Decision making and risks (preview)

Business owners and managers need to make decisions that involve business and legal concerns, as well as issues relating to cyberlaw. They will need to weigh various pros and cons, and occasionally seek advice of counsel. We dive into this in the following chapters.

37.12 References and resources

- *Chapter 37 resources*, https://johnbandler.com/cyberlawbook-resources-ch37
- *Business Basics and Law - An Introduction*, https://johnbandler.com/business-basics-and-law

37.13 Chapter questions

- Do you hope to own or manage a business some day? Briefly summarize.
- What business decisions might you have to make in life that are somehow related to law, and may require some knowledge of law, or even require legal advice?
- What is a main benefit of forming an entity for a business?
- How big do you think an organization needs to be to have a full-time lawyer on staff?
- If an organization does not have their own lawyer on staff, where do they obtain legal advice from?
- What percentage of organization legal issues do you think involve "cyber"? Explain.

38

Organization Management and Policy Work with the Five Components

In this chapter:

- Organizations need to manage themselves well
- This includes law, cyber and cyberlaw issues
- The Five Components for Policy Work
- The Three Platforms to Connect for Compliance

38.1 The Five Components for Policy Work and management

Executives, managers, and owners make many decisions and need to achieve their mission and legal compliance. The Five Components concept helps with this and can be applied to any type of organization to:

- Assess what is a legal requirement
- Comply with legal requirements
- Accomplish the mission
- Manage effectively.

Organization management, decision-making, and compliance principles can start with the Five Components for Policy Work, which are:

- *External rules*: Laws, regulations, and other legal requirements.
- *Mission* (business goals and business needs): The reason the organization exists in the first place.
- *External guidance*: Best practices and helpful and relevant voluntary guides for your actions and policies.
- *Internal rules*: Policies, procedures, and more.
- *Practice and action*: What is actually done by the organization and employees.

Here is a top view of the five components.

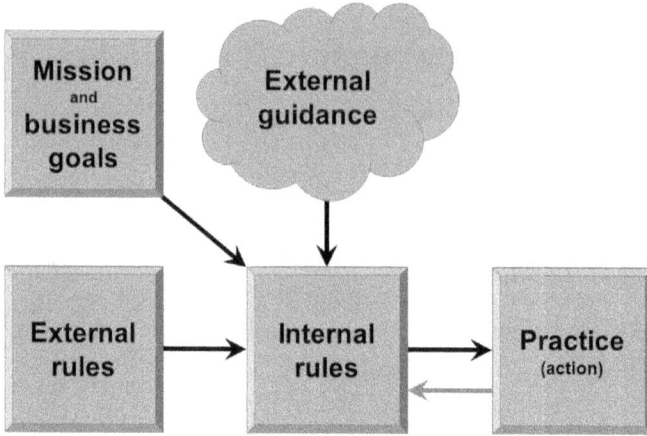

Bandler's Five Components for Policy Work

These components are four platforms and one cloud. The external guidance is depicted as a cloud because it is amorphous and infinite, while the other four components can be depicted as well-defined platforms.

We can transition our analogy and view with a front facing perspective, envisioning the organization working to align these four platforms.

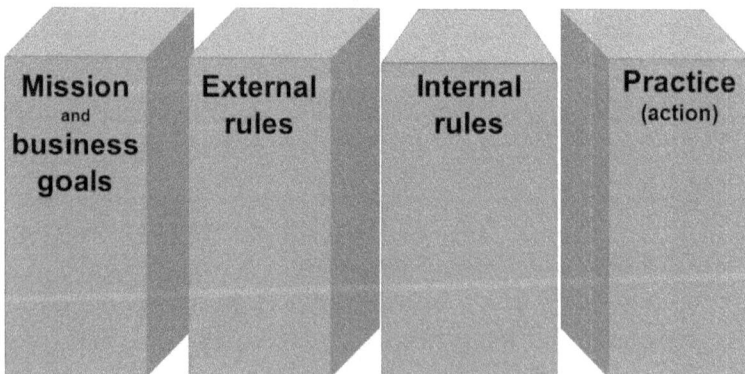

Bandler's Four Platforms to Connect

38.2 The Three Platforms to Connect for Compliance[577]

For a compliance focused view, we remove the mission platform, leaving Three Platforms to Connect for Compliance. This metaphor addresses how an organization complies with legal requirements.

The three components we look to for compliance related functions are:

- *External rules*, the laws
- *Internal rules* of the organization, whether written or unwritten
- *Practice and action*: What is done by the organization and employees.

The external rules platform is already built by the government, so it simply needs to be assessed, and then the organization builds the next two platforms to align with it.

If all three platforms are aligned, then the organization is in compliance with the law, and we can imagine an employee being able to safely walk across all three platforms.

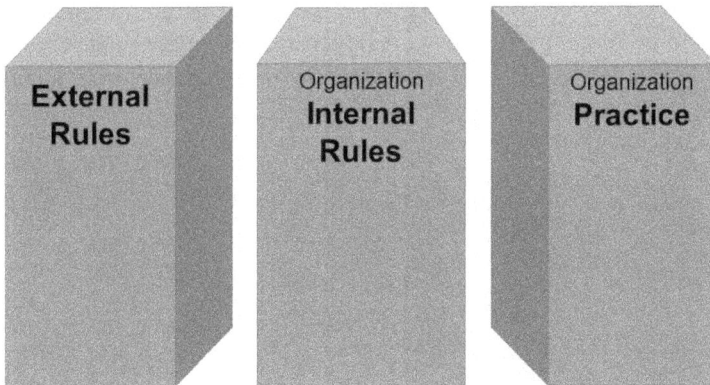

Bandler's Three Platforms to Connect for Compliance

38.2.1 Non-compliant organizations

Not every organization complies with the law and the news is full of examples where organizations were charged criminally with an offense (a rare circumstance) or held civilly liable (much more common).

---

[577] The Three Platforms was the start of an evolution that eventually led to the Four Platforms and then the Five Components for Policy Work.

If an organization's written policies conflict with laws, this non-compliance is easy to detect. Whatever the written rules, sometimes the actions of the organization or employees don't comply with or violate a law. We can depict those circumstances with these misaligned platforms.

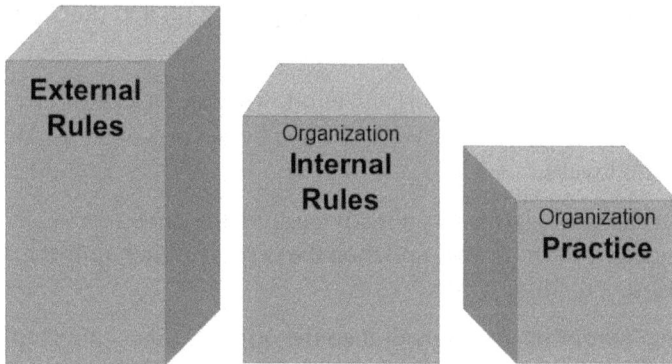

Noncompliant organization

Some organizations may have "good policies on paper" but do not follow them, and perhaps employees were never trained on them or never heard of them. The cracks and holes in their rules and practices will become evident and can be depicted like this.

Noncompliant organization

John T. Bandler

38.3 Compliance

Compliance is essentially the process of following (complying with) laws and other legal requirements.

Compliance should be incorporated into the mission and operations of each organization. Good organizations understand their legal obligations and do their honest best to comply. Some mistakenly view it as a "cost center" and a hinderance to revenue earners who want to go faster.

Whatever the title or department of a person, they should have both compliance and mission first and foremost in the mind they go together.

Organizations want to be able to truthfully say things like this:

✓ *"We comply with all applicable laws and regulations."*

✓ *"We have compliant policies and procedures, and we follow them."*

✓ *"We have designated people in charge of compliance and other important areas, and they dedicate sufficient time to those duties."*

Organizations do *not* want to say things like this:

✗ *"We have compliant policies on paper but don't really follow them."*

✗ *"We have a compliance officer on paper, but they don't really have time to work on it."*

38.4 A deeper dive into the Five Components[578]

⏭️ Skippable section – deeper dive ⏭️

If you have a good understanding on what the five components are and are not currently involved in management or policy work, then you can skip this section. Otherwise read on for more details.

---

[578] We provided a short one-sentence summary of each component earlier. This section has some more details and my book *Policies and Procedures for Your Organization* covers it in greater depth.

38.4.1 External rules are the legal requirements

External rules are legal requirements such as laws and regulations that come from outside an organization.

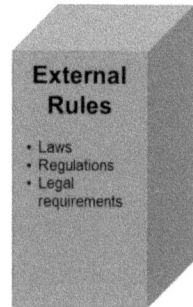

This book has covered a wide variety of traditional law and cyberlaw, but there are other areas of law that organizations need to be aware of.

The external platform includes all legal requirements the organization needs to comply with, including:

- Statutes (federal and state, criminal and civil)
- Regulations (federal and state, primarily civil)
- Court decisions
- Negligence law (considering a duty of diligence and reasonable care)
- Contractual requirements.

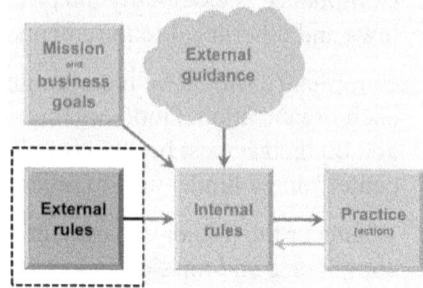

We call them "external rules" to distinguish them from the "internal rules" which the organization creates itself.

38.4.2 Internal rules are built by the organization

Internal rules are built by the organization. They include governance documents of all types (*e.g.*, policies and procedures) and include unwritten rules, verbal instructions, and culture.

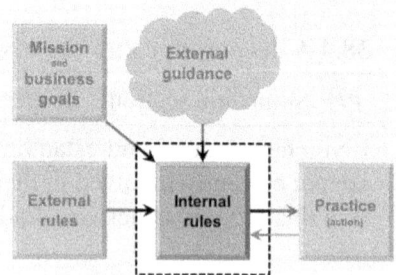

Internal rules come with many different configurations, sizes, and names. Organizations may define them differently and call them different things.

A start-up or small business may not have a single written policy yet and that does not necessarily mean they are noncompliant, negligent, or failing to perform their due diligence. Eventually some rules need to be put in writing. There are a lot of different ways to write a rule, from an email, memo, detailed procedure, general policy and more.

A fuller list of these internal rules includes:

- Culture and tone
- Verbal rules
- Policies (general rules, high level, don't need to be changed too often)
- Standards (more detailed rules)
- Procedures (highly detailed steps to accomplish a task, may need frequent update)
- Guidelines (guidance, not technically a rule, but we apply the rulemaking process to it)
- Plans
- Handbooks
- Manuals
- Charters
- Bylaws
- Articles of organization
- Incorporation documents
- Governance documents (a general overarching term that includes many of the above)
- Signage
- More.

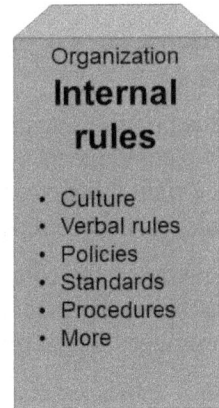

Internal rules are essential to accomplish the mission and for compliance. Organizations need rules because the leaders and managers need to set the direction and practices of the organization and employees.

Once created, these rules have legal significance.

- Policies are often the first item requested and inspected by a regulator or plaintiff.
- Policies will become exhibits in any litigation, inspected and referenced by attorneys, witnesses, judges, and juries.
- Some policies are required by law.

Regarding cyber issues, most organizations will need written internal rules that address cybersecurity, privacy, and incident response.

38.4.3 Practice is what we do

Practice (action) is what organizations do.

It is possibly the most important of the five components because they need to do the right things to accomplish the mission and comply.

Practice is the component where the rubber meets the road. How products are built and sold, how services are provided, and so on.

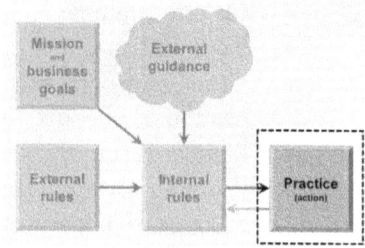

38.4.4 Mission is what we need to accomplish

Mission and business goals (business needs) are the top priority for every organization.

"Mission" may sound too militaristic for some, but many businesses incorporate that language and expressly refer to their "mission" or "mission statement."

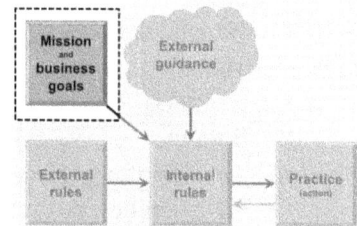

Every organization exists for a reason—that's their mission. It might be called goals, objectives or something else, and along with it comes business needs.

At the root of it, every good organization's mission is something like this:

- Do good and help individuals, businesses, and society
- Provide value with a necessary service or product
- Earn revenue and profit (which pays business owners and shareholders, employee salaries, rent, utilities, etc.)
- Obtain donations or grants (for nonprofits)
- Survive, provide livelihood
- Thrive and grow.

In the for-profit sector, this usually means selling services or goods. They need customers and clients; they need to generate revenue. In the non-profit sector organizations have important missions too, providing goods, services, information, food or shelter. In government sectors, mission also comes first, whatever that governmental organization is doing, citizens and residents need it.

38.4.5 External guidance

External guidance comes from outside the organization and is consulted to avoid having to reinvent the wheel.

It might be called "best practices," "industry norms" or something else.

People may disagree on which external guidance are the "best" practices, and how to adapt or follow them. Common sense, practicality, and reasonableness remain our guideposts.

Examples include:

- A book (like this book)
- A reputable website
- Government resources
- A cybersecurity framework
- Lawyers and consultants.

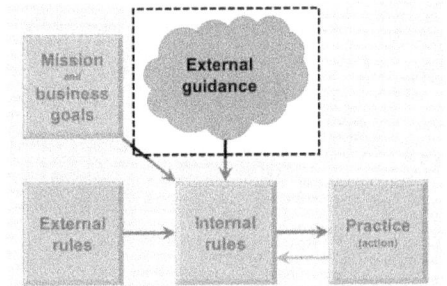

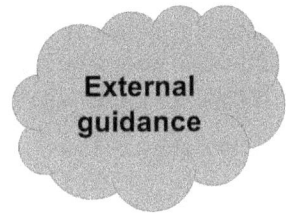

We depict this needed guidance as a cloud (rather than a platform) because it is seemingly infinite and amorphous, we need to search and find what is helpful from it.

38.5 Applying the Five Components to cyber (example)

Let us walk through how the Five Components is applied to an organization's information governance issues.

Organization A is assessing its cyberlaw compliance requirements, its cybersecurity program, privacy program, incident response plan, reviewing its practices and updating its policies.

Person B is responsible for this, and initially is overwhelmed and confused by how much information is out there, often conflicting. Then they realize they can organize according to the Five Components of Policy Work and use this book on cyberlaw as a guide.

They get to work and start assessing:

Mission: The first step, understanding the organization's mission, business needs, and future plans. They realize whatever they do needs to align with the mission.

External rules are the laws that must be complied with. They think about applicable laws for the organization such as:

- Data breach reporting laws
- Cybersecurity laws
- Privacy laws
- Contractual requirements (including with vendors and for cyber insurance)
- Negligence law considerations
- Federal laws
- State laws
- Any sector specific requirements.

External guidance is the voluntary guidance the organization can follow in part, fully, adapt, or disregard. Person B will remind others in his organization about the difference between this voluntary guidance and the legal requirements.

Examples are:

- This book
- Additional resources and references cited by this book
- Guidance from regulators (e.g. state attorney general, Federal Trade Commission)
- Four Pillars of Cybersecurity
- NIST Cybersecurity Framework
- NIST Privacy Framework
- Best practices or anything else that is not a law or legal requirement.
- Other reliable guidance.

Practice/action: Assess what the organization currently does, and what the organization should be doing.

The first is the "as-is" or "current" state, the next is the "to-be" or "future" state. Then there is a gap that needs to be closed.

Internal rules: Assess the existing internal rules, including those in writing and those that are not in writing. Compare that to practice and consider the current (as is) and desired future (to be) states of these internal rules. The organization may decide it needs to create (or update) its privacy notice, privacy policy, cybersecurity policy, and incident response plan.

By assessing these five components, organizations can better discuss issues appropriately and reasonably, separating issues worthy of separation while also seeing how they interact.

This can be a continual, cyclical process. They resolve to spend a reasonable amount of time working on it (person hours) and to make some solid steps forward (even if small) by a reasonable deadline.

In sum, Person B (and the project team) will seek to answer:

- What is our mission?
- What are the laws and our compliance requirements?
- What external guidance should we use?
- What *are* our current practices?
- What *should* our practices be to accomplish the mission and comply?
- What *are* our current internal rules?
- What *should* our internal rules be to have good practices (to accomplish the mission and comply)?
- How do we get from where we are now, to where we should be?

Regarding cyberlaw related issues, most organizations will need to create written internal rules (*e.g.*, policies, procedures, etc.) regarding:

- Cybersecurity and information security
- Incident response (and data breach reporting)
- Privacy (e.g., privacy policy and/or privacy notice).

38.6 Additional reading and references

For more on the concepts discussed above, you can visit:

- *Chapter 38 resources*, https://johnbandler.com/cyberlawbook-resources-ch38
- *Five Components for Policy Work*, https://johnbandler.com/five-components-for-policy-work
- *Three Platforms to Connect for Compliance*, https://johnbandler.com/bandlers-three-platforms-to-connect
- *Fourth Platform to Connect*, https://johnbandler.com/bandlers-fourth-platform-to-connect
- *Policies and Procedures for Your Organization* (2024 book)

38.6 Chapter questions

- List the Five Components for Policy Work
- What do you think of the Five Components for Policy Work? Is anything missing? Explain.
- List the Three Platforms to Connect for Compliance
- What do you think of the Three Platforms to Connect for Compliance? Is anything missing?
- How important is compliance for most organizations? Explain.
- List some cyber external rules an organization might need to assess.
- List some cyber external guidance an organization might need to consult.
- List some cyber internal rules an organization might create.

39

Managing Cyber Issues
(and Others Too)

- Practical decision-making principles to help you apply cyberlaw to your organization
  - o Your current business
  - o Your future business
- Risk

39.1 Overarching considerations for cyber (and anything else)

Throughout the book, we have built a foundation of law and cyberlaw, a layer of basic business law, then organization management with the Five Components for Policy Work.

This chapter adds a few more principles to aid with practical decision making.

The first touchstone for all organizations should be:

Be diligent and reasonable, never sloppy or negligent.

This means doing some research (investigation), assessing options, and then deciding on the path forward based on facts and logic.

Let's explore.

39.2 Information governance is our keyword

Cyberlaw, cyber issues, and technology affect information systems and information technology. Information systems are critical for the mission, cybersecurity, privacy, incident response, and other cyber issues.

All this falls under the umbrella of information governance, which is information management: how you manage and run information systems and assets.

Organizations should be managed well, and principles of good management should extend throughout the organization, including and especially for information systems.

Principles of good management are like good principles for students and learners and include:

- Gather and assess information, assess what is accurate, reliable, relevant (research and investigate).
- Manage risks: weigh pros and cons, assess risks and the potential for harm or benefit.
- Identify and weigh options to arrive at the best decision.

39.3 Information governance value and breadth

Organizations have people and departments with different priorities. Some departments may be viewed as non-essential or as a "cost center" which cost the organization money but do not bring in any revenue.

Cybersecurity, privacy, and compliance can be incorrectly viewed as just such a cost center. It brings in no money and can be perceived by others as something that slows them down.

Information technology can be taken for granted and expected to perform reliably on its own, even without investment or involvement.

Those working in the fields of information governance[579] need to be advocates for their cause for the good of the organization, as well as for their own professional development.

Information assets and systems are critical for the work of the organization. Managing them well ensures efficiency, protection, and compliance. Managing them poorly can lead to cybercrime attacks, outages, compliance issues, and other ills.

Work to persuade and motivate the organization and individuals within it towards effective information management and cybersecurity with a triad of reasons:

- Mission
- Protect
- Comply.

---

[579] Information governance includes the areas involving information systems, information technology, cybersecurity, and privacy. Sometimes this is called data governance, though data has a more "cyber" connotation.

Comply
with legal requirements
for cybersecurity

Mission
Improve efficiency
and effectiveness of
information assets

Protect
From cybercrime

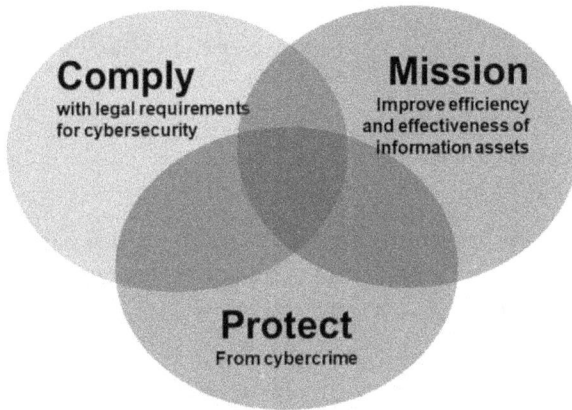

Bandler's Cybersecurity Philosophy

Mission is first, because that is the reason the organization exists (no organization exists simply to comply or prevent cybercrime). By realizing that and prioritizing it, you can better focus on the other goals. A failure to comply or protect can lead to nasty and costly events.

39.4 Fact finding, research, and investigation (recap)[580]

Good decisions and actions require facts—meaning accurate information.

Sometimes it is hard to obtain and assess that accurate information. There is contradictory guidance, people pass along information that has not been verified and may not be accurate, some people deceive.

Whatever we are deciding, accurate information, properly assessed, is essential. This includes when we are:

- Responding to a cyber incident
- Planning and writing a cybersecurity or privacy policy
- Deciding what software tools are needed
- Deciding what vendor or supplier to choose
- Deciding who to hire, when to discipline, when to fire.

The need to obtain accurate information applies to all other areas of business and life.

More complex business decisions require greater investigation, thought and analysis, a process we can call "diligence."

---

[580] Chapter 3 discussed this in the context of learning as a student and these skills are important throughout life.

39.5 Management and leadership

Management includes supervision and leadership. Organizations need to manage themselves well for optimal efficiency.

Poorly run organizations cannot accomplish their mission well and may fall out of compliance with legal requirements and may be subject to lawsuit or regulatory action.

Management means appointing certain people to be "in charge" of what other people do. As they direct what other people do, and what the organization does, some instructions are verbal, and some need to be put into writing.

Leadership is related but a little different because it addresses some of the non-tangible, unwritten aspects of an organization, such as how to motivate and influence culture in a positive way.

39.6 Risk and risk management

Risk analysis and risk management should be done when assessing options and deciding.

We do this all the time in life without realizing it,[581] and we should remember that we cannot eliminate *all* risk in life and should not try. It is just one factor to evaluate.

Risk and risk management are areas that some organizations and individuals have focused a great deal of research, developed frameworks to categorize, manage and protect the organization.[582]

---

[581] In our daily lives, we decide when to cross the street, whether to wear a helmet while riding a bike, wear our seatbelt while riding in the car, or how fast to drive. These decisions are the result of evaluating our risks perhaps without even knowing it.

[582] Consider that NIST has developed special publication (SP) 800-37, *Risk Management Framework for Information Systems and Organizations*. The document itself is 183 pages not including supplemental materials to help organizations make risk related decisions in the context of yet more documentation. *See* SP 800-37 at the NIST website, https://nvlpubs.nist.gov/nistpubs/SpecialPublications/NIST.SP.800-37r2.pdf.

Risk departments in large organizations also use risk related spreadsheets or software tools tracking hundreds of categories.

Insurance companies devote extensive resources to this.

Do not lose sight of the big picture. We want to understand some basic risk terminology and use some of these concepts to help us make reasoned, logical decisions.

- Threat: A person or thing that can cause a harm (negative event)
- Harm: A negative event
- Magnitude of harm: The amount of the negative event
- Probability of harm: The likelihood of a harm occurring within a period of time
- Frequency of harm: The number of times the harm might occur within a period of time
- Risk: The assessment of harm and it's probability, frequency, and magnitude
- Risk mitigation: The process of reducing risks (such as by reducing harm, probability, frequency, or magnitude)
- Risk transfer: The process of transferring a risk to someone else
- Risk management: the process of assessing risk and making decisions about whether and how to mitigate, transfer, or accept risks.

One way some may attempt to quantify a risk is with this equation:

$$\text{Risk} = \text{Harm} \times \text{Probability}$$

Expressed in words: the quantity of risk equals the magnitude of harm times the probability of the harm occurring.

There are other ways to try quantifying risk, but nothing is exact, and the future is hard to predict—anyone who could properly predict the future would be rich.

Before deciding, we can consider:

- Potential for various harms
- Probability of harms and potential frequency
- Magnitude of harms
- Whether and how to manage those risks
    - Do nothing? (Accept the risk)
    - Mitigate risk? Reduce likelihood of harm or magnitude of harm
    - Transfer some risk? (Insurance, indemnification clauses).

Risk management is often focused on harms and does not address potential benefits. To decide, we need to weigh both the risks (cons, or negatives) and the potential benefits (pros).

39.7 Decision making

To decide, one needs some options, then to weigh them.

First identify valid options. Then weigh the potential pros and cons of each, which will involve some judgments (educated guesses) about the future, risks, and benefits. Fact finding, diligence, analysis and discussion may be necessary. Eventually you want to arrive at a reasonable decision you can justify.

While some decisions can be made "on-the-fly" or with "instinct," good snap decisions are sometimes simply rapidly and subconsciously applying these principles.

Breaking the process down with more details:

1. Research and obtain relevant, accurate facts and information
2. Apply logic, reason, and common sense
3. Try to break bigger decisions into smaller parts
4. Try to identify what decisions are independent of others, and which are connected to others.
5. Where two or more decisions are connected to each other, try isolate and identify what the connections are and what effects they have
6. Try to identify which decisions need to come first ("threshold issues")
7. When you have isolated a decision point, identify options
   a. When you are identifying options, it helps to identify obvious options, extreme options, and terrible options
   b. Extreme and terrible options are sometimes helpful to identify boundaries (but don't spend too much time on them)
8. After you identify all the options, identify the pros (potential benefits) and cons (risks and potential harms) of each, using common sense and risk analysis.
   a. Risk analysis means evaluating the potential harms and magnitudes of those harms. Predicting the future is hard and approximate.
   b. Don't forget to evaluate the potential benefits of each option. As above, predicting the future is hard.

John T. Bandler

  c. Rule out the extreme and terrible options. That should be easy.

  d. Evaluate the remaining options with greater detail and discussion.

9. Good decision-making means evaluating all the factors and making a reasonable choice.

10. Consider the "business judgment rule," a legal concept that indicates decisions should be made in good faith, with reasonable care, acting in the best interests of the organization.[583]

11. Solicit necessary feedback, inform and consult as needed

12. Consider who needs to approve the decision

13. If needed, make recommendations for the decision to the approver, stating reasons for the proposed decision.

39.9 Charting the course for each organization

Each organization is different and needs to assess itself using the Five Components of Policy Work, as we covered in the prior chapter. This means assessing applicable laws, best practices, its own mission and actions, and internal rules. Then it needs to decide on the course forward, with many choices along the way, big and small.

Good management usually requires some written rules. Organizations should create the written rules that they need and that they can commit to following and keeping updated.

Larger organizations need a greater degree of documentation relating to many areas of management, including cyber issues such as cybersecurity, incident response, and privacy. The quantity of documentation should be commensurate to the size and business of the organization. A behemoth tech company or bank will have hundreds of people working on these issues and perhaps thousands of pages of documentation. A small business with a few dozen employees needs a smaller and simpler set of documents.

We see from this book that cyber issues permeate all areas of law and life, and data law may require special treatment.

---

[583] Generally, it means doing one's best to make the right decision for the right reason, recognizing that not every decision works out perfectly in the end. More technically, it is a shield from certain liability when decisions are made in an appropriate manner. *See* Cornell LII, *Business judgement rule*, https://www.law.cornell.edu/wex/business_judgment_rule.

Consider:

- Cybersecurity and information security[584]
- Incident response (and data breach reporting)
- Privacy (privacy policy and/or privacy notice).[585]

39.8 References and additional reading

- *Chapter 39 resources*, https://johnbandler.com/cyberlawbook-resources-ch39
- *Five Components for Policy Work*, https://johnbandler.com/five-components-for-policy-work
- *Internal rules*, https://johnbandler.com/internal-rules
- *Mission*, https://johnbandler.com/business-needs-and-mission
- *Risk*, https://johnbandler.com/risk
- *Free Starter Cybersecurity Policy*, https://johnbandler.com/cybersecurity-policy-free-version
- *Your organization's privacy policy — and privacy notice*, Reuters article available at https://johnbandler.com/organization-privacy-policy-notice
- *Policies and Procedures for Your Organization* (2024 book)

39.9 Chapter questions

- Write the first touchstone for all organizations, according to the chapter.
- What is information governance?
- What are the triad of reasons why an organization should manage its information assets well, including with good cybersecurity?
- What should your risk tolerance be in life and business? Explain.
- Does cyber require a special type of decision making, or just careful decision making?

---

[584] For small organizations with limited resources, I offer a free cybersecurity policy (with incident response plan) at https://johnbandler.com/cybersecurity-policy-free-version.

[585] Technically speaking, a *policy* would be an internal document, while a *notice* would be a public facing document. Many organizations publicly post what they call a "privacy policy" though opinions differ on that practice. See my article cited in the references.

40

Cybersecurity and Privacy Guidance (Frameworks)

In this chapter:

- Cybersecurity frameworks explained
- Learn the names of some common frameworks
- NIST Cybersecurity Framework (CSF)
- Privacy frameworks explained
- Early privacy frameworks
- NIST Privacy Framework

40.1 Cybersecurity frameworks are best practices

Simply put, a cybersecurity framework is a set of best practices to help manage an organization's cybersecurity.[586]

There are many useful best practices for cybersecurity to help organizations with the complex task of managing and securing their information assets.

Within the context of the Five Components for Policy Work these cybersecurity frameworks are "external guidance" and thus voluntary, not mandatory. Organizations may choose to follow, adapt, or disregard these frameworks.[587]

---

[586] Cybersecurity is a subset of information security, though many use the terms interchangeably. These may be referred to as information security frameworks.
[587] In contrast, a cybersecurity law is a mandatory requirement (if it applies to an organization) and we call that an external rule. The organization would not be able to simply disregard or "adapt" the law but must abide by it.
   Interestingly, some cybersecurity laws have a provision to presume compliance with the law if the organization is properly following a framework.
   There might also be circumstances where a "voluntary" framework becomes mandatory thanks to a contract or other requirement. For example, a contract to use a payment card processing system requires compliance with the PCI-DSS standards which can be considered a framework.

Cybersecurity is complicated so we cannot expect every organization to reinvent the wheel as they secure themselves.[588] On the one hand, every organization is different so one size does not fit all. On the other hand, the practice of effective cybersecurity is well understood with many resources available.

The main point is that people and organizations have developed best practices in this area, and some are excellent. Any best practice needs to be adapted to the organization, and that requires effort.

40.2 Frameworks are from multiple places

Anyone can create frameworks or other guidance. Many frameworks are written by excellent teams of smart people in reputable organizations.

Some come from the government, such as from NIST.[589] The NIST frameworks are created and maintained by qualified people in our government, paid for with federal tax dollars, and made publicly available at no cost and with no license agreement. NIST should be a first stop for anyone researching frameworks.

Some frameworks come from for-profit or not-for-profit organizations. Some may be available for easy inspection and review; others may require a fee or membership. Occasionally licensing agreements (a contract) are involved to protect their intellectual property and their business models.

I created a cybersecurity framework called the Four Pillars of Cybersecurity. It is simple and free and valuable and can get any organization started, as we cover in the next chapter.

Some of the frameworks are complex and beyond what the average person can understand and therefore too complex for most small organizations. My framework concepts are rapidly understandable with the ability to layer in more detail later.

---

[588] Similarly, house builders and auto mechanics consult best practices also. An auto mechanic doing a complicated repair on your car may consult a manual that tells them the steps to complete the repair. An architect or builder uses software tools and references to plan and build their creation.

[589] Remember that NIST is the National Institute of Standards and Technology, an agency of the U.S. Department of Commerce.

40.3 Who are the frameworks for?

The main frameworks are geared for readers with a high degree of technology and information security knowledge, meaning they are primarily for organizations with sufficient information security programs and staff. They could be too technical for most laypersons to understand, too complex for most smaller organizations to implement.

Some framework developers have created guides to help small and mid-sized organizations handle the basics. The recent update to the NIST Cybersecurity Framework does this nicely.

40.4 A quick listing of cybersecurity frameworks

The following list contains my framework plus several well-known cybersecurity frameworks. The point is not to memorize them but to be familiar with the names and where you can learn more about each.

- Bandler's Four Pillars of Cybersecurity (more next chapter)
- Critical Security Controls (CSC) from the Center for Internet Security (CIS) (now at 18 CSC, previously was 20)
- Frameworks from NIST
  - NIST Cybersecurity Framework (CSF) v 2.0[590]
  - NIST SP 800-53 Rev 5: NIST Special Publication 800-53, Security and Privacy Controls for Federal Information Systems and Organizations[591]
  - NIST SP 800-171 Rev. 3, Protecting Controlled Unclassified Information in Nonfederal Systems and Organizations[592]
- Cybersecurity Performance Goals (CPGs) from CISA (in coordination with NIST)[593]
- International Organization for Standardization (ISO) 27001 (27000 series) standard for Information Security Management Systems (ISMS). This framework comes with an industry of independent third-party certification services.[594]

---

[590] Covered next section.
[591] NIST SP 800-53 Rev 5, https://csrc.nist.gov/pubs/sp/800/53/r5/upd1/final.
[592] NIST SP 800-171 Rev 3, https://csrc.nist.gov/pubs/sp/800/171/r3/final.
[593] CISA CPG, https://www.cisa.gov/cybersecurity-performance-goals.
[594] ISO/IEC 27001:2022, https://www.iso.org/standard/27001.

- Control Objectives for Information and Related Technology (COBIT) from ISACA[595]
- American Institute of Certified Public Accountants (AICPA) Statement of Standards for Attestation Engagement (SSAE) No. 18 Service and Organization Controls (SOC) 2 & SOC 3. This is found in the AICPA 2017 Trust Services Criteria for Security, Availability, Processing Integrity, Confidentiality, and Privacy. These also have an industry of third-party attestation services.
- Payment Card Industry (PCI) Data Security Standard (DSS) (security for credit and debit cards and more, and may be required by contract for merchants)[596]
- North American Electric Reliability Corporation (NERC) Critical Infrastructure Protection (CIP) Cybersecurity Standards
- HITRUST Common Security Framework (CSF) (framework and ability for third party attestation services)
- Cybersecurity Maturity Model Certification (CMMC) from Department of Defense (DOD).[597]

There are even more. Each framework above sets forth a process and method to protect information systems and all the complexities that come with that. Each has similarities but also many differences, including with organization, categories, terminology and priorities.

40.5 NIST CSF

The NIST Cybersecurity Framework (CSF) version 2.0 was released on February 26, 2024.[598]

The NIST CSF is valuable cybersecurity guidance, free to access and use with just the click of a mouse, with no registration, no fee, and no licensing agreement. It was created and updated by smart people with a rigorous process, paid for with U.S. tax dollars, so organizations should take advantage of it.

---

[595] ISACA, COBIT, https://www.isaca.org/resources/cobit. ISACA was previously known as the Information Systems Audit and Control Association, now goes by just the initialism.

[596] PCI DSS, https://www.pcisecuritystandards.org/standards/pci-dss.

[597] DOD CMMC, https://dodcio.defense.gov/CMMC.

[598] It replaced version 1.1 which had an official title "Framework for Improving Critical Infrastructure Cybersecurity" and was released April 2018. Version 2.0 adopts the prior nickname as the official name.

Version 2 is much more accessible than the prior version and has multiple quick start guides. Still, it still may be too technical for many individuals to understand, and for many smaller and mid-sized organizations to implement.

The NIST CSF has a substantial page and word count, including with all the accompanying documents and guides. It is a complex read where some readers might need to research some of the terms and might not understand it. If an organization is going to follow the NIST CSF, they need someone in the organization who will read and understand it, some organizations do not have that person.

The NIST CSF v. 2.0 is organized into six main "functions" of:

- Govern
- Identify
- Protect
- Detect
- Respond
- Recover.

The framework recognizes the effort of cybersecurity through these six functions in an ongoing, cyclical process. These functions are further subdivided into categories, and they are laid out below:

- Govern (GV)
    - o Organizational Context (GV.OC)
    - o Risk Management Strategy (GV.RM)
    - o Roles, Responsibilities, and Authorities (GV.RR)
    - o Policy (GV.PO)
    - o Oversight (GV.OV)
    - o Cybersecurity Supply Chain Risk Management (GV.SC)
- Identify (ID)
    - o Asset Management (ID.AM)
    - o Risk Assessment (ID.RA)
    - o Improvement (ID.IM)
- Protect (PR)
    - o Identity Management, Authentication and Access Control (PR.AA)
    - o Awareness and Training (PR.AT)
    - o Data Security (PR.DS)
    - o Platform Security (PR.PS)
    - o Technology Infrastructure Resilience (PR.IR)

- Detect (DE)
  - Continuous Monitoring (DE.CM)
  - Adverse Event Analysis (DE.AE)
- Respond (RS)
  - Incident Management (RS.MA)
  - Incident Analysis (RS.AN)
  - Incident Response Reporting and Communication (RS.CO)
  - Incident Mitigation (RS.MI)
- Recover (RC)
  - Incident Recovery Plan Execution (RC.RP)
  - Incident Recovery Communication (RC.CO).

CSF v.2.0 added the function of "govern," a welcome emphasis because management and governance are an essential part of cybersecurity.

The NIST CSF's method for organizing the process of cybersecurity is helpful. Remember that other frameworks do it differently, with different categories and terminology.

40.6 Four Pillars of Cybersecurity introduced

The Four Pillars of Cybersecurity suggests a focus on four items:

1. Improve *knowledge* and awareness (to make better decisions)
2. Secure computing *devices*
3. Secure *data*
4. Secure *networks* and use of the internet.

Repeat the process for continual improvement.

It is simple and intuitive, with more details in the next chapter.

40.7 Privacy frameworks

As with cybersecurity frameworks, a privacy framework is simply a best practice for managing privacy in an organization. Here is a summary of some important privacy frameworks.

The NIST Privacy Framework is relatively recent, created to assist organizations in managing their privacy programs.[599] The NIST Privacy Framework was released in January 2020 (Version 1) and Version 1.1 is

---

[599] *See* article *NIST Privacy Framework*, https://johnbandler.com/nist-privacy-framework; NIST Privacy Framework landing page, https://www.nist.gov/privacy-framework.

in the works. This is designed to work nicely with the NIST Cybersecurity Framework.

It suggests organizations have six privacy functions (each is followed by a "P" to indicate it relates to privacy, since the cybersecurity framework shares many of the function category names).

- Identify-P
- Govern-P
- Control-P
- Communicate-P
- Protect-P.

The NIST Privacy Framework should be an organization's first privacy framework research step because it is free, reliable, and respected.

Fair Information Practice Principles (FIPPs) started in the U.S. in the 1970s and included some now established privacy principles of consumer access and amendment, accountability, authority, data minimization, data quality, data integrity, individual participation, purpose limitation, security, and transparency.[600]

The *Organisation for Economic Co-operation and Development* (OECD) privacy guidance was first issued in 1980 and was updated in 2013. It is a highly respected framework.[601]

The *Asia-Pacific Economic Cooperation (APEC) privacy framework is* for that region and can be enforced through a Cross-border Privacy Enforcement Arrangement (CPEA).[602]

---

[600] *See* U.S. Federal Privacy Council, *Fair Information Practice Principles (FIPPs)*, https://www.fpc.gov/resources/fipps.

[601] Like many privacy frameworks, it suggests attention to important privacy areas it categorizes as: limit collection of data, data quality, specific purpose, limit use, security, openness (transparency), individual rights (learn, obtain, correct), and accountability for the organization.

See the OECD main website, https://www.oecd.org/en.html; OECD, *Recommendation of the Council concerning Guidelines Governing the Protection of Privacy and Transborder Flows of Personal Data*, Amended 10/7/2013, https://legalinstruments.oecd.org/en/instruments/OECD-LEGAL-0188.

[602] Principles of the APEC privacy framework include; prevent harm, notice, limit collection, limit usage, choice, accuracy, security, access and correction rights, accountability. APEC's main website is https://www.apec.org. The 2015

40.8 References and additional reading

- *Chapter 40 resources,* https://johnbandler.com/cyberlawbook-resources-ch40
- *Cybersecurity frameworks and guidance,* https://johnbandler.com/cybersecurity-frameworks-and-guidance
- *External guidance,* https://johnbandler.com/external-guidance
- *NIST Cybersecurity Framework,* https://johnbandler.com/nist-cybersecurity-framework
- *NIST Privacy Framework,* https://johnbandler.com/nist-privacy-framework
- *NIST Cybersecurity Framework landing page,* https://www.nist.gov/cyberframework
- *NIST Privacy Framework landing page,* https://www.nist.gov/privacy-framework
- Four Pillars of Cybersecurity, see Chapter 41

40.9 Chapter questions

- What is the difference between a cybersecurity framework and a cybersecurity law?
- How can frameworks help an organization with their cybersecurity or privacy program?
- Who issues cybersecurity frameworks?
- Who are cybersecurity frameworks for?
- Who are privacy frameworks for?
- What cybersecurity framework is free, respected, and courtesy U.S. taxpayer dollars? Write out the name and provide a link to it.
- What privacy framework is free, respected, and courtesy U.S. taxpayer dollars? Write out the name and provide a link to it.

---

version of the APEC Privacy Framework is available at https://www.apec.org/publications/2017/08/apec-privacy-framework-(2015).

41

The Four Pillars of Cybersecurity
(More Cybersecurity External Guidance)

In this chapter:

- Four Pillars of Cybersecurity
  - Improve **knowledge** and awareness
  - Secure computer **devices**
  - Secure **data**, applications and accounts
  - Secure **networks** and internet usage
- Repeat

The Four Pillars in a nutshell

The Four Pillars of Cybersecurity is a cybersecurity framework anyone can understand, a good starting point for individuals, families, and small to mid-sized organizations.

The four pillars of cybersecurity are:

1. Improve *knowledge* and awareness
2. Secure computing *devices*
3. Secure *data*
4. Secure *networks* and use of the internet.

Repeat this continual process of improvement.

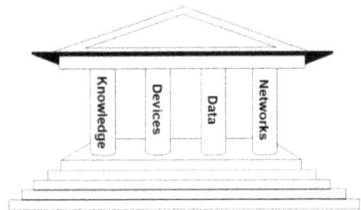

Bandler's Four Pillars of Cybersecurity

This conceptual framework is simple and efficient, understandable for every person from the newest hire to the head of the organization, from the luddite to the IT professional. That is how it should be, since cybersecurity is for everyone, from end users to the leaders who make the decisions about information assets.

As organizations using the Four Pillars framework increase in size and cybersecurity maturity, they can begin to transition towards a more complex and detailed framework, such as the NIST Cybersecurity Framework, or the CIS Critical Security Controls.

Even after such a transition, the more complex frameworks are difficult for some individuals to understand, but the Four Pillars remains a helpful touchstone.

1. Knowledge and awareness

Every person needs a degree of knowledge and awareness to make good decisions about technology, cybersecurity, and cybercrime. A person's lack of knowledge might result in a devastating cybercrime, or a disastrous decision regarding information technology and security.

Imagine trying to secure your home without knowing how a door operates, or how to engage the lock. Imagine trying to drive a car safely without understanding basic principles of how a car works, rules of the road, or the simple rules of nature like "slippery when wet."

Knowledge and awareness of cybersecurity should extend to:

- Legal requirements
- Organization internal rules (including written policies, procedures, and more)
- Cybercrime threats, including:
    - Email based funds transfer frauds ("business email compromise" and "CEO Fraud")
    - Malware, including ransomware
    - Data breaches and data theft
    - Social engineering (con artistry) and similar threats aimed at people
    - Phishing
    - Identity theft
- Privacy threats
- Basic information security principles
- How computers work
- How networks and the internet work
- How to implement basic security measures
- Risk management, decision making, and making good security decisions
- The importance of cybersecurity in the home, and how security at work and home are interrelated
- How working remotely creates and increases security risks.

2. Protect computing devices

Computing devices need to be secured. This includes smartphones, tablets, laptops, desktops, servers, networking devices, printers and more. This means:

- Inventory all devices (to a reasonable degree of detail)
- Develop a process for bringing devices into service securely (commissioning) and taking them out of service securely when no longer needed (decommissioning)
- Ensure physical security and control over these devices. Devices need to be protected from loss, damage, or theft
- Configure devices properly
- Update (patch) of devices
- Protect against malware
- Protect against intrusion
- Control access
- Periodic review of security and privacy settings.

3. Protect data and online accounts and applications

Data needs to be protected from breach and data needs to be available when needed. Certain data breaches could trigger reporting requirements and halt business operations.

This means:

- Inventory data (to a reasonable degree of detail)
- Inventory applications (to a reasonable degree of detail)
- Inventory cloud-based services and apps (to a reasonable degree of detail)
- Secure cloud accounts properly with complex, unique passwords, and a second factor of authentication (multi-factor authentication, MFA, or 2FA)
- Control access to data
- Secure data in a manner commensurate with its sensitivity
- Encrypt certain data as warranted
- Delete unneeded data
- Back up data regularly and securely.

4. Protect networks and safe use of the internet

Data is constantly flowing between our internal devices and through the internet. Key concepts include:

- Inventory network hardware and physically secure it
- Securely configure routers and switches
- Use unique (and non-default) passwords
- Keep devices patched (updated)
- Disable unneeded features
- Encrypt Wi-Fi networks and require a strong password to join and change this password periodically
- Consider intrusion prevention and monitoring
- Understand the route that data takes as it flows
- Avoid or minimize the use of public networks
- Encrypt data in transit whenever practical
- Consider encrypting certain data at the file level for transmittal.

Repeat (continually improve)

Cybersecurity is never "done" so we take small continual steps and work to continually improve security and the strength of each of the four pillars.

Four Pillars as a simple entry point for organizations and people

The Four Pillars is perfect for individuals, small organizations, and many medium sized organizations. It is helpful for individuals in larger organizations to better understand cybersecurity since more complex cybersecurity frameworks are not for laypeople.

Four Pillars is defensible and extensible

The Four Pillars of Cybersecurity is defensible and comprehensible for every organization employee.

It can be supplemented and extended with other guidance, including from NIST and other reputable organizations. These can add greater detail, and organizations can adopt more complex frameworks as they increase in size and maturity.

It is simple for the organization to begin a transition by supplementing with more complex and detailed guidance, such as the NIST CSF, or the CIS Controls. Even as organizations mature, the Four Pillars is a helpful concept because cybersecurity is a responsibility of every employee, and not every employee can understand the more complex frameworks.

You can craft a cybersecurity policy from it – or use mine

The Four Pillars of Cybersecurity is suitable for adapting to an organization's written cybersecurity policy. In fact, I have done that for you with my free policy.

References and additional reading

- *Chapter 41 resources*, https://johnbandler.com/cyberlawbook-resources-ch41
- *Four Pillars of Cybersecurity*, https://johnbandler.com/bandlers-four-pillars-of-cybersecurity
- *Cybersecurity Tips*, https://johnbandler.com/cybersecurity-tips-from-john-bandler
- *Free Cybersecurity Policy*, https://johnbandler.com/cybersecurity-policy-free-version
- Once you have digested the Four Pillars and related materials, try reading a more complex framework, such as the NIST Cybersecurity Framework.

Chapter questions

- List the Four Pillars of Cybersecurity, according to the chapter.
- Do you think Bandler's Four Pillars of Cybersecurity is sufficient for most individuals and small businesses? Explain.
- Do you think Bandler's Four Pillars of Cybersecurity is understandable by the average person, with the average level of technology knowledge?

John T. Bandler

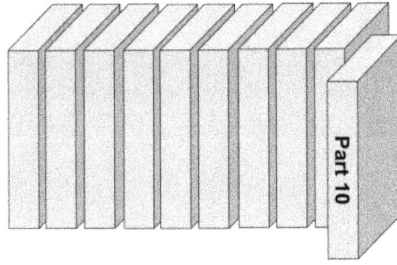

Part 10

Conclusion
and
Resources

("Appendix")

- Conclusion
- Glossary
- References and additional reading
- My journey to write the book
- List of diagrams
- Index

John T. Bandler

42

Conclusion

Did you skip here just to see how the book ended?

If you read it all the way through, it ends with a solid understanding of cyberlaw and traditional law.

I hope the book was informative and will remain a helpful reference and resource for the future. Feel free to reach out and connect or provide a kind constructive note about how I can make it better for the next edition and next readers.

Every person is different. What is helpful or enjoyable for some may land differently for others. It helps me when I hear what readers think as I plan the next edition.

Interested in more books of this type? My "to do" list includes books on:

- Introduction to Law[603]
- Cybersecurity for the Home and Organization.[604]

Thank you for getting here.

Our system of law is integrated with our system of government; far from perfect, but better than many places. We should not take it for granted, nor assume it is self-perpetuating and immune from negative influences. We need to be vigilant and diligent residents, citizens, and voters.

More resources follow.

---

[603] My "Introduction to Law" book will expand upon the introduction to law material within this book and minimize the coverage of cyberlaw.

[604] My first book in 2017 was *Cybersecurity for the Home and Office*, my thinking has evolved considerably, and it is time to write a new book.

John T. Bandler

43

My Journey to Write this Book

- Here's how this book came to be
- This chapter in the back to avoid cluttering the rest of the book and since some people may not want to read it.

My entry into cyberlaw arguably began as a state trooper, where I began to deal with criminal law and some of the unfortunate things people do, including theft, stealing, and the new at-the-time crime of identity theft.

Then came law school and my work as a prosecutor. While I was a junior prosecutor I happened upon the tip of an iceberg of cybercrime and kept investigating. A minor crime eventually led to an entire global economy of cybercrime, identity theft, and virtual currency payments and money laundering. That's the Western Express case you read about.

This was long before these crimes were in the public's awareness, and the case lasted eight years, during which time I evolved from a junior prosecutor to one with considerable experience in these complicated areas plus dealing with issues across state and country lines. Then the months-long trial that involved over fifty witnesses and a mountain of physical and digital evidence.

Eventually I moved into private practice and focused on cybersecurity, cybercrime investigation, and privacy.

Along the way, I was asked to teach. First to teach a course on cyberlaw for undergraduate students. I needed to build the entire curriculum for it, assign readings, create assignments and slide decks, and teach the class. Each semester I tried to improve it.

Then I was asked to build and teach a law school course on cybercrime and cybersecurity. Then to teach another class for graduate students about law and information systems, where the existing syllabus tracked an expensive textbook which did not seem like a good value for the students.

There are lots of books on cyberlaw, none align with my view and experiences, and some cost hundreds of dollars.

Many years ago, I proposed a book on cyberlaw to a publisher, but it was not the right time. The publisher needed a book on cybercrime investigations, so that book got written, including with a significant portion on law. It is a great book but not the perfect cyberlaw book.

Over the years my thinking, teaching, and writing has evolved. I updated and built out articles to supplement my teaching and to serve clients.

Then came book three (Policies and Procedures) and I learned new skills for writing and creating books. I learned I can publish myself (with help), bring it to market rapidly, and set the price much lower than any publisher would for book in this category.

Finally, it was time for this book on cyberlaw, covering it the way I wanted, in the format I wanted. My fourth book.

I thought I was going to put it together quickly and simply. I was wrong.

I got to work in earnest while preparing for the Fall 2024 semester of teaching, and during the semester I continued to build and refine it. The book grew and the complexity became clear, so I enlisted a growing number of readers to help, each with valuable perspectives to help improve it in many ways. From expert practitioners to students in law school and college, each of them helped make the book so much better than it would have been. It would have been a folly to try do this book without their help.

In this process, I have thought much about law and our legal system in the country, and I learned a lot. I hope your journey through the book has been as rewarding as mine.

44

References and Additional Reading

This is a very general list of references and additional reading.

Within the book, see the footnotes throughout, and references at the end of each chapter. That is a lot of references already.

Then remember the main resources webpage, which has links to each chapter resource page which has those references and many more.

As the scope of this book and my research increased, the number of references cited increased. It became impossible to include them all within the text or in this end section.

I decided not to keep all that research to myself but to put it on my website for others so they could use what I have done and start where I finished. We will see how it goes.

Find my cyberlaw resources and reference list online

The cyberlaw book resources main landing page has links to resource pages for each chapter.

https://johnbandler.com/cyberlawbook-resources

Then, the resources page URLs are formatted like this:

- https://johnbandler.com/cyberlawbook-resources-ch00 (an explainer page on the chapter resources)
- https://johnbandler.com/cyberlawbook-resources-ch01

And so forth.

The QR code at the end of each chapter takes you to that chapter resources page.

Major works of John[605]

- JohnBandler.com (my website)[606]
- John Bandler, *Cyberlaw: Law for Digital Spaces and for Information Systems* (Bandler Group LLC, 2025) (This Book!)[607]
- John Bandler, *Policies and Procedures for Your Organization: Build solid governance documents on any topic ... including cybersecurity* (John Bandler, 2024).[608]
- John Bandler and Antonia Merzon, *Cybercrime Investigations: A Comprehensive Resource for Everyone* (CRC Press, 2020).[609]
- John Bandler, *Cybersecurity for the Home and Office: The Lawyer's Guide to Taking Charge of Your Own Information Security* (American Bar Association, 2017).[610]
- Online courses, https://johnbandler.com/online-courses/

Citations throughout

- A hybrid citation format is used throughout this book for reader convenience and to reduce word count and clutter.
- Webpages may change or cease to work. All links cited were checked shortly before the publication date.
- We frequently cite to the Cornell Law School Legal Information Institute (LII) at https://www.law.cornell.edu. A great resource.

---

[605] I build upon my prior works and cite to them throughout. Many of my prior works had help from pre-publication readers who provided feedback.

[606] There is a symbiotic back and forth between my website and other writings. I borrowed heavily from my website, adapting as appropriate. Then I build out my website further based on my book writings.

[607] Some may question if it is proper to use this book as a reference for itself? It keeps this list complete and if someone copies out these references for future use, they will not forget about the book.

[608] I also borrow and adapt from this book, which discusses organization governance documents and management, cybersecurity, the Four Pillars of Cybersecurity, Five Components of Policy Work, and more. *See* https://johnbandler.com/policiesbook.

[609] This was written with a co-author who also put prodigious work into it, which discusses many important topics and laws and techniques for cybercrime investigation. For more *see* https://johnbandler.com/cybercrime-investigations.

[610] My first book and where I formed the Four Pillars of Cybersecurity. *See,* https://johnbandler.com/cybersecurity-for-the-home-and-office.

45

Frequent abbreviations

- Different books and references abbreviate differently
- Here are some abbreviations for this book for your speedy reference
- Also see the index

- AI, artificial intelligence
- C.F.R., U.S. Code of Federal Regulations (main federal regulations)
- C.P.L., New York Criminal Procedure Law
- DANY, New York County District Attorney's Office, Manhattan DA's office
- DFS, New York Department of Financial Services
- LLM, large language model (regarding artificial intelligence)
- Manhattan DA, New York County District Attorney's Office (DANY)
- NY, New York State
- NYS, New York State
- NYSP, New York State Police
- N.Y. C.P.L., New York Criminal Procedure Law
- N.Y. P.L., New York Penal Law
- P.L., New York Penal Law
- Penal Law, New York's Penal Law
- U.S. DOJ – U.S. Department of Justice
- U.S.C. or U.S Code, United States Code (main federal statutes)
- USSC, United States Supreme Court, Supreme Court of the United States, SCOTUS

John T. Bandler

46

Glossary

Words mean different things to different people, especially in different contexts.

This is what these words mean to me for the purpose of this book and in the simplest of fashions.

I'm not trying to be fancy or hyper-technical and I'm not trying to lawyer it up with legalese. I simplify and provide information in a simple format. If you need greater detail or precision, you might find it in the book (most of these terms are indexed). My website might have information too.

Consult other reliable sources and consider context. Others have spent time defining terms. Semantics matters and words have different meanings depending on the individual issuing or receiving them, and the context.

If a law or regulation defines a term, that has legal significance for compliance purposes so read that. Frameworks define terms for the purpose of that body of work. Consider the context in which you use a word.

Appendix: Sort of what I call Part 10 since it is a common term. But I am not a fan of it because the appendix in a human is an unnecessary organ that sometimes causes a pain, whereas this part is necessary and helpful information and causes no pain.

Compliance: The process of complying with external rules (laws and regulations and other legal requirements), as well as compliance with internal rules (policies and procedures).

Component: A generic term to indicate a part of a whole, such as a component like a platform or a cloud. *See* Five Components for Policy Work.

Cyber: A much-overused term that is used alone and in combination with almost every other dictionary term (it seems). It mostly means related to computers, networks, and the internet. Related to digital things.

Cyberconflict: Cyber + conflict. Usually in the context of nation-state conflict and operations that use cyberspace.

Cybercrime: Cyber + crime. When someone violates a criminal statute using computers and the internet. Most cybercrime is ultimately about theft and there are many typologies and also other motives.

Cyberlaw: Cyber + law. The areas of law relating to computers and the internet, including areas of criminal law, cybersecurity, privacy, nation-state conflict, and more. The subject of this book!

Cybersecurity: Cyber + security. The process of securing digital information (and information assets while we are at it) and protecting from cybercrime. In practical terms, think of it being the same as information security. The objectives of cybersecurity are confidentiality, integrity, and availability (CIA) of digital assets.

Cyberspace: That virtual area where data and networks exist, electrons move, and it is not our tangible, brick-and-mortar physical space. Still, cyberspace is intertwined with our "regular" space.

Cyberspeech: Speech and expression online.

Data governance: See information governance, though "data" has a more digital (cyber) connotation.

Data law: The law around data, or that portion of cyberlaw created specifically to deal with our newer issues with data, to include laws for privacy, cybersecurity, and data breach notification.

Decision making: The process of making choices, hopefully effective ones. Hopefully all reasonable options were considered and there was a reasonable process to consider facts and risks, and a reasonable decision was reached.

Easter Egg: A surprise or hidden joke. If I put something in this book that has nothing to do with cyberlaw or if I make a ridiculous joke, it is probably an Easter Egg. If you find a typo or error, that too is an Easter Egg (but please let me know so I can fix it).

External guidance: Best practices, expert advice, or anything from outside the organization that the organization could use or adapt to guide its policy or practice. One of the Five Components for Policy Work.

External rule: A law, statute, regulation, court decision or legally binding contract. One of the Five Components for Policy Work.

Five Components for Policy Work: A concept from John Bandler applicable for policies and management that focus on external rules, internal rules, practice, mission, and external guidance.

Four Pillars of Cybersecurity: A concept (framework) from John Bandler for organizing cybersecurity that everyone can understand, which involves building people's knowledge and awareness, securing devices, secure data, and secure networks. Repeat and keep improving.

Framework: A set of best practices, or "external guidance" that is not legally mandated. For example, the NIST Cybersecurity Framework.

Glossary: You're in the glossary now. A glossary is just one person's definition of terms.

Governance: Governance is basically just management. The process or act of overseeing or managing.

Governance documents: Documents from the organization that tell the organization and people within it what to do. Examples include policies and procedures, also bylaws, articles of incorporation, standards, handbooks, etc.

Governance, risk, and compliance (GRC): A term where these three items are often grouped together to comply with external rules (compliance), address risks, and also how the organization is managed.

Government: A vague term used to describe the systems and people managing our country and states. We have a federal government and state governments, with three branches of government in each, and many regulatory agencies. There are also local governments.

Identity theft is essentially when a defendant assumes the identity of the victim to obtain goods or services, steal, or commit some type of crime. See the relevant criminal statute for its exact definition.

Information assets: Assets of an organization relating to information systems, including people, computer devices, data, networks and communication methods.

Information governance: The process of managing information assets and information systems. Similar to data governance though "data" has a more digital connotation.

Information security: Similar to cybersecurity, but it has been around longer and could include non-cyber information (paper, verbal statements, etc.). For practical convenience think of it being the same as cybersecurity. The objectives of information security are confidentiality, integrity, and availability (CIA) of information assets.

Information system: A system to collect, process, store, and distribute information. Often used regarding a "computer information system" which involves computers (hardware, software, networks, data).

Information technology (IT) and information and communications technology (ICT), the fields regarding computers, networks, data, including the hardware and software and systems involved.

Internal rules: Within the Five Components for Policy Work, internal rules are those made by the organization, including verbal, written, policies, procedures, etc.

Johnbandler.com: The domain name for a website with excellent information. Please give me some views, clicks, and shares.

Law (as a concept): A vast area of government rules for conduct and a process for resolving disputes. Hard to explain in a glossary, but kind of what this book is about.

Law (as in statute): A duly enacted law, passed by the legislature, signed by the executive (president or governor).

Legal requirements: A broader term to encompass legally binding obligations which could come from law, regulation, or contract.

Management: The process of managing (governing or directing) an organization. Good management is what we strive for.

Organization: An entity of some sort, whether for-profit business, non-profit organization, or government agency or unit. This is my catch-all term because other words like "business," "corporation," are more specific and might exclude certain organizations.

People: Humans, or Homo Sapiens, indisputably the most difficult and destructive of all species on our planet, even the universe.

Pillars: An upright column, usually supporting something else. One of my metaphors of choice. *See* the Four Pillars of Cybersecurity.

Platforms: A structure you could stand or walk on. Another metaphor of choice. See for example the Three Platforms to Connect for Compliance, and the Four Platforms.

Practice (action). What you do. Your practices. The actions and practices of the organization.

Privacy: "The right to be let alone" and a growing area of law and compliance and policy regarding consumer data. Privacy also includes a cybersecurity component.

Procedure: A governance document that is a step-by step instruction on how to accomplish a task. It has many details and might need to be updated frequently.

Regulated sector: a sector that is regulated by the government, where government has special rules for it, requires licenses, etc. Examples include health, finance, education, utilities, and more.

Regulation: A government rule put forth by a regulatory body, usually under the authority of a related law.

Regulator: The governmental entity responsible for enforcing a regulation or law. Often this term relates to a regulated sector.

Regulatory type: A governmental entity responsible for enforcing a regulation or law, though not necessarily a "regulator" for a regulated sector. For example, a state attorney general might enforce data breach notification laws, even for entities that might not be in a "regulated" sector.

Research is the process of finding and analyzing information. Research is a type of investigation.

Risk: A downside, a "con," a potential harm that could occur because of a threat. We also factor in the probability, potential frequency, and magnitude of that harm.

Risk management: The process of managing risks. Risks should be managed reasonably and diligently. Still, we can't eliminate all risks. Risk is related to decision making.

Rules: An instruction to be followed. Rules could be written or unwritten. Organizations need rules (internal rules), governments create rules too (known as laws).

John T. Bandler

47

List of Diagrams

I created these diagrams, which are largely an evolution of diagrams I created for my website, prior books, speaking, or teaching.

Their goal is to convey or reinforce the concepts and break up the text.

48

Index

The notation "n" indicates the term is found in a footnote on that page.

Bitcoin, 145, 190, 248
Bluesky, 416
Branches of government, 41, 46, 69, 479
Brandeis, Louis, 359
Brandenburg v. Ohio, 108n
Breach notification laws, 15, 326, 327, 333-340 (Ch 30)
Breach notification rule (HIPPA), 294, 382
Briefing a case, 25
Budapest Convention, 237-238, 395n
Burdeau v. McDowell, 116
Business email compromise, *see* Email based funds transfer frauds
Business judgment rule, 451
Business law, 423-431 (Ch 37).
See also Cyberlaw

C

California data laws, 329, 330, 361, 364
Cambridge Analytica, 152-153, 366, 412
Center for Internet Security (CIS), 344, 455
CEO fraud, *see* Email based funds transfer frauds
Chaplinsky v. New Hampshire, 108n
ChatGPT, 308, 369. *See also* Artificial intelligence
Child pornography, *see* Child sex abuse material (CSAM)
Child sex abuse material (CSAM), 217
Children's Online Privacy Protection Act (COPPA), 362, 383
China, 238n
Citation, 25, 28,
style in this book, 5n, 474
Civil law, 40, 48-51, 52-53, 87-92 (Ch 9), Part 5, Part 6
CLOUD Act, 236
Code of Federal Regulations (CFR), 292n

Commodities and Futures Trading Commission (CFTC), 248, 250
Common law, 47, 268
Communications Decency Act (CDA), 415-416
Compliance, 15, 244, 426-427, 433, 437, 446-447
Three Platforms for compliance, 435-436
Component, *see* Five Components for Policy Work
Computer Fraud and Abuse Act (CFAA), 204, 207-208, 219, 267-268
Constitution,
as a type of founding document, 39, 41, 46
state constitutions, 23, 47
U.S. Constitution, 23, 24, 46, 59-67 (Ch 7), 80
Consumer Financial Protection Bureau (CFPB), 250, 298n
Contract business considerations, 424, 427, 438, 442
Contract law, 14, 175, 182, 283-290 (Ch 26), 321
See also Delta v CrowdStrike
Control Objectives for Information and Related Technology, (COBIT), 456
Controls (cybersecurity controls, safeguards), 172-173, 321, 344, 346-348, 380
Conversion (digital advertising), 151
Conversion (tort), 264, 267
Cooperative Cyber Defence Centre of Excellence (CCDOE), 393
Copyright, 303-308, 371, 376
Council of Europe Convention on Cybercrime (the Budapest Convention), 237-238, 395n
CPL, *see* Criminal procedure law
Crime, 69-85 (Ch 8), Part 4 and throughout
cybercrime and ID theft, 139-147

Fair Information Practice Principles (FIPPs), 360, 459

False imprisonment, 264

Family Educational Rights and Privacy Act of 1974 (FERPA), 351, 364,

Federal Financial Institutions Examination Council (FFIEC), 299, 350-351

Federal Information Security Management Act (FISMA), 352

Federal question jurisdiction, 91, 120

Federal Trade Commission (FTC) and FTC Act, 298, 300, 329, 349, 361, 362, 381, 442

Financial Crimes Enforcement Network (FinCEN) 237, 248, 249, 296

Financial regulation, 190, 244, 294-299

Financial Services Modernization Act (Gramm-Leach Bliley Act GLBA), 299, 341, 350-351, 363

FinCEN, *see* Financial Crimes Enforcement Network

First Amendment of U.S. Const. 65-66, 95-109 (Ch 10), 135, 217-219, 270, 405-408

Five Components for Policy Work, 424, 433-443 (Ch 38), 445, 479

Flat Earth belief, 414

Foreign influence or interference, 398-400, 412-413

Foreign Intelligence Surveillance Act (FISA), 395-396

Foreign Intelligence Surveillance Court, 395-396

Four Pillars of Cybersecurity, 169, 175, 442, 458, 461-465 (Ch 41)

Fourth Amendment of U.S. Const., 65, 66, 111-118 (Ch 11), 226-227
cyberspace application, 117-118, 136, 183, 225-227 (Ch 21)
search warrant req't, 112-114
evolution of, 62, 115-116
exclusionary rule, 78, 81, 115

Frameworks (best practices), 175, 344-345, 442, 453-459 (Ch 40), 479
CIS CSC, 344, 455
cybersecurity, 344-345, 453-458
Four Pillars of Cybersecurity, 461-465 (Ch 41)
privacy, 360, 458-459
NIST AI, 376
NIST cybersecurity, 456-458
NIST privacy, 458-459

Free speech (phrase), 97-98, 406, 410

G

Gambino v. United States, 116

General Business Law of NY, 77, 300, 335

General Data Protection Regulation (GDPR), 364-366

Generative AI, 133, 307, 369-377 (Ch 33)

Geneva Conventions, 390

Gilberto Valle, see *U.S. v Gilberto Valle*

GLBA, *see* Gramm-Leach-Bliley Act (GLBA)

Glossary, 477-481

Going dark debate, 255-257

Governance,
documents, 438-439
of information systems, 445-452 (Ch 39)
of organizations, 433-443 (Ch 38)
of U.S., 45-58 (Ch 6)

Gramm-Leach-Bliley Act (GLBA), 299, 341, 350-351, 363

H

Hague Conventions, 390

Hardware components, 159

Health Information Technology for Economic and Clinical Health Act (HITECH), 294, 382

L

M

N

data breach reporting law, 335-340
Department of Financial Services (DFS), 299
DFS Rule 500, 348-349, 380
State Police, 71n, 82n
NIST Cybersecurity Framework (CSF), 175, 344, 456-458
NIST Privacy Framework, 360, 458-459
NIST, *see* National Institute of Standards and Technology,
Noncompliant organization, 436
NYSP, see New York State Police

O

Office of International Affairs (OIA), 237, 240
Organisation for Economic Co-operation and Development (OECD), 360, 459
Organized Crime Control Act (OCCA), Enterprise Corruption, 192, 215
Organized crime, 191, 192, 204, 211, 215

P

Pace University, 13n
Patent, 314-318
Payment Card Industry (PCI) Data Security Standard (DSS), 345, 453, 456
PCI-DSS see Payment Card Industry (PCI)
People, *see* Homo Sapiens
Personal jurisdiction, 80, 119, 120
Policy (policies), as a type of organization rule, 438-439
Practice (action), 433, 435, 440
Precedent (precedence), 24, 26, 41, 47, 62, 63, 180
Preemption (preempt), 331
Premises liability, 155, 276, 277-278

Privacy, 15, 130, 135, 149-153 (Ch 15)
data laws, 326, 357-366 (Ch 32)
frameworks, 360, 458-459
invasion of, 88, 103, 264
policies and notices, 150, 153, 285, 287-288
rule of GLBA, 299, 362-363
rule of HIPAA, 382-383
Product liability, 88, 279, 288, 376
Prosecutor, 6, 48, 49, 51, 70, 73, 78
Protected health information (PHI)
Protecting Americans from Foreign Adversary Controlled Applications Act (PAFACA), 413
Proxies, 166-167

Q

QR code, 9, 10

R

Racketeer Influenced and Corrupt Organizations (RICO), 211
Ransomware, 145-146, 208, 462
Rational basis test, 66, 107
Reasonable cybersecurity, 175, 343, 360
Red Flags Rule, 298
Reno v. American Civil Liberties Union, 415
Research, 22-27
Risk management, 171, 448-450, 481
Roe v. Wade, 63, 359
Rule 500 (NYS DFS), 299, 340, 348-349
Russia, 238, 393, 399

S

Sarbanes-Oxley Act of 2002 (SOX), 299, 351
Search and seizure, *see* Fourth Amendment

John T. Bandler

Search warrant, 72, 78, 112-113, 229-230
Secret Service, *see* U.S. Secret Service
Secure data disposal, *see* Data disposal laws
Securities and Exchange Commission (SEC), 249, 351, 353-354
Sergei Aleynikov case, 220-221
SHIELD Act of NY, 335, 346-348, 379-380
Social engineering, 146, 405, 409, 462
Software components, 160
Solar Winds, 353
Solid-state drive, 159
Sources of law, 41, 45-47
Stare decisis, 24, 41, 47, 62
State action, 98, 112
State police, *see* New York State Police
Stored Communications Act, 209, 229, 230, 241, 267
Strict scrutiny test, 66-67, 108, 413
Supreme Court, *see* U.S. Supreme Court

T

Tallinn Manual, 393-394
Terry v. Ohio, 117
The New York Times Co. v. Sullivan, 271
Theocracy, 41, 60
Think like a lawyer, 56, 179-180
Think like a prosecutor, 84, 202
Three branches of government, 46, 69, 479
Three Platforms to Connect for Compliance, 435
Three priority cybercrime threats, 145-147
TikTok, 413-414
Tor (The Onion Router), 166-167
Torts,
    intentional, 263-272 (Ch 24)
    negligent, 275-281 (Ch 25)

Trade secrets, 220, 304, 318-321
Trademark, 303, 304, 308-313
Trespass, 264
    computer, 216, 267, 268
Trial, 54, 81-83, 90, 91-92
Twitter (X), 133, 136
Two factor authentication, 173, 343

U

U.N., *see* United Nations
U.S. Constitution, 23, 24, 46, 59-67 (Ch 7), 80
    First Amendment, 65-66, 95-109 (Ch 10), 135, 217-219, 270, 405-408
    Fourth Amendment, 65, 66, 111-118 (Chapter 11), 226-227
U.S. Department of Commerce, *see* National Institute of Standards and Technology (NIST)
U.S. Department of Education (ED), 351, 364
U.S. Department of Health and Human Services (HHS), 294, 382
U.S. Department of Justice (U.S. DOJ), 73, 126
U.S. DOJ Office of International Affairs (OIA), 237, 240
U.S. legal system (introduced), 45-58 (Ch 6)
U.S. Patent and Trademark Office (USPTO), 310, 314, 316
U.S. Secret Service (USSS), 73n, 74n, 191, 194
U.S. Supreme Court (USSC), 24, 63, 116
U.S. v Gilberto Valle, 208, 218-220, 415
U.S. v Sergei Aleynikov, 220
U-boat cart, 195
Uniform Law Commission (ULC), 318n
Uniform Trade Secrets Act (UTSA), 318-320

United Nations, 18
   Charter, 390-391
   Cybercrime convention, 238-239
Unlicensed money transmitting, *see*
   Money transmitting

V

Valle, *see U.S. v Gilberto Valle*
Venue, 81, 125-126
Virtual assets, 133, 245-246, 249,
   294, 297
Virtual currency, 17, 145, 182-183,
   243-251 (Ch 22), 294, 296
Virtual private network (VPN), 166
Virtual reality (Metaverse), 132,
   221-222, 272
VPN, *see* Virtual private network

W

WebMoney, 144, 189, 190, 247, 250
Weeks v United States, 115, 116
Western Express cybercrime case,
   144-145, 187-200 (Ch 19)
White House, 352, 375
Wiretap, 116, 209-210, 229, 230-231
Writing, 19-20, 27-28

X

X (Twitter), 133, 136

Y

YouTube, 133

Z

Zealous representation, 56n, 180

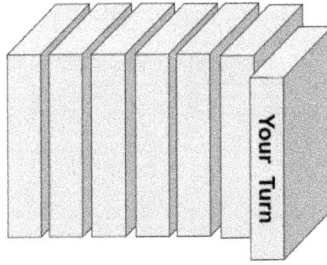

Part 11

Your Turn

A few pages for your notes.

John T. Bandler

John T. Bandler

www.ingramcontent.com/pod-product-compliance
Lightning Source LLC
Chambersburg PA
CBHW070347200326
41518CB00012B/2159